The Unified Process Transition and Production Phases

Best Practices in Implementing the UP

Scott W. Ambler and Larry L. Constantine,
Compiling Editors

Masters collection from

CRC Press
Taylor & Francis Group
Boca Raton London New York

CRC Press is an imprint of the
Taylor & Francis Group, an **informa** business

CRC Press
Taylor & Francis Group
6000 Broken Sound Parkway NW, Suite 300
Boca Raton, FL 33487-2742

Visit the Taylor & Francis Web site at
http://www.taylorandfrancis.com

and the CRC Press Web site at
http://www.crcpress.com

ISBN-13: 9781578200924 (pbk)
ISBN-13: 9781138436367 (hbk)

To my niece,
Sarah Vivian McGrath.
— Scott Ambler

To Dave Jasper,
a mentor who helped me learn the meaning of
software production.
— Larry Constantine

Table of Contents

Preface

A wealth of knowledge on how to be successful at developing software has been published in *Software Development* magazine and in its original incarnation, *Computer Language*. The people who have written for the magazine includes many of the industry's best known experts: Karl Wiegers, Ellen Gottesdiener, James Bach, Jim Highsmith, Warren Keuffel, and Martin Fowler, to name a few. In short, the leading minds of the information industry have shared their wisdom with us over the years in the pages of this venerable magazine.

Lately, there has been an increased focus on improving the software process within most organizations. Starting in the mid-1990s, Rational Corporation was acquiring and merging with other tool companies. As they consolidated the companies, they consolidated the processes supported by the tools of the merging companies. The objective of the consolidation was to arrive at a single development approach. They named the new approach the Unified Process. Is it possible to automate the entire software process? Does Rational have a complete toolset even if it is? We're not so sure. Luckily, other people were defining software processes too, so we have alternate views of how things should work. This includes the OPEN Consortium's OPEN process, the process patterns of the Object-Oriented Software Process (OOSP), Extreme Programming (XP), and Agile Modeling (AM). These alternate views can be used to drive a more robust view of the Unified Process, resulting in an enhanced lifecycle that more accurately reflects the real-world needs of your organization. Believing that the collected wisdom contained in *Software Development* over the years could be used to flesh-out the Unified Process — truly unifying the best practices in our industry — we undertook this book series.

Why is a software process important? Step back for a minute. Pretend you want to have a house built and you ask two contractors for bids. The first one tells you that, using a new housing technology, he can build a house for you in two weeks if he starts first thing tomorrow, and it will cost you only $100,000. This contractor has some top-notch carpenters and plumbers that have used this technology to build a garden shed in the past, and they're willing to work day and night for you to meet this deadline. The second one tells you that she needs to discuss what type of house you would like built, and then, once she's confident that she understands your needs, she'll put together a set of drawings within a week for your review and feedback. This initial phase will cost you $10,000, and, once you decide what you want built, she can then put together a detailed plan and cost schedule for the rest of the work.

Which contractor are you more comfortable with? The one that wants to start building or the one that wants to first understand what needs to be built, model it, plan it, then build it? Obviously, the second contractor has a greater chance of understanding your needs — the first step in successfully delivering a house that meets them. Now assume that you're having software built — something that is several orders of magnitude more complex and typically far more expensive than a house — and assume once again that you have two contractors wanting to take these exact same approaches. Which contractor are you more comfortable with? We hope the answer is still the second one; the one with a sensible process. Unfortunately, practice shows that most of the time organizations appear to choose the approach of the first contractor; that of hacking. Of course, practice also shows that our industry experiences upwards of 85% failure rate on large-scale, mission-critical systems (in this case, a failure is defined as a project that has significantly overrun its cost estimates or has been cancelled outright). Perhaps the two phenomena are related.

In reality, the situation is even worse than this. You're likely trying to build a house and all the contractors available to you only have experience building garden sheds. Even worse, they've only worked in tropical parts of the world and have never had to deal with the implications of frost, yet you live in the backwoods of Canada. Furthermore, the various levels of Canadian government enforce a variety of constantly changing regulations that the contractors are not familiar with. Once again, the haphazard approach of the first contractor is likely to get someone into trouble.

The Transition Phase

In the enhanced lifecycle for the Enterprise Unified Process (EUP), the Transition phase is the fourth of five phases — Inception, Elaboration, Construction, Transition, and Production — that a release of software experiences throughout its complete lifecycle. The primary goal of the Transition phase is to turn over your system to your user community. To accomplish this, you need to:

- Test and validate your complete system
- Operate the system in parallel with any legacy systems that you are replacing, if applicable
- Convert legacy databases and systems, as appropriate, to support your new release
- Train users, operations staff, support staff, and maintenance developers
- Deploy the system into production

The most important thing that you can do during the Transition phase is to ensure that your system works in production. This doesn't just mean that your system is operational. It implies that the actual operational needs of your users are met by your system. You need to ensure that your system doesn't cause harm to other systems, that your users understand how to work with the system and know how to get help when they run into trouble, and that the system is available when users need it.

The Production Phase

The lifecycle for your system isn't complete just because you have transitioned it into the hands of users. In fact, most of your users would claim that your system has just begun its lifecycle. The Production phase is the fourth of the five phases of the EUP. The primary goal of the Production phase is to operate the system and support users working with it. To accomplish this, you need to:

- Monitor the system, acting appropriately to ensure continued operation
- Operate and maintain relevant jobs, logs, and supporting systems
- Respond to help requests, error reports, and feature requests by users
- Manage your change control process so that defects and new features may be prioritized and assigned to future releases

It is critical that you recognize that it isn't sufficient to merely deliver a system into production — you also need to keep it there. The EUP, an instance of the Unified Process as is the Rational Unified Process (RUP), includes the Production phase because the operation and support of systems once they have been delivered to users is a cold, hard reality for real-world organizations. Just as the best developers take maintenance issues into account when they are building a system, the best organizations take production into account when they are managing their portfolio of computer systems.

This book collects articles written by industry luminaries that describe best practices in these areas. One goal of this book, and of the entire book series, is to provide proven alternative approaches to the techniques encompassed by the Unified Process. Another goal is to fill in some of the gaps in the Unified Process. Because the Unified Process is a development process — not a software process — it inevitably misses or short-changes some of the concepts that are most important for software professionals. Fortunately, the writers in *Software Development* have taken a much broader view of process scope and have filled in many of these holes for us.

About This Series

This book series comprises four volumes: one for the Inception phase, the Elaboration phase, the Construction phase, and a fourth one for the Transition and Production phases. Each book stands on its own, but for a complete picture of the entire Enterprise Unified Process (EUP), you need the entire series. The articles presented span the complete process without duplication among the volumes.

It has been a challenge selecting material for inclusion in this compilation. With such a wealth of information to choose from and only a limited number of pages in which to work, narrowing the choices was not always easy. If time and space had allowed it, each of these books might have been twice as long. In narrowing our selections, we believe the articles that remain are truly the *crème de la crème*. Furthermore, to increase the focus of the material in each book, we have limited the number of workflows that each one covers. Yes, most workflows are pertinent to each phase, but as Table 1 indicates, each book covers a subset of the workflows to provide you with a broader range of material.

Table 1   Overall organization of this book series.

Workflow/Topic	Inception Phase (vol.1)	Elaboration Phase (vol. 2)	Construction Phase (vol. 3)	Transition & Production Phases (vol. 4)
Business Modeling	X	X		
Requirements	X	X		
Analysis and Design		X	X	
Implementation			X	
Test	X	X	X	X
Deployment				X
Operations and Support				X
Configuration and Change Management			X	
Project Management	X	X	X	X
Environment	X			
Infrastructure Management		X	X	X

About The Editors

Scott W. Ambler

An avid reader of *Computer Language* and then *Software Development* for years, I started writing for the magazine in 1995 and eventually became the object columnist in 1997. I started developing software in the early-1980s, writing code in languages such as Fortran and Basic, and later in the mid-1980s in Turing (don't ask), C, Prolog, and Lisp. In the late 1980s, I realized that there was more to life than programming and started picking up skills in user interface design, data modeling, process modeling, and testing while I programmed in COBOL and a couple of fourth-generation languages for IBM mainframes. Disillusioned with structured/procedural techniques, in 1990 I discovered objects and readily jumped into Small-talk development, then into C++ development, then back to Smalltalk.

Having worked at several organizations in mentoring and architectural roles, I decided to combine that experience and apply my skills gained as a teaching assistant at the University of Toronto and get into professional training in the mid-1990s. I quickly learned several things. First, although I like delivering training courses (and still do so today), I didn't want to do it full time. Second, and of greater importance, I learned how to communicate complex concepts in an easy-to-understand manner, such as how to develop object-oriented software. This lead to my first two books, *The Object Primer* (Cambridge University Press, 1995), now in its second edition (2001), and the Jolt Productivity award-winning *Building Object Applications That Work* (Cambridge University Press, 1997/1998) which describe the fundamentals of object technology from a developer's point of view. I then decided to follow up with two books on the Object-Oriented Software Process (OOSP), *Process Patterns* (Cambridge University Press, 1998) and *More Process Patterns* (Cambridge University Press, 1999), describing the hard-won experiences I'd gained working for one of Canada's leading object technology consulting firms. Since then, I've helped several organizations — large and small, new and established — in a variety of industries to improve their internal software processes. My latest writing endeavors include this book series and *Agile* Modeling (John Wiley & Sons, 2002), as well as co-authoring *The Elements of Java Style* (Cambridge University Press, 2000) and *Mastering EJB 2/e* (John Wiley & Sons, 2001). I am now President of Ronin International (www.ronin-intl.com), a Denver-based process and software architecture consulting firm, and a freelance writer with my own web site, www.ambysoft.com, where I post a variety of white papers. I am also the thought-leader of the Agile Modeling (AM) methodology, described at www.agilemodeling.com. I think I've found my niche.

Larry L. Constantine

My association with *Software Development* and its forerunner, *Computer Language*, has been both long and fruitful, and my association with software development and computer language goes back even further. From my first Fortran program back in the dark ages of computing, I have been keenly interested in figuring out how to do things better and to help others do them better — interests that soon led me beyond technology into management and process issues as well as the essential matter of the usability of the products we design and build. Throughout my nearly 40 years in the field, I have continued to criss-cross that river that too often divides the people side from the technology side. In my view, success in software development hinges on an understanding and a mastery of material from both sides of this divide, and this has been reflected in my writing for the magazine and elsewhere. That work now spans over 150 articles and papers and 14 books, including, now, this collaborative compilation with Scott Ambler. With Scott's concurrence, some of my own columns and articles in the magazine have been included in these volumes. Others appear in *The Peopleware Papers* (Prentice Hall, 2001), which reprints, in its entirety, the contents of my long-running "Peopleware" column, and in *Beyond Chaos: The Expert Edge in Software Development* (Addison-Wesley, 2001), which incorporates the best from the popular "Software Development Management Forum" that appeared at the back of every issue for nearly four years.

In recent years, my professional interests have been particularly focused on increasing the usability of software, which has led to the development of usage-centered design and to the book with Lucy Lockwood, *Software for Use: A Practical Guide to the Models and Methods of Usage-Centered Design* (Addison-Wesley, 1999). The magazine honored us by giving that book the Jolt Product Excellence Award for best book of 1999. Of late, it seems I cross oceans even more often than rivers, because, although I live in the United States, I also teach at the University of Technology, Sydney, Australia, where I am an Adjunct Professor of Computing Sciences. Despite the title, I teach a mix of management and design topics. I am also a working trainer, designer, and consultant helping clients around the world build software that is easier to use. With Lucy Lockwood, I founded Constantine & Lockwood, Ltd. (www.forUse.com), where I am Director of Research and Development and currently working on the integration of usage-centered design with the Unified Process and Unified Modeling Language, among other things.

Chapter 1

Introduction

1.1 Introduction

What is a software process? A software process is a set of project phases, stages, methods, techniques, and practices that people employ to develop and maintain software and its associated artifacts (plans, documents, models, code, test cases, manuals, etc.). Not only do you need a software process, you need one that is proven to work in practice, a software process tailored to meet your exact needs.

Why do you need a software process? An effective software process will enable your organization to increase its productivity when developing software. First, by understanding the fundamentals of how software is developed you can make intelligent decisions, such as knowing to stay away from SnakeOil v2.0, the wonder tool that claims to automate fundamental portions of the software process. Yes, tools are important, but they must support and accommodate the chosen process, and they should not introduce too much overhead. Second, it enables you to standardize your efforts, promoting reuse, repeatability, and consistency between project teams. Third, it provides an opportunity for you to introduce industry best practices such as code inspections, configuration management, change control, and architectural modeling to your software organization. Fourth, a defined software process establishes a baseline approach for greater consistency and future enhancements.

An effective software process will also improve your organization's maintenance and support efforts, also referred to as production efforts, in several ways. First, it should define how to manage change and appropriately allocate maintenance changes to future releases of your software, streamlining your change process. Second, it should define both how to smoothly transition software into operations and support and how the operations and support efforts are actually performed. Without effective operations and support processes, your software will quickly become shelfware.

An effective software process considers the needs of both development and production.

Why adopt an existing software process or improve your existing process using new techniques? The reality is that software is growing more and more complex, and without an effective way to develop and maintain that software, the chance of achieving the required levels of quality decreases. Not only is software getting more complex, you're also being asked to create more software simultaneously. Most organizations have several software projects currently in development and have many times that in production — projects that need to be managed effectively. Furthermore, the nature of the software that we're building is also changing, from the simple batch systems of the 1970s that structured techniques are geared toward to the interactive, international, user-friendly, 7/24, high-transaction, high-availability online systems that object-oriented and component-based techniques are aimed at. And while you're doing that, you're asked to increase the quality of the systems that you're delivering and to reuse as much as possible so that you can work faster for less money. A tall order, one that is nearly impossible to fill if you can't organize and manage your staff effectively, and a software process provides the basis to do just that.

1.1.1 The Unified Process

The Unified Process is a framework from which a software process may be instantiated (Jacobson, Booch, & Rumbaugh, 1999). The Rational Unified Process (RUP) is one instantiation of the Unified Process and is the latest software process endeavor of Rational Corporation (Krutchen, 2000), the same people who introduced what has become the industry-standard modeling notation the Unified Modeling Language (UML). The heart of the Unified Process is the Objectory Process, one of several products and services that Rational acquired when they merged with Ivar Jacobson's Objectory organization several years ago. Rational enhanced Objectory with their own processes and those of other tool companies that they have either purchased or partnered with to form the initial version (5.0) of the RUP officially released in December of 1998.

Figure 1.1 presents the initial lifecycle of the Unified Process, comprised of four serial phases and nine core workflows. Along the bottom of the Figure 1.1 you see that any given development cycle through the Unified Process should be organized into iterations. The basic concept is that your team works through appropriate workflows in an iterative manner so at the end of each iteration you produce an internal executable that your user community can worked with. This reduces the risk of your project by improving communication between you and your customers. Another risk-reduction technique built into the Unified Process is the concept that you should make a go/no-go decision at the end of each phase — if a project is going to fail, then you want to stop it as early as possible. Granted, the important decision points are actually at the end of the Inception and Elaboration phases (by the time you've hit the end of the Construction phase, you've likely left it too late to be worthwhile cancelling). An important concept in an industry with upward of an 80–90% failure rate on large-scale, mission-critical projects (Jones, 1996).

Figure 1.1   The Initial Lifecycle of the Unified Process

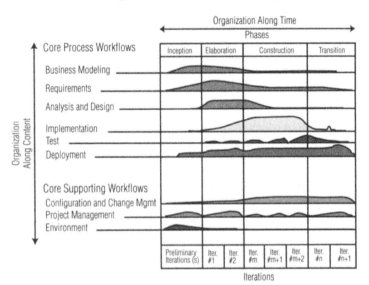

The Inception phase is where you define the project scope and the business case for the system. The initial use cases for your software are identified, and the key ones are described briefly. Use cases are the industry standard technique for defining the functional requirements for systems. They provide significant productivity improvements over traditional requirement documents because they focus on what adds value to users as opposed to product features. Basic project management documents are started during the Inception phase, including the initial risk assessment, the estimate, and the project schedule. As you would expect, key tasks during this phase include business modeling and requirements engineering, as well as the initial definition of your environment including tool selection and process tailoring.

You define the project scope and the business case during the Inception phase.

The Elaboration phase focuses on detailed analysis of the problem domain and the definition of an architectural foundation for your project. Because use cases aren't sufficient for defining all requirements, a deliverable called a Supplementary Specification is defined which describes all nonfunctional requirements for your system. A detailed project plan for the Construction Phase is also developed during this phase based on the initial management documents started in the Inception phase.

You define the architectural foundation for your system during the Elaboration phase.

The Construction phase is where the detailed design for your application is developed, as well as the corresponding source code. The goal of this phase is to produce the software and supporting documentation to be transitioned to your user base. A common mistake that project teams make is to focus primarily on this phase, often to their detriment because organizations typically do not invest sufficient resources in the previous two phases and therefore lack the foundation from which to successfully develop software that meets the needs of their users. During the Inception and Elaboration phases, you invest the resources necessary to understand the problem and solution domains; during the Construction phase, there should be very few "surprises," such as significantly changed requirements or new architectural approaches. Your goal is to build the system.

You finalize the system to be deployed during the Construction phase.

The purpose of the Transition phase, described in this book, is to deliver the system to your user community. There is often a beta release of the software to your users, typically called a pilot release within most businesses, in which a small group of users work with the system before it is released to the general community. Major defects are identified and potentially acted on during this phase. Finally, an assessment is made regarding the success of your efforts to determine whether another development cycle/increment is needed to further enhance the system. It is during this time that your nonfunctional requirements, including technical constraints such as performance considerations, become paramount. You will focus on activities such as load testing, installation testing, and system testing, all activities that validate whether your system fulfills its nonfunctional requirements.

You deliver the system during the Transition phase.

The Unified Process has several strengths. First, it is based on sound software engineering principles such as taking an iterative, requirements-driven, and architecture-based approach to development in which software is released incrementally. Second, it provides several mechanisms, such as a working prototype at the end of each iteration and the go/no-go decision point at the end of each phase, which provides management visibility into the development process. Third, Rational has made and continues to make a significant investment in their RUP product (http://www.rational.com/products/rup), an HTML-based description of the Unified Process that your organization can tailor to meet its exact needs. In fact, the reality is that you must tailor it to meet your needs because at 3,000+ HTML pages it comprises far more activities than any one project or organization requires. Pick and choose out of the RUP the activities that apply, and then enhance them with the best practices described in this book series and other sources to tailor an effective process for your team. Accepting the RUP right out of the box is naïve at best. At worst, it is very likely a path to failure.

The Unified Process also suffers from several weaknesses. First, it is only a development process. The initial version of the Unified Process does not cover the entire software process;

as you can see in Figure 1.1, it is obviously missing the concept of operating and supporting your software once it has been released into production. Second, the Unified Process does not explicitly support multiproject infrastructure development efforts such as organization/enterprise-wide architectural modeling, missing opportunities for large-scale reuse within your organization. Third, the iterative nature of the lifecycle is foreign to many experienced developers, making acceptance of it more difficult. The rendering of the lifecycle in Figure 1.1 certainly does not help this issue.

The software industry has a capacity for almost infinite self-delusion.
— Capers Jones

In *The Unified Process Elaboration Phase* (Ambler & Constantine, 2000a), the second volume in this series, we show in detail that you can easily enhance the Unified Process to meet the needs of real-world development. We argue that you need to start at the requirements for a process, a good start at which is the Capability Maturity Model (CMM). Second, you should look at the competition, in this case the OPEN Process (Graham, Henderson-Sellers, and Younessi, 1997) (http://www.open.org.au) and the process patterns of the Object-Oriented Software Process (Ambler 1998, Ambler 1999) and see which features you can reuse from those processes. From this we formulate an enhanced lifecycle based on what you've learned and support that lifecycle with proven best practices. This lifecycle summarizes our instantiation of the Unified Process, what we call the Enterprise Unified Process (EUP).[1]

The Unified Process is a good start but likely needs to be tailored and enhanced to meet the specific needs of your organization.

1.1.2 The Enterprise Unified Process (EUP)

The major addition that the EUP makes over the standard Unified Process or the current version of the RUP is that it redefines the scope of the Unified Process to include the entire software process, not just the development process. This implies that software processes for operations, support, and maintenance efforts need to be added. Second, to be sufficient for today's organizations, the Unified Process also needs to support the management of a portfolio of projects, something the OPEN Process has called "programme management" and the OOSP has called "infrastructure management." These first two steps result in the enhanced version of the lifecycle depicted in Figure 1.2. Finally, the Unified Process needs to be fleshed out with proven best practices, in this case found in articles published in *Software Development*.

---

1. This is the first use of the term EUP in this book series, even though this is the last book in the series. This new name is the result of the realization that we needed a name for our instantiation of the Unified Process; the term "enhanced lifecycle for the Unified Process" wasn't sufficient. Because the main difference between this instantiation and others, particularly the RUP, is that our scope focuses on the needs of an real-world enterprise and not just that of a single development team we felt that the name Enterprise Unified Process was appropriate.

Figure 1.2 The Lifecycle for the Enterprise Unified Process (EUP)

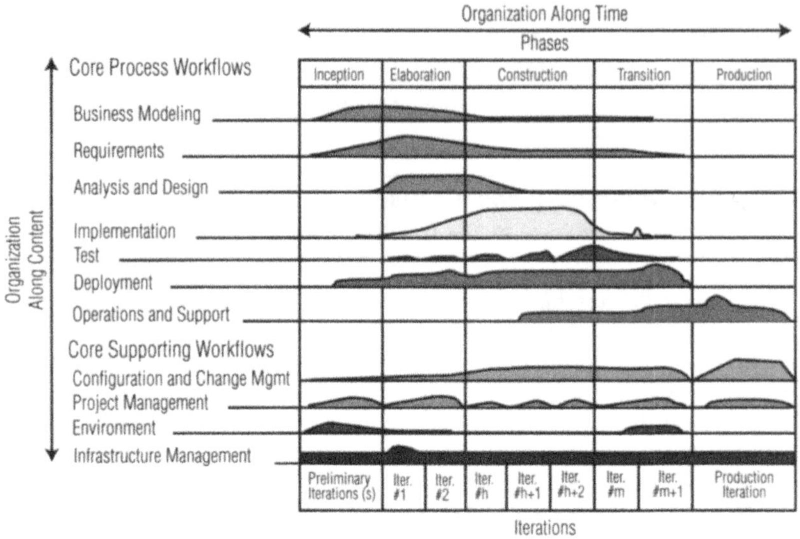

The EUP includes a fifth phase, Production, representing the portion of the software lifecycle after a version of a system has been deployed. Because on average software spends 80% of its lifetime in production, the Production phase is a required feature of a realistic software process. Explicitly including a Production phase also enhances the 20% of the lifecycle that you spend in development because it makes it clear to developers that they need to take production issues into account and provides greater motivation to work towards a common architecture across projects. As the name of the phase implies, its purpose is to keep your software in production until it is either replaced with an updated version, from a minor release such as a bug fix to a major new release, or it is retired and removed from production. Note that there are no iterations during this phase, or there is only one iteration, depending on how you wish to look at it, because this phase applies to the lifetime of a single release of your software. To develop and deploy a new release of your software, you need to run through the four development phases again.

The Production phase encompasses the post-deployment portion of the lifecycle.

Figure 1.2 also shows that there are two new workflows: a core workflow called Operations & Support and a supporting workflow called Infrastructure Management. The purpose of the Operations & Support workflow is exactly as the name implies, to operate and support your software. Operations and support are both complex endeavors, endeavors that need processes defined for them. This workflow, as do all the others, span several phases. During the Construction phase, you will need to develop operations and support plans, documents, and training manuals. During the Transition phase, you will continue to develop these artifacts, reworking them based on the results of testing. Finally, during the Production phase, your operations staff will keep your software running, performing necessary backups and batch jobs as needed, and your support staff will interact with your user community who are working with your software. This workflow basically encompasses portions of the OOSP's Release stage and Support stage as well as the OPEN Process's Implementation Planning and Use of System activities. In the Internet economy where 7/24 operations is the norm, you quickly discover that high-quality and high-availability is crucial to success — you need an Operations and Support workflow.

The Operations and Support workflow is needed to ensure high-quality and high-availability of your software.

The Infrastructure Management workflow focuses on the activities required to develop, evolve, and support your organization's infrastructure artifacts, such as your organization/ enterprise-wide models, your software processes, standards, guidelines, and your reusable artifacts. Your software portfolio management efforts are also performed in this workflow. Infrastructure Management occurs during all phases; the blip during the Elaboration phase represents architectural support efforts to ensure that a project's architecture appropriately reflects your organization's overall architecture. This includes infrastructure modeling activities such as the development of an enterprise requirements/business model, a domain architecture model, and a technical architecture model. These three core models form your infrastructure models that describe your organization's long-term software goals and shared/ reusable infrastructure. The processes followed by your Software Engineering Process Group (SEPG) — which are responsible for supporting and evolving your software processes, standards, and guidelines — are also included in this workflow. Your reuse processes are included as well because practice shows that to be effective, reuse management is a cross-project endeavor. For you to achieve economies of scale developing software, to increase the consistency and quality of the software that you develop, and to increase reuse between projects, you need to manage your common infrastructure effectively — you need the Infrastructure Management workflow.

Infrastructure Management supports your cross-project/programme-level, activities such as reuse management and organization/enterprise-wide architecture.

Comparing the enhanced lifecycle of Figure 1.2 with the initial lifecycle of Figure 1.1, you will notice that several of the existing workflows have also been updated. First, the Test workflow has been expanded to include activity during the Inception phase. You develop your initial, high-level requirements during this phase, requirements that you can validate using techniques such as walkthroughs, inspections, and scenario testing. Two of the underlying philosophies of the OOSP are that you should test often and early and that if something is worth developing, then it is worth testing. Therefore testing should be moved forward in the lifecycle. Also, the Test workflow needs to be enhanced with the techniques of the OOSP's Test In The Small and Test In The Large stages, two process patterns which apply the techniques of the Full Lifecycle Object-Oriented Testing (FLOOT) methodology (Ambler, 2001).

> *Test early and test often. If it is worth creating, it is worth testing.*

The second modification is to the Deployment workflow, by extending it into the Inception and Elaboration phases. This modification reflects the fact that deployment, at least of business applications, is a daunting task. Data conversion efforts of legacy data sources are often a project in their own right, a task that requires significant planning, analysis, and work to accomplish. Furthermore, our belief is that deployment modeling should be part of the Deployment workflow and not the Analysis & Design workflow as it currently is, due to the fact that deployment modeling and deployment planning go hand in hand. Deployment planning can and should start as early as the Inception phase and continue into the Elaboration and Construction phases in parallel with deployment modeling.

> *Deployment is complex, and planning often must start early in development to be successful.*

The Environment workflow has been updated to include the work necessary to define the Production environment, work that would typically occur during the Transition phase (you could easily do this work earlier if you wish, but the Transition phase often proves the best time for this effort). The existing Environment workflow processes effectively remain the same, the only difference being that they now need to expand their scope from being focused simply on a development environment to also include operations and support environments. Your operations and support staff need their own processes, standards, guidelines, and tools, the same as your developers. Therefore you may have some tailoring, developing, or purchasing to perform to reflect this need.

The Configuration & Change Management workflow is extended into the Production phase to include the change control processes needed to assess the impact of a proposed change to your deployed software and to allocate that change to a future release of your system. This change control process is often more formal during this phase than what you do during development due to the increased effort required to update and re-release existing software.

> *Change control management will occur during the Production phase.*

Similarly, the Project Management workflow is also extended into the new Production phase to include the processes needed to manage your software once it has been released. This workflow is currently light on metrics management activities and subcontractor management, a CMM level 2 key process area, a key need of any organization that outsources portions of its development activities or hires consultants and contractors. People management issues, including training and education as well as career management are barely covered by the Unified Process because those issues were scoped out of it. There is far more to project management than the technical tasks of creating and evolving project plans; you also need to manage your staffs and mediate the interactions between them and other people.

There is far more to project management than planning, estimating, and scheduling.

1.1.3 The Goals of the Transition Phase

During the Transition phase, your project team will focus on testing and validating your complete system, operating the system in parallel with any legacy systems that you are replacing (if applicable), converting legacy databases and systems to support your new release, training the customers of your system, and deploying your system into production. As you perform these activities, you will create and/or evolve a wide variety of artifacts:

- Final product baseline (also known as a production baseline) of your system
- Training materials for your system
- Documentation, including user manuals, support documentation, and operations documentation

The phase is concluded with the Product Release milestone (Krutchen, 2000). To pass this milestone you must:

- Show that your users are satisfied with the system.
- The actual expenditures versus the planned expenditures are still acceptable.

1.1.4 The Goals of the Production Phase

During the Production phase, you will focus on operating your system and supporting your users working with it. This includes monitoring the system and acting appropriately to ensure continued operation; operating and maintaining relevant jobs, logs, and supporting systems; responding to help requests, error reports, and feature requests by users; and managing your change control process so that defects and new features may be prioritized and assigned to future releases. As you perform these activities, you will create and/or evolve a wide variety of artifacts:

- Software problem reports (SPRs) summarizing potential defects or new features for future releases
- Problem resolution strategies to be followed by users requiring support
- Appropriate metrics summarizing system usage, system performance, and user satisfaction

The phase is concluded with the System Replacement milestone. To pass this milestone you must achieve one of the following:

- A new version of the system is deployed into production.
- The system is replaced by a new one.
- The system is removed completely from production, an event called "sunsetting."
- Your organization ceases system operations.

1.1.5 How Work Generally Proceeds During the Transition and Production Phases

A fundamental precept of the Unified Process is that work proceeds in an iterative manner throughout the activities of the various workflows. During the Transition phase, your focus is on testing and deployment of your system, whereas during the Production phase, your focus is on operations and support. As Figure 1.1 indicates, the workflows mostly applicable during the Transition and Production phases are:

- Requirements (covered in Volumes 1 and 2, *The Unified Process Inception Phase* and *The Unified Process Elaboration Phase,* respectively)
- Analysis and Design (covered in Volumes 2 and 3, *The Unified Process Elaboration Phase* and *The Unified Process Construction Phase,* respectively)
- Implementation (covered in Volumes 2 and 3, *The Unified Process Elaboration Phase* and *The Unified Process Construction Phase,* respectively)
- Deployment (Chapter 2)
- Test (Chapter 3)
- Operations and Support (Chapter 5)
- Configuration & Change Management (covered in Volume 3, *The Unified Process Construction Phase*)
- Project Management (Chapter 4)
- Infrastructure Management (Chapter 6)

1.1.6 The Requirements Workflow

The purpose of the Requirements workflow is to engineer the requirements for your project. During the Transition phase, you will identify new requirements based on testing results. You will be discovering new requirements as your users work with your system during alpha/beta/pilot testing, as well as use acceptance testing. These requirements, as well as defect reports, need to be handled by your configuration and change management efforts and reassigned to iterations during this current phase. Changes assigned to iterations within the transition phase will need to be explored via your normal modeling workflow efforts, including that of the Requirements workflow.

The Production phase does not include Requirement workflow efforts because this workflow pertains to development efforts handled during the Inception, Elaboration, Construction, or Transition phases of a future release (from the point of view of the Production phase). This includes the development efforts of new jobs to support operations and support efforts — work that should be treated as a miniproject with its own development phases.

1.1.7 The Analysis and Design Workflow

The purpose of the Analysis and Design workflow is to model your software. During the Transition phase, your modeling efforts are likely to address last minute changes due to new requirements (see above) and/or as the result of addressing defects. As with the Requirements workflow, the Analysis and Design workflow is not pertinent to the Production phase.

1.1.8 The Implementation Workflow

The purpose of the Implementation workflow is to write and initially test your software. During the Transition phase, your implementation efforts will focus on the rework of your system to address new requirements and/or defects. As with the Requirements and the Analysis and Design workflows, the Implementation workflow is not pertinent to the Production phase.

1.1.9 The Deployment Workflow

The purpose of the Deployment workflow, the topic of Chapter 2, is to ensure the successful deployment of your system. During the Transition phase, the Deployment workflow will include several key activities:

1. *Finalize of your deployment plan.* Deployment of software, particularly software that replaces or integrates with existing legacy software, is a complex task that needs to be thoroughly planned. Your deployment planning may have begun as early as the Inception phase and evolved throughout the Elaboration and Construction phases.

2. *Finalize your deployment model of the current environment.* As you work towards installing your system you will find that you need to model last-minute changes pertaining to the deployment of the existing systems, at least those applicable to the system that you are building, within the current environment. Deployment modeling was originally an activity of the Analysis and Design workflow in the initial version of the Unified Process (Krutchen, 2000); this work has been moved into the Deployment workflow for the EUP. The reason for this is simple: deployment planning and deployment modeling go hand in hand and are the main drivers of your actual deployment efforts. This is a stylistic issue more than anything else.

3. *Deploy your system into production.* This effort includes the installation of your software, hardware, and middleware as well as any support systems and jobs. It also encompasses training your user community, your support staff, your operations staff, and your maintenance developers (if any) that will be taking over further development of the system. You will need to deploy relevant documentation to these groups of people as well.

1.1.10 The Test Workflow

The purpose of the Test workflow, the topic of Chapter 3, is to verify and validate the quality and correctness of your system. During the Transition phase, you will focus on testing in the large activities (Ambler, 1999), including function testing, system testing, user acceptance testing, and alpha/beta/pilot testing. During the Production phase, limited testing will occur, often performed by support personnel in conjunction with maintenance developers, to verify problems reported by your users.

1.1.11 The Operations and Support Workflow

The purpose of the Operations and Support workflow, the topic of Chapter 5, is to perform the activities required to successfully operate and support your software. During the Transition phase, you will continue to develop operations and support plans, documents, and training manuals, reworking them based on the results of testing. During the Production phase, your operations staff will keep your software running, performing necessary backups and batch jobs as needed, and your support staff will interact with your user community whom are working with your software.

1.1.12 The Configuration and Change Management Workflow

The purpose of the Configuration and Change Management workflow is to ensure the successful evolution of your system. During the Transition phase, this workflow focuses on the categorization, prioritization, and assignation to iterations or future releases of defects found during testing. This activity is critical to your success because you need to trade off the goal of your system meeting the needs of its users with the necessity to reduce the amount of rework so you can actually deliver your software. You will still need to place project artifacts under configuration management control, and will want to define the production/final baseline for each artifact before final delivery of your system. Configuration management (CM) is essential to ensure that you have the proper versions of your project artifacts in place so that your system may be further evolved in future releases.

1.1.13 The Project Management Workflow

The purpose of the Project Management workflow, the topic of Chapter 4, is to ensure the successful management of your project team's efforts. During the Transition phase, the Project Management workflow focuses on several key activities:

1. *Identify potential risks.* The project team must ensure that the project's risks are managed effectively, and the best way to do that is to ensure that the riskier and/or more important requirements are assigned to earlier iterations.

2. *Assess the viability of the project.* At the end of the Transition phase a project viability assessment should be made (also called a go/no-go decision) regarding the project. You may find that the results of your testing show that your system simply isn't ready to be delivered, that it either needs to be reworked or scrapped completely and therefore should not be put into production.

3. *Develop a detailed plan for the Transition phase.* An important part of project management during any project phase is the definition and continual update of a detailed project plan for that phase. Your planning efforts will include the testing and rework of your system, training efforts, and actual deployment tasks.

4. *Navigate the political waters within your organization.* An unfortunate fact of software development is that softer issues such as people management and politics are a reality for all software projects.

5. *Perform a project retrospective.* During the Transition phase, as well as at the beginning of the Production phase, it is an ideal time to learn from your experiences (Ambler, 1999) by performing a project retrospective (Kerth, 2001).

6. *Manage the team's efforts.* A key activity of project management is to manage the people on the project team, ensuring that the team works together effectively and that the personal career goals of each team member are being met to the best of your abilities.

During the Production phase, your project management efforts revolve around the management of your operations and support staff as well as your configuration and change control efforts. You may find that you need to lobby for support to begin work on a new release of your system or even to begin work on a related system. People management issues are still relevant, such as career management efforts as well as training and education efforts for your staff. Remember, many activities performed by information technology (IT) staff are not performed within the scope of the development of a system, activities that still need to be managed.

1.1.14 The Infrastructure Management Workflow

The Infrastructure Management workflow, the topic of Chapter 6, encompasses activities that are outside of the scope of a single project yet are still vital to your organization's success. This includes activities such as strategic reuse management and support, software process management and support, enterprise modeling, organization/enterprise-level architectural modeling, standards and guidelines management and support, and programme management. During the Transition and Production phases, all of these efforts are important, although because your team is at the end of a development effort, there should be a focused software process improvement (SPI) based on the results of your project retrospective(s).

1.1.15 The Organization of This Book

This book is organized in a simple manner. There is one chapter for each of the Deployment, Test, Project Management, Operations and Support, and Infrastructure Management workflows. Each of these chapters is also organized in a straightforward manner, starting with our thoughts about best practices for the workflow, followed by our comments about the *Software Development* articles that we have chosen for the chapter, then the articles themselves. The book finishes with a chapter looking beyond the Unified Process to alternative techniques, particularly agile techniques such as Extreme Programming (XP) and Agile Modeling (AM).

_2_

Chapter 2

Deployment

2.1 Best Practices for the Deployment Workflow

If you can't get software into your user's hands, then what is its value? Absolutely nothing. Software deployment is a complex endeavor, all too frequently ignored in favor of sexier topics such as distributed object development, components, or the latest version of the Java development kit. The Deployment workflow includes efforts such as your system's initial release planning, including identifying your deployment audience's potential release window, and general deployment strategy — will you release the software all at once or incrementally? It also includes efforts such as training your customers, including the end users of your system as well as the operations and support staff that will be working with it. It also includes actual installation of your system into your staging and production environments. Why is the Deployment workflow important? The answer is simple: you may be able to create the greatest software in the world, but if you can't deploy it, it really doesn't matter.

In the article "Effective Software Deployment" Scott W. Ambler overviews the activities of the Deployment workflow by phase. He shows that when you are deploying a system, you need to consider three basic tasks: preparing for release, releasing your system to operations and support, and finally releasing your system to your user community. During the Inception phase the Deployment workflow focuses on your system's initial release planning, including identifying your deployment audience's potential release window, and general deployment strategy. During the Elaboration phase you must define the deployment configurations for your system as part of your architectural efforts. During the Construction phase the majority of your Deployment workflow efforts often focus on legacy data conversion considerations, detailed deployment modeling, development of operations and support documentation, and detailed deployment planning, including the development of scripts and tests to perform the actual conversion. During the Transition phase you must finalize and accept the user, support, and operations documentation before deploying the system. Actual deployment occurs toward the end of the Transition phase. At this point, you perform any required data conversion or run the new system in parallel with the existing system for several weeks to ensure that it actually works in production. You may also choose to operate a pilot release with a subset of your user community verifying that it runs before you "inflict" the system on everyone. The Deployment workflow does not explicitly extend into the Production phase of the enhanced life cycle for the Enterprise Unified Process (EUP). Note, however, that because your user community is constantly changing — people are transferred, hired, and move on to other organizations — you may need to deploy systems to new users, particularly for systems requiring components deployed on user's workstations.

2.1.1 Preparing to Deploy

Careful preparation is required if your deployment efforts are to succeed. Scott W. Ambler in "Planning for Deployment" shows that when you're developing complex software (the kind of systems typically tackled with modern technologies such as J2EE or .NET), your deployment efforts can be similarly complex. Therefore, whether you're building a replacement system or plowing a fresh "greenfield" development, adequate planning is essential for successful deployment. Your planning efforts must take into consideration the following tasks:

1. Development of installation and de-installation scripts
2. Development and distribution of documentation
3. Development and implementation of multilevel training to your customers
4. Negotiation of release dates, including your system as well as for of other systems or interfaces to those systems that yours interacts with
5. Upgrading your users' technical and/or physical environments
6. Upgrading your support environment
7. Developing and then communicating a release announcement
8. Deployment of your system

In "Planning the Right Rollout" Jeff Weinberg provides complementary advice for successful preparation. He points out that it is critical that you get your support and operations staff involved early. Everyone, including your team as well as operations and support staff, need proper training and preparation before executing the rollout. He believes that your initial focus when deploying your system is to build relationships within your user community and to identify people who can learn to master the application. He advises that you should thoroughly document the installation process, validating and updating it on your first installation efforts (installation testing is described in Chapter 3), thereby learning from your experiences. Part of your deployment modeling efforts should be to determine the differences that exist between locations, differences that may cause you to vary your installation procedures. He also points out the importance of training, describing the various strategies you may want to follow. Finally, Weinberg focuses on the importance of post-deployment efforts, in other words the Production phase, when he describes the need to define a plan for supporting the application after the rollout, setting expectations and training your support staff, and the need to keep a team of developers available for ongoing maintenance and enhancements (especially right after the rollout when the biggest problems are likely to occur).

Andy Barnhart describes deployment best practices in "Creating Good Installations." As both a software developer and a product reviewer for *Software Development* magazine (www.sdmagazine.com), he has significant experience installing and de-installing software. He believes that a very short list of problems accounts for most installation procedures, including no uninstall procedures, file overwrites, the removal of shared files, and failure to include a new system component. He suggests that you should put off creating the installation until the last moment because it is a development project in its own right, the implication being that you must design it, implement it, and thoroughly test it, and doing this properly takes time. Issues to consider when creating an installation procedure include your naming strategy for files, your system's ability to tolerate different versions of other system components (such as shared databases, shared DLLs, …), and your understanding of how your system interacts with other system components. Finally, because installation is difficult, he stresses the importance of installation testing.

A significant issue to consider when you are deploying a system is how it interacts with other systems currently in production — few systems are truly brand new. Instead, it is more common to see applications that reuse functionality and data that already exist within your production environment. In "Manageable Migrations" Brian Black argues that the only way to be successful at developing hybrid systems, those that use new and legacy functionality together, is one where a laser-sharp focus remains on how the legacy environment will be impacted. He shows that there are functions within the legacy environment that you do not want to interfere with because of reliability and response time issues. When reusing existing functionality, it is important to quantify the impact that the planned user load will have on the system. To do this you need to perform capacity planning that builds a picture of how the new system's processing will be split between the new and legacy environments. You should identify the major functions being accessed and the frequency and performance impact of that access. With this information you are in a position to develop the architecture for your system in such a way that you can deploy it in the least invasive manner possible. Viable architectural strategies for hybrid systems include transaction gateways, data replication, log sniffing, and batch manipulation. Taken in this light, it is clear that to common advice to do a "simple" data conversion is often insufficient for many systems that you are likely to build. In short, this article is important because it gives you insight into how you need to plan the deployment of a hybrid system.

Finally, in "UML Deployment Modeling and Beyond" Scott W. Ambler describes how to create UML deployment diagrams and apply them effectively throughout the software process. A deployment diagram depicts a static view of the run-time configuration of processing nodes and the components that run on those nodes. It shows your system's hardware, the software installed on that hardware, and the middleware that connects the disparate machines together. A common best practice is that deployment modeling is performed cooperatively by both the development and engineering folks responsible for building the system and by operations folks who are responsible for operating it and supporting it once in production. This is advantageous because the engineers know how to build the system, whereas the operations people will have a better understanding of your system's current environment and important operational considerations that the engineers may not fully appreciate.

2.1.2 Deploying Your System

A critical part of the deployment workflow is the transitioning of your system to your customers, including your operations staff, your support staff, and your end users. When you are deploying a system, not only do you need to install the software and hardware, but you must also distribute appropriate documentation to your customers. In "Place Tab A in Slot B" Scott W. Ambler argues that when you are building a system, you want to ensure that it can be maintained and enhanced over time after it's been deployed. These goals are supported by sufficient system documentation — written descriptions of the applications, not just comments in your source code. In this article Ambler describes a collection of documentation best practices, including recognizing that people need a road map to understand the system; documenting only to fulfill clear, important, and immediate needs; identifying each document's customer, remembering that different customers have different needs; determining each document's medium based on its use; keeping documents as simple as possible; traveling light (Beck, 2000; Ambler, 2002) and therefore minimizing the number of documents that you create and maintain; and finally letting the customer and not the developer decide whether system documentation is sufficient.

No requirements document starts with the assumption that the new system will be initialized with bad data, yet this is often the case in practice. John Boddie describes how to handle many of the challenges that you'll experience with legacy systems in "Waste Management." Boddie argues that controlling and cleaning up the garbage is as central to good software development as it is to modern living. We do not all have to become waste management specialists, but every manager needs a grounding in the rudiments of data migration, along with an appreciation for the complexities of dealing with messy data. Part of system deployment is conversion of legacy data and systems, and/or integration with them. This means that you require an understanding the semantics of the legacy systems and data you are dealing with, the business practices that use the current systems, and the way these are expected to change, as well as the technologies that the new system, the old systems, and the migration environment use. When migrating data, you do not have the luxury of dealing with the clean abstractions that are hopefully implemented in your system; instead you must contend with idiosyncrasies from years of legacy system operation, including data elements that have been redefined, multiple applications of data fields, and obsolete values. Boddie goes further by pointing out that you can't assume that your new system is the only one using the migrated data. (This points to the importance of programme management, one of the activities of the Infrastructure Management workflow.) If the data you are migrating is used by multiple downstream systems (not an unusual situation), then you may need to provide data feeds to those systems as well. If legacy integration or data conversion is an issue for your project, then Boddie's article is a must read.

2.2 The Articles

2.2.7 "Place Tab A in Slot B" by Scott W. Ambler

2.2.8 "Waste Management" by John Boddie, edited by Larry Constantine

2.2.1 "Effective Software Deployment"

by Scott W. Ambler

Deploying software is a complex endeavor, one that you should plan for early in the development life cycle.

If you can't get software into your users' hands, then what is its value? Absolutely nothing. Software deployment is a complex endeavor, all too frequently ignored in favor of sexier topics such as distributed object development, components, or the latest version of the Java development kit. I've learned about successful software deployment from developing and releasing mission-critical, object-oriented software in a variety of environments.

Figure 2.1 Lifecycle for the Enhanced Unified Process

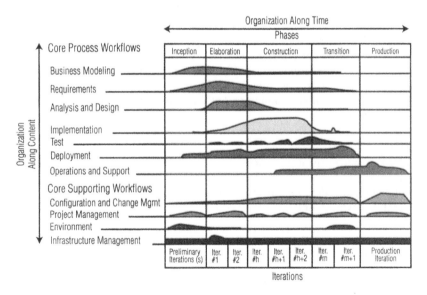

Figure 2.1 depicts my extended life cycle for the Enterprise Unified Process (EUP). I've extended the Deployment workflow to begin in the Inception phase, as opposed to the Construction phase in the initial version of the Unified Process (*The Rational Unified Process* by Philippe Krutchen, Addison Wesley Longman, 1999). Because deployment can be quite complex, especially when your user base is physically dispersed or you have a wide range of system configurations, you must start planning early in your project life cycle.

Figure 2.2 Deployment Support Process

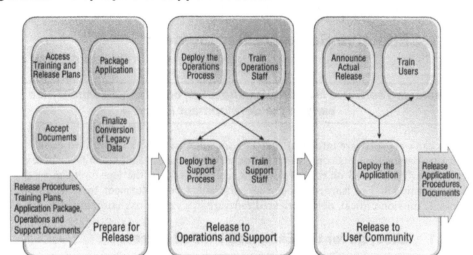

To meet the real-world demands for deploying mission-critical software, apply the "release stage" process pattern shown in Figure 2.2 (reprinted from my *More Process Patterns,* Cambridge University Press, 1999). When deploying a system, consider three basic tasks: preparing for release, releasing the application to operations and support, and releasing the application to your user community. Let's map these tasks to the Deployment workflow on a phase-by-phase basis.

Inception Phase

You tackle key management documents — your initial risk assessment, estimate, and plan — during the Inception phase. The Deployment workflow focuses on your system's initial release planning, including identifying your deployment audience's potential release window, and general deployment strategy — will you release the software all at once or incrementally?

Understanding your deployment audience is critically important to your project. There are at least three distinct groups to consider: your users, your operations staff, and your support staff. You must also determine the level of control that each group has over deployment. For example, both operations and support departments often have defined criteria for the release of new software. Further, I once worked for an organization where all software had to be first accepted by union representatives before it could be deployed. Identify early in your project the deployment hoops that you'll have to jump through.

Elaboration Phase

The Elaboration phase focuses on detailed analysis of the problem domain and defining an architectural foundation for your project. When you define architecture, you must define the deployment configurations for your system — each individual deployment configuration should be documented with a UML deployment model that shows how you'll organize actual software and hardware components. Deployment modeling is arguably part of the Analysis and Design workflow, but it should be part of the Deployment workflow because it is a key deployment artifact.

Data conversion is key to deploying a new software system. It's a complex effort that should start early in the software life cycle, typically during the Elaboration phase. You must analyze your legacy data, which entails identifying the legacy data sources, using a persistence model to model the legacy schemas, and choosing official sources for each data attribute that is stored in several places. You must understand your existing legacy data schema so that you can convert it to your new schema, which will be finalized as part of your Analysis and Design workflow efforts during the Construction phase.

During elaboration your deployment plan will evolve, likely based on one of several common installation approaches. Perhaps someone will visit every user and install the software by hand or perhaps the software will be physically distributed for users to install on their own. You might decide to have users log on to a specific location, such as a web site or internal server, to download and install it from there. Perhaps your software will automatically install itself when a user logs in one day, a possible built-in feature of your organization's technical infrastructure. Regardless of your general installation strategy, you've got some planning to do.

Construction Phase

During the Construction phase, you develop detailed design and source code for your application. The majority of your Deployment workflow efforts during this phase will focus on legacy data conversion modeling and planning, including the development of scripts and tests to perform the actual conversion. A related effort is legacy equipment conversion; you might need to upgrade user desktops or internal application servers to run your new system. The earlier you perform equipment conversion the smoother your eventual deployment will actually go. Attempting to upgrade hardware and software simultaneously can be very difficult, so separate these two efforts if possible.

Another important effort is developing operations, support, and user documentation, the potential artifacts of which are summarized in Table 2.1. You will probably need one or more technical writers on your team to develop this documentation. In parallel with writing the documentation, your team must assemble the installation package, which includes procedures and documentation.

Deployment planning continues during the Construction phase. You'll probably need to negotiate your deployment plan with the operations and support departments, as well as with other projects that are also planning on deploying software, to ensure that your project fits into your overall corporate deployment system. An important feature of a good deployment plan is that it includes go/no-go decision points during the actual installation. If at defined times during the installation you have not reached a certain point in the overall installation process, you can roll back your efforts and try to install again at a future date. This is a critical concept for projects that have very stringent deployment requirements, such as software to replace existing mission-critical systems. As Figure 2.2 indicates, your release plan should be accepted towards the end of the Construction phase or early in the Transition phase.

Transition Phase

The purpose of the Transition phase is to deliver the system to your user community, making the Deployment workflow a key focus of this phase. As shown in Figure 2.2, you must

Table 2.1   Documentation Needs for Each Customer Group

Operations

    Backup procedures
    Batch job and printing requirements
    Data extraction/sharing requirements
    Installation procedures
    Resource requirements
    Configuration definition
    Release notes

Support

    Contact points within development and operations
    Escalation procedures
    Support call recording process
    User documentation (all versions)
    List of new features

Users

    Reference manual
    Support user's guide
    Tutorial manual
    User manual
    List of new features

finalize and accept the user, support, and operations documentation before deploying the system. Packaging is also important, although in the case of the Unified Process this is an effort that is split between the configuration and change management and the Implementation workflows. To finalize your software packaging, you'll define its deployment baseline, a configuration management activity, and to perform a "final" build for the software, an Implementation workflow task.

Spreading the Word

Training and education are often key to your deployment success. If the learning curve is too steep, users will quickly abandon it. Further, your operations staff needs to understand how to keep the new technology running properly. Announce the anticipated deployment schedule, including the expected training and installation dates, and train your operations, support, and user communities appropriately during the Transition phase.

During the Transition phase, and perhaps even during the Construction phase, hold regular release meetings with the key players involved in the actual deployment. Discuss testing with quality assurance staff, implementation with developers, and current production with operations staff. Be sure to meet with support and user representatives, so they can inform you of their issues.

Actual deployment occurs toward the end of the Transition phase. At this point, you perform any required data conversion or run the new system in parallel with the existing system for several weeks to ensure that it actually works in production. You may also choose to send a pilot release to a subset of your user community verifying that it runs before you "inflict" the system on everyone. Do the same for the support department so they can simulate production problems when users contact them for help. Finally, as Figure 2.2 indicates, you may also need to deploy a corresponding support process for your system. Regardless of how you go about it, you should plan these efforts first.

As shown in Figure 2.1, the Deployment workflow does not explicitly extend into the Production phase of the enhanced life cycle for the Unified Process. Note, however, that because your user community is constantly changing — people are transferred, hired, and move on to other organizations — the Operations and Support workflow must include installation and deinstallation of your system once it is in production.

Successfully releasing software requires analysis, planning, and implementation. Deployment efforts occur almost from the very start of development and continue through the four Development phases of the enhanced Unified Process life cycle. You must consider the needs of, and work closely with, three distinct groups: users, operations staff, and support staff. Why is the Deployment workflow important? The answer is simple: you may be able to create the greatest software in the world, but if you can't deploy it, it really doesn't matter.

2.2.2 "Planning for Deployment"

by Scott W. Ambler

Never underestimate the complexity of launching your latest system.

It isn't enough to build software — you must also deploy it, so you can operate and support it effectively once it's in production. When you're developing complex software (the kind of systems typically tackled with component-based technologies such as J2EE or .NET), your deployment efforts can be similarly complex. Therefore, whether you're building a replacement system or plowing a fresh "greenfield" development, adequate planning is essential for successful deployment.

Step by Step

First, you must identify your system's customers. The business side includes direct users of the system, along with indirect users such as managers who receive reports based on data generated by your system. With respect to deployment, your primary technical customers are the operations and support staff, two groups who clearly need to be involved with deployment planning efforts. Once you know who your customers are, you can identify what they need from the system and related artifacts, discover their potential roles in the overall deployment effort, and negotiate their actual involvement.

The next major issue is developing your deployment strategy: Will you run the new system in parallel with the existing one or perform a cutover? Running the systems alongside each other lets you easily back out to the original system if the new one runs into problems. However, parallel operations require significant effort on the part of everyone involved: Your users will need to do double entry, the operations staff must run both systems, the support staff will have two systems to support, and the development staff may need to create integration code that temporarily works behind the scenes to synchronize data. For many systems, particularly those supporting online customers via the Internet, a cutover is the only option — few customers would be willing to place their book order with both Amazon version N and Amazon version N+1. With a straight cutover, you'll need to plan for the downtime when the cutover occurs, a period that could last from a few seconds to a few hours or even a few days, depending on the system being deployed. The ability to back out becomes critical with this approach, requiring additional resources to develop and test "de-installation scripts." In fact, many system deployment efforts fail miserably because the development team didn't consider how to back out of their new system, only to discover that they had to do so because of an unforeseen problem during installation. An effective installation routine will include go and no-go checkpoints at which you determine whether deployment efforts are on time and working smoothly. If you don't have these crucial checkpoints, you need to consider stopping and de-installing to a known and safe state from which to attempt deployment at a later date. Never assume that your deployment efforts will go smoothly.

From Back to Front

Working backward is an effective technique for deployment planning. Envision the system in production — users working with it, operations professionals keeping it going, support staff helping users to work with it, and developers modifying it to address defects and implement new requirements — and ask what has to happen to get the system to that point. Then compare that vision with the current environment to determine what you must do to successfully install your system. In my experience, forward planning generally isn't sufficient for system deployment, because the requirements often don't reflect issues pertinent to your system's production phase — that is, the need to operate and support your software is often assumed and therefore not explicitly reflected in your requirements. This problem can be exacerbated when your project life cycle doesn't explicitly include a production phase or even an operations and support workflow. What is out of sight is often out of mind.

Start deployment planning early in the project life cycle, particularly when deployment may be a complex issue. For example, I was once involved with a project for which we needed to physically install a system at 450 separate locations. Our users were geographically dispersed and computer illiterate. Depending on the location, we had to either replace existing hardware or install new equipment. At each location we needed to run a data backup and conversion program, and we had to deploy the system at night so as not to disturb the day-to-day operation of the business. For another project, we had to deploy our systems into a dynamic environment in which several systems worked together, shared common components, supported 24/7 operations and had very limited deployment windows due to service level agreements. As you can see, deployment can be very complex — it may be the most difficult issue that your team faces. Accordingly, it should be considered early, because if you can't deploy your system, you shouldn't build it.

An early focus on deployment not only enables you to avoid problems, it also lets you take advantage of your experiences during development. For example, take notes on what works and what doesn't when you're deploying software into your staging area (see the article "J2EE Testing" in Chapter 3); these notes can serve as the backbone of your installation scripts. For example, when deploying an Enterprise JavaBean (EJB) application for the first time, you'll encounter several common "gotchas," such as how to define XML deployment descriptors, where to put them and how to deploy EJB JAR files.

During development, you'll also discover dependencies between your system and others — dependencies that should appear on your deployment model, but affect your deployment plan because they imply the order in which updates to the various systems must be installed. You'll need to negotiate deployment efforts with the other teams that own the systems that your system depends on, effectively creating a cross-project effort that would be included as part of your Infrastructure Management workflow efforts (assuming that you're following the enhanced life cycle of the Unified Process). If your system's interface changes, or if you need new ways to access their systems, they may also need to release all or part of their systems before yours.

Training your project customers is always an important part of deployment. They may even need training beyond how to work with your application. For example, this might be the first time that some users are working with a PC, a browser or even a mouse. Similarly, this may be the first time that your operations staff works with a new technology that your system uses, such as an EJB application server, and therefore they'll need to be trained in that technology to be qualified to work with your system.

The "Don't Forgets" of Deployment Planning

When planning your system's release into production, remember that you may need to:

1. Develop both installation and de-installation scripts.
2. Distribute corresponding documentation.
3. Provide multilevel training to your customers.
4. Negotiate release dates of other systems or interfaces to those systems.
5. Upgrade your users' technical and/or physical environments.
6. Upgrade your support environment.
7. Develop and then communicate a release announcement.

Pump It Up

When building a new system, you often discover that the existing environment isn't sufficient to support it; therefore, any deployment efforts must include activities to perform required upgrades. These upgrades could include changes to hardware, operating systems, databases or middleware. If you don't know the current status of your technical environment, you'll also need to plan for activities to perform the required legacy analysis. If you're upgrading your database, you may be upgrading the software itself or the database's schema; consequently, you'll need to include data conversion activities in your deployment plan. Physical considerations should also be considered when performing environment upgrades. Is sufficient power available? Are working areas in place? Is there sufficient space in the building(s) that you're deploying to? Are there enough network drops to accommodate new workstations?

You may also need to plan for upgrades to your support environment. Are your existing change management process and required tools in place and sufficient for your needs? If not, you need to plan for appropriate development, training and installation of said tools and procedures. Your support department may need to have their support problem simulation environment or help desk product (which they use to track defects and enhancement requests) upgraded, as well.

A good reality check for your deployment plan is your deployment model; in fact, I often develop the two in parallel. Different deployment architectures, as described by your deployment model, will require different strategies for installation, and therefore will demand different plans. For example, a fat client system requires an installation script that can be operated by your users, whereas an n-tier thin-client application requires an installation script that can be followed by your operations folks: Different customers for the installation script require different levels of script sophistication, and of the strategies used to develop and test those scripts.

Don't forget to distribute the documentation for your system, particularly user documentation (see the article "Place Tab A in Slot B" in this chapter). Electronic documentation can be deployed along with your software, but physical documentation will need to be distributed appropriately. Will physical documents be distributed as part of training sessions, on demand via some sort of document order process, or as part of the system installation itself (in the box for shrink-wrapped software or distributed via your mail system for internally developed software)? Thinking these issues through in advance will save you headaches later.

Now Presenting...

A small but critical part of deployment is the release announcement, a task that may require significant preparation. Your announcement could be an e-mail to your customers, a press release, or even advertisements on television, in magazines, or on the Internet. Release announcements are important because people want to know how and when the new system will affect them, if at all. Remember, you're disrupting their lives, and your deployment efforts should respect this fact.

Deployment planning is an iterative task, one that starts early in the project life cycle and continues until the actual deployment of your system. Most projects don't need a separate deployment plan, but the fact remains that deployment activities must be planned, regardless of the nature of your project. Never underestimate the complexity of software deployment.

2.2.3 "Planning the Right Rollout"

by Jeff Weinberg

Managing the rollout of a complex distributed client/server application is initially challenging. Taking the time to do it right will not only make deployment easier — it will reduce support problems down the road.

You've just finished one or two years of design and development on your latest client/server application. You've employed all the latest and greatest techniques by using prototypes, conducting iterative reviews with users, and thoroughly testing the new application. But, if you're like many team leaders, your job is far from over. Your next step is getting the application into production and into the hands of hundreds — maybe thousands — of users.

You and your development team don't want to see all your hard work result in one of those never-used applications that ends up on the shelf. A successful rollout will make sure this doesn't happen. But where do you begin? Myriad details can haunt you in the middle of the night: When is the phone going to start ringing nonstop? Will a server crash? What if bugs start appearing just after my programmers are reassigned?

Following are some basic guidelines for planning and executing your rollout. They will help improve the success of your application and hopefully let you get some quality sleep at night.

Train Your Team

For starters, it is critical to get your technical support team involved early. Your team needs proper training and preparation before executing the rollout. By the nature of the tools and technology, your team may expect to install the application with a simple batch file, and not see a need to adequately plan the rollout. However, it is imperative to create a plan early and communicate it to them. You can even involve them in the planning, but also be sure to communicate it to the business managers, support personnel, and so forth. If done correctly, you can swiftly and successfully get the application into the users' hands.

Implement with a Pilot Program

Your team probably believes most or all of the bugs have been caught and fixed during the testing process. However, you probably haven't done your testing in a true-to-life scenario, where the application runs in the user environment with developers nearby. You can be certain that as the first users get started with the application, they will quickly find bugs and other problems that weren't caught during formal testing.

In anticipation of these problems, establish a pilot program to provide an opportunity to run the application with users and developers working side by side. A subset of the development team is sufficient. These developers must be readily available and responsive to making adjustments and fixes. This initial focus will filter out problems and ease future rollouts.

It is critical that the initial application users realize its benefits and learn to use it quickly. These users must become experts at working with the application because they are the ones who will promote it throughout your company.

Your primary focus when first rolling out the application is to build relationships within your user community and to identify people who can learn to master the application. Avoid selecting people who won't be critical enough. Also, don't select your best friends — they'll be too easy on you. The squeaky wheel gets the grease, so find the most vocal, critical people to work with. It frightens me every time I take this approach, but the results are often amazing.

By choosing the right people, you are guaranteed they'll find the glitches. Because they are demanding, it takes a little extra effort up front to work with them. Once you have trained them, however, half the deployment battle is won. By nature, these people like to brag. Let them brag about something that will help you champion your application.

Get the Ball Rolling

When you implement the pilot program, you'll be installing your application for the first time. Until you get started, you don't really know how things will work out. Be sure to thoroughly document this first installation process. You also need to install the database components, including triggers, stored procedures, and other necessary items. In a Windows environment, you will likely be using ODBC, device drivers, and other DLLs. Documenting the processes and procedures at this time significantly eases the remaining installations. This documentation can also come in handy when you are required to troubleshoot an installation at one of your sites. It also becomes a useful tool for delegating the installation effort.

Plan Your Success

Schedule your rollout at the right pace. If it's too slow, the users may feel the application is of little value or importance. If it's too fast, you may inadequately prepare the users for the application's full capabilities. In either case, you run the risk of alienating the people who have the most to gain.

When you begin planning your rollout, determine the differences that exist between locations. For example, larger corporations often install the application on different versions of a database that runs on multiple hardware platforms. You may deploy your application to all locations with Oracle Version X. However, some locations may be running Oracle X.1.6 on a Sun platform while other locations are running Oracle X.2.0 on Hewlett Packard hardware. You want to minimize problems like this during the rollout. If you must support multiple platforms, minimize the risk by rolling the application out one platform at a time.

Again, document your experiences in order to reduce the risk of recurring problems. I typically create a simple database of the steps involved with the rollout, and then use it to track experiences and knowledge gained with each new installation. If you create documentation for the users (which is highly recommended), use it during the pilot program to ensure it corresponds with actual usage. You can use the pilot program to fine tune the user documentation. Incorporating feedback into your training program also helps build rollout momentum. Again, during the pilot program, the focus of this training should be on building experts and leveraging them to champion the application to the remaining users within your company.

Training, It's in the Bag

Training is an essential part of the rollout, and can be executed in many forms. The most important planning aspect of training is to understand the users' needs and backgrounds. Power users don't need much more than a quick walk-through, and only limited support early in the rollout. Other users may not have much background with PCs or with the Windows environment. They need hands-on training and considerably more support. I find that brown bag lunch sessions are a great method to get people up to speed on the pending changes that will occur with the new system. These sessions are informal, fun, and they go a long way to leverage the experts you work so hard to create.

Play Nice in the Sand Box

Define a plan for supporting the application after the rollout. Initially, a central team will roll out the application. However, because of time and cultural differences, especially for multinational companies, you may not want to use a centralized support approach. In these cases, a central support person plans and coordinates the rollout for all geographic regions. This person also works closely with regional or local support staff during the rollout's early stages. Over time, the plan should shift responsibility back to regional or local sites.

Base where and when to use local support on site-specific need. If many users reside at any one location, support there may be justified. Our experience finds that support should be located as close to the users as possible. Simply put, knowledgeable support must be available, in person or by phone, whenever a user requires help. If this isn't the case, users may become disenchanted and abandon the new application.

When establishing support, a help desk function can be useful. Typically, it's not a good idea to have your developers provide this type of support. Developers are too close to the application and they often don't have the patience necessary to help people through a problem. Depending on the application and where it's installed, you may be required to make support available 24 hours a day, seven days a week. If this is difficult or impossible to support within your organization, a good alternative is to outsource the help desk function. Many companies offer this service on a customized basis.

It is equally important to set expectations and train your local support personnel. Budget and time constraints may prevent you from bringing your support people to one location. To avoid this, empower the users to assume some of the support. Hands-on training allows people to share experiences early. Encourage users to continue to share experiences, and to teach and learn from each other.

I find that investment in remote control software provides significant value for companies. Remote control software lets you run the application over regular telephone lines. Your organization may already support this software over the LAN. Before even rolling out the application, you can use remote control software to bring local support personnel up to speed. On one project, I used Symantec's PC Anywhere to demo an application to technical personnel in Singapore and in Orleans, France. PC Anywhere allowed remote users to operate our PCs and I was able to train them from thousands of miles away. Offering informal training in this manner allows support personnel and users to get hands-on experience with the application before it's rolled out.

Client/Server Rollout Tips

1. Get your technical support team involved early.
2. Establish a pilot program with users and developers working side by side.
3. Train the most vocal and critical users to become experts.
4. Thoroughly document the first installation process.
5. Minimize risk by rolling the application out one platform at a time.
6. Implement a step-wise rollout--not too fast, not too slow.
7. Brown bag lunch sessions are a great method to get people up to speed.
8. Locate support as close to the users as possible.
9. Keep the application versions the same across all installations.
10. Communicate, communicate, communicate.

Supply and Demand — Providing Version Control

One of the toughest aspects of managing the rollout of a complex distributed client/server application is dealing with installing bug fixes, revisions, and new features. Although not recommended, program changes are sometimes necessary even after the application has been rolled out. Once development is complete, assign some of your developers to the rollout — some to make bug fixes and some to new projects. It's a good idea to keep a small team focused on ongoing maintenance and enhancements, especially right after the rollout.

As more users begin to use the new application, you will get more requests for changes and enhancements. Don't succumb to pressures to change the application right away. If a bug crashes it, you need to make a fix immediately. If a new feature is requested, collect enhancements and implement them simultaneously. Your job is to keep the application versions the same across all installations. Early in the rollout, you may need to update the executable code as often as once a week. For enhancements, update the code no more than once a month. Resist pressure to make too many changes. And remember, test, test, and retest the changes before you roll them out to users.

Rolling out your distributed applications successfully can be challenging. It can also be a fun and rewarding experience. Look at your rollout as part of your overall project effort. Plan ahead and set aside enough time to get the job done right the first time. Don't underestimate the need to communicate throughout the project. Make sure to communicate the rollout plan, the expected benefits the new application will provide, and the realistic effort required for users to come up to speed. Pay extra attention to users during the initial rollout and identify potential experts. Most important, pay close attention to the installation process and make sure the application is installed properly before moving to a new site. A successful rollout will ensure the intended benefits of the application will take place, and will also provide the required return on the investment in your company.

Your applications are written to improve a company's revenue stream and productivity. Following a solid rollout plan will make sure people use your software.

Sweet dreams.

2.2.4 "Creating Good Installations"

by Andy Barnhart

A few simple development tips will help you ensure your application won't damage or disable other programs on its way on or off the user's hard drive.

I recently did a thorough cleaning of my home office. One of the biggest piles of clutter was software submitted in hopes of a review or mention in the column. I really hate to throw the stuff out without taking a peek, so I went through my normal review routine — I back up my hard drive, then install the packages, try them out, then uninstall them. Then I blow away the hard drive, boot from floppy, and restore from tape.

Does this seem a bit extreme? It does to me. But if I don't do it, I often find that I slowly lose disk space or that once-stable products suffer some inexplicable decay. In the long run, I find it more efficient to rebuild a system than to uninstall and hope that my system has been restored to its former state. The few times things go terribly wrong, I can spend weeks trying to cope with the problem, then days trying to exorcise it. Even when things go well, space keeps disappearing slowly.

How does this happen? There is a very short list of problems that accounts for most of the inconveniences I have suffered:

- No uninstall
- DLL overwrites
- Removal of shared files
- Failure to include a new system component

No Uninstall

The first is rather straightforward: no uninstall. Programs that fall into this category are often 16-bit Windows applications that never had to earn the Windows 95 logo. Many shareware programs, even 32-bit implementations, also have this problem. Even some applications that have an uninstall don't properly remove themselves. Perhaps a better description is "applications that won't go away by themselves."

DLL Overwrites

DLL overwrites is a category that has four subcategories. The first is simple and welcome — something newer and better is available, so your old buggy DLL was replaced and the world is better for it. The second subcategory is potentially destabilizing — an older version has been copied without regard to the date of the current DLL. Often, this case is proliferated by the third subcategory — newer, yet unstable DLLs. I ran into this one recently, and it required a reinstall of Windows 95 to correct it. The fourth category, which I refer to as completely wrong DLLs, only comes up in odd cases where a third-party DLL has a name that conflicts with a system DLL or a DLL from another third-party provider. Interesting variations of the Win32 operating system often result from this mistake.

Removal of Shared Files

Removal of shared files occurs in a couple of different scenarios. In one case, an uninstall removes unconditionally, using the logic that "since I put it there, I can blow it away." If you've installed another application that needs the file in the meantime, it will now have a problem. The second scenario occurs when an application doesn't register shared file usage properly. Uninstalling another application that seems to have sole usage of the shared file removes it.

Failure to Include a New System Component

As developers, we tend to stay current with regard to new releases of operating systems or service packs for existing releases. Sometimes, new APIs are added or bugs are fixed in an existing API. You should do a quick check for a new system component in the knowledge base to see if there are bugs in earlier versions. You must make sure it existed in the earliest version of the operating systems you plan to support. If you have to include a new component, you must make sure it can coexist in an earlier version of the operating system. You may need to consider "raising the bar" — restricting operating systems you are supporting to only the more current ones.

The Installation Process

As developers, part of our job is to try to avoid the causes of these problems. Before I get into a few specific tips, let me offer a general one: don't put off creating the installation until the last moment. It is a development project in its own right. You must design it, implement it, and thoroughly test it — and doing this properly takes time.

Some of the design phase tips may affect the product being installed, and the product certainly affects the installation. Thus, I strongly suggest a team approach using product development resources in creating the install. Examples of this are giving consideration to static linking, naming files, and version tolerance.

Static Linking

Static linking is not possible in all environments, and isn't always a good thing to do even if it is possible. For example, if you use C++ and MFC, I don't suggest static linking to the class library. The MFC DLLs are well named (more on that shortly) and the class library is large. But if you use a third-party product that is relatively small, poorly named, or is unlikely to be used by other applications, link it statically if you can. It's just one less potential headache.

Naming Files

Naming files should not be taken too lightly. Despite the emergence of long file names, I suggest sticking with 8.3 names for program files. This protects users from losing the file by backing up or copying using a utility or file system that doesn't support long names. The extensions for executable programs and DLLs are fixed, so this only leaves eight characters for you to work with. Some files may need to support coexistence of different versions, and should use a version number in the name, as the MFC DLLs do. I like the idea of a two-character abbreviation for the product or company at the beginning of the name; this groups the files together in an alphabetic sorted view (the default for Windows Explorer). Search everywhere — knowledge bases, the World Wide Web, news groups, and machines at your site — to look for duplicate names and avoid them. It amazes me how often I come across USER.EXE or SERVER.DLL.

Version Tolerance

Version tolerance is a tough issue. I've often had a new, improved version of a DLL break an existing application. The flip side of this is that some applications refuse to work when it's quite likely the new version of a DLL or operating environment will cause no problem. You have to address this on a case-by-case basis. One of my biggest pet peeves is having an application demand a later version of a system component, but not supply it. Watch out for this one.

Shared Files

A shared file can cause a lot of grief in installs and uninstalls. The two tips I suggest are that you watch out for public placement of private files and consider private placement of some public files. There is no reason to put all your DLLs in the Windows system directory. Co-locating them with the executable (which should be in a product-specific directory) is the best approach for your private files. You have to be careful in deciding what is public vs. private. Third-party DLLs should usually be considered private. Be especially wary if there is a source code purchase option for a library, whether you choose to exercise it or not. Another application may overwrite it with a modified version and break your application.

You should rarely use the second tip — considering private placement for public files. Windows gets fussy when you mismatch versions of some of its core DLLs. But in some rare circumstances, an application requires a specific version of a system DLL that can peacefully coexist with a later version being used by other applications. In this case, placement of the DLL in your program's directory is a better option than forcing the user to remain at a fixed environment level.

Shared files are also a source of problems in uninstall. In some rare circumstances, you might consider leaving files untouched even if the registry indicates no other application uses them. DLLs that you might consider to be system extensions are candidates for consideration.

ActiveX components add a layer of complexity that I don't have room to fully explore in this article, but a good synopsis would be that you should consider each component as a separate installation (handled in batches — don't force the user to do too many installs).

Once you've designed your install, there are a number of approaches to consider for implementation. You might "roll your own," use an installation wizard that comes with your development environment, use a third-party installation utility like Sterling Software's InstallShield or Great Lakes Business Solutions' Wise, use an intranet or Internet approach by downloading components from CAB archive files, use a configuration management tool, or do nothing at all. That last option might surprise you, but there are a lot of cases where it makes sense. If you have a self-contained executable and savvy users, why waste development resources? Sometimes an e-mail informing users where to find a program and how to copy and run it is adequate. In corporate environments, you can often "coat-tail" another program that installs all the needed DLLs.

Testing

Finally, do not overlook installation testing. It is impossible to exhaust all possibilities, but you should try as many different situations as you can. You should make sure that you have tested on all supported platforms, within each platform, on the oldest version you support, and on the most recent available.

Don't limit testing to installation; check your uninstall as well. Download REGCLEAN from the Microsoft Web site (www.microsoft.com) and use it to ensure you don't leave any registry entries. Check disk space and file counts before and after installation, then again after uninstall.

You must also pay attention to interaction with other products. This is very difficult to test if you have a wide distribution. You need to make sure other common applications work after installing your application, and that your application still works after installing other applications. Intertwine installation and uninstall of your product and other common products. Office suites tend to be great testing tools; they are notorious for upgrading Windows and are very picky about having all the proper versions of support DLLs.

Take a Deep Breath

It's important to note that some problems are outside your control or are too costly to fix in the installation. In such cases, carefully document any known problems and work arounds. Make this information available to users as well as technical support staff.

Much of what I discussed seems like common sense. Although difficulties can and do occur, I have never felt that many technical problems prevent products from having good installs. The biggest obstacle is getting time and resources committed to do the work. It's an important issue that deserve attention.

2.2.5 "Manageable Migrations"

by Brian Black

Building hybrid systems that combine new technologies with legacy environments is very possible — provided you make allowances for the impact the hybrid system will have on existing systems.

A former manager of mine had a favorite saying when staff members complained about how difficult a particular task was: "If it was that easy, you could buy the answer at the local mall." This remark is not particularly motivating, but it is thought-provoking, particularly when put in the context of using new software development products. For some reason, new products are always quantum leaps ahead of their predecessors, marketed as easier, faster, cheaper, and better. More important, the prospective user's existing information technology investment is persistently denied. The plain fact is that the great majority of shops are faced with a considerable integration effort when considering something new (like the World Wide Web, for example) for a nontrivial application. New technology may indeed enable the desired system, but technology alone cannot magically create the business solution. Instead, the system must be engineered using solid principles and disciplines so that business objectives can be met.

Building hybrid systems that use new technologies in conjunction with existing legacy investments is possible. Experience has shown, however, that the only successful approach is one where a laser-sharp focus remains on how the legacy environment will be impacted.

Moving Forward

When contemplating a hybrid system, it's worth asking the fundamental question, "Why do this at all?" The simple answer is that there are functions within the legacy environment that you do not want to interfere with for many reasons (including reliability, predictability of response times, and so forth). However, there are also additional functions you should implement, but that are not for use with the legacy platform. Such an approach usually means some combination of the following:

- Capacity in the legacy environment is limited.
- Implementation costs using a hybrid approach are more advantageous.
- Time-to-market considerations require a more rapid development cycle.

This situation summarizes the chief information officer's dilemma: Existing mainframe systems provide the reliability to support key business functions, but the environment is costly to maintain and slow for the development of new systems. A hybrid approach can be considered as one born out of necessity, but it is still an unnatural act because new hardware and software is being grafted onto existing legacy machines. To proceed requires the concurrent execution of two major activities: capacity planning and analyzing function and data interactions.

Capacity Planning

In any project like this, no matter how small, it's important to quantify the impact that the planned user load will have on the system. The legacy environment is constrained in the sense that it either has to sustain performance-critical workloads or has limited excess capacity. The hybrid system will affect it, and establishing an idea of to what degree is essential. This involves getting answers to some basic questions:

- What volumes of business activity must this new system support? Are there any significant time variations (such as seasonal peaks, month end, quarter end, and so on)?
- What is the existing capacity use of the legacy environment; and given current business conditions, how will it change in the future?
- What will the new transactions and queries look like? (This will require further analysis of the business requirements to see if these new loads will interact with existing legacy maintained data, or if they will require the creation of additional data elements that will reside on the new hardware.)
- What additional load will the new demands place on the existing legacy hardware?

Answering all the questions at the beginning of a project may be difficult, but using existing performance data and educated guesses is helpful. The objective is not to be 100% accurate right away, but to have enough data to build a predictive performance model. You can use this model to evaluate different implementation options, and you can refine it as more information is gathered. The process is the "performance conscience" of the project because it can indicate what the impact of different decisions will be. More detailed information that you can feed into the model will be obtained from subsequent tasks.

Function and Data Interactions

Conventional analysis that is used in the design of a system will generate several deliverables. Two are of particular interest:

- A hierarchy of functions that the new system will support and enough detail to specify the major transactions, queries, and reports that must be developed
- A high-level logical data model complete with full attribute definitions

What is important is the overlay of the two in a matrix that indicates the interactions between them, as shown in Table 2.2. Given the correct input and storage, some of the CASE tools on the market will generate this diagram. This is known as a CRUD Matrix (Create, Read, Update and Delete), which is an unfortunate name for a very important piece of analysis. The term "function and data interaction matrix" seems more appropriate.

It is important to build a picture of how the new system's processing will be split between the new and legacy environments. To gain this insight, the capacity planning exercise should identify the major new workloads. It should also, by interpretation, identify the frequency of the functions that are detailed in the y axis of the matrix. Mapping the individual attributes in the x axis of the matrix to each environment completes the picture. Finally, the functions should be sorted in descending order of frequency, indicating which of the CRUD operations are carried out. By multiplying the function frequency by the data size of each attribute, you can calculate the total amount of data processed per time period.

Table 2.2   Function and Data Interactions (CRUD Matrix)

	Entity 1			Entity 2		Entity 3			Entity 4		
	Att #1	Att #2	Att #n	Att #1	Att #2	Att #1	Att #2	Att #3	Att #1	Att #2	Att #3
Function 1									x	x	x
Function 2		x				x					
			I								
			V								
Function N			x	x			x			x	

Developing the Architecture

Given the constraints on the legacy environment, the objective must be to develop a system that is the least invasive. The function and data interaction analysis provides a picture of the total amount of data processed in both components, and the further analysis of this data and other information drives the decision-making process. The function and data analysis checkpoints follow.

Check 1.   For the legacy environment only, what percentage of the total data manipulation is read activity? If the percentage is high, this is good news because it means you can copy data out of the legacy environment and into the new hardware for browsing. (This minimizes the load that is placed on the legacy hardware). Conversely, if the percentage is low, this means a lot of data creation, updating, and deleting must be carried out on existing data elements in the legacy environment. (This reduces the chances of off-loading processing).

Check 2.   What sort of response times do users want for the new functions? Is it within seconds, minutes, or hours (letting the results be delivered by some form of batch reporting)?

Check 3.   Of the functions that alter data elements that reside on the legacy hardware, are there any existing coded production transactions that carry out the same operations? (Again, we are not looking for an exact fit; an existing transaction could manipulate additional attributes above those in which we are interested).

Scoring the Results.   You should tabulate the information from the checks as shown in Table 2.3. This matrix provides a structure for making the decision of how to architect the hybrid system. A predominance of read activity among the high-volume functions suggests that you can off-load data from the legacy environment (with the caveat that the response time objectives can be met). If the high-volume functions require alterations to the data, the legacy system will have to do the work.

Evaluating the Options.   You can pursue three strategies for a hybrid environment: transaction gateways, data replication, and batch manipulation. Without considering cost, each strategy has advantages and considerations, as shown in Table 2.4.

The data gathered previously will help narrow the choices. If the legacy environment's existing transactions do not map well to the requirements of the new functions, a transaction gateway is not an option. Also, if the legacy environment does not use an RDBMS, the data replication options are reduced. But the capacity implications of these strategies are not known, and given the constraints of the legacy environment, you should evaluate the options.

Table 2.3   Information Gathered via Function and Data Analysis Checkpoints

Function	Frequency (Per Day)	Response Time Required			Total MB of Legacy Data Processed		Existing Transaction
		Seconds	Minutes	Hours	Read	Other	
Function 1	100,000	x			5	30	Tran3004
Function 2	83,000		x			78	-
Function N	100			x		5	
Total MB						354	1,296

Table 2.4   Evaluating the Strategies for a Hybrid Environment

Response Time Requirements	Hybrid Strategy	Comments	
		Pros	Cons
Seconds	Transaction Gateway	• Uses existing legacy trans-actions • Existing data for capacity planning activities	• Additional legacy system online load • Little scope for tuning; uses production code
Minutes	RDBMS Data Replication	• Lets specific granularity of data be pushed out • Refresh cycle can be cus-tom-tuned	• No good for legacy DBMSs • Substantial production infastructure
Minutes to Hours	Log-Sniffing-Based Data Replication	• Less invasive than other strategies	• Requires a lot of post pro-cessing to extract data • Infrastructure implications
Hours +	Batch Manipulation	• Least impact on legacy sys-tems if designed correctly	• Capacity issue: Batch windows already under pressure

Capacity Planning (Revisited)

It's time to dust off the models that have already been created, and to use them to evaluate the viable hybrid strategies.

Transaction Gateways.   This should be relatively easy, as the new functions will use existing production transactions. Existing data on per-transaction CPU and I/O counts should be available. The additional volumes for the new functions are known. Multiplying the two will give you the additional demands on the system.

RDBMS Data Replication.   The implementation of this feature varies between products. In most cases, replication results in additional SQL queries being generated. Given background performance statistics, and the volumes of new functions, some estimate of the incremental load can be made.

Log Sniffing. Depending on the legacy DBMS and the operational standards that are in place, log archiving is probably already taking place. However, some degree of post-processing must take place to extract the relevant data elements. It would be preferable to off-load the log data to the new hardware and carry out the processing there. This could mean minimal impact on the legacy environment. If the legacy hardware is chosen, you should run an evaluation benchmark to get performance data that you can put into the model.

Batch Manipulation. The major issue here is that batch windows are under pressure. This is because they cannot be expanded to be used for increased business volumes. Any additional jobs will eat into this scarce resource. If data on existing, comparable jobs exists, use it to provide an estimate. If not, you should run an evaluation benchmark and take measurements.

Informed, Objective Decisions

The process of updating and rerunning predictive models should be thorough, as it is the only objective way of evaluating decisions before they are implemented. Any time there is a change in any significant piece of data, you must rerun the model. Further, how will the new hybrid system perform as workloads grow? You can leverage the investment made in generating performance models into predicting when the hybrid system will no longer function.

This begs the question: if there is a cost in people and time to generate an answer from a model, is it worth it? A colleague of mine once put it quite succinctly. He said, "What is the cost of obtaining the information? If it costs $50,000 in burdened people costs to evaluate purchasing a $30,000 upgrade, why not just order the upgrade?"

If you are dealing with an environment that has a finite capacity, and the potential exists for adversely affecting existing production system response times, blind guesswork is just not acceptable.

2.2.6 "UML Deployment Modeling and Beyond"

by Scott W. Ambler

Incorporating the UML deployment diagram into your system development efforts will increase your chances of delivering your system successfully.

The Unified Modeling Language (UML) describes many models that may or may not be useful to you, depending on your project's needs. Many writers in this field tend to concentrate on a few "core" diagrams — such as class diagrams, use-case diagrams, and scenario diagrams — when they write about UML modeling, while neglecting the other important diagrams. Among these overlooked diagrams is the UML deployment diagram. This month, I will discuss how you can apply UML deployment diagrams throughout the software process.

A deployment diagram depicts a static view of the run-time configuration of processing nodes and the components that run on those nodes. In other words, it shows your system's hardware, the software installed on that hardware, and the middleware that connects the disparate machines together. A deployment model is a collection of one or more deployment diagrams with their associated documentation.

You should create a deployment model for applications that are deployed on several machines. A good candidate for a deployment model would be a point-of-sale application running on a thin-client network computer that directly accesses a centralized database server. Another would be a customer service system deployed using a distributed object architecture such as CORBA. You also need deployment models for embedded systems designs to show how the hardware and software components work together. In short, all but the most trivial system will require a deployment model.

Figure 2.3 Example of a Deployment Diagram

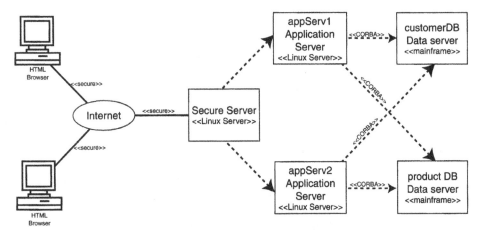

Figure 2.3 presents an example of a UML deployment diagram for a simple Internet-based electronic commerce application. Users use browsers to interact with the system (because you can't get this information directly from the deployment diagram, you need to indicate this in the corresponding documentation or put a UML note on the diagram), then the browsers interact with your application via the Internet. All requests pass through a secure server that has a firewall installed on it. The requests are multiplexed to different application servers which, in turn, interact with your organization's data servers.

I've applied several stereotypes in Figure 2.3 that are worth discussing. Stereotypes, indicated with the <<some text>> notation, are a UML mechanism for extending the modeling language by defining common types appropriate to your problem domain. In this instance, stereotypes indicate that the connection between the browser and the secure server is secure (potentially using secure sockets), that several servers use the Linux operating system, that the two data servers are deployed to mainframe technology, and that the Linux boxes interact with the mainframes via CORBA. By applying stereotypes to your diagram, you communicate important information to the diagram users consistently and understandably.

Also note how Figure 2.3 uses solid lines to indicate communication connections from the browsers to the secure server, and dotted lines with arrowheads to show dependencies between the servers. There are dependencies between the servers because each server directly invokes operations on the other servers it interacts with: the secure server invokes specific operations on the application servers. The application servers, in turn, invoke operations on the data servers. If an operation on the mainframe is changed, the potential result will be changes to the code deployed to the application servers; hence, the application servers depend on the interfaces provided by the data servers. The browsers, on the other hand, don't depend on the secure server that simply serves them standard HTML and 100% pure Java applets: the HTML and the applets could change and, as long as they remain standard and pure, you would not need to change the browsers.

Now for some modeling tips. First, the diagram doesn't actually show that a firewall has been installed on the secure server. You would either need to include this information in the associated documentation or use a UML note. Notes are graphical means for including important information in your diagrams that doesn't fit elsewhere. My experience is that notes quickly clutter your diagrams and make them difficult to use, so you should put this sort of information in the appropriate documentation. Notes are useful when you want to resolve questions about a portion of a diagram — once the issue is resolved, you can remove the note and update the diagram and documentation.

Second, deployment modeling should be performed by both the development and engineering folks responsible for building the system and by operations folks who are responsible for operating it and supporting it once in production. The engineers know how to build the system, whereas the operations people will have a better understanding of your system's current environment and important operational considerations that the engineers may not fully appreciate.

Third, the modeling team should consider a bevy of issues, such as: What existing systems will your system need to interact or integrate with? How robust does your system need to be (will there be redundant failover hardware in case of a system failure)? What and who will need to connect to and interact with your system, and how will they do it (via the Internet, exchanging data files, and so on)? What middleware, including the operating system and communications approaches and protocols, will your system use? What hardware and software will your users directly interact with — PCs, network computers, browsers, and so on? How will you monitor the system once you deploy it? How secure does the system need to be — do you need a firewall, physically secure hardware, and so on?

To determine whether you need to create a deployment model, ask yourself the following: if you knew nothing about the system and someone asked you to either install or maintain and support it, would you want a description of how the system's parts fit together? When I ask the project teams that I work with this question, we almost always decide to develop a deployment model. More important, practice has shown that deployment modeling is well worth it — deployment models force you to think about important deployment issues long before you must deliver the actual system.

You should perform deployment modeling early in your project's life cycle, and update it throughout your project as needed. According to the Rational Unified Process (RUP) life cycle depicted in Figure 2.4, deployment modeling is an important part of your architectural modeling efforts, typically performed during the Elaboration phase as part of the Analysis and Design workflow. When you consider this approach from Rational's 4+1 architecture view shown in Figure 2.5, this makes sense: it contains a deployment view that is documented using a deployment model. However, I disagree with the RUP philosophy on this. I believe that deployment modeling is actually a key component of the deployment workflow.

Figure 2.4 **The Rational Unified Process (RUP)**

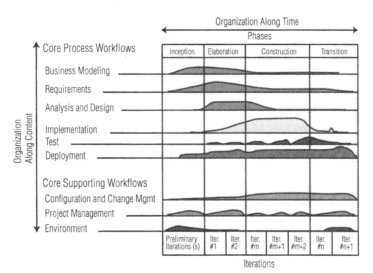

Figure 2.5 **The 4+1 Architecture**

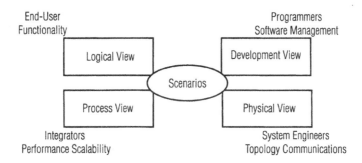

In my experience, deployment is a difficult process that you should start early in the life cycle. It begins with requirements definition during the Inception phase, continues with deployment modeling and deployment planning during the Elaboration and Construction phases, and then results in the actual deployment of your system during the Transition phase. The RUP, for reasons unknown to me, has the deployment workflow starting late in the project life cycle. The key to the Transition phase is to have a realistic and workable deployment plan, not something you can simply pull out of your hat: deployment is an important issue during the full project life cycle, not a last minute consideration.

When developing a deployment plan in parallel with your deployment model, you must take many issues into consideration. How will your system be installed? Who will install it? How long should it take to install? Where can the installation possibly fail? How do you back out if the installation fails? How long does it take to back out? What is your installation window (during what time period can you install your system)? What backups do you need to make before the installation? Do you need to do a data conversion? How do you know that the installation was successful? If different versions of the system will be in production at the same time, how will you resolve differences? What physical sites do you need to deploy to and in what order? How will you train your support and operations staff? Do you need to deploy a production support system so that the support staff uses their own environment to simulate problems? How will you train your users? What documentation, and in what formats and languages, do your users, and support and operations staff need? How will updates to the documentation be deployed? As you can see, deployment planning is more complicated than it appears on the surface.

Many of the mistakes made in system design are the result of unqualified people picking inappropriate technology. Earlier, I discussed using standard HTML and 100% pure Java — this is a perfect example of choosing to use appropriate technology. There are wacky schemes out there for how to deploy client code that are usually for the tool vendor's benefit and not yours, the disadvantages of which quickly become apparent once you perform deployment modeling. Deployment modeling is a technique for describing the overall approach to delivering your system, showing both hardware and software, letting you communicate your approach to others for their review and input. Deployment modeling, and the deployment workflow in general, is an important part of your system development efforts that will increase your chances of successfully delivering your system.

Recommended Resources

The Unified Modeling Language User Guide by Grady Booch, James Rumbaugh, and Ivar Jacobson (Addison-Wesley Object Technology Series, 1999)

UML Distilled: Applying the Standard Object Modeling Language by Martin Fowler and Kendall Scott (Addison-Wesley Object Technology Series, 1997)

The 4+1 View Model of Architecture by Philippe Krutchen (1995) www.rational.com

The UML and Beyond by Scott Ambler (1998) www.ambysoft.com/umlAndBeyond.html

2.2.7 "Place Tab A in Slot B"

by Scott W. Ambler

The key to writing sufficient and successful documentation is to work with your users.

When you're building a system, your primary goals are to ensure that the system works, that it meets its users' needs and that it provides value to your organization. You also want to create software that can be maintained and enhanced over time after it's been deployed.

These secondary goals are supported by sufficient system documentation — and that means written descriptions of the applications, not just comments in your source code. While design models, requirement specifications and user manuals potentially make the grade, management artifacts such as project schedules don't.

Here, I'll discuss the post-development write-ups that support systems in the production phase. What types of documents do you need to deliver and when do you know if they're sufficient? The answers may surprise you.

Guiding Principles

Let's start with some guiding principles — first, Extreme Programming (XP)'s (www.extreme-programming.org) and Agile Modeling (AM)'s (www.agilemodeling.com) tenet of traveling light. Your project team will be more agile, hence more effective, with minimal baggage. The fewer documents you create and maintain, the more time you'll have for development. However, you must remember the people who will operate, maintain and use your system. Individuals who weren't actively involved in development (and in a large organization, that can be a lot of people) will need a way to understand and work with your system effectively.

Summary documentation is one means to that end. Simplicity, another fundamental value shared by XP and AM, teaches that the best documentation is the simplest that gets the job done. Don't babble on for 50 pages when five will do. Don't create an intricate diagram when a sketch will suffice. Don't repeat information found elsewhere when a brief reference will do. Furthermore, rough-draft system documentation created during active development can help to streamline the entire development process. Of course, you have to keep progress and documentation in balance; remember that any in-development documentation must be updated to reflect midstream changes. This can increase your documentation burden and impede your development velocity.

Finally, "develop with a purpose" — a fundamental principle of AM. Document only to fulfill clear, important and immediate needs.

The Fundamentals of System Documentation

Tips for providing your customers with documents they'll value.

1. Recognize that people need a road map to understand the system.
2. Document only to fulfill clear, important and immediate needs.
3. Identify each document's customer, remembering that different customers have different needs.
4. Determine each document's medium based on its use.
5. Keep documents as simple as possible.
6. Travel light: Minimize the number of documents that you create and maintain.
7. The customer decides whether the documentation is sufficient.

Who Needs What?

I don't believe that an application is truly delivered until it's in production and the required documentation rests in the appropriate hands. What system documentation should you include when your project is ready for production? You must identify your documentation's potential customers, determine what information they believe they need, and then work with them to produce documents that address their actual requirements.

System documentation customers span varied personnel: the users themselves, the operations staff that will run the system, the support staff that help users work with the system and the maintenance professionals who will adjust the system over time. Ask them what they do, how they do it and how they want to work with the system documents. Then listen to their answers.

So, what types of documents will you need to produce? Your users may require a reference manual, a users guide, a support guide and even training materials. Different requirements demand different media: Electronic documents are OK for quick lookups and additional help, but users guides and extensive training material often require a paper format. I learned long ago to base my users guide and training materials on the use cases for the system — use cases describe how people work with the system, and so provide a firm foundation on which to base both of these documents.

Operations personnel are often concerned with a system's interaction with other systems, databases and files. This documentation should be easy to produce because you've already handled these types of questions throughout the development phase.

I've always found it useful to meet with my operations folks early in the project's life cycle. Because I wanted to discover their requirements as early as I can during any project, I extended the deployment workflow into the Inception phase of the enhanced life cycle for the Unified Process (www.ronin-intl.com/unifiedProcess.htm).

Some operations departments will require an intricate deployment model ("Effective Software Deployment," Nov. 1999) that delineates each type of hardware node in the system, the software deployed to them, the middleware between them and any relationships they have with external systems (and vice versa). I've also worked with operations departments that wanted only release notes listing the various system components, their version numbers and their interdependencies. Most operations departments will also want documented backup procedures, the availability and reliability requirements for the system and the expected load profile of your system. And, of course, they need to know the system's contact personnel and how to reach them. It's clear that your operations department may require a wide range of documentation, so be prepared.

Your support department will probably request system training materials specific to their needs. This may be as simple as a page or two of notes for your development team to follow when training new employees, or as complex as manuals for both the instructor and trainees, a video tutorial or even a computer-based training system. For problem-solving reference, support staff will also want access to any documentation provided to your users. A trouble-shooting guide, perhaps in the form of an online knowledge-base that support staff can update as they solve new problems, may also be required. Escalation procedures for handling difficult problems will also be necessary. Support departments often have these in place already and may need only minimal updates.

For maintenance professionals, the primary artifact is quality source code, and Andrew Hunt and David Thomas's book, *The Pragmatic Programmer: From Journeyman to Master* (Addison-Wesley 2000), provides excellent advice for writing such code. In addition to well-documented source code, your system's maintenance team will require an overview of the system and an indication of where to go for more detail. I like to write a "Good Things to Know" document during development. Typically short and to the point (usually fewer than 10 printed pages), it summarizes key information such as the system's mission, primary user contacts, development tools and technologies, and critical operating processes (both development and production). I also include references to important project artifacts such as the location of the source code (the project name in the source-code control system is often sufficient), the critical models pertaining to the system (if any), and other essential data.

Enough is Enough

When is a document sufficient? When it's as small and simple as possible, but still gets the job done. To pare a document to fighting trim, I'll ask my customers how they intend to use it and why they're using it that way. It's not enough to say, "We need a logical data model because our procedures say we do" or "We need a logical data model because we tell you so" — they must explain why they need it. With a little persistence, patience and tact, you can effectively ease your project's documentation burden. Sometimes you can trim to the point where you don't need an artifact at all; at the least, you can usually condense the artifact itself — a brief list of bullet points might well replace a users manual written in full prose.

Negotiating an artifact down to its minimal qualities can be a straightforward process — when you are working with reasonable people. But sometimes, reason takes a back seat, and you'll be in for a bumpy ride. People can be threatened by new ideas, such as basing a physical data model on a class model instead of a logical data model or using pair programming techniques to write cleaner code. When negotiation comes to a halt, you must be willing to take another approach, such as moving the decision up the management chain. This requires exquisite finesse: Remember, there is no such thing as a politics-free software project.

The Customer is King

In your zeal for reducing documentation, keep in mind the teeter-totter of excess and insufficiency: Remember that the customer, not the writer, determines what's necessary. Years ago, I worked for a large Canadian financial institution that had the wise policy of requiring the artifact's customer — be it a maintenance developer to whom you were transitioning your code or a user for whom you were building the system — to accept that artifact. Individual artifacts were inspected by the customer, and if they weren't deemed up to par, the development team returned to the drawing board, sometimes working with customers to ensure a successful round two. This practice provided a fair and effective checks-and-balances system for both developer and customer.

To best determine whether a document passes muster, let a representative of its target customer base work with it. Does the document provide needed information, and is it accurate? Does the document offer more data than is necessary? A developer new to your team can check out the "Good Things to Know" document, user acceptance testing can provide a perfect venue to evaluate user documentation, and an operations engineer can try out the backup procedures.

Supporting artifacts, particularly documentation, are a vital element of modern systems. To move your system successfully into production, you need to create concise, thorough system documentation that meets the needs of its customers. This doesn't mean that you must create something whose size puts the Encyclopedia Britannica to shame — by working with, not against, your project stakeholders, you can often travel much lighter than you expected, and create documentation that is both succinct and sufficient.

NOTE: I'd like to extend thanks to Martin Fowler and Neil Pitman for providing input for this article.

2.2.8 "Waste Management"

by John Boddie, edited by Larry Constantine

Improving data quality is an important endeavor to any development project — and it's something all managers need to understand.

This is the day — the payoff for the technical risks, the weekends spent in front of a terminal, and the mind-numbing requirements meetings. The boss is here, along with the vice president of development and her equivalent from the user community. After a few remarks about all the hard work, you start the demo. It looks good. The user you've carefully coached moves confidently through the screen sequences. Response time is great. The user interface draws pleasing comments.

Then someone says, "That can't be right."

"What can't be right?"

"That order. You're using real data, aren't you?"

"Yes. We wanted you to see the system in a production setting."

"Well, McDongle and Crashmore has five sites and you only show two."

Stay cool. You tell the user at the terminal to go to the customer profile screens, but she can only find two sites.

The user's vice president looks at your boss's boss and says, "Are you sure this new technology is worth giving up 60% of our customer base?"

You never planned on this, and therein lies the problem.

Trash Compactors

Software development strives for new functionality and new ways to deliver data to users. In practice, what we often do is reinvent the trash compactor. You remember — the kitchen marvel that turned a 20 pound bag of trash into 20 pounds of trash.

Alas, no level of tool or user interface sophistication can overcome the burden of bad data. Although it is one of the key determinants of development success, the process of converting data from old systems into data for new ones receives almost no attention from the development community.

Developers build trash compactors because they are focused on the processing and not the content of the data. A trash compactor doesn't care if it's crushing milk cartons or old broccoli, and our systems don't care if a customer's telephone number is right or wrong. We conveniently overlook the fact that referential integrity rules in our databases can be satisfied with data that isn't related in the real world. Bad data, we say, is "not our problem."

Trash compactors can be wonderfully complex and great fun to build. Trash itself is much less interesting. Most developers would not consider "making sure the parts list is correct" a career-enhancing opportunity. Typically, such assignments fall to the most junior staff — when they can't be fobbed off on the users. But by leaving these jobs to junior programmers, what are the chances of difficulties when you attempt to deploy the system? When these difficulties show up (and they will), will everyone still think you did a great job?

Face it, these are assignments nobody wants. Cleaning up legacy data is like being a referee, any news you have is probably bad. I'm currently leading a data migration effort for a telephone company and so far we've only found data for about 70% of the routers they installed in the field. Results like these create long faces at project meetings.

The View from the Landfill

In my opinion, data migration and data quality improvement are two of the most complex and valuable data processing areas. Ask any business process owner what is the first priority, accurate data or a really nice interface, and you already know the answer. Nevertheless, chances are that you will spend far more time thinking about the interface and working on it than you ever will dealing with the data's accuracy.

Even if you want to clean up the data, you may not have the technical skills required. Java development expertise doesn't easily translate into interpreting VSAM files or using Wang utilities.

Data migration work requires an understanding the semantics of the data you are dealing with, the business practices that use the current systems, and the way these are expected to change, as well as the technologies that the new system, the old systems, and the migration environment use. In my current project, the data sources include Wang, Oracle, Microsoft SQL Server, Microsoft Excel spreadsheets, Microsoft Access databases, direct feeds from telephone switches in the network, direct feeds from Cisco and Newbridge routers, Lotus Notes, proprietary databases, and flat-file outputs from mainframe systems.

In data migration, you do not have the luxury of dealing with the clean abstractions that are collected into the new system requirements. No requirements document starts with the assumption that the new system will be initialized with bad data, yet this is often the case in practice.

When migrating data, you must contend with idiosyncrasies from years of legacy system operation, including data elements that have been redefined, multiple codings of data fields, obsolete status values, and the like. You cannot disregard or arbitrarily correct these. If you can't find location data for a $25,000 piece of equipment, you can't leave it out of the new system just because it doesn't fit your model. Data migration can make you feel you are turning over rocks by a river after a major storm. You will start to notice odd-looking things when you start dealing with the details that have accumulated over the years.

Primary Treatment

When migrating data, identify the data source for your new system first. This is not simply a matter of identifying what system will be replaced. If the system being replaced gets its data from other systems and they, in turn, get it from other ones, the chances are slim that the most accessible data is the most accurate.

Identifying data sources can be difficult. In most companies, systems environments have become so complex that data processing groups don't really understand the "big picture," and users can't identify all their data sources and data streams. In fact, one of the first things the development teams of these companies probably have to do is examine the current system and "extract the business rules." If users really understood the process details, this step would be unnecessary.

In many cases, new systems will be replacing multiple legacy systems whose data is supposed to be identical. When it isn't, you must know how the data came to be in each of the systems in order to choose which of the supposedly identical data items is correct. This involves looking at the business processes as well as the systems.

For example, my current project combines data from legacy systems for order entry and billing. Each contains customer account data, including account status, contact address, and billing address. About 20% of the records are inconsistent in at least one of these attributes. The obvious choice is to use the data from the billing system as the correct data whenever billing and order entry attributes differ. However, contact information is updated in the order entry system, and these updates are often not made in billing. Likewise, accounts may be made inactive in the billing system but are not updated in the order entry system unless the user calls and requests it specifically. Knowing these things, we can make a rule that the data for the new system should include the billing address and status from the billing system and the contact address from the order entry system. We still need to produce reports showing the discrepancies between the order entry and billing systems. One report might show all customers where the billing address differs and the account is more than 60 days overdue, which may indicate that the billing address was updated in the order entry system but not in the billing system.

Looking at the "last edit date" for records is not as useful as it might appear, since it's difficult to determine what changed in the record. Was it a contact name? Was it an area code in the phone number? Change dates provide collateral information, but they seldom drive adjudication in those cases where data sources contain different values.

You must map all the sources and destinations to a meta data model. To manage data migration, you must create a meta data model and keep it current. It will be your most valuable management tool. It will track source systems and databases, the destination system and its database, and all the attributes including their formatting and coding. You will use the meta data to establish and enforce conventions, such as always using "Ave." instead of "Avenue" or "Ave" (without the period).

You can't assume that the new system is the only destination for the migrated data. If the system being replaced provided data for multiple downstream systems (not an unusual situation), then the data you are cleaning up may be a candidate for migrating to these systems as well.

All of this analysis work may sound a lot like developing software. In fact, much of it is the same, except there is more detail and more riding on understanding what all of the data really means. Since data migration always shows up early on the critical path, the work that supports it must also be accurate early.

Secondary Treatment

Data systems that include errors are likely to get new errors every day. Reducing the influx of errors means spending a lot of time dealing with users who don't have a lot of time to worry about data migration.

Downsizing information technology personnel adds its own challenges. The people who understood the legacy systems and data have moved on, and those who are left are so overworked that they hardly have time to breathe. On the plus side, most people still working with the legacy systems are interested in doing what they can to improve the data's quality because they understand that good data makes their jobs easier. These people also understand that more new systems are promised than are actually delivered and that the work you are doing with data migration may benefit them over an extended period. You need to find ways to let these people help you make the data better with as much efficiency and as little disruption to their regular work as possible.

In most cases, this work involves generating reports that show both the current legacy data and its expected values, and then either developing code to migrate good data back into the legacy systems that should have it already or providing worksheets that let users examine the data and make the necessary changes directly. You need to coordinate the worksheets with the screens the users will be invoking to make the changes.

You also need to determine with the business process owner how the errors were introduced into the system. For example, if sales representatives include dummy site address information to get sales approved faster and commissions credited earlier, it may be necessary for the process owner to curtail this practice. If not, then the data migration work needs to be conscious of orders received after a given date, knowing that the site addresses may be erroneous.

Trash to Steam

In the real world, turning trash into steam sounds like a great idea. Unfortunately, it is also complex, expensive, and subject to regulations, hearings, and even public protests.

The software development equivalent of trash to steam is phased implementation. In phased implementation, data migration is no longer a simple matter of concocting files of relatively good data and loading them into a new system. It becomes a complex enterprise with transactional processing, application modification (both legacy and target), special purpose middleware, and shifting objectives. Developers who have been through the process assert that the cost and difficulty of migrating from system A to system B in phases is likely to be more costly than the development of A and B combined.

Typically, phased implementation requires that the new system and the old system be run in parallel. This means that migration now becomes a two-way street. If the defined phases include both functional and organizational or geographical steps, you'll need "retrofits" to bring previously migrated data up to the current standard. You might need requirements for new data and functionality as a consequence of business process changes. If multiple systems are involved, this is a complex undertaking.

Phased implementations are often the result of mergers or acquisitions. In these situations, further complications can arise from the cultural differences between organizations and from differences in business processes, terminology, and even legal requirements. When migrating data to support a new system, none of this is an abstraction. You'll need to deal with it every day.

Now ask yourself, do you want to leave all of data migration's complexity in the hands of junior programmers and newly-minted managers? Do you still believe that data migration and quality improvement are "not your problem?"

Chapter 3

Test

3.1 Best Practices for the Test Workflow

It isn't enough to simply develop software — you need to build software that works. And there is only one way to prove that your software works: test it. During the Transition phase you will be focused on system and user testing efforts, something often referred to as testing in the large (testing performed during the Inception, Elaboration, and Construction phases is referred to as testing in the small). Figure 3.1 depicts the solution to the Test In The Large process pattern (Ambler, 1999), which includes a subset of the techniques of the Full Lifecycle Object-Oriented Testing (FLOOT) methodology (Ambler, 2001), and Table 3.1 summarizes the techniques depicted in the figure. The arrow on the left side of the diagram represents the inputs coming into the process and the arrow on the right side represents the outputs created by the effort. The first step is to accept your master test/QA plan, a task that often includes updating the plan so that it reflects all testing to be performed. Final validation of the current release begins once the test plan is accepted. As you can see, this is comprised of two general tasks — system testing in which the development community tests the application and user testing in which the user community tests the application. Testing in the large is typically organized into system and user testing because your development team wants to first ensure, to the best of its ability, that your system is ready for testing by your users before it makes it available to them for their own testing efforts. Throughout both types of testing, you must regression-test the application, and you must record defects discovered in the application.

Table 3.1   The Solution to the Test In The Large Process Pattern

FLOOT Technique	Description
Alpha testing	Testing in which pre-release versions of software products, products that are often buggy, are released to users who need access to the product before it is to be officially deployed. In return these users are willing to report back to the software developers any defects that they uncover. Alpha testing is typically followed by a period of beta testing.
Beta testing	Similar to alpha testing except that the software product should be less buggy. This approach is typically used by software development companies who want to ensure that they meet as many of their client needs as possible.
Function testing	A part of systems testing in which development staff confirm that their application meets user requirements specified during analysis.
Installation testing	The act of ensuring that your application can be installed successfully.
Operations testing	The act of ensuring that the needs of operations personnel who have to support/operate the application are met.
Pilot testing	A testing process equivalent to beta testing that is used by organizations to test applications that they have developed for their own internal use.
Regression testing	The act of ensuring that previously tested behaviors still work as expected after changes have been made to an application.
Stress testing	The act of ensuring that the system performs as expected under high volumes of transactions, users, load, and so on.
System testing	A testing process in which you find and fix any known problems to prepare your application for user testing. System testing includes function testing, stress testing, installation testing, and operations testing.
User acceptance testing	A testing technique in which users verify that an application meets their needs.
User testing	Testing processes in which the user community, as opposed to developers, performs the tests. User testing techniques include user-acceptance testing, alpha testing, beta testing, and pilot testing.

Figure 3.1   Techniques for Testing in the Large

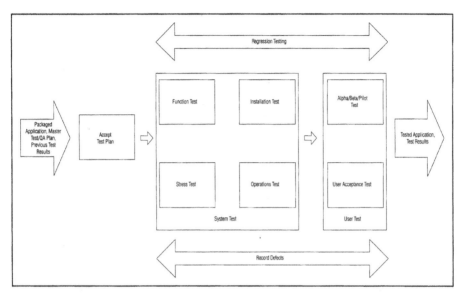

During the Production phase limited testing will occur, often performed by support personnel in conjunction with maintenance developers, to verify problems reported by your users. This is often the equivalent of function testing where the support engineer explores the problems reported by users, testing that is often repeated in a more thorough manner by the developers responsible for addressing the problem (this effort would likely occur during the Elaboration or Construction phase efforts of a future release of your system).

So what are best practices for the test workflow? First, recognize that testing during these phases is difficult, as you can gather from Figure 3.1, and different than the testing in the small efforts that you would have performed during the Inception, Elaboration, and Construction phases (testing in the small was covered in detail in *The Unified Process Construction Phase*). Second, you should put your testers first and treat them with the respect that they deserve because they are valuable members of your development team. Third, you should adopt common testing best practices and integrate them throughout your entire system lifecycle. Fourth, recognize that it isn't over until it's over — bugs may get past you and be found once your system is in production, bugs that need to be dealt with swiftly and effectively.

3.1.1 Putting Testers First

In "Recruiting Software Testers" Cem Kaner argues that decisions made during the hiring process affect the efforts of your testing group, and, in the long run, of your organization. He describes best practices for hiring testers, such as initial verification of the candidate's resume, delving into their testing knowledge and philosophy, and evaluating the candidate's technical breadth.[1] Kaner believes that a good test engineer should recognize that different application issues call for different approaches, a belief consistent with the variety of techniques that you see in Figure 3.1. When he interviews senior candidates he wants to discover their opinions on common testing issues and hear a description and evaluation of the tools they've used. He suggests giving a testing candidate an extremely simple program for which they should generate a list of interesting test cases, a task that testers will actually do in practice — analyze a program and figure out ways to test it. He also points out that writing skills should be verified because writing a bug report is a basic and important part of a tester's job.

Hiring good people isn't enough. You also need to train them. James Bach provides advice for doing so in "Training Testers." He believes that few universities offer courses on testing and commercially available courses are not up to par; so as a result he believes you will need to train yourself and members of your team on the job. The article describes fundamental best practices that are applicable to training any type of staff member, not just test engineers. An interesting philosophy of Bach's is that training and mentoring on a personal level may occur from peer-to-peer or manager-to-employee — a concept coincidentally captured in Agile Modeling's (Ambler, 2002) "Everyone Can Learn From Everyone Else" principle. Bach argues that training on the job of testers occurs as the result of the inspection of test cases and test plans: not only do you uncover defects, you also distribute knowledge about testing across your staff — individual best practices become common practices as a result. Hands-on experience is also important because performing a task not only helps students remember how to do it, it also helps them develop a more intimate relationship with it. Self-study is also critical, taking on the form of reading books, journals, or working with computer-based training. Finally, Bach describes a competency-based training approach that organizes learning activities around well-defined, observable, business-related outcomes. To be effective you must define a competency list, identify a means of assessing students in the items on the list, develop training for those items, and determine a strategy for deploying the training into your environment. Definitely an article worth reading.

Another aspect of putting your testers first is managing them effectively within the scope of your overall development efforts. In "Running a Stellar Testing Team" Len DiMaggio describes how to do just that. He argues that there are cliques within your project team, and your testers are often one such clique. For these cliques to cooperate rather than regard each other as adversaries, you must clearly define the roles, rights, and responsibilities up front. Regardless of whether your software team is integrated with or independent of the developers, they will succeed only if you first quantify their deliverables and dependencies. What should you expect from your testers? They should test early and often, define and maintain the test environment, adopt or build appropriate testing tools, and act as a knowledge base for the project team. A critical best practice is to establish the rules of engagement between your testing team and other groups, including: sharing of access, information, and tools; protocols for release notes and software handoffs; and testing activities themselves. DiMaggio believes that your development and test groups should be independent but closely integrated, with both teams working together and sharing information with each other. DiMaggio also shares several of his testing philosophies in the article. First, he believes that testing begins long before a line of code is written — never underestimate your planning and organization efforts. Second, one of the most difficult tasks in testing software is isolating the root cause of a bug, a fact that reinforces the need for good tools and for developers and testers to work together effectively. Third, he suggests that one of your goals should be to design and build a

---

1. The article "Tips for Technical Interviewing" was reprinted in *The Unified Process Elaboration Phase*.

complete set of test tools in parallel to the actual system being developed, so that when development is complete the tests are also complete. This concept is supported by Extreme Programming (XP)'s test-first design approach (Beck, 2000) — XP is covered in Chapter 7.

3.1.2 Effective Testing Practices

John D. McGregor & Melissa J. Major in "Selecting Test Cases Based on User Priorities" describe fundamental best practices for planning your system testing efforts. They point out that regardless of your approach to system design, one thing holds true: the frequency with which each type of user uses the system will reflect the relative importance of the specific system features. In the article they describe a set of extensions to existing use case and actor documentation templates that capture information relevant to testing. For use cases, they focus on the frequency and criticality fields in the template — the criticality indicates how necessary a use is to the successful operation of the system and the frequency indicates how often a specific use is triggered. With respect to actors, the major attribute is the actor's use profile, which ranks the frequency with which this actor triggers each individual use. McGregor and Major show how to combine the individual actor's use profiles to rank each use case, so that once the priorities have been determined you can compute the number of tests to be associated with each use case. This enables you to maximize the return on investment of system testing, because test cases are selected so that those operations users depend on most are triggered most often. An additional benefit is that the technique also links the system's actors, uses, and tests; when usage changes you can easily identify which tests to change, and when tests fail you can easily find the affected use cases. This supports traceability, a topic covered in detail in Chapter 7 of *The Unified Process Construction Phase*.

Scott W. Ambler describes a wide range of testing techniques in "A J2EE Testing Primer." He argues that modern software development, typified by the Java 2 Enterprise Edition (J2EE) and Enterprise JavaBean (EJB) environments (Roman et al., 2002), is typically distributed across several types of logical components such as firewalls, Web servers, EJB application servers and database servers. Testing in this environment is difficult, if only for the simple reason that functionality is distributed across several interacting platforms (and there is far more to it than this). In this article Ambler describes best practices critical to your testing success, regardless of whether you are working in a J2EE environment or not. These best practices include:

1. Test throughout the project's entire life cycle.
2. Develop your tests before you develop an artifact.
3. Test all artifacts.
4. Test continuously.
5. Determine the specific cause of a defect.
6. Do more, not less, testing of objects.
7. Make the goal of testing to find bugs, not cover them up.
8. Automate your regression tests.
9. Invest in simple, effective testing tools.
10. Have separate personal, integration and staging areas.

In "Real-World Acceptance Testing" Randy Sparks and Timothy Seevers describe best practices for your acceptance testing efforts during the transition phase. They suggest building an ever-improving, automated acceptance test through an iterative cycle of test development and coverage analysis. They argue that in modern testing environments that an acceptance test should be automated and human intervention minimal. If possible, intervention should only occur at the beginning to start the test and at the end to check the test results. They also believe that an acceptance test be short, although they argue that it's foolish to put an exact time on this because projects differ. They suggest that you automate your build process so that there is both a release build and a debug build for each release of code.

3.1.3 It Isn't Over Until It's Over

Testing during the Transition phase isn't enough, because problems will get past you into the Production phase, problems that are often centered on performance issues that are typically found early in the production lifecycle of an application. In "Surviving Performance Fire Drills" Benson Margulies argues that despite the best preparation, catastrophes will occur with little or no warning. Margulies believes that the first order of business is chaos-containment because when you are "managing a fire drill" you may find yourself surrounded by people who are running around like chickens with their heads cut off. The source of the panic is typically that whatever the problem it has to be fixed "right this minute," although Margulies' experience is that maybe it does, and maybe it doesn't. He has found that the urgency will often evaporate when you ask hard questions, and therefore you should push back as appropriate. One of the biggest problems that you will find when dealing with performance issues is the lack of hard data because problems are often reported in qualitative and impressionistic terms. Margulies suggests that you use the scientific method to validate a problem: define the problem, state a hypothesis, and perform tests and record the results. For performance tuning to succeed, you need timing data from the production environment, data that is often obtained through effective testing. If you know where the time is going, you know where to focus in fixing the problem.

You cannot only improve your software through testing but your software process itself. In "Don't Waste Your Bugs" Stephen and Timothy Shimeall show that defects can be a very effective source of information for modeling and controlling the software process. For this to work it is important to know which defects to track, and which not to, how to use them, and how to apply the knowledge you gain from them.[2] The authors argue that software defects provide a key indicator into the code's maturity. By monitoring the impact of changes to code in terms of the number, scope, size, and type of bugs introduced, you can estimate how far along your software is, determine the potential impact of proposed changes, or even decide when it's time to discard some code and redesign it. An important best practice is to look at what point the defect was introduced into the software and why it wasn't detected earlier in the process. Defects are introduced during all aspects of software development, hence the need for full lifecycle testing (Ambler, 2001); so discovering where defects are introduced will help you identify potential areas for improvement in your software process. The authors advise you to look for defects that show up in more than one individual in the group and to look for defects that hint at underlying problems. You should also attempt to identify related

---

2. Software metric management is covered in detail in *The Unified Process Inception Phase*.

problems that occur across projects or products, an aspect of your programme management efforts in the Infrastructure Management workflow (Chapter 6). Identifying the circumstance under which these defects occur, the source of the errors, is also critical to your success. Apparently there is more to testing than testing.

3.2 The Articles

3.2.1 "Recruiting Software Testers" by Cem Kaner, Ph.D., J.D.
3.2.2 "Training Testers" by James Bach
3.2.3 "Running a Stellar Software Testing Team" by Len DiMaggio
3.2.4 "Selecting Test Cases Based on User Priorities" by John D. McGregor and Melissa L. Major
3.2.5 "A J2EE Testing Primer" by Scott W. Ambler
3.2.6 "Real-World Acceptance Testing" by Randy Sparks and Timothy Seevers
3.2.7 "Don't Waste Your Bugs!" by Stephen Shimeall and Timothy Shimeall
3.2.8 "Surviving Performance Fire Drills" by Benson I. Margulies

3.2.1 "Recruiting Software Testers"

by Cem Kaner, Ph.D., J.D.

Staffing decisions that can make or break a company often come down to asking effective questions during interviews.

One of the most difficult functions any manager has is selecting good staff. Decisions made in the hiring process ultimately will make or break the mission of the group — and, in the long run, the company.

After initially defining staffing needs, a manager must establish requirements for the job, examine the motivations of people wanting to get into software testing, and gather information about — and phone screen — job candidates.

Ultimately, though, staffing decisions usually come down to the results of a rigorous interview process. How does the candidate approach testing, and how deep is her knowledge of the field? Does he have project-management experience? How does she relate to her peers, supervisors and staff? Are his bug reports comprehensive and insightful, or terse and ungrammatical? How well does she perform on tests and puzzles specially designed for candidates? These are the key questions that will separate the qualified from the unqualified.

Testing Philosophy

Once I've done my homework on the résumé and ascertained the basics about the candidate's education and past employment, I delve into his testing knowledge and philosophy. For supervisory or senior positions, I ask the following questions:

- What is software quality assurance?
- What is the value of a testing group? How do you justify your work and budget?
- What is the role of the test group vis-à-vis documentation, tech support, and so forth?
- How much interaction with users should testers have, and why?

- How should you learn about problems discovered in the field, and what should you learn from those problems?
- What are the roles of glass-box and black-box testing tools?
- What issues come up in test automation, and how do you manage them?
- What development model should programmers and the test group use?
- How do you get programmers to build testability support into their code?
- What is the role of a bug tracking system?

I'm not looking for the one right answer about how testing should be done. I simply want to know if the candidate has thought about these issues in depth, and whether his views are roughly compatible with the company's.

These questions, for example, are designed for a company that focuses on testing with little regard for process standards. Therefore, the candidate's answers should assure me that he would be comfortable working in a group that doesn't follow process standards such as ISO 9000-3 or the Capability Maturity Model.

Technical Breadth

After covering philosophy and knowledge, I evaluate the candidate's technical breadth. Though the actual questions depend on the particular company and application area, the following elicit the many facets of an interviewee's experience:

- What are the key challenges of testing?
- Have you ever completely tested any part of a product? How?
- Have you done exploratory or specification-driven testing?
- Should every business test its software the same way?
- Discuss the economics of automation and the role of metrics in testing.
- Describe components of a typical test plan, such as tools for interactive products and for database products, as well as cause-and-effect graphs and data-flow diagrams.
- When have you had to focus on data integrity?
- What are some of the typical bugs you encountered in your last assignment?

The answer to "Should every business test its software the same way?" indicates a candidate's open-mindedness and breadth of exposure to the field. I believe the correct answer is no, and I expect to hear that more rigorous testing and process management should be applied to life-critical applications, than the here-today, new-version-tomorrow web-based application.

A candidate also should believe that different application issues call for different approaches. For example, testing a financial application that is written in COBOL and works with a huge database would require different techniques than those used to test the interactive competence of a word processor. Also, an exceptional candidate should discuss the different paradigms of software testing, or how different people view core issues in the field.

Within the black-box world, for instance, James Bach identifies domain testing, stress testing, flow testing, user testing, regression testing, risk-based testing and claim-based testing as separate techniques (*Tripos: A Model to Support Heuristic Software Testing*, 1997, available at http://www.stlabs.com/newsletters/testnet/docs/tripover.htm). However, in my course on testing, I identify nine paradigms that aid testers in determining the different criteria that create effective test cases or suites: domain testing, stress testing, risk-based testing, random testing, specification-driven testing, function testing, scenario-driven testing, user testing and security testing. A candidate shouldn't believe that there is one correct partitioning of paradigms but should recognize that different groups with different approaches to testing can both be right.

When I interview senior candidates, I want to find out their opinions on common testing issues and hear a description and evaluation of the tools they've used. I'm not looking for agreement. Rather, I want to determine whether the candidate has a well developed, sophisticated point of view. The data-oriented questions, for example, would be excellent for probing a candidate's sophistication in the testing of databases and test tools used. Of course, the questions need to be changed to match a candidate's skill set and the class of application. There would be little value in asking a highly skilled tester or test manager for interactive applications such as games or word processors about databases and their test tools.

Another Simple Testing Test

Draw a simple Open File dialog box on a whiteboard, explaining "This is an **Open File** dialog. You can type in the file name (where it says **File4** at the bottom), or you can click on the open button to open it." Hand the marker to the candidate and ask her how she would test the dialog. Make it clear that she can have as much time as she wants, can make notes on the whiteboard or on paper, and that many candidates take several minutes to think before they say anything. When the candidate begins presenting her thoughts, listen. Ask questions to clarify, but don't criticize or challenge her. When the tester pauses, let her be silent. She can answer when she's ready.

White Board Test

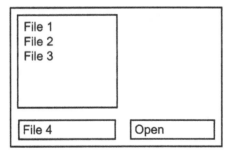

This is a remarkable test in the extent to which answers can vary. One candidate might stay at the surface, pointing out every flaw in the design of the dialog box: There is no cancel button or dialog title, no obvious way to switch between directories, and so on. Another candidate might skip the user-interface issues altogether and try testing the opening of large and small files, corrupt files, files with inappropriate extensions or remote files (specified by paths that she types into the file name box, such as `d:\user\remote\File4`).

Because of the variation in responses, over time I've changed how I use this test. Now, I present the dialog as before, giving the candidate a marker and whatever time she needs. I compliment the analysis after she has finished her comments, regardless of her performance. Then, I show her the types of tests that she missed. I explain that no one ever finds all the tests and that sometimes people miss issues because they are nervous or think they have been rushed. I spend most of the time showing and discussing different types of tests and the kind of bugs they can find. Finally, I erase the whiteboard, draw a **Save File** dialog that is just as poorly designed, and ask the tester to try again.

Because the differential practice effects are minimized by the initial practice test and coaching, the real test is the second one. The candidate receives feedback and is reassured that she isn't a dolt. In fact, most testers are substantially less nervous the second time through.

The second test allows me to find out if this candidate will be responsive to my style of training. Did the candidate understand my explanations and do a substantially better job in her next attempt? If the answer is yes, I have a reasonable candidate (as measured by this test). If the candidate's second analysis wasn't much better than the first, she is unlikely to be hired. She might be a bright, well-intentioned, interesting person, but if she doesn't learn when I teach, she needs a different teacher.

Occasionally, I have dispensed with the second test because the candidate did impossibly poorly during the first test or was extremely defensive or argumentative during my explanation of alternative tests. This usually means that I'm finished with the candidate. I'll spend a little time looking for a polite way to wrap up the interview, but I won't hire him.

Project Management

As a matter of course, supervisory candidates must be queried on their personnel and project management philosophy. However, I also do the same for potential mid-level or senior testers. At some point in seniority, a tester becomes largely self-managing, assigned to a large area of work and left alone to plan the size, type and sequence of tasks within it. Peter Drucker (*The Effective Executive,* HarperCollins, 1966) defines any knowledge worker who has to manage his or her own time and resources as an executive. I've personally found understanding the managerial nature of my mid-level contributors a great insight.

Here, then, are some questions for supervisors or self-managers:

- How do you prioritize testing tasks within a project?
- How do you develop a test plan and schedule? Describe bottom-up and top-down approaches.
- When should you begin test planning?
- When should you begin testing?
- Do you know of metrics that help you estimate the size of the testing effort?
- How do you scope out the size of the testing effort?
- How many hours a week should a tester work?
- How should your staff be managed? How about your overtime?
- How do you estimate staff requirements?
- What do you do (with the project tasks) when the schedule fails?
- How do you handle conflict with programmers?
- How do you know when the product is tested well enough?

Staff Relations

This series is, again, primarily for supervisory staff. However, I ask the test-group manager questions, which are quite enlightening, of managerial candidates.

- What characteristics would you seek in a candidate for test-group manager?
- What do you think the role of test-group manager should be? Relative to senior management? Relative to other technical groups in the company? Relative to your staff?
- How do your characteristics compare to the profile of the ideal manager that you just described?
- How does your preferred work style work with the ideal test-manager role that you just described? What is different between the way you work and the role you described?
- Who should you hire in a testing group and why?
- What is the role of metrics in comparing staff performance in human resources management?
- How do you estimate staff requirements?
- What do you do (with the project staff) when the schedule fails?
- Describe some staff conflicts you've handled.

If a candidate's picture of the ideal manager is dramatically different from my impression of him or from his image of himself, I would need to determine whether this difference is a red flag or a reflection of genuine humility. On the other hand, I would not immediately assume that a candidate whose description exactly matches his perception and presentation of himself is pathologically egotistical. It's possible he's just trying to put himself in a good light during the interview. This is fine, as long as he doesn't exaggerate or lie. Finally, if a candidate's description of the ideal manager differs fundamentally from the expectations of the company, then I wonder whether this person could fit in with the company culture.

Tests and Puzzles

Some managers use logic or numeric puzzles as informal aptitude tests. I don't object to this practice, but I don't believe such tests are as informative as they are thought to be. First, there are huge practice effects with logic and numeric puzzles. I had my daughter work logic puzzles when she was in her early teens, and she became quite good at solving them.

Her success didn't mean she was getting smarter, however. She was simply better at solving puzzles. In fact, practice efforts are long lasting and more pronounced in speeded, nonverbal and performance tests (Jepson, A.R., *Bias in Mental Testing*, The Free Press, 1980). Second, speed tests select for mental rabbits, those who demonstrate quick — but not necessarily thorough — thinking. Tortoises sometimes design better products or strategies for testing products.

A Simple Testing Puzzle

An old favorite among commonly used speed tests is G.J. Myers' self-assessment (*The Art of Software Testing*, John Wiley & Sons, 1979). The candidate is given an extremely simple program and asked to generate a list of interesting test cases. The specific program involves an abstraction (a triangle). I prefer this puzzle because it tests something testers will actually do — analyze a program and figure out ways to test it. However, there will still be practice effects. Average testers who worked through Myers before will probably get better results than strong testers who have never seen the puzzle. Additionally, I suspect that cultural differences also will produce different levels of success, even among skilled testers. Someone who deals with abstractions, such as geometric abstractions or with the logical relationships among numbers, has an advantage over someone who tests user interfaces or a product's compatibility with devices.

Bug Reports

Writing a bug report is one of the most basic and important parts of a tester's job. Nonetheless, there is a lot of variation in the quality of bug reports, even among those written by testers who have several years' experience.

To test this ability, find a reasonably straightforward bug in part of your software that is fairly easy to understand and have the candidate write a report. If none of your product's bugs fit the bill, www.bugnet.com can provide one. It's easy to recognize an excellent bug report; however, having sample reports from your staff can help you determine the quality of the attempt. There are many other good puzzles and tests in use, and all are based on a common premise: If you can find a way to present a portion of the job that the tester will actually do, you can see how well the tester does it. You have to make the test fair by designing it so that someone who doesn't know your product can still do well. That's challenging. But if you can come up with a fair test, the behavior that you elicit will be very informative.

Having comprehensively questioned and tested all your promising candidates, you'll have ample data with which to make your decision — and choose a winner.

3.2.2 "Training Testers"

by James Bach

Turn your engineers into surefire bug-zappers — even if you lack funds and the time for formal training.

Throughout most of my career, I've struggled with the problem of teaching people the art of software testing. As a test manager and consultant in the competitive packaged software business, this struggle has been long and lonely. Since few universities offer courses on testing, and commercially available courses usually seem out of touch with reality, I've had to do my best to train myself and help members of my team learn on the job.

Because no state-of-the-art software testing exists, especially in packaged software, many companies must scrape together their own ideas of testing competence or hire outside consultants who can provide useful training, all the while limping along to get today's work done. Even if your company cannot invest in a formal training program, you can take some steps to help your testers quickly gain critical skills.

How Testers Learn

As a company evolves, an untrained testing staff generally won't anticipate new risks that threaten the success of its products. Untrained testers don't know how to maximize their chances of finding all of the important bugs. They frequently miss entire categories of bugs, their bug reports tend to be poorly written and include many issues that aren't problems at all, and they usually cannot effectively plan, schedule, document, repeat, or justify their work.

Novice testers will discover useful principles and rules of thumb as they gain experience, but their knowledge is usually specific to the particular product they've been testing or the company where they work. They absorb the local folklore but don't gain the general skills to deal efficiently with new and different testing challenges. Let's consider some of the ways testers can learn the craft.

Invention

People who consider themselves creative problem-solvers often prefer to invent methods rather than follow someone else's path. Those who invent their own testing practices tend to have a deeper understanding and appreciation for them. Invention is usually a slow and painful process, however. Testing skill involves so much abstraction that the invention process leads to many different and often conflicting ideas about theory and practice. Many people don't have patience with the tinkering and failing process that goes along with inventing.

Observation

Some people learn testing by watching others test on the job. The problem with observation in the testing sphere is that the most important aspects of testing — the judgments made about what techniques to use and when — are not directly observable.

One-on-One Training

Training or mentoring on a personal level may occur from peer to peer or manager to employee. This is a powerful method, but it takes a lot of time to do well, and no working person can handle more than a few students at any one time. I made this my job at Software Testing Labs, and quickly became swamped with questions and meetings as we added staff.

When I was in this mode of training at Borland, I found that my maximum capacity for one-on-one training was nine testers per six months. That is to say, I was mentoring nine junior testers every minute of every working day until they got their sea legs, which took about six months.

Peer Reviews

Inspections of test cases and test plans not only uncover defects, they also distribute knowledge about testing across your staff. Individual best practices become common practices. In time, people stop making the same foolish errors, so quality arises all by itself. Reviews make it possible and even convenient to both establish and ensure compliance to standards. In fact, quality goes up the moment testers discover their work is going to be reviewed. Wouldn't you take a bit more care if you knew your work was going to be minutely examined by a group of your peers?

Inspections and reviews don't come for free, however. They take a lot of time, but when done well, they are extremely valuable. The main problem with peer reviews is making room for them in the social and technical fabric of the organization. If you can't afford a full-blown training program, but you can afford to commit to a major new process, peer reviews may be an excellent substitute.

Practice

Practice may not necessarily make perfect, but it does drive a lesson home. Performing a task not only helps the students remember how to do it, it also helps them develop a more intimate relationship with it. They feel ownership of the skill and gain confidence in their abilities. Practice doesn't help much, though, if the method hasn't been settled.

Self-Study

Self-study may take the form of reading books, journals, or working with computer-based training. I know of no computer-based training for software testing, and most of the books and journals seem aimed at an audience of scholars or life-critical software developers. Here's a simple method for determining the applicability of a book or paper:

- *Count mathematical equations.* If there are no mathematical equations, that's good. If you see a few, beware. If you see more than a few, ask yourself whether you really have the patience and passion to slog through the material.

- *Look for evidence of preaching.* Books that imply that there is a good way and an evil way to develop software or do software testing generally have little to say about how to cope with limited resources and office politics. If you're taking the time to read a testing book, you're already past the need for preaching.

- *Look for questionable assumptions about the development environment.* Does the book assume that you are starting with a complete specification? That you are fully staffed? That your management understands and supports the cause of testing? That you have source code and the time to perform white-box testing? Make sure the assumptions are in line with your working situation. The best book I know of in this regard is *Testing Computer Software* (International Thomson Computer Press, 1988), by Cem Kaner. It is also the preferred text of testing groups at Microsoft.

- *Look for hand-waving and ambiguity.* Most testing books don't include examples of specific test cases, making it harder to visualize the actual process of testing. Some that provide more specifics include: *Black Box Testing*, by Boris Beizer (John Wiley & Sons, 1995), *Software Testing: A Craftsman's Approach* (CRC Press, 1995), by Paul Jorgensen, and *The Craft of Software Testing*, by Brian Marick (Prentice Hall, 1995).

Even with excellent learning materials, however, the real problem with self-study is the "self" part. Few people will follow a discipline of systematic self-education.

Classroom Training

Well-designed classroom training is a great way to train a lot of people systematically and quickly. Unfortunately, most classroom training is not well-designed. Few instructors who know about testing also know a lot about the art and science of education. Many commercially available testing training programs and courses include droning lectures oriented toward overly analytical, white-box testing methods. These methods are usually presented outside of any practical context, and typically assume the tester has access to a complete specification, complete source code, and all the time needed to do the job right. Another problem with commercial training is that it is presented over only a few days. It takes a lot more time and effort to gain testing skills.

My approach to maximizing the value of classroom training or conference talks is to pepper the instructor with questions about the relevancy of the material — but this strategy isn't for everyone. If you dislike public confrontation, quietly separate the useful ideas from the useless. Listen to the lecture or review the course materials in the same manner you'd use for testing books. The value of the conference or class is not likely to be an entire model or program of testing from specifications to bugs, ready to go. Its value may turn out to be a single idea or a couple of slides that help you see the world more clearly.

Receptivity of Testers to Training

The challenges of training testers vary depending on the type of person you're working with. People with no testing experience and no computer science training are in many ways the easiest group to train. Although they have difficulty absorbing all the technical trivia that goes along with testing particular technologies, they're usually very open to seeing testing as a valuable, learnable discipline. The gems of this group are the people who have lots of professional experience in other fields of problem-solving. One of my best students was a former auto mechanic.

To train people who are true neophytes in the art of testing, you should start lightly on concepts and provide a lot of examples. Show them the process first, so that the concepts have a place to roost as you get more deeply into them.

People with computer science backgrounds are a more difficult group to train. While their knowledge of computer science is useful, recent computer science graduates may not be motivated to learn testing. They often take testing jobs because they see it as a stepping stone to get into software development. This kind of student seems to prefer examples — especially examples slanted toward technology. Teaching testing using a hot technology, like Java, may hold their interest better.

People with testing experience are the most difficult people to train because they usually think they already know enough. In addition to being less motivated as a group than either neophytes or computer science graduates, they have the additional baggage of the habits they've already acquired. The general challenge for a trainer or mentor is to honor the student's experience, and then relate the lessons to that experience while simultaneously helping them see the value of a broader way of thinking. Another important challenge is that the trainer must know the subject very well, both in theory and in practice.

For this group, I think a strong "concepts first" approach is better than giving "examples first." They already have the experience — now show them how their experience relates to a consistent model of testing. Consider including your most experienced people in the process of developing or tailoring the course. Do that, and your potentially harshest hecklers become your staunchest supporters in the classroom.

Competency-Based Training

Training is an important issue at Software Testing Labs, because we provide outsource software testing services. The competence of our staff is paramount if we are to continue growing. Our training program combines self-training, internal classes, and external classes. We offer six hours of classroom training every week for every tester in the lab.

The entire training program revolves around the competency-based training approach, which organizes a learning activity around well-defined, observable, business-related outcomes. Competency-based training requires that we define a competency list, determine a means of assessing students in each item on the list, develop the training, and determine a strategy for deploying the training in our lab.

As a first step, we defined a body of knowledge that everyone working in the lab had to master. Next, we created a job ladder for our lab employees and mapped the body of knowledge to it. The job ladder for a second-level associate engineer, senior-level engineer, and staff-level engineer is shown in Table 3.2.

Table 3.2   Results of Tests

	Title	Lead Track	Engineer Track
Job Ladder	**Staff** The staff-level engineer or lead is a strategic resource for STL, who has unique or extraordinary skills, understands the software quality industry, and otherwise directly improves our stature in that industry. Staff-level people drive their own education and have the resources and contacts to support rapid learning. *Minimum six years relevant experience in addition to required education and other professional experience.*	We expect successful staff leads to manage multiple innovative, critical, or otherwise very challenging projects from beginning to end. We expect them to pioneer new services and processes for the company and to train other leads to administer them.	We expect successful staff engineers to execute all aspects of risk-based test projects, as well as other kinds of test projects, using industry-recognized professional processes.
	Senior The senior-level engineer or lead is a role model within STL. He or she has diverse skills and experience, as well as the versatility to anchor a wide variety of projects. *Minimum three years directly relevant experience in addition to required education and other professional experience.*	We expect successful senior leads to manage multiple projects from beginning to end. They may manage other leads. We expect them to contribute substantially to the improvement of both services and processes.	We expect successful senior engineers to plan and execute all aspects of a risk-based test project, use a wide range of test techniques and tools, and have sufficient technical knowledge to anticipate, observe, discuss, and resolve esoteric quality problems.
	Associate 2 (A2) The second-level associate engineer or lead has skill and experience in software testing or development, and a demonstrated ability to follow our internal Software Quality Assurance practices. The A2 is a recognized specialist in some area of general technology. *Minimum one year directly relevant experience in addition to required education and other professional practice.*	We expect successful lead A2s to organize and execute routine test projects, including day-to-day leadership and mentoring of test engineers.	We expect successful A2s to create and execute a systematic test plan for a routine project and to produce all relevant reports. We expect them to have knowledge of typical technologies sufficient to recognize quality problems in those areas.

Defining competencies, and the means to assess students against them, is difficult for an intellectual art like testing. How can you say, objectively, how well-written a particular bug report is? Or how well-designed a particular test is? There is no objective answer, and you don't need one. As long as you provide broad guidelines for the quality of work you expect, the judgment of the instructor or qualified test manager is enough to verify competence. You only need to create competencies that make sense for your company, not necessarily the entire universe of software testing. An example of the competency list at Software Testing Labs is shown in Table 3.3.

Table 3.3 Example Competencies: Software Quality Assessment

General Competencies
• Ability to explain why overall quality is unmeasurable, even though individual quality factors are measurable.
• Ability to identify, for a specified quality factor, at least method of observation that is practical for use at STL.
• Ability to communicate levels of quality in qualitative terms.
Additional for A2 Level
• Ability to construct accurate and usable displays and graphs from sample data.
• Ability to explain how quality is measured at a good packaged software firm.
• Ability to describe common bug metrics and how they are used to assess quality.
• Ability to explain the responsible use of bug metrics, identifying common errors of analysis and how to avoid them.

How exactly do these competencies map to the job ladder? Some competencies only appear at certain levels of the ladder, while for many others the following levels of mastery are recognized:

- *No familiarity*: the student has no consistent understanding of the topic.
- *Academic familiarity*: the student can talk about it but can't perform it.
- *Inefficient practice*: the student can perform if necessary, but lacks speed, versatility, or quality of the result.
- *Efficient practice*: the student is able to perform quickly and produce a good quality result.
- *Mastery*: the student can perform superbly in a wide variety of situations.

Competency-based training works well because it explicitly aligns the activity of training to the skills needed to succeed. This makes training more flexible, because students can learn the material any way they want, as long as they demonstrate the required level of competency.

As we have pursued this training program at Software Testing Labs, we've run into some interesting problems. For instance, we discovered that our training development committee is ideally suited for creating the core testing classes that involve policies and methods. However, it works too slowly to meet the need for quick and dirty technology training such as classes in the basics of HTML or Windows 95. We found that defining competencies is not enough. We also have to explain to the students the precise connection of the competencies to the work they do. Another challenge with a full-blown competency-based training program is the administrative problem of assessing and recording everyone's competency levels over hundreds of competencies.

One resource for learning about competency-based training is the book *Logolearning*, by Dale Parnell (Center for Occupational Research and Development, 1994).

Any way you slice it, the starting point of meaningful training is understanding of what performance means and what skills are necessary to perform. This understanding is difficult to achieve in the domain of software testing. But if you take the effort and time to do it, you have a solid foundation on which to train testers.

3.2.3 "Running a Stellar Software Testing Team"

by Len DiMaggio

Developers and testers often have a contentious relationship, which can be exacerbated by nebulous roles and responsibilities. Clear rules of engagement enable the key QA activities to take place.

How do you get the cliques comprising a project team to cooperate rather than regard each other as adversaries? Clearly define the roles, rights and responsibilities up front. Be it integrated or independent, your new software test team will only succeed if you first quantify the group's deliverables and dependencies. For example, the developers rely on the testers to document all bugs encountered during testing, while the testers rely on the developers to ensure that the software is sufficiently stable to permit testing.

What can you expect from a testing group? It should test early and often, maintain the test environment, build appropriate tools and act as a knowledge base. But first, you must establish the rules of engagement between the testing team and the other groups. These should cover three main areas: sharing of access, information and tools; protocols for release notes and software handoffs; and smoke tests. In establishing rules for these tasks, remember that you must walk a fine line between imposing too little structure, thereby risking anarchy (and bugs), and imposing too much structure, thereby risking stifled creativity and turf wars.

Sharing Access, Information, and Tools

One of the main effects of the Internet on your everyday life is that you must constantly think about security. In order to protect information or source code, you build walls to keep outsiders out. In the course of doing so, however, sometimes you make it difficult for insiders to gain data.

The most effective relationship for the development and test groups is for each to be independent but closely integrated. There are really no good reasons to hide project information and deny access to tools and data from other members of the project team. There are, however, some bad reasons. Perhaps you are denied access to a set of tools because the programs are so hard to use that only their original author can make them run. If this is the case, then the tools are worthless to the project.

There are also no good reasons to deny test groups access (or at least read-only access) to the product's source code. There is a hackneyed view, still held by some software developers, that having test engineers read the code is a form of cheating, because they will lose objectivity by knowing how the code works (see Boris Beizer's *Software Testing Techniques,* Coriolis

Group, 1990; reprint, Van Nostrand Reinhold, 1982). It's an interesting way of looking at things — similar to the concept of not telling your accountant the whole story of your real estate losses before an IRS audit.

Don't forget that the information flow on a project is a two-way street — or a 10-way street. The test group must ensure that any information it uncovers is available to the rest of the product team. For example, marketing and development may make assumptions about the compatibility between two products. The actual compatibility testing may prove that while the products are, strictly speaking, compatible, the memory required to keep both applications open at one time is more than the "required system minimum" defined for each product.

Documenting Software Handoffs

The key moment in a relay race is when the baton is passed from one runner to the next. If it's done correctly, the runners never lose stride. If it's done badly, they lose time, and maybe the race. Similarly, great effort is spent developing and testing software, but time is often lost transferring software from the coders to the testers.

It sounds like a simple task, doesn't it? It should be as simple as copying files onto a diskette or making them available from a Web server, right? Wrong! It's easy to create a program; it's hard to create a product. A software handoff submitted for testing (I use the term "software test package" or STP) is, in effect, the software packaged as a product. The customer is the test group. Question: What do customers have regarding products? Answer: Requirements.

The most crucial testing requirement for an STP is information. Specifically, it is a definition of the software to be tested. Why is this necessary? Why can't the test group simply rely on the product's functional or design specifications? Because the release note is a snapshot that describes the product's current condition at that moment in time. It may be that, of the 10 major functions planned for the product, only three are actually implemented or testable. The development team's goal in submitting the STP for testing may be to verify the operation of these first three functions before work on the remaining functions begins. Why is it necessary to document the STP in a release note? Conversations are forgotten. E-mail can get lost. An archive of STP release notes in a central, accessible location such as a group Web server is a recorded history of the project. This history can be used to track progress and highlight trouble areas (say, the same bug being fixed and then reappearing). Use a standard format for the release notes to enforce a level of discipline and ensure that each note is comprehensive (see sidebar).

The Classes of Information that Belong in a Release Note

Product Information
This section uniquely identifies the software referenced by the release note. The patch or software test package (STP) number must be unique within each product release to ensure that bugs test results are accurately tracked against the correct STP.

Goal for this Section: To eliminate any confusion about just what version of the software is being tested at a particular time, and what bugs are present in what STP, so that you won't waste time trying to figure out if a code change was included in yesterday's build, the current build or the final build.

Release Purpose

States the objectives for which the software referenced by the release note was built (for example, to implement new functions or to solve problems in existing software with a patch). It also includes a description of the changes in the software referenced by the latest release.

Goal for this Section: To ensure the software changes relative to the previous STP are known. Areas that have been changed represent those most at risk (and most in need of testing).

Bugs Fixed

Lists, by bug report number, the bugs resolved in the software referenced by the release note. It is not necessary to restate the details of any specific bug resolutions in the release note, as this information is written into the bug reports.

Goal for this Section: To ensure that all bugs fixed are clearly identified. Listing the bugs by bug report number makes it much easier to verify the bug fixes.

Files Changed

Lists all new, changed and removed files relative to the software previously submitted for testing.

Goal for this Section: To ensure that all changed source files are clearly identified. Listing the source files makes it easier for the test group to review the code changes and ensure that new bugs are not inadvertently introduced.

Known Bugs and Restrictions

Lists all known problems and incomplete functions in the software referenced by the release note.

Goal for this Section: To ensure that quality assurance tests are not inadvertently performed (and bug reports not logged) in functional areas known to be unready for testing.

Installation Notes

Describes the steps necessary to install the software referenced by the release note. If the project has a standard set of installation instructions, it is sufficient to simply refer to those instructions in the release note.

Goal for this Section: To ensure that the test group is able to correctly install and configure the software to be tested. In many cases, spurious bugs result from improper installation or configuration.

Unit Tests and Tools

Lists the unit tests performed on the software referenced by the release note before it was submitted for QA testing. It includes references to any development test documents or test tools.

Goal for this Section: To avoid duplicating efforts.

The ultimate objective behind documenting each STP is saving time in the project schedule. The up-to-date product definition contained in the release notes enables the test group to exclusively concentrate its efforts on those areas in the product that are at risk and require testing; they do not waste time testing areas that are not ready for testing or reporting bugs that are already known. The goal of creating the notes is not just to produce a collection of documents. The release notes are only a means to an end.

Smoke Tests

The last thing anyone needs is another "cheesecake" bug. What's a great example of a cheesecake bug? Development delivers a software handoff to the test group and it fails to install. Or it installs, but its most basic or newest functions completely fail. Bugs such as these run up the "body count" on a project, but they're a waste of testing resources. They're also a waste of development resources, as the software handoff in which they're found must immediately be replaced.

The answer is simple enough: smoke tests. The name comes from tests performed by hardware engineers who would carefully apply power to a newly developed (or patched) board or component and watch for smoke. No kidding. I actually saw this happen once at my first job after college. A senior hardware engineer plugged in a prototype CRT and wham! Sparks flew and smoke poured out of it. It was fun to watch, but I decided to stick with software.

So, what constitutes a software smoke test? That depends on the software. You have to tailor the set of individual tests that comprise the smoke test to fit the product and the software handoff in question. For example, the smoke test for the initial handoff for testing will concentrate on verifying (or at least quantifying) the operation of new features, while the smoke test for the final release of the same product will concentrate on verifying the final bug fixes. Likewise, a smoke test for a Web-based front end to a mutual fund database will be very different from the smoke test for a sign-up form for dishwashing soap coupons.

What are the constants in all smoke tests? Here's a hint: I also refer to smoke tests as "sanity tests." In practice, the smoke test for a handoff of any given product while under development includes the following classes of tests:

- *Installation and Configuration.* Tests for these two tasks may sound overly obvious. After all, how can the software fail during its own installation? If a file or a shared library is missing, or if a file has its ownership or access permissions incorrectly set, then the act of installing or configuring the software may fail. How can bugs like this arise during testing when the software in question had been performing without error in the development environment? Well, strange things do happen the first time software is run outside of its development environment. For example, the assembling of the software into a portable package may appear to be complete, but files may be missing.
- *Verification of Newly Added Features.* The code most at risk in any software build is the code that has changed relative to previous builds. (Other code may also be at risk, as the cause and effect of bugs is not always direct.)
- *Verification of Bug Fixes.* As is the case with adding new features, fixing bugs can also put the software at risk, because new bugs may be introduced.
- *Limited Test of Each Logical Subsystem and Feature.* Here is where it gets a little fuzzy. This set of tests constitutes a regression test of the software. How many of these tests should you perform? It's directly related to the project under test. Specifically, it's related

to the extent to which you've been able to build an automated set of tests, and to the project history. If changes in source code are not tracked and reviewed on an ongoing basis, and if the team has a record of making unnecessary changes and introducing new bugs, then you have no choice but to run more tests on each subsystem to ensure that the entire product is ready for extensive testing.

The tests are performed in the sequence listed previously, so that each class of tests builds on the class that came before it.

In order to be effective, the smoke test should be performed twice: first, by the development group within its own environment to ensure that the software is ready to be submitted for testing, and again by the test group in its environment to ensure that the software performs the same outside development as it does inside development. Note that the development testing should be performed on separate systems to eliminate the "missing file" problem. Performing the smoke test in each environment will reduce the number of bugs found by the test group that the development group is unable to reproduce or debug. This will also reduce the number of times "Gee, it works in my lab" is heard during the project.

The Tasks

The test group performs four crucial functions: testing early and often, maintaining the test environment, building tools and acting as a source of knowledge.

Testing Early and Often

In order for the test engineers to be effective, they must be involved in the project from its planning and design stages, not simply when the code is being written and the testing is performed. This early involvement enables test engineers to understand the design and implementation of the software product to be tested.

There is another crucial reason for the test group to be involved on the project from its earliest stages: to remove bugs before they are ever put into the product.

This is practicing bug prevention at the lowest level, by ensuring that the design itself is bug-free. As sure as there is no free lunch, there is no bug-free software, you may say. There is, however, software that is less buggy than other software. Very often, the test engineers will have the most vivid memories of problems caused by some sections of a program. It may seem strange, but the more bugs that are found in a section of a program, the more likely additional bugs will be found there (see Glenford J. Myers' *The Art of Software Testing,* John Wiley & Sons, 1979).

Don't let anyone tell you that this type of bug detection and design review is not testing. It's the most cost-effective kind of testing there is. Bug detection is the goal of every test. Bug prevention, however, is much more efficient because there is no corrected code, no testing to verify the fix (and to verify that the fix doesn't cause a new bug), no slipping schedule and no embarrassed programmers (see Beizer's *Software Testing Techniques*).

Every bug found costs something to fix. This cost is less, however, the earlier in a project that the bug is found. Each bug not only rings up charges for equipment, schedule and personnel resources to fix the bug, but also hurts your credibility with your customers. The cost of fixing a bug is geometrically related to its degree of public exposure (Boris Beizer, *Software System Testing and Quality Assurance,* Van Nostrand Reinhold, 1984). The most expensive bug of all, of course, is the bug found by a customer.

An important aspect in trying to prevent bugs involves thinking about the implications of the design. Some design bugs are obvious. I remember a problem where a file server for some early 1980s PCs made use of a hardcoded "F:" as its remote file server, while the disk partitioning software permitted partitions to be assigned the letters C through Z. What happened if the local disk was configured with an "F:" partition? Well, at least it didn't take too long to reformat the disk.

I encountered a subtler problem a few years later when I was working on a network traffic measurement project. The goal of the project was to provide a report of exact numbers for the amount of traffic flowing through a telephone company's central voice mail system. The reports included several subsections and would take minutes to generate from dynamic counters. These counters would continue to increment while the reports were being run. The result was that the later sections of the reports would include additional data beyond that included in the earlier sections. Subtle to you and me, but it would have been a serious problem for a telephone company auditor to find.

This type of built-in testability is not only helpful during the development and testing of a product before it is released, it's also useful in debugging problems that customers encounter in a product after it is released.

Maintaining the Test Environment

Do you ever find yourself constructing and maintaining a hardware and software environment, only to end up lending it out to development groups because they don't have a clean setup in which to debug their work? This happens to me with some frequency. Some time ago, I encountered an environment-sharing problem while testing an Internet firewall. It was a fairly complex product to test, because it required two networks (one inside and one outside), internal and external DNS (Domain Name Service) servers (to provide address-to-host-name resolution), routers, and Unix and PC test hosts. The developers had a habit of working as individuals on "their own" parts of the product. As a result, they never took the time to build a complete network in which to debug their work as a whole. Instead, they begged to borrow my test network. I let them do this for short periods of time, but I always warned them that it was a temporary solution.

This is clearly not an acceptable way to do things. The only way I could have been sure of my test environment was to format the disk of any host they used during their debugging before I could begin testing. Why would this be necessary? To avoid situations like the following:

1. Development engineer installs a software release to debug…
2. …but then discovers files are missing.
3. To save time, the software is not completely rebuilt; the missing files are simply installed separately.
4. Debugging is successfully completed.
5. The same software release is successfully tested by test group on the same systems in which the missing files were installed.
6. The software release is sold to a customer who installs it and…
7. …watches it fail as files are missing.

How could this have been avoided? By starting step five with a "clean" system. In this context, "clean" means "in the same state as the customers' systems." This may be a simplistic example, but I've seen it happen. The real cost is not the setting up of the network; it's the maintenance. Indeed, the cost of maintenance is frequently overlooked when test automation is estimated.

Tool Building

The stereotype that frequently comes to mind when someone mentions testing software is that of a engineer performing the tedious task of manually running hundreds of tests over and over again and then manually verifying the results. The stereotype is no longer the rule, it's the exception. Software life cycles have become so short, and the software itself so complex, that no one has the time or ability to manually run hundreds of tests. Besides, it's boring and ineffective; problems can be missed and results misinterpreted.

While there are times when only human judgment can determine the success or failure of a test, it is much more likely that the test — and the verification of its results — can be automated. Creating test tools (programs or scripts) is one of the best ways to ensure the quality of a product. If the tedious, human-error prone testing tasks can be automated, the test group can concentrate on finding more insidious bugs. What's more, you can even supply these test tools to the developer group, so they can debug the software before it's submitted to the test group.

Here is a good example: A few years ago, I was working on a telephone voice mail network switch statistics program. One of the features of the program was a summary report generated on a daily basis. The report was created in a binary file that used a complex record format. For example, the value of the first four bytes reflected the number of calls measured in thousands. This was done in order to store as much data as possible in a small file. File size was important, since the file was transmitted over a slow data link to the customers' sites. The development engineer checked his work by creating a report, printing out the hexadecimal values of the data in the file and manually comparing the printout to his input data.

This seemed like a form of torture suitable only for IRS auditors. I didn't enjoy watching him repeatedly perform such a menial task. I also didn't like the idea that he could easily miss bugs because the testing process was so error-prone. And I really didn't like the idea of having to perform the same types of tests myself! So I wrote a short program to reformat the binary file into human-readable form and compare it with a defined set of expected results. Then, I tested the program to ensure that it could handle the range the binary file supported and that it would report format errors in that file. I gave it to the developer. He thanked me, but he seemed sad. I later learned that he was working as a contractor and was being paid by the hour.

There is another benefit to developing tools: satisfaction. One of the great joys of writing software is the ability to create new programs, and one of the joys of testing software is breaking those programs. One of the more interesting joys of testing software is creating your own program that in turn breaks another program — sort of an antimissile-missile.

A Source of Knowledge

People always ask me about the products on which I work. Sometimes the questions come from marketing folks, other times from support personnel. Recently, I've been getting a lot of questions from development engineers. This might strike some people as strange. After all, if they're writing the software, they must know everything about it, right?

In fact, they usually know a great deal about the parts of the product they're working on, but they may not have much of an idea about what anyone else is doing. Engineers get tunnel vision. It's in situations like this that bugs are found when the program is integrated.

Test engineers must have a broader view of the product. In order to plan and execute a complete test of a product, the test engineers must not only understand how the pieces of the program work, they must also understand and have knowledge about how they work together and how the program must work with the other parts of the environment (such as the operating system or other programs).

The main beneficiary of this knowledge is the test group itself. The other beneficiaries are the development, marketing and customer-support groups. Each has a unique perspective: The test group's goal is to uncover bugs, the developers want to create their design, customer support wants to verify solutions to specific bugs, and marketing wants to see customers' needs (and sales quotas) fulfilled.

Rules and Roles Revisited

A common cause of conflict between individuals and groups is when expectations are not met (often because they are not correctly set). Despite the best efforts of everyone involved, the relationship between a software development team and its testing counterpart is often contentious, or even adversarial. These troubles can be exacerbated if the roles and responsibilities of the groups are not clearly defined. Once this framework is in place, the four key testing activities can take place.

First, testing begins long before a line of code is written. It begins during the earliest stages of a product's design and planning. A successful test is one that uncovers a bug, and the best bug to find is the one that never happened because the flaw that would have caused it was found during a design review before the program was written.

Second, one of the most difficult tasks in testing software is isolating the root cause of a bug. What makes this task difficult is that typically there are a large number of variables affecting the performance of the software under test. One set of these variables comprises the test environment. The test environment consists of both the hardware (CPU, memory, disk size and so on) and software platform (operating system and utilities) required by the software under test as well as the software itself. It may sound like a trivial or automatic task to maintain a stable, well-defined test environment, but, like so many things in software engineering, nothing is automatic. If you fail to maintain the environment, you may miss legitimate bugs and spend your time chasing down problems that are not in the software under test but in your own test configuration.

Third, in starting a new software project, my (as yet unachievable) goal is to be able to design and build a complete set of test tools at the same time the actual product is being developed, so that when product development is complete, the tests are also complete. Regardless of schedule pressures, reusable test tools must be built and shared between the development and test groups. Engineers in each group will approach this in different ways. Development engineers will better understand the product's operation, but they may only exercise the software within its intended boundaries. For example, if the software under test is a program with a Unix shell (command line) interface, a developer may create a tool that presents the program with all of its valid inputs, while a test engineer may build a tool that volleys a barrage of invalid inputs. The most cost-effective approach is for the two to collaborate.

Finally, it's easy for people working in a technical field to lose track of the world around them. Test engineers, however, generally see not just the parts of the product, but their sum performance. By doing so, they fulfill an important role: ensuring the integrity of the product as a whole.

3.2.4 "Selecting Test Cases Based on User Priorities"

by John D. McGregor and Melissa L. Major

The road to more reliable software is paved with customer — not developer — intentions. An operational profile built from use cases can guide you in testing the most popular system functions and eliminating the defects users would encounter most often.

Your product's release date looms. Though you're scrambling to cover every testing contingency, a worry still gnaws at you: will the user base curse your name in three months' time as a poorly coded module repeatedly causes problems? How do you know you've done every reasonable, appropriate test?

If your system-test strategy is implementation-based, you will attempt to test every line of code, or even every path through the code. You'll certainly find defects, but the process is expensive — and impossible for those portions of the system for which you only have access to the executable, or where there are infinite paths. Specification-based techniques, on the other hand, will cover all of the assumptions and constraints that were imposed by the software's developers.

Table 3.4   The Use-Profile Process

1. Define complete set of actors.
2. Define a complete set of use cases including associations with actors.
3. Construct the use profile for each actor.
4. Compute the frequency attribute for each use case from the actor use profiles.
5. Combine the frequency and criticality ratings for a single use case into a "test priority" value.
6. Allocate test cases based on the test priority of the use case.
(Source: McGregor, John D. and Sykes, David A., *A Practical Guide to Testing Object-Oriented Software*, Addison-Wesley.)

Figure 3.2 A Unified Modeling Language Use-Case Diagram

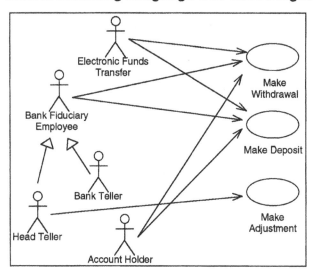

To illustrate the use profile technique, we'll model a simple banking system with which customers can directly access their accounts through automated teller machines. The bank employees access the same accounts directly through the system under development. Customers can add or remove money from their accounts or check their balances. According to the UML notation, actors are stick figures and uses are ovals. A dependency arrow shows the association of an actor to a specific use. The actors in the example system include a bank customer, a teller, a head teller and the electronic funds transfer system.

However, neither approach addresses a crucial point of view: your users' priorities. If you are in the shrink-wrap software business, you may have made some vague assumptions about your users; by contrast, if you are building a product after a formal request for proposals, you may be following precisely defined user profiles. Regardless of the rigorousness of your design process, one thing holds true: the frequency with which each type of user uses the system will reflect the relative importance of the specific system features.

In system testing, this frequency of use has traditionally been represented by an operational profile, which guides the selection of test cases so that the most popular system operations are tested most frequently. This is an effective technique for discovering defects that users would encounter the most. While operational profiles are easy enough to construct after accumulated experience with the system, they are harder to build prior to release — which is when, of course, they are most useful.

The familiar use-case model of system requirements can play a part in computing the relative frequency of use, thus guiding the selection of test cases for the system. We have developed a set of extensions — including an expanded description of the system actors — to existing use-case templates that capture information relevant to testing.

Increasing System Reliability

The reliability of a software program, as defined by John Musa in *Software Reliability Engineering* (McGraw-Hill, 1999), is the probability of failure-free operation in a specified context and period of time. During system testing, it's possible to estimate the reliability of the system as it will be experienced in normal operation. Accurate estimates require that you must specify the context, which is in part comprised of the system functions that will be exercised. The context should also include a description of the operating environment consisting of the operating system version number, the run-time system's version (if applicable), as well as version specifications for all DLLs used. One technique for specifying the system functions' portion of the context is to use the same operational profile that drives system testing.

Reliability requirements are stated in terms of a specified period of failure-free operation (for example, "no failures in 24 hours"). The frequencies of operation shown in the operational profile should be based on the user's actions within the same time period as expressed in the reliability requirement. This relationship between the two time periods provides a clear direction for system testing. Using an operational profile designed for the appropriate time interval to direct the tests, and then repairing the failures encountered produces the fastest possible improvement in system reliability.

Actors and Use Cases[3]

The use-case technique, incorporated into the Rational Unified Process, provides an easy-to-understand representation of the functional requirements for a system. The technique identifies all external forces (or actors) that trigger system functionality. Each use case provides a description of a use of the system by one or more of the actors.

An actor can represent a human user of the system or a stimulus from another system. However, because each actor actually represents a type rather than a specific user, each will interact differently with the system.

Use cases describe the details of system functionality from the user perspective, with scenario sections detailing the system's response to specific external stimuli. The scenario section also outlines what triggers the use and provides the information needed to establish the criteria that will determine whether the system passed the test. Additionally, the use case describes the preconditions that must be established prior to the execution of the test case.

For our purposes, let's focus on the frequency and criticality fields in the use case template. The criticality attribute defines how necessary a use is to the successful operation of the system; the frequency attribute defines how often a specific use is triggered. By combining these two attributes, you can prioritize uses and tests and thus test the most important, most frequently invoked uses. In our simple banking system, making deposits and making adjustments might have about the same frequency, but making deposits would have a higher criticality and should be tested more rigorously.

---

3. This template is derived by Software Architects based on work from Ivar Jacobson's *Object-Oriented Software Engineering: A Use-Case Driven Approach* (Addison-Wesley, 1992) and the work of Alistair Cockburn (compiled at http://members.aol.com/acockburn). We have modified Cockburn's priority attribute to more clearly distinguish between frequency and criticality and have also added a risk attribute.

Table 3.5   A Unified Modeling Language Template

Use Case ID:	Make Deposit
Use Case Level:	System Level
Scenario	
Actor(s):	Electronic Funds Transfer, Bank Fiduciary Employee, and Account Holder
Preconditions:	Account must be open and active
Description:	Trigger: Actor initiates a deposit to an account
	The system responds by adding the deposit amount to the pre-existing balance.
	The system updates counters measuring account activity.
	The system checks if amount of deposit requires IRS notification and generates notification if required.
	Relevant requirements: Ability to increase account balances
	Post-conditions: Balance has been increased by the amount of the deposit
Alternative Courses of Action:	If account is not active, first activate the account and then make deposit.
Extensions	
Exceptions:	Invalid account number
Concurrent Uses:	Making a withdrawal
Related Use Cases:	Making a withdrawal
Decision Support	
Frequency:	
Criticality:	
Risk:	
Modification History	
Owner:	MLMajor
Initiation date:	12/20/99
Date last modified:	12/20/99

Criticality is easy for an expert to judge, so this field can be completed as the use case is constructed. Frequency is more difficult to quantify, however, because different actors may trigger the same use at very different rates.

Actor Profiles[4]

Each actor is described by a brief profile. The major attribute is the actor's use profile, which ranks the frequency with which this actor triggers each individual use. It is usually easy to determine the relative frequency with which a specific actor does this, either by analyzing the responsibilities of the actor or by simply reasoning about the domain.

You can note the frequency attribute with relative rankings (for example, first, second or third), implied rankings (high, medium or low) or the percentage of invocations that are applied to this use (0 to 100 percent). However, the actors seldom trigger each use the exact same percentage during each program execution, making this last approach less accurate.

Table 3.6 Actor Profiles

Name: Bank Fiduciary Employee Description (Role): Has access to money accounts Skill Level: Varies Actor's Use Profile:	Abstract: Y/n
Use Case Name	Relative Frequency
Make Withdrawal	High
Make Deposit	Medium
Make Adjustment	Low
Name: Bank Teller Description (Role): Directly interfaces with account owners Skill Level: Trained but varied amounts of experience Actor's Use Profile:	Abstract: y/N
Use Case Name	Relative Frequency
Make Withdrawal	Medium
Make Deposit	High
Make Adjustment	N/A

---

4. Each actor is described by a brief profile. The major attribute is the actor's use profile, which ranks the frequency with which this actor triggers each individual use.

Table 3.6   Actor Profiles (Continued)

Name: Head Teller Description (Role): Supervises Bank Tellers and manages accounts Skill Level: Expert Actor's Use Profile:	Abstract: y/N
Use Case Name	Relative Frequency
Make Withdrawal	High
Make Deposit	Medium
Make Adjustment	Medium
Name: Account Holder Description (Role): Owns the account and can trigger account activity Skill Level: Novice Actor's Use Profile:	Abstract: y/N
Use Case Name	Relative Frequency
Make Withdrawal	High
Make Deposit	Medium
Make Adjustment	N/A
Name: Electronic Funds Transfer System Description (Role): Triggers account activity within constraints Skill Level: Expert Actor's Use Profile:	Abstract: y/N
Use Case Name	Relative Frequency
Make Withdrawal	Medium
Make Deposit	Medium
Make Adjustment	N/A

Though the ranking values are identical, it's often easier to attach meaning to high, medium and low than to 1, 2 and 3. On the other hand, combining numeric rankings is more intuitive than combining subjective values.

Use-case Profiles

Now, you can combine the individual actor's use profiles to rank each use case. Record the ranking in the frequency attribute of the use case (we also summarize it in a table for ease of reference). Combine the actor profile values with a weighted average (the weight represents the relative importance of the actor).

For simplicity, in our example we treat all the actors equally, each with a weight of 1. The values in the abstract actor use profile aren't included in the computation, but they do help determine the value for specialized actors.

The test priority column is determined by combining the frequency and criticality columns, typically with either a conservative or an averaging strategy. While averaging is self-explanatory, the conservative strategy — choosing the highest rating by default — often comes into play with life- or mission-critical systems.

Allocating Tests

The technique presented here doesn't change the basic process of selecting types of tests and specific input data, nor does it change the calculation of how many test cases can be constructed given the available resources. What does change is that now you can systematically distribute test cases to specific use cases with a calculated test priority.

Once the priorities have been determined, you can compute the number of tests to be associated with each use case. One easy method is to value the use cases' test priorities numerically. In our example, the ranks of high, medium, and low are replaced with 3, 2 and 1, which sum to 6. Assume that there is time for approximately 100 tests. Then, assigning 3 to high, use case number 1 would rate 100 * 3/6, or 50 tests. Use case number 2 would rate 100 * 2/6 tests, or 33 tests, and use case number 3 would rate 100 * 1/6, or 17 tests.

When you calculate the number of tests in this fashion, adopt a standard for determining which test cases to construct. In general, allocate your tests to the sections of the use-case description in the following order of priority: first, the basic scenario; second, exceptions; third, alternative courses of action; and last, extensions.

Although the basic scenario and exceptions should be the focus of the majority of the tests, do be sure to evaluate each section to a greater or lesser degree.

Maximizing Testing ROI

Prioritizing the uses of the system produces a weighted operational profile, or use profile. Many of the steps might seem straightforward enough in the context of the simple example presented here, but in a larger project, determining which use cases to stress and which to cover only briefly can be tricky.

Indeed, building use profiles maximizes the return on investment of resources allocated to system testing, directing system testing in such a way that the reliability of the software increases the fastest. That is, test cases are selected so that those operations users depend on most are triggered most often.

Table 3.7   Summary Table of Use-Case Profiles

Use Case Name	Frequency	Criticality	Test Priority
Make Withdrawal	High	High	High
Make Deposit	Medium	Medium	Medium
Make Adjustment	Medium	Low	Low

The individual actor's use profiles are combined to rank the frequency of each use. For the Make Withdrawal use case, the average frequency is calculated as: Medium + High + High + Medium/4 = High. For the Make Deposit use case, the average is calculated as: High + Medium + Medium + Medium/4 = Medium. For the Make Adjustment use case, the average frequency is calculated as: Medium/1 = Medium.

To save space in this example, the criticality value for each use case is placed in the table. The Make Adjustment use has a low criticality rating because the head teller could use combinations of deposit/withdrawal to achieve the required result. Withdrawal is rated as more critical than deposit, simply because we must be able to return money that we have accepted. The test priority column is then obtained by combining the frequency and criticality columns, using the same method.

Figure 3.3   Test-Case Diagram

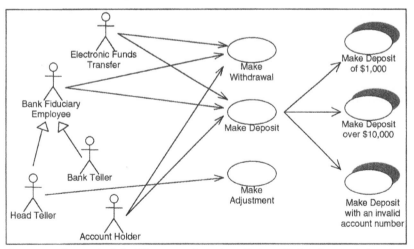

The test case diagram extends the UML use case diagram to provide traceability from the actors to the system test cases that an actor triggers. Changes to an actor may result in a need to change specific use and test cases. Test reports can easily provide a "by actor" summary of failure. You can then systematically distribute a portion of the possible test cases to specific use cases using a calculated test priority.

The technique also links the system's actors, uses and tests; now, when uses change, you can easily identify which tests to change, and when tests fail, you can easily find the affected uses.

To illustrate the use profile technique, we'll model a simple banking system with which customers can directly access their accounts through automated teller machines. The bank employees access the same accounts directly through the system under development. Customers can add or remove money from their accounts or check their balances. According to the UML notation, actors are stick figures and uses are ovals. A dependency arrow shows the association of an actor to a specific use. The actors in the example system include a bank customer, a teller, a head teller and the electronic funds transfer system.

3.2.5 "A J2EE Testing Primer"

by Scott W. Ambler

It takes a wide range of tools and techniques to evaluate the quality of distributed software.

It isn't enough to simply develop software — you need to build software that works. And there's only one way to prove that your software works: test it. Due to the inherent complexity of software developed with Java, particularly software based on the Java 2 Enterprise Edition (J2EE) platform, testing often proves more difficult than it first appears. With J2EE, you're developing logic using a wide range of technologies including Java Server Pages (JSPs), servlets, Enterprise JavaBeans (EJBs) and relational databases — therefore, you need to apply a wide range of testing techniques and tools. This month, I explore several best practices for testing J2EE-based software and describe how to organize your environment to support effective software testing.

Fundamental Testing Concepts

Get back to basics with these essential tips.

Although the focus here is on J2EE, these fundamental concepts of software testing are independent of your development environment:

1. Test throughout the project's entire life cycle.
2. Develop your tests before you develop an artifact.
3. Test all artifacts.
4. Test continuously.
5. Determine the specific cause of a defect.
6. Do more, not less, testing of objects.
7. Make the goal of testing to find bugs, not cover them up.
8. Automate your regression tests.
9. Invest in simple, effective testing tools.
10. Have separate personal, integration and staging areas.

EJB Testing Best Practices

First, it's critical that your project team and stakeholders understand that J2EE testing is difficult. In "Object Testing Patterns" (*The Unified Process Elaboration Phase*, Chapter 7), I described several process patterns for testing object-oriented software and summarized a collection of techniques, such as inheritance regression testing and function testing, applicable to the testing of J2EE software. That article was just the tip of the iceberg, as Robert Binder's 1,190-page book, *Testing Object-Oriented Systems: Models, Patterns and Tools* (Addison-Wesley, 2000) suggests. There is a wide range of testing techniques at your disposal — techniques that you must understand to be able to apply appropriately.

Second, J2EE presents unique testing challenges. J2EE software is typically distributed across several types of logical components such as firewalls, Web servers, EJB application servers and database servers. The logical components are then distributed onto physical processors that are often organized into farms of machines for scalability and performance purposes. Organizations new to J2EE, often neophytes to testing distributed software, may not be prepared to handle the task. To test distributed software, you need tools and techniques that enable you to run both single-machine and cross-machine tests. For example, a typical end-to-end test may originate in a browser and connect to a Web server to access a servlet, which interacts with session beans that may access the database through Java Database Connectivity (JDBC), and/or interacts with entity beans that access the database through the EJB persistence container. The beans produce a result that the servlet passes to a JSP to produce HTML that can be displayed in the browser. Whew! To make matters worse, many aspects of J2EE are encapsulated (for example, the internal workings of your EJB persistence container); therefore, you're often limited to black box testing techniques. This can make finding the true source of defects a challenge — sometimes requiring excruciating effort to determine a bug's cause. Furthermore, Web-based applications present a novel set of security challenges to watch out for.

Another critical best practice for J2EE testing is the automation of your regression tests. When you take an iterative approach to software development (the most common way to develop J2EE-based software), it's critical to prove that previous functionality still works after you've made changes (the focus of regression testing). Without the ability to press a button and rerun all tests against the system, a developer can never feel safe making a change to his code.

Anything the team can build, they can test: requirements, review design models, user documentation and source code. After all, if something isn't worth testing, it probably isn't worth building. Your testing process must address more than source code testing — you can and should test all important project artifacts.

An important best practice is to recognize that silence isn't golden. Your goal is to identify potential defects, not to cover them up. Good tests find defects: Tests that don't find any defects may well have failed.

Your team should test often and test early. First, because most mistakes are made early in the life of a project: Developers tend to make more errors when gathering and analyzing requirements than when designing and writing source code. Second, the cost of fixing defects increases exponentially the later they are found. This happens because of the nature of software development — work is performed based on previous work. For example, your code is based on your models, which in turn are based on your requirements. If a requirement was misunderstood, all modeling decisions based on that requirement are potentially invalid, and all code based on the models is also in question. If defects are detected during requirements definition, where they are likely to be made, then they will probably be much less expensive to fix — you have only to update your requirements model. For best results, you need to test throughout the project's entire life cycle.

Also consider writing your testing code before you write the "real" code, as developers following Extreme Programming (XP) techniques do. This forces them to think about what they are developing, to ensure that it meets the actual requirements, and that, in fact, it can be tested. You'll have to write the test eventually, so you might as well benefit from its side effects.

Finally, plan for rework. Testing your system means little if you don't intend to make repairs. Include time in your project plan to rework your system before it's delivered to your users. Too many project teams fail to plan for this and, as a result, schedules slip.

Java Testing Environment

In addition to an effective testing tool suite, you also need a software environment that reflects the realities of testing. For example, in many organizations, it's quite common for development environments to differ from production environments: Perhaps developers are working on Intel-based machines running Windows NT, whereas the production environment is made up of Sun servers running Solaris. This begs the question of organizing your work to reflect this reality, particularly with regard to testing. Figure 3.4 presents a common solution to this problem, depicting three distinct technical environments: a development area, a staging area and a production area.

Figure 3.4   How to Test Different Development and Production Environments

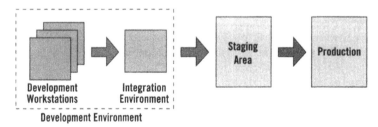

Programmers do the bulk of their work in the development area, writing and unit testing software on their personal workstations and then integrating their results with the work of their teammates within a shared integration environment. This environment typically consists of one or more machines to which programmers deploy their work on a regular basis (often daily or even hourly) to perform integration testing. A common development best practice is to continuously integrate your source code — a core XP practice that requires an integration environment to support continuous integration testing of code.

Your staging area serves as a testing ground for software that will be released into production. This enables development teams to determine how a system is likely to work within your production environment without putting actual production systems at risk: Your system may work fine on its own, but it could have adverse effects on existing systems, such as the corruption of shared data or the reduction of the runtime performance of higher-priority applications.

Ideally, your staging area should be an exact replica of your production environment, although it's often a reduced version due to replication costs. For example, your production environment may be a cluster of 50 Sun servers, whereas your staging area is a cluster of three Sun servers. The important thing is to provide a hardware and software environment that is as close as possible to your production environment.

Your production environment is where your systems run to support the day-to-day business of your organization. It's typically the domain of your organization's operations department. One of your operations department's primary goals is to ensure that no software is deployed into production until it's ready. To move your system into production, your project team will often have a long list of quality gates that it must pass through, such as proper testing in your staging area.

Java Testing Tools

Try out these tools to reduce your test anxiety.

Testing is a difficult process, but it can be eased by purchasing one or more testing tools. Luckily, there is a wide variety for Java-based software:

Bean-test (www.testmybeans.com) by RSW Software performs scalability (load and stress) testing on EJB applications. EJBQuickTest (www.ejbquick.com) simulates method invocations by clients of your EJB application, supporting regression testing, generation of test data, and performance and stress testing. Man Machine Systems' (www.mmsindia.com) JStyle critiques the quality of your Java source code, including the generation of code metrics. Parasoft's (www.parasoft.com) JTest supports sophisticated code testing and quality assurance validation for Java, including white box, black box, regression and coding standards enforcement. Sitraka Software's (www.klgroup.com) JProbe is a profiler and memory debugger for Java code, including a server-side version for EJB and a client-side version for ordinary Java code. JUnit (www.junit.org), a favorite among XP practitioners, is an open source framework for unit- and code-testing Java code that enables you to easily implement continuous code testing on your project.

Which tools should you adopt? The Extreme Modeling (XM) methodology (*Thinking Objectively,* Nov. 2000 and Apr. 2001) provides several insights to guide your tool selection efforts. First, use the simplest tools that will do the job. Simpler tools require less training and less effort to work with, and are often less expensive to purchase and install. Second, adopt tools that provide value. A tool should reduce the overall effort a task requires — if it doesn't, it detracts from your project and your organization. Do the least work possible to finish the job, so you can focus on the myriad remaining tasks necessary to deliver your project to your users. To find out more about XM, visit www.agilemodeling.com. If you want to add your two cents' worth to the discussion, you can join the XM mailing list (www.agilemodeling.com/feedback.html).

So, how do you use these environments effectively? Throughout an iteration, your developers will do their work in the development environment. Toward the end of an iteration, they'll schedule a minor release of their system into the staging area. It's important to understand your organization's processes and procedures for releasing software into the staging area because the area is typically shared among all project teams; the managers of the staging area also need to ensure that each team gets fair access to the environment without adversely affecting the other teams' efforts. Finally, once your project has passed your final testing in the large efforts, you'll take your release one step farther and move it from the staging area into production.

J2EE Testing Is Difficult

At the best of times, software testing is hard. Testing object-oriented software often proves more difficult than structured and procedural software because object technology is used to address more complex problem spaces. Distributed technology is harder to test than nondistributed technology because of the additional complexities inherent in multinode deployment. J2EE is a distributed, object-oriented software development platform, which means that it's one of the most difficult platforms to test. To be successful, you need to use many, if not all, of the best practices that I've described, and to adopt a productive software environment that supports the realities of developing, testing and then releasing software into production.

3.2.6 "Real-World Acceptance Testing"

by Randy Sparks and Timothy Seevers

Acceptance testing is like qualifying rounds at the Indianapolis 500. It eliminates unworthy software releases before the big race: full-blown regression testing.

Here's the assignment: improve the quality of your company's software without lengthening the product schedule. At first glance, these two forces may seem to be pulling you in opposite directions. Though there will probably always be some trade-offs between quality and time to market, there is a process you can (and should) put in place to minimize the problem.

The process, simply stated, involves building an ever-improving, automated acceptance test through an iterative cycle of test development and coverage analysis. You probably know by now that seemingly simple ideas are often difficult to actually implement. So, we will attempt to break down the process into pieces, define what these pieces are, and try to help you avoid the pitfalls you may run into as you put the process in place.

What an Acceptance Test Is

You can think of an acceptance test in the same way you would think of the qualifying rounds at the Indianapolis 500. It serves two purposes. First, it eliminates the drivers that are not qualified so the actual race isn't bogged down with slow and perhaps unsafe drivers. (An unsafe driver, like poorly developed software, is likely to crash.) Second, it provides a feeling of confidence for those drivers who did make the cut. They can go on to the big race because they've proven themselves worthy.

Acceptance tests serve these same two purposes. The drivers, however, are now releases of software that must pass the acceptance test (the qualifying round) before they can go on to a full-blown regression test (the big race).

What an Acceptance Test Should Be

First, an acceptance test should be automated. Human intervention should be minimal. If at all possible, this intervention should only occur at the beginning (to start the test) and at the end (to check the results). How this is accomplished largely depends on the environment in which the software must run. For example, you can drive the graphical interface portion of Windows 95 or Windows NT applications by using tools like Rational's Visual Test or Mercury Interactive's WinRunner. Underlying DLLs are often best tested with internally written test tools that poke directly at the published APIs the DLLs support. Often, you must drive embedded systems from the same points of entry that the user would exercise.

In any case, the test is a standard black box test in which you try something, get a result, check the result against what was expected, and log the information. The important thing here, as stated previously, is that this process must be automated.

Second, an acceptance test should be short. It's foolish to put an exact time on this, but ideally it should not last longer than an hour. Often, it's possible to reduce the duration of the test to a matter of minutes. The main goal is to get the information the test provides as quickly as possible.

Finally, you should always develop an acceptance test in conjunction with the information provided by a code coverage analysis tool. This approach will greatly help you put together a short test that also maximizes code testing. Before we go further into the benefits, let's talk in more detail about code coverage analysis.

Code Coverage Analysis

Earlier, we discussed how you can think of an acceptance test as the qualifying round for a development release of code. In a similar fashion, you can also think of code coverage analysis as the qualifier for the acceptance test (and regression tests in general). It is perhaps the most important measure of software test quality. The information code coverage can provide includes the test functions, executed lines of source code, executed lines of assembly, and a percentage of each as it relates to the whole. Some tools will also provide the percentage of call pairs and branches that were hit as a result of the test, and as an added bonus, they may throw in dead code information.

Code coverage tools accomplish this in several ways. One way requires you to recompile your source code while letting the tool add some source code of its own to perform the magic of determining which code was executed. The preferred method lets the tool use the debug symbols to determine executed code. At the very most, this will require you to recompile your code with debug symbols turned on. Since no new source code is entered into the system, it is easier to get the tool functioning on your code. In addition, the lack of outside source code will help eliminate the possibility that the tool will be the cause of a functional problem.

Some code coverage tools available include VisionSoft/TEST from VisionSoft (www.vsonline.com); Green Hills Software test suites (www.ghs.com); TracePoint's Visual Coverage (www.tracepoint.com); and C-Cover from Bullseye Testing Technology (www.bullseye.com).

Putting Code Coverage in Place

If you're not already using code coverage, you're probably thinking the information it provides is powerful stuff, and you would be correct. That is the good news. Now for the bad news. Getting code coverage to work in your environment may not be a trivial matter. If you are working with an embedded system, you may have a very limited choice of tools, if any at all. Embedded systems also have the added difficulty of how to get the coverage data back out of the system. Even if you are working in a ubiquitous environment such as Windows 95, getting a tool to work on your application can take some trial and error.

Before you begin using the coverage numbers that your tool is spitting back at you, it is important to independently verify that the numbers appear realistic and accurate. This is especially true the first time you attempt to use a new tool.

Once you have a coverage tool with which you are comfortable in place, you should automate your build process so there is a release build and a debug build for each spin of code. You should never use the debug build in your actual acceptance or regression test. It is only used as a determination of how good your set of tests are and where you can make improvements. Since the debug build is never going to reach the customer's site, there is no point in testing its quality.

Once you have accurate test coverage data to report to your management team, keep one thing in mind: these numbers are of no value unless you do something with them. That something is to feed that information back into the development of your acceptance test bucket. If your coverage is low, determine which code is not getting executed and add a test to hit it. If your acceptance bucket takes all day, use your coverage analysis data to determine where you have redundant tests. If you have dead code, discuss this with your development team to determine whether it should be removed, especially in an embedded system where code space is critical. This is an iterative process that will last until you have coverage numbers that satisfy both you and your management team.

The Functional Specification: Knowing Your Audience

The functional specification will usually serve many audiences including documentation writers, software testers, managers, and follow-on software developers (those who do post-release maintenance and development). As a result, it's difficult to balance the amount of detail the functional specification should contain. You will likely serve your respective audiences better if you maintain two documents: a user interface specification and an architectural design.

A user interface specification details only what you can access from the user interface. Another way to phrase this is that the user interface specification is the where and what of the software application and not the why or how. This document will serve some of your audience members completely, including documentation writers, black box software testers, and nontechnical managers. Documentation writers will love this document because, if done well, it can be the basis of the documentation that goes with the product. Black box testers' needs are met because black box testing is only concerned with the defined inputs (the user interface) and the expected outputs (the result). Finally, nontechnical managers are happy because you won't be boring them with details that do not pertain to their "bottom-line" world.

Some of your audience members need more. This is where the architectural design comes into play. This document should contain the details of why and how your software relates and flows. This could include items such as APIs, code module responsibilities and relationships, and design patterns (if any). Clearly, follow-on developers will become useful team members more quickly with this information. In addition, white box testers will find this information useful for evaluating code metrics and implementing code coverage.

Knowing that your audience has different needs, and targeting those needs with separate documents, will help you ensure the supporting members of the software development process will remain satisfied and productive. Some testers are concerned with the use of the product, some with the design, and some (probably your best) are concerned with both user interface and architectural design.

Benefits of Coverage Analysis and Acceptance Testing

It takes out the guess work.   You've been there before. You're in the middle of a regression test and your manager asks you how much of the code you have exercised so far. If you're not using code coverage analysis, then you may as well base your answer on a random number generator. The fact of the matter is, you just don't know. On several occasions, I've been surprised by how poor my test coverage was. Though I may have been blissfully ignorant, I was not in a position to increase quality and drive down product delivery cycles until I made the move to coverage analysis.

It exposes holes in the functional specification.   As hard as the development team may try, it doesn't always have the most complete, accurate, or up-to-date specification for the product you are testing. There may even be functions you didn't know existed. Sometimes, the only way to find these hidden functions is through coverage analysis. If you have a test for every functionally specified scenario, yet your coverage data shows you're missing big chunks of code, then the functional specification probably needs some work.

Putting Code Coverage Analysis Tools in Place

Unless you are testing the latest version of "Hello World," you'll probably experience some pain when you first attempt to apply a generic code coverage tool to your specific application. Here are some hints that might help you achieve success without having to learn from your own mistakes:

- Choose a code coverage tool that does not require source code modification. This type of tool provides the same coverage analysis information as the packages that require source code modification. Yet, not having to modify code eliminates the one step in the process that has traditionally been the most difficult.
- If your application runs as part of the operating system and it does not shut down unless the operating system is shut down, then find a tool that will let you take a snapshot of coverage in time. Some tools will only provide accurate data once the application being tested is closed.

- Choose a coverage tool that provides good technical support. Often, code coverage analysis tools are developed with leading edge technology. These tools are also generic and may not have been designed to support your specific requirement. In either case, you will need strong technical support to work with you on your specific needs.
- Build close relationships with the key developers of the product being tested. The developers' knowledge of the code is an obvious value if you run into problems or need special instructions on the toolset or the build process. At the very least, you will need access to the code, and usually that cannot be accomplished without the developers' support.

It encourages communication between test and development. Test development driven by code coverage requires more direct knowledge of what a section of code actually does. The best source for this information is the developers who wrote the code. Initially, developers may be skeptical, or worse, fearful of some tester poking around in their code. But, over time, they should see the benefit of such practices. The specific benefits are: faster test turnaround time, more intelligent test development, test tools that developers can use prior to release, and, since the testers now have a better understanding of the code their tests run on, more intelligent bug reporting.

It eliminates redundant tests. An acceptance test that does the same thing repeatedly is a waste of time. Remember, one of the original goals of an acceptance test is that it should be short. Redundant tests increase the test time with little gain. You can use a coverage tool to determine which tests are redundant through a process of trial and error. In other words, try removing a test you feel may be redundant and check the coverage numbers to see if there is a drop in coverage. If not, you've probably lost very little in terms of benefit to the acceptance test.

Do not misunderstand: there is a place for redundant tests in a full-blown regression, especially if you are tracking down memory leaks. However, the acceptance phase is not the time to perform repeated tests.

Pitfalls and Fallacies

As hard as I try, I can't reach 100% coverage. If you're driving yourself crazy trying to get to 100% coverage, then I have some advice for you: stop trying. In every program, code is included (I hope) to handle errors or exceptions. Attempting to write a test for every possible exception is probably not the best use of your time. Hit the main exceptions and move on to the next project where you can get more bang for your buck.

My acceptance test hits 95% of the functions; therefore, it can't get much better. Just because your coverage tool shows you've entered a function does not mean you've executed all or even most of the code in that function. If your functional coverage is excellent, you must determine the level of line coverage before you ask for that big raise. It is possible to hit 90% of the functions, yet miss the majority of the code in the application.

My acceptance test hits 90% of the code; hence, regression testing is unnecessary. Executing a block of code with success one way does not mean it will execute successfully under all conditions. While it's O.K. for acceptance testing to ignore this, it's not acceptable for regression testing to ignore it. Consider what could happen if the block of code was entered with different state conditions. Code coverage is the first primary data point to consider in determining the quality of your test suite. However, it doesn't guarantee a bug-free release in and of itself.

Making the Grade

Software testers are in a challenging yet rewarding position. To meet the demands of today's software market, you must use or create tools that automate your acceptance and regression tests. In addition, you should use code coverage analysis to determine how good your tests are. In this way, you will be a step closer to improving your company's software quality, while at the same time reducing product development schedules.

3.2.7 "Don't Waste Your Bugs!"

by Stephen Shimeall and Timothy Shimeall

Who says bugs always have to be a nuisance? Turn the coin and make them work for you.

For most people, the preferred reaction to finding a bug is to fix it, do some testing to make sure it's gone, and forget it. But, believe it or not, you can gain full value from your bugs. In today's increasingly competitive and cost-limited world, doing so can become a competitive edge.

One of the major testing discoveries over the last decade has been that bugs don't happen randomly. Instead, they happen for a reason — and that reason can be a key to improving your software and the process that builds it. Bugs can be a very effective source of information for modeling and controlling the software process. Organizations that want to improve the efficiency and quality of their software process are well-advised to view their bugs as valuable management data.

From a tactical standpoint, it is important to know which bugs to track, how to use them, and how to apply the knowledge you gain from them. In this article, a bug is considered to be an erroneous section of software source code that results in either undesired performance or a lack of performance altogether.

Using Bugs to Define Code Maturity

Software bugs provide a key indicator into the code's maturity. You can judge whether it's immature, mature, or obsolete by looking at the numbers and kinds of bugs found.

For example, as the code is first implemented, problems are typically due to unknown or misinterpreted requirements, unexpected or improperly defined interfaces with other software, and similar types of startup problems. Midlife bugs that occur after the software's first release are usually due to modifications in the code and new features that are added by staff unfamiliar with the original design. With these changes come logic errors in the new code, incompatibilities between the new use and the original design, and so forth.

As changes pile on top of each other, the code becomes less coherent in its design, complexity increases, and the potential for errors goes up. At some point, the software will become difficult to maintain. Ultimately, it will become obsolete. At this point, it is cheaper to throw out the code and rewrite it than to risk changes to correct bugs or add features.

By monitoring the impact of changes to code in terms of the number, scope, size, and type of bugs introduced, you can estimate where the software is in a cycle, determine the potential impact of proposed changes, or even decide when it's time to throw out a given section of code and redesign it. In turn, this knowledge permits designers and managers to more accurately judge the costs and risks of potential design changes, get a better feel for when software is ready for release, and objectively evaluate the potential benefits of reengineering the code.

One methodical way of using bug-based maturity data is to incorporate it into a predictive quality management model. A large number of these models exist, and they typically require time-of-detection, time-of-correction, and criticality data for each of the bugs. Using this data, the models extrapolate (based on prior experience and on the modeling assumptions) the number of remaining bugs, the likely operational reliability, or the degree of risk associated with releasing the software at its current level of maturity. Over time, organizations that retain bug data can calibrate the models by adjusting the values of the modeling constants. With this information, they can obtain relatively trustworthy numerical estimates of the software's behavior. This helps to build a culture of quantitative, predictable engineering in the software development process.

Using Bugs in the Development Process

Look at two areas when you detect bugs: at what point the bug was introduced into the software, and why it wasn't detected earlier in the process. Clearly, no process will completely eliminate the chance of human error, so bugs will be introduced during any nontrivial software development project. But looking into where they are introduced during development will help you identify problematic steps and indicate possible improvements in development practices.

Quality Checks

Looking at why a bug was not detected by the intervening parts of the development process will give you insight on the quality checks in those intervening parts. Specifically, you should closely examine any intervening inspections and the documentation used therein. To analyze the inspections, you must look at the identified location of the bug in the source code. If that portion of the code was omitted in the inspection process, you must revise the inspection instructions to ensure a more even code coverage. If the bug location was inspected, be sure to revise the inspection instructions to encourage inspectors to view the code in a way that might reveal the bug. When a bug is found during inspection, you must make sure the fix completely deals with it rather than with only selected aspects. These revisions will help you discover future bugs in a more cost-effective manner.

Bug Repository

A bug repository is basically a cumulative database of bugs discovered in the software produced by your organization. The type of information in the repository is dictated by the improvements you want to gain by using your bugs. For common predictive quality models, you will want to record the following:

- The portion of the code that contains the bug (name of routine and type of routine)
- The identities of the coder, designer, and tester of that portion of the code
- The time to detection as a measure of the subtlety of the bug (both in terms of wall clock time and cumulative CPU time)
- The time to correction (once detected) as a measure of the difficulty of the bug (both in terms of wall clock time and CPU time)
- If the criticality level of the bug is trivial, troublesome, critical, catastrophic, or infectious (For obsolescence tracking, you must record the portion of the code containing the bug by name of routine.)
- The size of the bug (in relative terms of how much of the input data it affects)
- The scope of the bug (in relative terms of how much of the source code must be changed)
- The type of the bug, using some common bug taxonomy.

This may seem like a lot of data, but much of it may already be available from your development tracking process and your testing records. Using this information in quantitative models lets you flexibly track quality and overall process improvement.

Documentation

Lack of documentation quality can also result in bugs. Look at the documentation that describes the code containing the bug to see if any omitted detail has resulted in a lack of communication to the developer working on the code. Bugs due to this kind of omitted detail often include interface bugs. Another way documentation may cause bugs is in inconsistent details between or within documents. Too much detail can be another source of confusion from documentation. Documentation with too much detail is often the result of the lack of good abstraction. In addition to excess work, it can cause bugs by increasing the complexity of the code and by introducing potential problems with interpretation of the document.

Some bugs escape detection due to problems with the documentation used in the intervening quality checks. Documents that omit, heavily abstract, or inconsistently present needed information may cause confusion between correct and incorrect behavior. Documents that contain a lot of extraneous information may obfuscate proper emphasis on software behavior. When a bug is detected, a review of the documentation associated with the software and its behavior may indicate needed changes to improve future maintenance, debugging, and testing. Tracking which portions of which documents are associated with bugs will help you indicate revisions in documentation content and style.

Teamwork

A development process is only as good as the people who perform it. Without appropriate motivation, team members will not be as diligent and effective as they could be. The technology does not yet support the use of personnel reviews as appropriate feedback in this area. While an individual may have made a mistake that led to a bug in the software, a large number of factors could have played into the situation. Often the presence of bugs points to process-related problems at least as much as they do to individuals. Process-related problems include lack of training, inattention due to lack of expertise in a given area (or due to overambitious scheduling that contributes to fatigue), using programmers as "interchangeable parts," and lack of time to come up to speed in the software or application area. All of these show up as problems that tie back to individuals.

Several key techniques can help you remedy this. First, look for individual bugs that show up in more than one individual in the group. Second, look for individual bugs that hint at underlying problems. Third, identify related problems that occur across projects or products. Fourth, identify the circumstances under which these bugs occur — the source of the errors. And last, publish the information about the bugs and the circumstances under which they can occur to the developers and managers. As you complete these activities, you will identify solutions. In other cases, where the underlying source cannot be corrected, the increased awareness will cause the bugs to be identified earlier in the development process, reducing correction time and schedule impact.

One method of using bugs to enhance the software development environment and promote a culture of engineering is to publicize selected bugs (a "bug of the month" system). Without careful selection and motivation, however, the "bug of the month" will turn into an inside joke. The purpose here is not to turn it into a competitive exercise, either negative or positive, but to select technically significant or interesting bugs as a means to teach how an entire class of bugs comes about — and how to avoid them.

Another approach is to review the kinds of bugs encountered during periodic bug meetings. The purpose of these meetings should not be to put anyone on the spot, but to use the expertise in the development group itself. This way, you can identify common problems, increase group awareness of the problems' potential, and reduce the risk of bugs by correcting the underlying problems that cause them. You can also educate developers about how these bugs occur, how to spot them, and possibly how to avoid them.

In many organizations, bugs are a costly and valueless part of the overhead in creating software. You might not be able to eliminate the cost of finding bugs, but you can capture the full benefit from that cost. Viewed as costs and benefits, testing and debugging assume more of the role of investments rather than overhead. Then it's possible to recoup this investment in terms of code improvement, personal and team process improvement, and testing improvement. Recouping the investment from your bugs leads to better software that is produced more efficiently. It also forms a more stable base for future development.

Further Reading

Charles Adams, "Code Inspection for NPSNET," MS Thesis, Naval Postgraduate School, Monterey, Calif., March 1995.*

Lionel E. Deimel, "Scenes of Software Inspections," Technical Report SEI-91-EM-5, Software Engineering Institute, Carnegie Mellon University, 1991.

Lelon L. Ginn, "An Empirical Approach to Analysis of Similarities between Software Failure Regions," MS Thesis, Naval Postgraduate School, Monterey, Calif., Sept. 1991.*

S. S. Cha, Nancy G. Leveson, John C. Knight, Timothy J. Shimeall, "An Empirical Study of Software Error Detection Using Self-Check," *IEEE Transactions on Software Engineering*, April 1990.

Lawrence H. Putnam, "Progress in Modeling the Software Life Cycle in a Phenomenological Way to Obtain Engineering Quality Estimates and Dynamic Control of the Process," Proceedings, Second Software Life Cycle Management Workshop, IEEE Press, 1978.

*Contact the National Technical Information Service (NTIS) at (800) 553-6847 for a printed copy.

3.2.8 "Surviving Performance Fire Drills"

by Benson I. Margulies

Something as vague as 'slow code' can become an all-out crisis when customers aren't happy with the system. There are tense phone calls, threats of corporate disaster and all the usual theater. The pressure is on to act immediately.

Acute performance problems are a regular part of life for software developers and their managers. It is easy to fall into the trap of seeing them as natural disasters: You can't predict them, you can't prevent them, and you can't do much more than offer sacrifices to the local volcanoes to get rid of them.

Despite the best preparation, catastrophes will occur with little or no warning. However, there are better responses to them than trekking to the nearest crater. Indeed, techniques that you would never expect to use in a crisis can come in handy. Code inspection is one of them.

Code inspection is often seen as a measure favored by quality assurance engineers or methodology mavens. Many people think of it as part of a large, bureaucratic process in which code passes through many hands before it sees the light of day. Developers, and even managers, often consider it a waste of time imposed on them by some quality process (such as ISO-9000 or the Software Engineering Institute's Capability Maturity Model) rather than as an effective tool for solving or preventing problems.

In fact, code inspection can be a powerful tool for solving and preventing problems, including software performance nightmares — and there is a reason why I focus on performance as an example. Performance problems often come to our attention as situations that demand immediate response or "fire drills." If I can convince you that code inspection is an effective technique in a product performance crisis, I shouldn't have much trouble convincing you that it can help in less stressful situations.

Performance problems provide a good example for all kinds of unplanned fire drills. When a performance problem arrives, it arrives with a bang. There are tense phone calls, threats of corporate disaster and all the usual theater. Frequently, there are precious few data to back up an impressionistic problem characterization ("it's too slow"). There is plenty of pressure to act immediately.

The first order of business is chaos-containment. In managing a fire drill, you may find yourself surrounded by people who are running around like chickens with their heads cut off. If you allow this to spread to those who must fix the problem, you are finished.

The second step is fostering ownership. In many development organizations, software performance belongs to everyone and no one. At best, a separate quality assurance group might run some performance regression tests. The main developers don't think of themselves as performance experts or as responsible for solving or preventing performance problems. With these two steps in mind, let's look at how to convert a crisis from a hot potato to a routine concern.

We're in Trouble

One morning, you arrive at your office to find smoke coming out of your e-mail client: There is a performance problem. Perhaps the new version of the product is mysteriously slower than in the previous release, or it runs at a snail's pace at a particular customer site or for a particular application. It could be that someone has deployed it on a full production configuration for the first time, and it is not performing adequately. Or maybe seemingly trivial changes in the load or environment have led to a significant drop in performance.

Whatever the problem, it has to be fixed "right this minute." As with many issues that people think have to be fixed "right this minute," maybe it does, and maybe it doesn't. Perhaps the urgency will evaporate when you ask hard questions. Your first job is to push back as appropriate, but I don't have to tell you that.

Finger-pointing

How do performance problems happen? While this question may not help you very much in fixing the current mess, it deserves attention after the dust settles. Code can be defect-free, meet its specifications and still yield a performance crisis the day it is deployed for three main reasons: unclear requirements, code evolution and memory issues.

In the first case, it can be hard to predict the configuration and load requirements for a deployed product — assuming, of course, that someone tried to state performance requirements at all. If you don't see the answers to questions like "How many…" and "How fast…" and "With how many megabytes of memory in the machine…" in the specifications, then no one has thought through the requirements.

Second, seemingly trivial changes to the code to address functional requirements or defects can have alarmingly large effects on the performance of the code. A programmer repairing a defect may not know that the procedure she is adjusting is used in a performance-critical inner loop.

Finally, when code has buffers and caches, very small changes in the size of the input can produce large changes in the results.

Moving Targets

One of the biggest traps in dealing with performance issues is the lack of hard data. Problems are often reported in qualitative, impressionistic terms. And while the customers' subjective perceptions make the difference between success and failure in the marketplace, you can't solve a performance problem by chasing subjective targets. You, as the manager, must make sure that the performance problems are measurable and repeatable.

This is easiest when the code can be run as some sort of batch process that you can time. However, even if you can't do that, you can still impose some rigor on the problem definition. For instance, you can write a script to follow in such events to make sure that the people complaining and the people trying to fix the problem are observing the same problem.

In short, use the scientific method: define a problem, state a hypothesis, perform an experiment and record the results. A specific example might be:

- *Problem statement:* When I edit a drawing with at least 10,000 elements, group at least 10 and try to rotate them, the program is unresponsive for at least 20 seconds.
- *Hypothesis:* The background pagination process has gone haywire and is consuming all the time.
- *Experiment:* Disable the pagination process and go through the exact script from the problem statement, and see what happens.
- *Results:* A scientist's most important tool is the lab notebook. People involved in performance wars tend to forget what they have already tried. It is essential to keep good records of all the data and all the experiments. The notebook doesn't have to be a paper one. Spreadsheets work very well to record a series of experiments and data points.

Among the challenges in tracking down a performance bottleneck are instrumentation, unrepeatable testing conditions, complex modeling and tunnel vision. For instance, you can insert code (manually or with a tool) that measures time used in different parts of the code. It requires great care, however, to avoid spending so much time in the instrumentation code that it changes the program's behavior beyond recognition, or, worse yet, beyond usability.

Also, if the production environment is a $0.5 million server, it can be a little difficult to get an identical one that you can use for experiments. Say you'd like to construct a model of the parts of the system and how they interact in order to predict the performance of the code. It doesn't take much complexity for a system to become a very difficult modeling problem. Finally, snow blindness can strike developers: Once someone has been staring at the same code for long enough, he stops seeing it.

Grinding Through

In spite of the difficulties, performance problems are solved with a combination of all of the methods mentioned above — with the critical addition of a methodical process of experimentation. Code inspection is not a magic bullet that obviates all of that work. It's primarily a remedy for snow blindness, both individual and organizational. When a new person reads code for the first time, he carries different preconceptions and assumptions. He asks questions and challenges what he sees. It can be quite amazing to see the light bulb go on over the head of the original developer.

In a sense, you can think of code inspection as a way of generating specific, relevant materials for brainstorming. When a new person reads old code, he nearly always ends up with a laundry list of questions about how it works — or whether it works at all.

Code inspection is also useful at different scales. If you have managed to isolate a problem to a relatively small region of code, but the owner can't seem to find the smoking gun, code inspection can lead very rapidly to the critical problem.

If you are faced with a large mass of poorly understood code, I don't know of any alternative to reverse-engineering it to some extent, and, again, code inspection is the only way I know to approach that problem.

For larger bodies of code, a few days of examination can prove quite illuminating. Original authors tend to work on individual problems in isolation. An inspector may notice, for example, that the code is doing the same work in three different places.

Note that these tactics apply both to focused and broad performance problems. If a particular operation in a particular case is too slow, careful reading of the implementation of that operation can yield results very quickly. If the problem is general slowness of an entire program, an examination that attempts to understand what work gets where can turn up structural problems, such as bottlenecks or redundant computations.

So how do you define the problem, apply the right technical resources and choose management strategies to make a development group more functional in dealing with performance problems and less likely to have them in the first place? Code inspection holds many of the answers.

Defining the Problem

As discussed before, the most important thing you need to do in tackling a performance problem is to make sure that the problem is defined in terms of empirically measurable facts. This can be difficult. On the one hand, the people reporting the problem may present you with mushy, impressionistic complaints. You must convert those complaints into a specific characterization that you can measure. On the other hand, developers tend to respond to performance problems by spinning out hypothetical causes of the problem without any factual basis. I call these, after Rudyard Kipling, "Just So Stories." A Just So Story about a performance problem is a perfectly plausible explanation that usually comes with a proposed technical solution. "The object cache is too small, so we need to make it bigger;" or "the computation of intercept points is using floating point arithmetic, so we need to change it to scaled integers."

A Performance War Story

Inspection without measurement won't always solve the problem.

Once upon a time, I was hired to have a look at a very prominent Internet search engine. The Internet is always growing, so much so that a program is inevitably a constant source of performance issues.

I want to emphasize that, while some of the things I found will sound somewhat goofy, no one involved was incompetent or stupid. Collectively, they had tried to scale a solution and an approach until it no longer worked. At that point, they were so invested in what they had that it was hard to back off and see the problem from a fresh perspective. It happens to all of us.

The code in question is a multithreaded server written in ANSI C on Digital Unix. It ran on very large and expensive hardware — so large and expensive that the development group didn't have a machine with the same configuration as the production systems. Because it is on DU, there is no Quantify tool to help. There is a DEC (Compaq) tool called atom, but it is very focused on CPU time and on the leaves of the call graph (such as memcpy). It turned out to produce very misleading results in this case.

The hardware was so expensive and the scale of the problem growing so fast, that there was a great deal of management resistance to buying $0.5 million systems to increase capacity. Over the long run, the problems would have to be solved by a different architecture in which they could run a larger number of smaller systems instead of fewer large ones. In the short term, the requirement was to "fix the code" to run significantly faster.

The development organization had an unhappy track record of making changes that were intended to improve the performance. These changes had proven disappointing when deployed, even when they appeared to improve performance in controlled test runs.

There was no instrumentation in the code. Some data had been collected with the DU atom tool, but it attributed the time to low-level data copying primitives. At best, this failed to tell us what callers were using them. At worst, it was misleading, as it was a CPU-time only measurement, and it seemed very likely that there were real-time effects at work.

I started two efforts in parallel. I inspected the code, and I persuaded the owner to add real-time measurements over all of it and to try to get the version that contained them into service as soon as possible.

Code inspection yielded four big issues that seemed as if they might explain the problem:

- The code worked by reading and processing large amounts of data. A particular thread working on a particular task would read, say, 50 MB of data into memory all at once and then traverse it. This required very large buffers, needless to say. There was no I/O hardware that optimized such very large buffers. It seemed likely that the performance could be improved by reading in smaller chunks.
- The code was holding locks while reading the 50 MB chunks.
- The code was using a default thread-scheduling policy that used a round-robin rule. The meant that if the program ever started more threads than it could service with the available processors, the thread scheduler would thrash the CPUs among the threads. It would also give the CPU to new threads in preference to old ones.
- Several interesting pieces of code appeared to be duplicated.

The only one of these for which there was hard evidence was the thread-scheduling policy. The system was responding to extra load by mysteriously failing to complete queries. This was entirely consistent with a thread falling off the bottom of the scheduler's agenda. Further, it was very hard to imagine any way to test this theory other than to add the two lines of code needed to change the policy and measure the results.

The process that ensued was interesting. The owner of the code moved from vehement denial that any of these issues could be problems to a state of mind something like, "Gee. I haven't looked hard at the code in a while. Now that I look at it again, it sure looks peculiar."

Eventually, a version with real timers made it into service, and pointed at some computational code that hadn't looked especially suspicious to me. This code, it turned out, could be put on a diet by moving some computations around and moving some other computations out of the run time altogether. Note that if we had acted on the inspection alone, without measurements, we would not have found this.

It is important to note that the cost of this code was not news to anyone involved, except perhaps me. I never did figure out why it wasn't on the top of the list before I got involved. In this case, what I brought to the process was method: First collect the data, then look at it, and then choose a course of action. It sounds simple, but after a few too many fire drills, people get punchy and a little disorganized.

Long after I finished my work, the team succeeded in deploying a significantly faster version. Fixing the scheduling policy drastically reduced the incidence of mysterious timeouts, and fixing the CPU-intensive code reduced the cost of each query.

The only problem with Just So Stories is that there is no way of telling whether they are correct except to go ahead and implement the proposed solution. If the story happens to be correct, there is a happy ending. Even a blind pig finds an acorn once in a while, as the saying goes. (Of course, this isn't entirely fair. These ideas are often informed by a developer's deep understanding of the code. You would be surprised, however, at how often developers' intuitions are off.) If the story is wrong, you have used up valuable time to no avail.

Just as you have to insist that the original problem be defined in terms of measurable, repeatable phenomena, you should insist that proposed solutions be justified by measurable data. When someone proposes an explanation for a performance problem, the first step is to use some kind of instrumentation to find out if it is really an explanation. In general, only after you have instrumentation should you proceed to coding any proposed fixes.

Of course, you have to use judgment in deciding when to take a flyer. Given a choice between spending three hours trying an unsupported hypothesis and three weeks implementing a measurement scheme to test it, you may want to go ahead with the first option. The problem is that, before you know it, you may have used up three weeks on a whole series of experiments of this kind, and you have neither fixed the problem nor implemented enough instrumentation to find the problem. The cliché about making haste slowly is quite relevant here. Write it in big letters and hang it on your door.

Data Acquisition

The Holy Grail of performance tuning is timing data from the production environment. If you know where the time is going, you know where to focus in fixing the problem. This information can be elusive, but it is hardly ever impossible to get.

The easiest case is when you can use a tool that automatically instruments your code. My favorite for this purpose is Quantify, by Pure Software (which has since been swallowed up by Rational). Quantify modifies your executable image to add code that captures timing data at a line-by-line level. You run the modified executable, then use a GUI to poke around in the call graph and at annotated source listings, looking at where the time went. You can even call upon it to calculate the difference between two different runs as a way of getting a clearer picture of the effect of a change in the code or the input data.

You don't get something for nothing, however. An instrumented executable runs *v-e-r-y s-l-o-w-l-y,* so it can't be put into full production. A full run of an interesting case may take a very long time, to the point of impracticality.

That said, if the program can run a relevant case, even if it takes several hours, the resulting data is a gold mine of real, hard facts: "Fifty percent of the CPU time is being spent formatting date-time strings for the log, even when the log is disabled?" (I kid you not. I was involved in a performance stew with this eventual explanation.)

Quantify is available for Windows and a number of Unix platforms. There are a variety of competing products. I confess that I don't have experience with them and cannot offer a comparison. One that is ubiquitous on Unix is gprof. This is a much weaker tool that requires you to compile with special options and which attempts to capture function-level CPU time usage. Sometimes it can be very useful, but other times it's not.

Even with the best of tools, the analysis of the data is rarely completely trivial. Here is an example of why. It is quite common for a function-level profile to report that a significant amount of time is consumed in a common library routine. This does not imply that the library routine is the problem, however. More likely it means that some part of the code has an algorithmic problem such that it is making too many calls to the library routine. It can be hard to separate these issues. In a specific case, it is very common to see a CPU profile that shows a great deal of CPU time in the standard C strcmp function. This does not imply that this simple string comparison function needs to be rewritten. Rather, you have to look at the callers of the function and see why these callers call for so many string comparisons.

Another source of difficulty is real time versus CPU time. If the application's performance is bounded by some kind of I/O latency, nothing will be using much CPU time.

What do you do if you can't use an automatic instrumentation tool? You capture your own real-time measurements. Every operating system in common use has way to read a real-time clock. The trick is to find a way that is as inexpensive as possible. For example, on the RS/6000, you can create a tiny assembly procedure that reads a clock register.

Once upon a time, real timers were a mixed bag. If you are time-sharing a system, there is no telling when you will get a big real-time pause, courtesy of the scheduler. These days, you can almost always run your tests on a dedicated system. In such an environment, real times are, by far, preferable to CPU times.

For example, if you are working on a multithreaded server, and you have too many threads (or the wrong thread scheduling policy), your application may suffer from thrashing as it tries to share the CPU among the threads. In this case, CPU measurement shows nothing out of the ordinary, but real-time measurements show suspicious delays.

A set of real-time measurement routines should be part of the utility toolkit of any development group. In the event of a performance problem, a developer should be able to take them off the shelf, apply them to the code and get some numbers.

Once you have numbers, you have to be careful about how to interpret them. In many cases, some basic statistics are required. Never trust one measurement. Take 100, or at least 10. Plot a histogram, or run a standard deviation. Not all programs display wide variations, but you won't know if you are working on one that has wide variations until you try.

One thing to look out for is the outlier. That is, the single measurement that is much larger than the norm. If the original complaint is of the form, "Once in a while I click the mouse and it runs forever," then the outlier is the case you are seeking. Tracking these down may require additional instrumentation to correlate the long real times with other conditions in the program.

In these cases, you need to augment your real-timing tools with event-logging tools. Once again, the crucial problem is to avoid perturbing the performance by measuring it. A common error is to call a library routine (such as `printf`) to record an event. These routines are often single-threaded — or just plain time-consuming — and can completely alter the code's behavior.

A traditional technique is the in-memory log structure. Allocate a large buffer at the beginning of the run. Record the events by writing simple, binary information (numbers, for instance) into the log buffer. After the run is complete, format the log and write it to a file. Don't do input/output, don't format strings, and don't add anything extra during the measurement interval. A log of events with real-time stamps can be a powerful tool for understanding the performance behavior of your code.

Management Strategies

As a development manager, you are faced with helping a group productively apply the techniques described above.

The first thing you have to do is to model the appropriate attitude, which consists of the following truisms:

- If we run around like chickens with our heads cut off, we will end up as chicken salad.
- If we can't measure it, it doesn't exist.
- If we don't engage in a systematic process, we will never accomplish anything.
- We're here to hunt the problem, not the author of the problem.
- We need to keep records of what we do.
- We need to keep records of what we do.
- We need to keep records of what we do.

Strike a balance between the need to solve the problem quickly and the need to take enough time to solve the problem at all. Getting a group to engage (in the military sense) with a performance problem is a delicate balance between fostering individual expertise in using the tools and techniques described above and promoting an attitude of interest and responsibility in the entire group. I think of this as a circular process. You start with performance being everyone and no one's problem. Then you make it someone's problem in particular. Finally, you feed that person's work back into the group to get everyone involved in a productive way.

If you don't have anyone in the group with experience in measurement and instrumentation, you need to find one. Hiring an expert (at least full-time) is almost always impractical, so you have to figure out how to turn someone you already have into an expert.

The most important qualifications for a field promotion to "performance expert" are:

- Unfamiliarity with the code
- Tenaciousness
- Ancestors from Missouri (the "Show Me" state)
- Organization and record-keeping ability

Unfamiliarity with the code qualifies the individual as a code inspector. It can be much more effective to have a new person show up and start asking questions about the code in order to design an instrumentation strategy than to have developers add instrumentation. They will tend to neglect those areas that have escaped from their conscious picture of the code.

A performance issue is a great opportunity to get a relatively inexperienced person to step up to the plate and take on more responsibility and a more central role. An important role of the instant expert is to foment, with your assistance, brainstorming. Once you have some data, gather the usual suspects in a room and do the brainstorming thing. Open the floor for suggestions, however strange, and allow no critical commentary. Collect them all, and then collect opinion about which ones to investigate (with suitable measurement, of course), first.

The best thing about brainstorming is that even the most stressed-out developers usually relax and enjoy themselves. The whole process begins to look suspiciously like fun, and then your life is much easier.

A brainstorming session is your opportunity to ensure that the process finds the problem and not its author. (You may want to keep track of the author for future reference.) You want the author to see this entire process as a service, not as a cannibal feast in which he or she is the main course. The developer or developers may have been knocking themselves silly for an extended period of time, or been knocked silly by external parties, over performance issues. Giving them a process that allows them to make material progress on these issues should, with a little spin, improve their quality of life.

Solving the Problem Before It Arrives

Well, you've heard all this, taken it home and perhaps survived a file drill with fewer casualties. Now what? Well, I nearly don't have to tell you that all of this technique can be looped back into your process before someone shows up with a problem. You can set quantitative performance targets, instrument and measure as part of the development process and hunt down and fix performance problems before anyone knows you have them.

This process can be more fruitful that you might expect. Making relatively few simple changes can speed up almost any program significantly. It is much less time consuming to work on these issues within the development cycle than in response to an external crisis. So giving every release a basic performance once-over can pay.

Performance problems present themselves as fire drills. You have a choice. You and your development group can join the Keystone Kops, or you can stop, take a deep breath and apply an organized process to the problem.

Whether you use a Fagan-style inspection with a number of reader or reviewers, or just one other person reading the code and asking questions, this, combined with an appropriate methodology for gathering data and performing experiments, can be a powerful technique. You and your group will learn to treat performance as a central part of the product's quality — and you'll apply those lessons to solving problems before they escape to the field and come back around to bite you.

Chapter 4

Project Management

4.1 Best Practices for the Project Management Workflow

The purpose of the Project Management workflow is to ensure the successful management of your project team's efforts. During the Transition phase the Project Management workflow focuses on several activities, including:

- Managing your development team's efforts
- Risk identification and management
- Project assessment
- Updating your project schedule, estimate, and plan
- Managing your relationship with your project stakeholders
- Managing your relationship with vendors and contractors
- Navigating the political waters of your organization

During the Production phase your project management efforts revolve around the management of your operations and support staff as well as your configuration and change control efforts. You may find that you need to lobby for support to begin work on a new release of your system or even to begin work on a related system. People management issues are still relevant, such as career management efforts as well as training and education efforts for your staff. Remember, many activities performed by information technology (IT) staff are not performed within the scope of the development of a system, activities that still need to be managed.

Although project management has been covered in each volume of this four book series, there are still two major topics that have yet to be addressed: best practices for learning from your experiences and best practices for recovering from (near) disasters.

4.1.1 Learning From Your Experiences

Norm Kerth, author of *Project Retrospectives* (2001), describes how to benefit from project failures in "Making Lemons from Lemonade." If you've had a software project failure, you have a choice. You can be embarrassed and try to hide the fact, but you will then learn nothing and may be condemned to repeat the experience. Or, you can embrace the failure and turn it into something even more valuable than a success. When a project fails — when you fail — you can end up feeling discouraged, depressed, even degraded. But those are just feelings, you think, and this is just a job. There's more code to be cut and new projects to plan. Just get on with it! Right. In this article Kerth leads us in a different direction, confronting those feelings of failure head-on and suggesting that dealing with feelings may sometimes yield some unexpected payoffs for managers and developers. He shows that every failure is an opportunity to improve the way you work, but that to do so you must discuss what really happened to the people, the team, and the organization. You must face not only the technical and management issues, but also the people issues: what happens to self-esteem, confidence, relationships, and interactions? Furthermore, you must learn to avoid common but ineffective ways of coping with catastrophe, including:

- Declaring that failure is really success
- Saving face by blaming "factors out of your control"
- Waiting for the cavalry to appear and save you
- Conducting a witch-hunt for the guilty
- Claiming that your failure merely proved that you had taken on an impossible task to begin with

Kerth shows that to overcome a failed project you need to go through acceptance and discovery. During the acceptance stage participants in the failed project need to recognize that emotions of grief and loss are real, are part of the process of healing, and are appropriate for the workplace. During the discovery stage the participants should perform a project retrospective where they explore their experiences on the project. Retrospectives help you to identify lessons learned, often through painful experience. Project retrospectives address four fundamental questions:

1. What did we do that worked well and should be kept?
2. What did we learn as the project proceeded?
3. What do we want to do differently next time?
4. What still puzzles us?

Karl Wiegers and Johanna Rothman describe best practices for conducting project retrospectives in "Looking Back, Looking Ahead." They argue that retrospectives provide a structured opportunity to look back at the project or project phase you just completed — retrospectives can and should be held throughout a project, particularly at major milestones when you are trying to assess the viability of your project. During a retrospective you might identify practices that worked well that need to be sustained, or you might identify practices that didn't go well and even gain insight into how to improve them. Best practices for effective retrospectives include:

- Define your objectives.
- Use a skilled and impartial facilitator.
- Engage the right participants.
- Prepare the participants.
- Allow everyone to be heard.
- Respect the other person's experience and perspective.
- Avoid criticizing input and ideas from other participants.
- Avoid blaming people for past events.
- Identify root causes, not just symptoms.
- Focus on understanding, learning and looking ahead.
- Identify the action plan owner.

4.1.2 Recovering From Disaster

Often it isn't enough to simply to identify lessons learned from failures, you often need to recover from them and continue on or ideally avoid them in the first place. In "Lost in Chaos: Chronology of a Failure," Steve Adolph describes his experiences on a failed software development effort, providing significant insight into how problems get off track to begin with and therefore a list of potential problems to look for on your projects. He starts by identifying a few common warning signals that your project is in trouble, particularly management claims that "It's an aggressive schedule," "It's a challenging project," or "This project is on the fast track." Adolph advises that you should translate these claims to "We don't have time, so we're abandoning any software development process and, therefore, our ability to control the project." Why do developers do this? Adolph argues that the short-circuiting or total abandonment of process has a seductive appeal because there is no tedious production of requirements documents, no boring review meetings and no one telling you what you can or cannot put into the build. In the project that Adolph helped to recover one of the first warning signs should have been their cavalier approach to schedule estimation and the fact that they had set their project milestones too far apart: every six months. This period is too long to accumulate and then act on objective data indicating whether the project was on or off track. Another warning sign was the fact that requirements/analysis effort was effectively skipped — the project manager didn't want to produce a requirements model because he saw himself as an expert in the legacy system and thought he had a clear vision of what the new system needed to achieve. Adolph's experience is that when replacing a legacy system,[1] software developers often underestimate the risk because they assume the legacy system is one of the organization's core competencies and that it represents a set of stable requirements. He also believed that the architecture and design efforts were likely misguided, with an inordinate amount of time spent on "interesting" technical infrastructure features and not on addressing the true risks of the project. The project suffered a major blow when the project manager left the company, the person that was the only source of requirements. Without a single clear vision for

---

1. Legacy system issues are covered in Chapter 5 of *The Unified Process Elaboration Phase*.

the product, the project suffered feature creep on a monumental scale, and the project was canceled a year after it was started. Had the project followed a realistic process, one that included shorter iterations and a review mechanism to check the project status, management may have been able to detect and address the problems before they caused the project to fail.

Steve Furlong provides advice to do exactly this in "Saving a Project in Trouble." He believes that you know that a project is in trouble because it usually has the worst in project management, code quality, and customer expectations. To save a troubled project Furlong recommends a five-step process:

1. *Determine the project requirements.* Because there is typically little accurate documentation, you need to talk to the people responsible for creating the disaster in the first place. The previous developers generally have an idea of what the project was supposed to do. Although they may be hazy on the details, they are often willing to take the time to flesh out any sketchy notes they left behind.

2. *Figure out the source code.* Unfortunately, you can't rely on any documentation you might find. So you need to go to the source code — as the XP (Beck, 2000) community says, "Only the source code is in sync with the source code.". Requirements and design documents are typically out-of-date, if they exist at all; programmers' notebooks (if they exist at all) are often illegible and incomplete; and source comments are typically outdated, useless, or just plain wrong. Once you have understood the code, you still need to refactor it (Fowler, 1999).

3. *Plan your recovery strategy.* After you've cleaned up the source code, you can proceed through the development process, something that should run just like any other project.

4. *Do it.*

5. *Deal with the aftermath.* A "lessons learned" write-up might do you and your employer some good, so hold a project retrospective.

A valid strategy for recovering from a project failure is to simply focus on yourself and your own career, effectively moving on from the mess as best you can. This may include leaving your existing organization, moving on to a similar role on a new project team, or even transferring to a new position within your existing organization. In "Revamp Your Current Job" Peter Alexander describes best practices for staying within your current organization, practices that are important to you if you want to follow them yourself or use them to help retain your good employees — just because the project was a failure doesn't mean your people are failures too. Alexander suggests that you need to start by thinking about what would make a significant difference to your job satisfaction — know what you want before you try to change your situation. This may include more money, training, flexible schedules, an active role in the organization's overall effort, or a change to an area with another group culture. Once you understand what kind of change you want, you need to talk with your manager. Let him or her know that you want to discuss your job, and that you would appreciate some uninterrupted private time for the discussion. Alexander advises that it is best to assume that your manager does not know what your issues are — you likely didn't know yourself until you performed your own assessment — nor are they like to know yet what would make your job more rewarding. You must take the initiative to make your job and your career what you want it to be. Furthermore, as a manager you must be willing to help your staff to do the same. Either way, this is an excellent article that everyone can benefit from.

Another valid strategy for dealing with project failure is to dismiss some or all of the people involved in the project, albeit a harsh alternative. In "Painless Dismissals: Saying Good-Bye" Jess Wells provides cogent advice for effectively dismissing staff — an improperly handled dismissal can destroy team morale and potentially make your company vulnerable to a retaliatory lawsuit. By cutting a poor performer loose you may actually boost morale within your team — if you do it in a respectful, firm, and clear way. The message you send to your workgroup is that excellence is rewarded, slackers should look elsewhere, and you have the intestinal fortitude and sense of justice that it takes to handle the situation properly. Wells describes several best practices for smooth dismissals. Be sure you have policies that are based on fairness. Make sure those policies are enforced fairly. Provide performance reviews frequently, and gather thorough documentation of poor performance. Make sure you retrieve equipment, keys, IDs and other corporate property. Furthermore, make it a quick and clean experience. With these things in mind, dismissals can be a relatively painless part of improving your software development team. Finally, Wells suggests several alternatives to termination, including leaves of absence, reassignment, assignment to part-time status, and layoff. Project management is hard, and dealing with issues such as dismissing an employee or contractor is one of the hardest tasks that a project manager can take on. This article will help you through it.

4.2 The Articles

4.2.1 "Making Lemonade From Lemons" by Norm Kerth, edited by Larry Constantine
4.2.2 "Looking Back" by Karl Wiegers and Johanna Rothman
4.2.3 "Lost in Chaos: Chronology of a Failure" by Stephen Adolph
4.2.4 "Saving a Project in Trouble" by Steve Furlong
4.2.5 "Revamp Your Current Job" by Peter Alexander
4.2.6 "Painless Dismissals: Saying Goodbye" by Jess Wells

4.2.1 "Making Lemonade From Lemons"
by Norm Kerth, edited by Larry Constantine

Software teams will create a more people-oriented workplace as they begin to discover and accept the emotional issues involved in project failure and devise effective strategies to cope with them.

Let's admit it: too many software projects fail. When they do, the experts line up in rows to offer explanations and suggestions. They compile generic lists of reasons for failure and nod in solemn agreement about the sad state of affairs in software development. Armed with such lists, guides, and a generous dose of 20-20 hindsight, we readily second-guess the stupid or merely silly decisions that led up to the failure. We even divert attention by ridiculing someone else's project, secretly hoping we won't be next.

However, top 10 lists of reasons for project failure will not help you learn the most from your experiences with failure. Every failure is an opportunity to improve the way you work. Learning and improvement require you to discuss what really happened to the people, the team, and the organization. You must face not only the technical and management issues, but also the people issues: what happens to self-esteem, confidence, relationships, and interactions? You must discuss how to cope with failure — and learn from it.

Not long ago, I was invited to work with a software team that had experienced a project failure on a grand scale. It had spent two years and $10 million on a major new system intended to replace an aging but critical system that was riddled with Year 2000 problems. After several schedule slips, cost overruns, and reorganizations, the management concluded that nothing would ever be delivered, and the project was killed.

When I began listening to and interviewing people within the organization, I discovered that they were coping with the catastrophe in a variety of ineffective ways.

Failure is success. In this newspeak strategy, the project is simply declared a success regardless of what has been or will ever be delivered. Among those people who had declared the project a success, some were doing their best to make sure not too many questions were asked. A shroud of secrecy was being woven around the project, and developers who said too much about the project were labeled "disloyal." I was told, "We need to look positively to the future."

Saving face. Some spin doctors said the organization's priorities had shifted due to changes in the marketplace. The project had been "put on the shelf for a while," as the company's people resources were being applied in more productive ways on more pressing matters.

Waiting for the cavalry. Another story was that newly emerging third-party vendors were likely to provide cheaper and better solutions in the near future. Several people told me that "someone else" was investigating these possibilities. The truth was no one was actually looking at third-party options, and no one knew of any viable options. The hope that someone else was working on this problem, however, remained high.

Hunting for the guilty. It was common to hear detailed stories about individuals who were responsible for the failure. Management pointed to the developers and developers pointed to management. The calamity was always the fault of someone else: the customer, testing, vendors, or contractors. Many team members expected someone to be fired and had their own ideas of who should be at the top of the list.

Proving the impossibility. Another common position was: "We had the best people working on this project. We worked as hard as possible, harder than could ever be expected, and still it wasn't enough. We proved it couldn't be done. There is no shame in trying something aggressively and not reaching our goals. At least we know not to try that again."

Such coping strategies are natural ways for people to respond to failure, yet they are also ineffective in leading an organization toward learning from its failure. Each strategy prevents us from studying our mistakes and improving our abilities to manage them. These ways of coping are not unreasonable when you consider the strong push within our culture to succeed in all cases, and the lack of practice within our discipline to learn systematically from our failures. Our culture often punishes failure harshly — so much so that many adults learn over time to rarely take risks, if at all.

What is it all about? It's about grief and loss. When we first join a project, hope is usually high. As we work on the project, make decisions, solve problems, and overcome challenges, we become attached to the outcome. We develop systems as well as a sense of commitment — often a moral one — to the project's success. When things start to go wrong, we work all the harder, sometimes even sacrificing weekends and evenings or skipping vacations. In the process, we become even more invested in the success of the project.

When the project is canceled, we experience grief and loss in the same way that homeowners might grieve over the loss of a home in a disaster. The magnitude of grief might be different, but the feelings are essentially the same. The difference is that grieving over a lost project is not usually accepted in the workplace. We learn to hide or ignore our feelings and to substitute various ineffective coping strategies.

One alternative is to devise a business process that recognizes the emotional component of loss and supports grieving in productive ways appropriate to the culture of the workplace. The emotions that are often ignored or inhibited can help us at this time of loss to become all the more receptive to new lessons. Working through the emotions, we become better prepared to learn from the experience.

The process of grieving the loss of a project or a professional failure has two major stages: acceptance and discovery. In the first stage, participants in the failed project need to accept that emotions of grief and loss are real, are part of the process of healing, and are appropriate for the workplace. In the second stage, once the team members have accepted their loss, they are in a better position to discover the hard lessons that can be learned.

Achieving Acceptance

Psychologist and expert on the grieving process, Elizabeth Kubler-Ross, suggests the experience of grief and loss involves a number of common emotions: denial, anger, blame, bargaining, and depression — which eventually lead to acceptance. There is no particular order in which any person or team might experience these emotions, nor is there a certain amount of time to be spent on each.

Team members of a failed software project need a way to experience these emotions in a constructive manner. The workplace must be managed with an understanding that these emotions exist. If the grieving process isn't allowed or acknowledged in the workplace, team members will push the feelings underground. While these feelings may be experienced less acutely when this happens, the unresolved emotions will continue to influence people's actions and will be carried into later projects, where they can lead to counterproductive work habits and conflicted relationships among coworkers. For example, unacknowledged feelings of anger and blame can lead to chronic distrust, and depression can be transformed into habitual passiveness.

What is needed is not project psychotherapy but reasonable opportunity. I have used two simple techniques to help people through these emotions: quiet reflection, often through writing, and group discussions. The typical questions I ask include aspects of the past, the present, and the future. Here are some examples that project participants might be asked to reflect on, write about, or discuss:

Past: What did you hope would happen on this project for you? What did you sacrifice while working on it?

Present: What does it mean to you now that this system won't be finished? What did you learn about running software projects?

Future: Where do you want to go from here professionally? What excites you about this possibility? What do you need to get there?

A sense of safety in exploring these issues is vitally important. As an operating norm, I tell all team members that I believe they did the best they could, given what they knew at the time. I urge them to write about and discuss their feelings from that position. I make clear that participation is strictly optional and no one will be pressured into sharing anything he or she prefers not to reveal. I tell them whatever they write is personal and private unless they have something they want to share with the other team members.

Depending on the magnitude of grief and loss involved in your project failure, you may want to hire a professional facilitator or a consultant specializing in this area to help your team through this stage. For very serious failures, the recovery process could extend over months, perhaps even years, but for most situations I've seen, the process is much quicker.

With the particular team I mentioned earlier, I asked the members to send me e-mail about their feelings, after which I made a few follow-up phone calls. Then I set the stage for a team meeting where I interviewed the president of the company and her chief information officer. The topic of the interview was the failures in each of their own careers: What was the failure about? Why was it important? What happened in the short term and over the long term? What did they learn, and how did that help them later in their careers?

In the course of about an hour, the team made some important discoveries. They found out that even the top levels of the organization knew their project failed, but that no one was going to be fired. Perhaps most important, they realized that if the team did not learn how to prevent this kind of failure, it was likely to happen again. If another failure of similar magnitude were to happen in the future, a number of people would undoubtedly lose their jobs, including both the president and the chief information officer.

With these discoveries, the denial, anger, blame, bargaining, and depression finally ceased, and the team reached a state of acceptance. They were ready for the next stage.

Big Picture Learning

Once team members have accepted the failure of a project, having worked through their own feelings, they are ready for a project postmortem. Within the perspective that "everyone did the best they could given what they knew at the time," a postmortem can provide a productive opportunity for learning.

A postmortem can take many different forms. I usually involve the entire team, working for several days to review the project from start to end, so everyone can add his or her own piece of the story and because everyone can learn from the review. Since no one ever knows the entire story, leaving one person out of the process can create a hole.

During the postmortem, the team works together to construct the "big picture" of what happened. Members look at the project from each person's perspective and see how the same event can mean different things to different people. They discover events that were important to a few and ignored by the rest. They study how events affected other events and learn why some events were important.

Throughout this review, we looked for answers to certain questions. First, what did we do that worked well and should be kept? Second, what did we learn as the project proceeded? Third, what do we want to do differently next time? And fourth, what still puzzles us?

If run well, a postmortem can result in a great deal of healing and can dramatically change the energy of the community. The group I have been describing is a good example. As their review proceeded, the team discovered 23 actions they had learned that would have either prevented the failure or made it apparent early that there was big trouble that needed to be addressed.

More important, these learned actions were not yet known to the rest of the company. A similar failure was, therefore, likely to happen to any number of projects. The firm was quite vulnerable, but this team now knew how to reduce that vulnerability by leveraging off their failure. They knew changes needed to be made in their standard software development practices. Plans were made during the postmortem to organize training and take their message across the company.

Their message was driven by the energy gained from their experience of failure. One project leader summed up the experience: "The pain and cost of failure might have been worth it if we can prevent even one more failure. The issue is not that we had a failure, but what we are going to do now that we've had one."

If you've had a software project failure, you have a choice. You can be embarrassed and try to hide the fact, but you will then learn nothing and may be condemned to repeat the experience. Or, you can embrace the failure and turn it into something even more valuable than a success.

4.2.2 "Looking Back"

by Karl Wiegers and Johanna Rothman

Examining your last project can improve your next one.

Pat, a vice-president in an Internet start-up company, was proud of her team's previous product release but concerned about why it had shipped a few weeks later than planned. At the project's retrospective, Pat was astonished to hear several team members say, "I might have been done earlier, but I didn't know exactly what 'done' meant. If I had known when my part was really finished, we might have shipped the product earlier." It was a valuable comment, and Pat used the information on her next project to define clear release criteria, which helped improve her team's schedule performance.

Retrospectives provide a structured opportunity to look back at the project or phase you just completed. You might see practices that worked well that need to be sustained, or you might see what didn't go so well and gain insight into how to improve. The retrospective helps you identify the lessons you've learned from often painful experience.

An astute project manager will begin each new project by reviewing the lessons learned from previous projects for ideas that will save time and avoid sleepless nights. You might not be able to quantify the value of learning from past experiences. Nonetheless, the small investment you make in a retrospective will almost certainly save you more time than it costs. In today's speed-driven and bottom-line conscious development world, you can't afford to repeat past mistakes and encounter the same surprises project after project.

Retrospective Defined

A retrospective is a gathering of knowledge, insights, and possibly metrics and artifacts from a completed project or project phase. Metrics might include actual results for schedule, effort, cost and quality, which you can use to improve your future estimates. You can archive key project documents, plans and specifications to serve as examples for future projects.

A retrospective provides closure, a way for the participants to share their observations away from day-to-day pressures. Even if the project was a colossal failure, the lessons you learn from evaluating it can produce something positive from the experience and point to useful improvement opportunities.

It may seem silly to talk about what a retrospective is named, but names have powerful associations. When someone calls a retrospective a post-mortem, we wonder who died; sometimes projects are successful! And naming a retrospective a post-partum suggests that the new "baby" product may grow up someday, but is far from mature. Retrospective and post-project review are neutral terms that suggest a contemplative reflection on previous experience to gain practical wisdom.

Hold a retrospective whenever you want to gather information about your project or evaluate how the work is going. Many projects iterate through a series of development cycles, so you should gather lessons after each cycle to help you with those that remain. Reflecting on past experience is especially worthwhile any time something went particularly well or particularly wrong. It's easy to forget what happened early in a project that lasts longer than a few months, so hold a short retrospective after reaching each major milestone on a long project. The healing effects of time and the exhilaration of recent success can ease the pain you suffered some time ago, but those painful memories contain the seeds of future improvements.

The Retrospective Process

An effective retrospective follows the simple process depicted in Figure 4.1. The key players are the manager who sponsors the retrospective, the project team members and a facilitator.

Planning. Planning begins when the management sponsor who requested the retrospective works with the facilitator to determine the scope of the retrospective (the entire project or just a portion), the activities to examine and any specific issues to probe. During planning, you also need to identify who should be invited, choose an appropriate facility (preferably off-site and away from distractions), select the facilitation techniques you will use, and define an agenda.

Figure 4.1   The Retrospective Process

We've had different results with splitting participants into groups. In one retrospective, Karl and another facilitator led two separate discussion groups in parallel. One group consisted of six managers, while the other group was made of 15 software practitioners. The facilitators and the sponsoring manager believed that the practitioners would be reluctant to raise certain issues if their managers were in the room. Splitting the participants worked well in this situation, although we had to carefully merge and prioritize the issues from both groups. In another case, however, separating the participants proved unwarranted. The two groups involved were a software development team and a visual design team who had worked together on a major Web site development project. Karl underestimated the participants' collaborative mindset. Despite some points of friction between the groups, it would have been better to keep the entire team in the same room to discuss their joint issues.

Johanna has never separated participant groups, because she believes that separating the groups placates the people with the perceived power. It's important to prepare the managers by telling them that the retrospective may uncover issues that are uncomfortable for them. As Jerry Weinberg points out in *The Secrets of Consulting* (Dorset House, 1985), "No matter what it looks like, it's always a people problem," and sometimes people problems are management-generated. Consider requesting permission from the managers to ask them to leave the room if they seem to be inhibiting the discussion.

Kickoff. During a short kickoff session with all participants, the sponsoring manager introduces the facilitator and any other unfamiliar faces. The manager also identifies his objectives for the retrospective and thanks the participants in advance for their time and honest contributions. The manager should clearly state his commitment to taking concrete actions based on the retrospective outcomes. The facilitator then outlines the agenda. To establish the appropriate constructive environment, the facilitator defines some ground rules, including:

- Allow everyone to be heard.
- Respect the other person's experience and perspective.
- Avoid criticizing input and ideas from other participants.
- Avoid blaming people for past events.
- Identify root causes, not just symptoms.
- Focus on understanding, learning and looking ahead.

Data gathering. While some retrospectives collect hard data and project artifacts, the core activity is gathering issues, observations, and concerns from the participants. We explore three basic questions in a retrospective: What went well? (We want to repeat it in the future.) What could have gone better? (We might want to change it.) What happened that surprised us? (These might be risks to watch for on future projects.)

An experienced facilitator will use numerous techniques to elicit information from different kinds of participant groups. The traditional approach is to have a facilitator stand by a flipchart in front of the group and ask the participants to suggest issues. The facilitator marks what went well with plus signs and less favorable experiences with minus signs. A variation is the round-robin approach, where the facilitator asks each participant in turn to raise one issue and cycles through the audience until everyone passes. This approach to issue generation generally takes 60 to 90 minutes. After issue-generation is completed, the facilitator (or a scribe) records each issue raised on a separate index card. The participants then group the cards into related categories (affinity groups) and name the issue groups.

This traditional facilitation approach has several drawbacks.

- Sequential issue-generation is slow.
- It's easy for a few outspoken participants to dominate the input.
- It's easy to slip into an extended discussion of a single hot-button topic, instead of identifying additional issues.
- Some participants may be uncomfortable raising issues in a public forum.
- Influential or strong-willed participants might prevent others from speaking up.

If you're concerned about any of these factors, consider using alternative facilitation approaches. Silent techniques that let participants generate issues in parallel can be more efficient and comprehensive than the public, sequential method. In one such approach, the facilitator and the retrospective sponsor identify several categories in which issues are likely to arise prior to the retrospective meeting. Common categories for software development projects include communication, organization, teamwork, management, requirements, design, construction, testing, subcontractors, business issues and processes. You probably won't need all of these categories for every retrospective. There is a risk that defining the category names in advance will limit what comes out of the group, so you might prefer to group issues and name the groups after issue-generation is completed.

Write each category name on a separate flipchart page, and divide each page into labeled sections for what went well, what could have gone better and what lessons were learned. During the meeting, have the participants write each of their issues on a separate 3 by 5 sticky note, indicating the pertinent category. The facilitator places these in the right section of the appropriate flipchart page. Spend about 20 minutes clarifying the things that went well, then move on to what could have gone better for another 20 or 30 minutes. Participants can walk around the room and see what other people wrote on the flipcharts to stimulate their own thinking.

This approach addresses most of the shortcomings of the traditional facilitator-at-the-flipchart method. Participants working concurrently can generate more issues in a given amount of time. There is little chance of being distracted by discussions as each issue is raised. And people who might be reluctant to state their opinions aloud willingly contribute them silently and anonymously. However, the facilitator will have to read all the sticky notes on the flipcharts aloud to make sure each issue is clearly stated and properly classified. He must also group related issues.

To close the data-gathering portion of a retrospective, you might ask each team member two questions: What one aspect of this project would you want to keep the same on a future project? And what one aspect of this project would you want to change on a future project?

Issue prioritization. A successful retrospective will generate far more issues than the team can realistically address. You must identify those items that the participants agree would be the most valuable to pursue. Some high-priority issues might point to effective practices you want to institutionalize on future projects. Others will reflect shortcomings in current practices that you need to address promptly.

A classic prioritization technique is Pareto voting. Each participant gets a limited number of votes, usually about 20 percent of the total number of issues being prioritized. To simplify the data collection with a large group, some facilitators give each participant just three to five votes. Colored adhesive dots work well for this voting process. The participants walk around the room, examine the flipcharts and place their dots on the sticky notes with the issues they believe are most important to address. Those issues that gather the most dots are most ripe for early action. However, seeing the dots on the sticky notes can bias participants who might not want to "waste" votes on issues that clearly are not favored by earlier voters. To avoid this problem, participants can place their voting dots on the backs of the sticky notes.

Analysis. If you have time during the retrospective, spend 15 or 20 minutes discussing each of the top priority items. Otherwise, assemble a small group to explore those topics after the retrospective meeting. For items noted as going particularly well, determine why they succeeded and what benefits they provided. Find ways to ensure that each of those aspects of the project will go well again in the future. For high-priority "could have gone better" items, determine why each item didn't turn out as intended, the consequences of each and recommendations for doing it better the next time.

Retrospective Success Factors

A retrospective can succeed only in a neutral, nonaccusatory environment. Honest and open communication is essential. If a project has been difficult or unsuccessful, some venting is to be expected; however, the facilitator must limit that venting and channel it in a constructive direction. Make sure your retrospectives don't turn into witch-hunts. The retrospective must emphasize guilt-free learning from the shared project experience. Let's look at some retrospective critical success factors.

Define your objectives. As the sponsoring manager, you should identify your objectives for the retrospective and the specific project aspects on which it should focus, along with identifying the potential beneficiaries of the activity: Who will come out ahead if the information gathered during the retrospective guides some constructive process changes? Also, think about who might look bad if the root causes of problems are revealed. Remember, you're not looking for scapegoats, but you need to understand what really happened and why.

Use a skilled and impartial facilitator. It isn't realistic to expect the project manager to objectively facilitate a retrospective. The manager might have a particular axe to grind or want to protect his own reputation. Some project managers might unconsciously impede participation despite their good intentions. Other participants can be intimidated into silence on important points, or the manager might put his own spin on certain issues.

To avoid these problems, invite an experienced, neutral facilitator from outside the project team to lead the retrospective. The facilitator's prime objective is to make the retrospective succeed by surfacing the critical issues in a constructive, learning environment. Consider having someone who is not an active participant in the retrospective act as scribe to record the issues generated.

Engage the right participants. Of course, the essential participants are the project team members. Management representatives are invited to the retrospective only if they were actually members of the project team. However, you should provide a summary of lessons learned to senior management or to other managers in the company who could benefit from the information.

Some teams might be too busy, too large or too geographically separated for all team members to participate in a retrospective concurrently. In such a case, select representatives from the various functional areas that were involved in the project. If a large project was subdivided into multiple subprojects, each one should perform its own retrospective. Delegates from each subproject can then participate in a higher-level retrospective at the overall project level.

When people who we believe have key insights claim they're too busy to participate, we ask them if they think everything went well on the project. Generally, they have some important observations and constructive suggestions. We then help those people balance their current time demands against the need to hear their input on the previous project.

If the project involved multiple groups who blame each other for the project's problems or who refuse to sit down together to explore their common issues, you might begin by discussing the friction between the groups. Chances are good that you'll uncover important project issues. If the groups can't get along in the retrospective, they probably clashed during the project, too. The retrospective might address what needs to change for those groups to collaborate more effectively next time.

Prepare the participants. If the participants aren't accustomed to retrospectives, and if the project being studied had serious problems, an invitation to a retrospective can stimulate confusion or resistance. Some participants might be sick with anxiety, while others will be eager to let the accusations fly. Provide information and reassurance to the participants through the invitation material and during "sales calls" made to team leaders and key participants. Describe the process in advance and establish an appropriately constructive mindset by emphasizing that this is a future-oriented, process-improvement activity.

Focus on the facts. A retrospective should address the processes and outcomes of the project, not the participants' personalities or mistakes. The facilitator has to ensure the participants don't blame or placate others by concentrating on what actually happened. However, people often experience events in different ways. Understanding the different interpretations can release hard feelings and provide the opportunity for new insights.

Identify the action plan owner. Identify the person who will write and take ownership of an improvement action plan and see that it leads to tangible benefits. Assign each action item in the plan to an individual who will implement it and report progress to the action plan owner. This owner must carry enough weight in the organization to steer these individuals toward completing their action items.

Retrospective Action Planning

After the retrospective, don't tackle all of the identified issues immediately. Initially, choose up to three issues from the top priority list; the rest will still be there for future treatment. Write an action plan that describes your improvement goals, identifies steps to address them, states who will take responsibility for each activity and lists any deliverables that will be created. At your next retrospective, check whether these actions resulted in the desired outcomes. Remember, an action plan that doesn't lead to concrete actions is useless. Karl once facilitated retrospectives for the same Internet development group two years apart. Some issues that came up in the later retrospective had been identified two years earlier. Failing to learn from the past practically guarantees that you will repeat it, and nothing kills an organization's attempt to hold retrospectives faster than recommendations that aren't implemented.

Lessons Learned

For maximum organizational benefits, accumulate lessons learned from your retrospectives. We prefer to write lessons learned in a neutral way, so it isn't obvious whether we learned each one because something was done well or because the team made a mistake. The information in your "lessons learned" database could include:

- Statement of the lesson
- Lesson-learned subject category
- Date the lesson was entered into repository

- Project name
- Risks of ignoring the lesson
- Recommendations for implementing the lesson
- Work product involved
- Pertinent life cycle phase

The People Side

Because we're human, our personalities influence how we react to situations. During one retrospective that Johanna facilitated, a management participant had tears in his eyes when he described a particular concern. Johanna spoke to him at a break, and he said he felt that management didn't trust him, yet he didn't feel comfortable saying so. He agreed to have Johanna bring up this sensitive topic.

When the group reconvened, Johanna said that one participant did not feel trusted by management because of three points that she wrote on the flipchart. The room was silent for a minute. Then someone else said, "Me, too." Several others chimed in, and then they looked at the senior manager. Johanna reminded the group we weren't judging individuals, but rather airing our concerns so we could address them. The senior manager then asked, "Does anyone here trust me?" No one responded. It was a telling moment. The senior manager then listed lack of trust as a problem.

The project team is the best source of information about how a recently completed project or development phase really went. Use a retrospective to help the team assemble a whole picture of the project, so the project leader can use that information to create a more effective environment the next time. But remember that all organizational change takes time, patience and commitment from all stakeholders. If people don't want to change, they won't.

4.2.3 "Lost in Chaos: Chronology of a Failure"

by Stephen Adolph

On the surface, the ingredients for success were there: an enthusiastic and capable team, a competent manager and proper funding. So why was the project a disaster?

One of my favorite TV shows when I was growing up was "Lost in Space." I was particularly fond of the robot who would always warn the Robinson family about perilous situations with the now cliché phrase "Danger, Will Robinson, danger!" Today, I wish I had one of those robots standing behind me when someone describes a project to me using phrases like "It's an aggressive schedule," "It's a challenging project," or the ever-popular, "This project is on the fast track."

"Danger, Will Robinson, danger!" What these phrases really mean is "We don't have time, so we're abandoning any software development process and, therefore, our ability to control the project."

On the surface, the short-circuiting or total abandonment of process has a seductive appeal: no tedious production of requirements documents, no boring review meetings and no one telling you what you can or cannot put into the build. This approach to software development assumes that your project will never hit a crisis, no key personnel will leave, all third-party software will work as advertised, and the system will meet its performance requirements. Success is rooted more in faith and the tenacity of the developers than in a controlled, predictable process. This chaotic approach to software development is characteristic of immature organizations.

The Capability Maturity Model is a framework developed at Carnegie Mellon University in 1989 that outlines the elements of an effective software process. The CMM describes an evolutionary path from an ad hoc, chaotic process to a mature, disciplined one. It covers practices for planning, engineering and managing software development, which, when followed, improve the ability of an organization to satisfy cost, schedule, functionality and product-quality goals.

Unfortunately, many developers have a Pavlovian response to words like "process" and "methodology." They believe that process shackles their creativity and will prevent them from developing the creative solutions to the problems they have at hand. Often, the developers justify the belief that the CMM framework is not applicable by describing their project as different, too small or destined for an overly competitive market. After all, the CMM is for mega-programming ventures in the aerospace industry, not little applications like ours. Another popular justification is that, in the case of a legacy system conversion, a process is unnecessary because the legacy represents the company's core competency.

Although the CMM may originally have been adopted by large development organizations, its recommendations and goals are applicable to any development group. A software development group does itself a great disservice when it dismisses CMM out of hand.

Setting the Stage

Our story begins several years ago with a mobile dispatching business whose products were used by taxi companies, police and fire departments and utilities for dispatching their fleets.

The product for utility companies was nearing the end of its useful life and was therefore too expensive to maintain, modify or enhance. At the same time, the company had won an important contract to supply a dispatch system to a large utility company. We had a choice to make: Upgrade the legacy system to handle the customer's requirements, or take this as an opportunity to create the next-generation utility dispatching system. We decided to build the next generation. I had recently been hired by the company because of my technical expertise in UNIX software development, and it was going to be my job to serve as the team's technical leader.

The Legacy

The system that was about to launch us into chaos was in fact very simple. A dispatcher sat at a terminal and would receive a phone call from a client who might require, for example, a furnace repair. He would create a work order by entering the customer's information and a description of the required work into the system. The work order would be prioritized by urgency (from emergency calls to routine maintenance), and a service technician would be assigned to the work order, either by the dispatcher or the system. The service technician would receive the work order in her service vehicle on a mobile terminal, which she also used to report her status and request more information.

The system was based on UNIX System V and was written by a group of former mainframe programmers who did not trust UNIX. The original authors had decided to handle threading, file, terminal and memory management themselves rather than relying on the UNIX system services.

This was one of the finest examples of spaghetti code ever created, packed with hardware dependencies and corrupt with several years of undocumented enhancements and bug fixes. It was not unusual to fix a bug in one subsystem and have a completely new bug suddenly appear in an unrelated subsystem.

The programmers who maintained the system didn't enjoy the task; as a consequence, turnover was high. This threatened our ability to deliver because we could not keep our staff long enough for them to become experts in the system.

The system, the code and the programmers' disdain for the legacy were not our only problems. Our company was developing its next generation of mobile terminals, and many clients were clamoring to get them. However, the legacy system could only operate with one type of terminal, which meant all the existing terminals would have to be replaced with new ones. This was not an option that our existing clients would consider; they wanted to keep their existing terminals and add new ones as their fleets expanded.

Justifying Replacement

Our normal procedure for system delivery was to customize the software on a standard system. The customization requirements were usually straightforward: Configure the system to operate with the specific type of mobile terminal used by the client, customize the menus with the customer's name and adapt the host interface to match the communications requirements of the client's mainframe.

Our standard customization process had worked fine until an existing utility dispatch client requested new features that went well beyond our standard customization. The customer wanted to move to a client/server architecture with automatic fail-over for high availability and the incorporation of a commercial off-the-shelf relational database.

It should be clear by now that our utility dispatch product was old, limited and difficult to modify. Therefore, after estimating the cost of incorporating these new features into the legacy system, the decision was made to replace the legacy with a new system.

The Project Mandate

Management was not enthusiastic about replacing the legacy system (management never is) — and with good reason. Despite its technical flaws, the legacy was generating revenue for the company, and there was a great deal of reluctance to replace the product simply because programmers found it hard to maintain.

Management was concerned that the justification for the legacy replacement was being driven strictly by the technology rather than by business objectives. They were concerned that we were risking proven — albeit archaic — technology with a promise of wonderful vaporware. Our group was given a strict project mandate: Re-engineer the utility dispatching system to create a client/server architecture, operate with multiple mobile terminal types, decouple application functionality from the hardware, incorporate a commercial off-the-shelf database and add a high-availability feature.

We had 18 months to deliver a new architecture that combined the services of the legacy system as well as the new required features. In everyone's opinion, the project goals were aggressive but achievable.

Our team consisted of a very aggressive and capable hands-on project manager, two senior designers including myself (a contractor who frequently worked with the company), and four junior-to-intermediate developers, one who had good experience implementing the company's proprietary communications protocols and others who had customized the legacy system extensively. The team members were enthusiastic and got along famously.

One of the first warning signs should have been our cavalier approach to schedule estimation. We estimated a multi-million-dollar venture the same way three engineering students in college might estimate their term project. The senior developers simply met with the project manager and within two hours decided that we required six people over 18 months to satisfy our contractual obligations. This approach to estimation is typical of an immature, or CMM level one, development organization. What influence could following the CMM framework have had on this estimation effort if we had decided to move to at least level two in the maturity hierarchy?

One of the key practices of a level two organization is the tracking of project costs and schedules. This information forms a historic database that can be used in subsequent estimates. Of course, our software development group didn't have any historical data for making estimates, so the wet-finger-in-the-air approach was about the best we could do. However, we could have established short-term milestones — a key practice in many of the modern iterative software development processes — and then frequently compared our actuals to our estimates. That way, as the project progressed, we could have begun to use the historical database to produce higher-quality estimates.

Unfortunately, not only did we not follow this approach, we also set our project milestones too far apart: every six months. In other words, it would take that long to accumulate enough objective data to indicate whether the project was on or off track. For a project of our size, we should have set monthly milestones that would have forced us to compare our actuals to our estimates much more frequently.

Analysis or "We Don't Need No SRS"

The next warning sign should have come during the analysis phase, which, for all practical purposes, was skipped. Our wet-finger-in-the-wind style of estimating had almost panicked us into believing that we were under a great deal of schedule pressure. The approach to mitigating this risk was to abandon what we perceived as unnecessary steps in the software development process.

Having come from a very disciplined software development environment, I recommended the creation of a software requirements specification (SRS) as part of the requirements analysis process. This was rejected by the project manager for two reasons: First, it was considered unnecessary because the company had expertise in the field of mobile dispatching, and second, the schedule was the risk and all unnecessary activities — including the preparation of an SRS — needed to be pruned from the schedule.

There is a perception that creating an SRS is a time-consuming, paper-wasting exercise that doesn't contribute to a project. This perception is probably reinforced by published SRS standards such as the ANSI/IEEE 830 in the 1984 *IEEE Guide to Software Requirements Specification*.

The ANSI/IEEE 830 provides a comprehensive and complete format for an SRS. There are seven major sections covering everything from the information model and functional models, to validation criteria. A complete SRS for a moderately sized project (moderate being about

15 staff-years) can be more than 100 pages long, and one for a defense system (approximately 100 staff-years in effort) was said to have been shipped in a panel van! While it is inappropriate to prepare such a comprehensive document for a small project, that does not justify abandoning a document or other artifacts that serve the purpose of the SRS. The usefulness of the SRS is not in the volume of paper produced but rather in how well it communicates what the system should be to all project participants.

For a small project, the IEEE 830 standard becomes an excellent checklist for ensuring that all project participants know the functional requirements, the stored data model and the constraints on the system. Often, the objective of the SRS can be satisfied with a few bullet lists and a couple of class diagrams.

Our project manager didn't want to produce an SRS because he saw himself as an expert in the legacy system and thought he had a clear vision of what the new system needed to achieve. Regardless of that fact, abandoning the analysis process altogether is not a justifiable project management practice; without it, we have nothing that states the requirements for our project and nothing constraining it, other than the whims of its participants.

When replacing a legacy system, software developers often underestimate the risk because they assume the legacy system is one of the organization's core competencies and that it represents a set of stable requirements. This perception is true only if the replacement project's development team understands the legacy system and actually uses it to reduce the risks associated with uncertain requirements.

In *The Mythical Man-Month: Essays on Software Engineering* (Addison-Wesley, 1975), Frederick Brooks called this the "second system effect," writing "the second is the most dangerous system a man ever designs ... There is a general tendency to overdesign the second system using all the ideas and frills that were cautiously sidetracked on the first one."

Unfortunately, we were destined to find out how accurate Frederick Brooks's prediction was.

Design or "I Like This Part Best"

Based on the assumption that we were experts in the domain of mobile dispatching and that the majority of our functional requirements were captured in our legacy system, we short-circuited the analysis phase of our project and moved quickly into high-level design.

Our goal in the design phase was to create an executable architecture: a foundation for our new system that we would grow by adding new functionality as we went along. To satisfy our project mandate, the senior designers reorganized the monolith into a textbook three-tiered client/server architecture. This immediately satisfied our project mandate because it provided a clean separation of our business rules from our device interfaces for both dispatcher and mobile terminals.

The new architecture supported a variety of mobile terminal types. Now, all that was needed to add a new terminal type to the system was to write a device driver for it and add an entry for that terminal type to the configuration table. Unlike the legacy application, the system no longer had to be recompiled to add a new terminal type.

In design, we once again avoided the formal process, opting instead for having a couple of programmers confer with the project manager and sketch system components on a whiteboard. The programmers would write the code and rely on the project manager for midcourse corrections. Once the code was complete (that is, when a clean compile had been obtained), we would have a formal code walkthrough. The project manager, a senior designer and the programmer whose code was under review participated in the walkthrough.

There was one glaring exception to this informal process. Because the senior designers had placed a lot of emphasis on the communications backbone for the new client/server architecture, we published a formal document describing the APIs for the communications backbone and also created a guidebook to help the other programmers use the backbone's services.

As a result, the backbone was beautiful, heavily overdesigned and a reinvention of the remote procedure calls (RPC), a service readily available on most flavors of UNIX. There were several justifications for this reinvention, but the one that kept resurfacing was performance. High performance was necessary, and it was believed that our design had less overhead than the RPC.

The excessive attention paid to the design and implementation of the communications backbone was a result of what we had perceived as the risks to the system — probably diverting our attention from handling the true risks — and also a result of the fact that the senior designers found it interesting.

The First (and Last) Milestone

The departure of one of the senior developers, a contractor on the project, was the first blow. Suddenly we had no one with experience in the business services the system was to provide; without the de facto expert in the legacy system, it was extremely difficult to read and understand the legacy code. So, rather than trying to continue to recover the application logic from the existing code, we began to recover it from the only documentation we had — the user manual.

At this point, the legacy code was lost as a risk-reduction mechanism.

Six months into our project, at our first milestone, we were able to successfully demonstrate the executable architecture to our marketing group and corporate executive. It satisfied the mandate given to us by management, featured a client/server architecture that was nicely layered to decouple application functionality from the hardware and the system used a commercial off-the-shelf database. The system was dynamically reconfigurable and management was extremely impressed when we could change terminal types on the fly during the demo.

Our executives were happy. The demonstration gave them confidence in the system. Better yet, it boosted the confidence of the team. We started to become arrogant and forgot that this little performance had only demonstrated approximately 10% of the functional capability of the system — while we had used up 33% of our project time.

The second blow to hit the project occurred when the project manager left the company. He had acted as a living SRS and had often scrubbed feature changes recommended or desired by the project team. Under the fast-track process (or lack thereof) we were running, this was the fatal blow, although it would be another six months before anyone would notice the symptoms.

A former employee was brought in on contract as the new project manager. His management style was quite different from our previous manager. He believed strongly in employee empowerment, and he let the development team manage itself. One of the key requirements of empowerment, however, is that empowered employees must clearly understand what the project objectives are — and those had gone out the door with our living SRS. In the absence of well-defined goals, staff members created their own, based on what they thought important rather than what was important to their clients.

Beyond its spaghetti architecture, the legacy system had numerous technical and application problems. The design team often chose to invent new strategies rather than reuse techniques from the legacy system. There were good technical and application reasons for these new strategies. However, what was unseen was the element of risk these new strategies introduced.

Let's take an example. The unit of work assigned to a service technician was a work order. Only one service technician could be assigned to a work order; however, many of the tasks required more than one service technician, and each of the attending service technicians would be on the job for different periods of time. The legacy system handled this by linking work orders together so one work order became a kind of primary work order, and other work orders became secondary. There were numerous problems with this design, especially when trying to determine when the work order was complete.

We viewed the linking of work orders as a hack; it offended our collective sense of good design. We came up with a better idea: the concept of a job as a unit of work that a service technician performed on a work order. A work order was a set of one or more jobs. Now, knowing the work order, you could find the service people and their jobs.

The only problem with this beautiful scheme was that it completely changed how the system operated. It changed the user interface for both the dispatchers and technicians, which meant that all the documentation had to change. Furthermore, our field-service people would have to be retrained.

Nevertheless, the development team aggressively sold this idea to the new project manager, who approved it. Indeed, the new project manager endorsed most of the design team's suggestions and improvements without question. This led to situations where the design team would implement a feature and then decide later there was a better way to re-implement that feature. The existing code would be ripped out and an improved feature implemented. In all cases, there were good technical reasons for re-writing the feature. The problem was that the technical justifications conflicted with schedule requirements and, in some cases, caused the project to actually slide backward. Without a requirements scrub process — a hallmark of developmental maturity — and without a single clear vision for the product, we began to suffer feature creep on a monumental scale. The worst part was that this feature creep was self-inflicted.

Curtains

The legacy replacement project was canceled a year after it was started. Six months after the highly successful first demonstration, at our second milestone, management no longer clung to the hope that the development team could deliver the new system on time. We had less than 30% of the legacy system's functionality incorporated into the new architecture, despite the fact that we had expended nearly 70% of our project's allotted time and resources.

In retrospect, it's amazing that the team could let the situation deteriorate to the extent that it did. We were all too interested in how to make the system technically perfect to notice that we were in serious trouble. I had received praise from my manager and from my team for the architectural elements that I had created for the system. Unfortunately, I let these technical achievements delude me into believing that our project was well on its way to success. I had lost sight of the project mandate originally specified by our corporate management.

This is all too common an occurrence in immature development organizations. People have an amazing ability for denial, which is abetted by an absence of objective data. Perhaps this is the ultimate purpose of a software development process: to shake us out of complacency by pushing the hard facts right into our faces. If the project had been reviewed early and frequently, we would have had the opportunity to take remedial action.

The development team was redeployed to create wrappers around the legacy system so that it would minimally satisfy our client's requirements. Within two years of the legacy replacement cancellation, the company was out of the business of supplying application software for its mobile terminals.

The Final Analysis

Without a defined process, the project relied entirely on the first project manager's ability to maintain the project vision. When he left, all control was lost. Our justification for not applying a disciplined process was the tired cliché that our project was somehow different. We deliberately chose a chaotic approach to software development because of the belief that following a process would bog us down in miserable details.

Following a process does not mean turning a fast-moving software development organization into a plodding bureaucracy. The CMM provides a tailorable framework that shows progressive levels of process maturity with the goal of improving an organization's ability to meet goals for cost, schedule, functionality and product quality.

Each maturity level has a set of process areas that an organization should have in place to help it achieve the goals of the CMM. The mere production of documents does not satisfy the requirements of a process area. Therefore, it is more important to understand the risks that the process area mitigates rather than the format of an industry standard document for that area.

Had we made a commitment to improving the maturity of our development process and at least borrowed some elements from the CMM, we might have had a successful project.

For example, the first key process area of level two is requirements management, which establishes a common understanding of the requirements. We never produced a requirements document, assuming instead that our project mandate and the legacy system represented our requirements. As a consequence, there was no way to control changes to the requirements after the first project manager left.

Other level two process areas include software project planning, tracking and oversight, which establishes visible milestones to compare estimates to actual progress.

Finally, level two's emphasis on quality assurance gives management visibility into the process. This helps prevent long periods of developer denial due to the lack of objective data to shake them.

In retrospect, the task of maturing into a level two organization wouldn't have been very onerous, entailing perhaps the creation of a few short documents and the implementation of regular reviews. Perhaps we wouldn't have won the heart of an ISO 9000 auditor, but we might have succeeded in delivering our project.

4.2.4 "Saving a Project in Trouble"

by Steve Furlong

Are you joining a project after everyone with any sense has bailed out?
Here's how to get oriented, make sense of legacy code,
troubleshoot the crises, and save the day.

How did you get into this? You've just come on to a new project and you already know it was a mistake. The requirements are a mystery, the code is a disaster, the development team who worked on the job before you is long gone, and you have two months to get it out the door.

You know when a project is in trouble right away: it usually has the worst in project management, code quality, and customer expectations. You have to figure out the project requirements and make sense of source code you didn't write before you can begin to tackle the problems. Small projects that you might handle on your own or with only a few team members can be particularly difficult due to limited resources and support. The following steps will help you save a project in trouble — and keep your sanity in the process.

Step One: Determine the Project Requirements

Before you can fix the project, you must know what you're supposed to accomplish. This has three overlapping components: the requirements document, the minimal set of features needed, and short- and long-term issues.

You'll probably have some kind of requirements document. It may even be accurate, though, if the project were well-managed enough to have proper requirements tracking, it wouldn't be a disaster. Most likely, you'll have to rummage through a pile of binders and folders to find contract documents, meeting and phone notes, and so on.

One of the first things you'll want to do is find the programmers who worked on the project before you. No, not for programming instruction! The previous programmers generally have an idea of what the project was supposed to do. Although they may be hazy on the details, they might be willing to give you the nickel tour and flesh out any sketchy notes they left.

Projects for outside customers are likely to have a paper trail. This may not be a clear trail, what with written amendments, undocumented promises, and the like; however, it's a start. "Inside" jobs are more likely to be specified informally at best. The best procedure is to sort everything by date where possible, write up what you can, and have it reviewed. Expect changes, even if you did a perfect job of reconstruction, because user or manager requirements will have evolved.

While you're deducing the requirements document, divide the requirements into several categories, including "essential for the first version," "can wait for a later version," and "nonessential." The category of any feature doesn't matter much, but it is important to prioritize the features. You will be hard-pressed to get anything done in time, and you can't be burdened with nonessentials. (If management tells you that all features are mission-critical and first-priority, abandon ship; this lack of flexibility does not bode well for anyone's ability to pull this project together.)

Balance short- and long-term goals. You should want to build a masterpiece, but if the project is two delays from the chopping block, the final straw may be your effort on some long-term issue that doesn't get the product out the door next month.

Decide on the quality that must be present in the final product. Attention to quality usually results in reduced time and cost for new projects. I haven't seen any similar studies for projects that gained a concern for quality midway, but my experience generally supports the idea of striving for quality in coding and in meeting requirements. Be prepared for a tough fight with management on this. The idea of "ship it now, fix it later" is so obvious that every manager reinvents it. Studies, statistics, and logic don't persuade them, so either give in on the issue or insert quality on the sly.

Step Two: Figure Out the Source Code

Most programmers see the source code as the heart of the project. I don't quite agree. The requirements document and project management procedures have at least as much to do with the project's eventual success or failure. But I can see their point: if the source code doesn't make a working project, you've got nothing. Examining the source code is a universal step since every project will have it, but many don't have a requirements document, standards, or other frippery. The source code is, of course, its own documentation. (Yes, that's a joke.)

But it's not as much of a joke as it should be. Unfortunately, you can't rely on any documentation you might find. Requirements and design documents are notoriously out-of-date; programmers' notebooks are often illegible and incomplete; and source comments are typically outdated, useless, or just plain wrong. Odds are, the previous team made several variations of the project in different directories, and didn't document any of the locations or the reasons for making them. Also, version control probably isn't being used properly, if at all.

You'll usually have to go over the source code, line by line, to figure out what it's doing. That's not necessarily what it should be doing, but it's the baseline of where you'll start in making the project work.

Generally, the source code will not be of a quality that anyone would care to brag about. A big problem is inconsistency: in indentation, variable names, and everything else. It's not usually worth the time and effort to stop all work and bring all the code up to standard. Instead, it's O.K. to fix each module when you need to work on it for other reasons.

As an exception, you may wish to use a "code beautifier" — I use Emacs in C++ mode — to adjust the formatting of your source code. I've also seen source code and executables on the World Wide Web. Most of these tools let you specify indentation, comment placement, use of blank lines, and the like. You can run them in batch mode and fix all files in one pass.

The commercial tools have some bells and whistles and sometimes better documentation, but the freeware and shareware tools I've seen do the job just as well. Just download a few free packages, fiddle with them for half a day, and use what you like best; you'll get the job done with minimal effort and aggravation.

Break down large functions. Most projects in trouble seem to have a number of very large routines. This is probably because the programmers had sloppy habits and also were under the gun to add just one more feature or to patch an error, and thought that sloppy code could always be fixed later. In any event, code tends to accrete, comments get out of date, and any hypothetical clarity of design morphs into obscurity.

You'll want to break these large functions into smaller chunks, mainly for comprehension now but also for maintainability. One way is to lift large, relatively autonomous pieces and turn them into routines. Really messed-up code won't have any chunks that you can extract and call without a dozen or so arguments. In these cases, you might want to declare a type solely as an argument for that call, then stuff the myriad arguments into its fields.

Use literate programming. Another method of making sense of undocumented legacy code is literate programming, invented by Donald Knuth. I use literate programming extensively when I have to fix orphaned code. Literate programming is the combination of source code and documentation in the same source file, with emphasis on clear exposition for the human reader. The main audience of your program is not the computer, but other people. Your goal as a literate programmer is to describe the program in a technical article, which, incidentally, can be processed by a tool to create the program's source code.

A literate source file consists of blocks of descriptive text interleaved with blocks of code, most often called "chunks." Chunks may contain references to other chunks as well as target language code, and may in turn be contained in higher-level chunks. The program that makes the program code from your literate program is essentially a macro expander that starts from a root chunk and expands all references to other chunks until it ends up with straight source code.

A key point of literate programming is that the code chunks should be small enough that a reader can easily grasp the function of each chunk. You don't need to write chunks in the order in which the compiler needs to see them. Instead, present them in whatever order makes the program clearest to the reader. You can detail the interwoven discussion as you like, using mathematical equations, tables, diagrams, or anything else you need to get the point across.

Knuth's original WEB package of literate programming tools required the use of his TeX document description language as the text formatter, and many other literate programming packages have followed suit. This may have put off some potential literate programming users: TeX is much harder to get started with than WinWord. It's also much more powerful, but that's not apparent until you've learned to use it. Several literate programming packages since WEB use other text formatters (such as WinWordWeb) or are formatter-independent (such as CLiP). Some packages are designed for a particular programming language (WEB for Pascal, CWEB for C, and so forth), while others, like Norman Ramsey's noweb, are language-independent. I mainly use noweb for my literate programming work because I work with several programming languages and have come to appreciate TeX's advantages.

A trivial example, using noweb syntax, is shown in the Hello, World Program in Listing 4.1 (page 132). Chunks begin with <<chunkname>> and end with @. Utilities turn the literate source file into either compilable source code or human-readable documentation.

Usenet has at least one group devoted to literate programming: comp.programming.literate. The frequently asked questions list gives many resources for literate programming tools and papers. In particular, all of the tools mentioned previously are freely available from archive sites. The frequently asked questions lists many sites. You may also wish to obtain Donald Knuth's *Literate Programming* (Center for the Study of Language and Information, 1992). It is a collection of Knuth's papers on literate programming discussing its purpose and giving nontrivial example programs.

Now, let's apply literate programming to the analysis of legacy code. My usual technique is to make each routine (function, subroutine, whatever) into a single chunk, then work my way through the large chunk, extracting loops, conditionals, conceptual blocks, and the like into nested chunks. By the time I'm done, I'll have turned an 800-line function into a few dozen chunks of about 20 statements each, and most chunks will have a description of a few lines to a couple of pages. These are much easier to grasp than the original behemoth.

Listing 4.1   Hello, World Program Using Noweb Syntax

```
the printf statement.
<<print the message>>=
printf ("Hello, world!\n");
@
<<the program>>=
<<include files>>
void main()
{
    <<print the message>>
}
@
<<include files>>=
#include <stdio.h>
@
```

Determine calls between procedures. Determining the web of calls between procedures can be a daunting task, but it's necessary to understand the nature and scope of the project. Many modern compilers generate browser information, and third-party tools abound for common languages. Look for "call tree" in the tool's description when you browse an archive site.

Use metrics. Some metrics tools might come in handy. McCabe's Cyclomatic Complexity is a measure of code complexity. Leaving aside the merits of this metric compared to others, it is a useful method of automatically finding complex functions vs. functions with apparent but not actual complexity. Function points probably will not help you. Today's tools and methods work off requirements documents, not plain source code. Your project presumably does not have a correct requirements document in any condition for function point analysis.

Examine modules, functions, and data types for usefulness in meeting requirements, modularity, flexibility, and so on. For instance, a record describing an accounts payable voucher should have a "released for payment" field, even if that requirement was never spelled out. Unfortunately, in the absence of a complete and correct specification, you will probably need either domain experience or room for trial and error (that is, iterative development). You can design a function to easily accommodate change by branching to code based on a lookup table rather than cascaded ifs. A full discussion of these topics would take up more than this entire magazine, so let me just refer you to Chapters 5, 6, 11, and 12 of Steve McConnell's *Code Complete* (Microsoft Press, 1993).

Check private and public members. Types in object-oriented languages should not have too many externally visible data members. To use C++ terms, if all classes have only public members, the designer or programmer probably didn't understand the concept of object orientation and probably misused other concepts as well. In a badly designed project, you may well find many improperly public members. If you are under schedule pressure, it may not be worth making these private and putting in accessors unless you suspect data is being modified on the sly. A quick test to find out which functions make direct access to a public member variable is to make it private, recompile, and see what breaks. Most likely you'll get a slew of compile-time error messages for functions that are using the variable properly, with any incorrect uses buried in the listing.

Step Three: Plan Your Strategy

After you've cleaned up the source code, you can proceed through the development process, which should run just like any other project. As with any development task, you'll have to juggle several competing priorities: feature set, schedule, cost, quality, and maintainability. As we've seen before, you'll find some differences in procedures and priorities since you're fixing preexisting work. For instance, designing proper error handling and testability probably is no longer an option since the modules are already designed. On the other hand, developing and running a good set of unit tests will take a higher priority than would otherwise be the case. This is because you must find the problem children post haste.

It's important to plan some of the back-end steps ahead of time. Most projects run over, and important back-end tasks (you know, testing) get shortened or eliminated. Of course, you'll have to judge how much time you can put into these tasks without getting the project killed.

First, you'll need to revisit the feature list, and estimate the time and cost needed to bring each feature to the level of quality required. You'll have to include the time necessary to write the feature from scratch, as well as how long it will take to fix or completely rewrite the existing code that implements the feature incorrectly. If you're serving as the project manager, include the programmers in this decision. If you're serving as the technical lead, make sure your project manager includes your views on these decisions. Most likely, your guesses at the cost to implement features and fix errors will be just that: guesses. Until you know exactly what you're getting into, exactly where you're going, and exactly how productive you and your team members will be in this environment, you have no basis for reasoned judgment. This could be a justification for keeping productivity measures as you fix modules, but managers tend to flatly forbid such time-wasting busywork. In any event, the goal of this operation is to prune down the list of features into must-have, wanna-have, and next-version lists.

You must also specify the quality required of each feature: must work completely right; a few user interface faults are allowed if the data isn't corrupted; and so on. Yes, of course, we'd prefer to ship only perfect code, but problem projects are usually in "good enough" mode, with the "good enough" bar dropping with time. The best you can do in this case is to make sure the really important features don't get shipped with significant errors. After the feature list has been negotiated, draft the user's manual and other external documentation first. This will serve as the specification for the rest of development. Don't get too specific, though; you can expect changes in the requirements, particularly in a project managed badly enough to get into such poor condition.

Determine the tools you'll need to finish your development. You should also look into tools that are specifically for analyzing existing code. I've mentioned a few tools already. A lint-like tool is invaluable if one is available for your language and operating system. It will pick up questionable programming that you would never have suspected of causing potential problems. The lint tool is commercially available for C and C++ compilers on most platforms; the name is usually some variant on `lint`. Users of some C and C++ compilers, such as the Free Software Foundation's (freely distributable) GNU C++, have less need for `lint` because their compile-time warning messages are much more complete than most compilers. Freely available and commercial code checking tools are also available for other languages, such as Visual Basic.

The next major step is to put together test cases, input and output sets, and the like. This is pretty standard stuff. Writing a proper test suite takes a lot of time, so if you're working alone or with only minimal help, you may have to cut corners. As we have seen, some modules or features are less important to the project, and can be shipped with errors. Don't put too much time into these parts of the project; concentrate your efforts on the mission-critical areas instead.

You might want to give a low priority to writing internal documentation, such as detailed commentary on each function. The rationale is that the code is low-quality and should be tossed as soon as the project is released, so why bother documenting it? I disagree with this because code never seems to get tossed; it's always tweaked and expanded and stays around longer than the programmers. However, if you or your programmers hate writing documentation, this is a good excuse.

Finally, put together a timeline, complete with milestones. A PERT chart can help. While some say the chart's major purpose is giving managers something to look at, it can also help keep you on track and prevent you from wasting too much time on tasks that take much longer than expected.

Step Four: Do It

Implementing your plan should be straightforward. You presumably know how to write and test code, write help and documentation, resist schedule pressure and featuritis, and the other usual tasks.

There are several strategies for implementing the plan. Which one you'll choose depends on circumstances, mainly your boss's personality. One is to proceed in an orderly fashion, by examining, fixing, testing, and documenting each module feature in turn, according to a priority list. This is possible only if your manager is rational.

Another strategy is to examine and fix features with show-stopping flaws, perform sketchy testing, and write almost no documentation. This can be useful when the product is in use before release and you need to let customers get some work done with it before it is complete. It is also used when you need to make frequent builds with an appearance of progress.

A third strategy is to work on whatever features your boss complains about. These will tend to be user-interface issues, especially if your boss isn't technical.

You've probably noticed that these three strategies proceed from most effective to least effective. Unfortunately, in my experience, they also proceed from "unlikely to be allowed" to "almost certain to be required."

Step Five: Aftermath

O.K., you've got a working version with all of the required features in a "good enough" state. You're still not done. You can, however, do something that will help the product, the company, and your career.

Issue number one is maintenance. This starts with the usual area of fixing errors and expands to adding features not included in the first release. You might also need to work on the user's guide and online help; if these were produced under the same abbreviated schedule as the source code, they'll probably have plenty of errors and sections that need revision.

Unless you were able to redesign and rewrite almost the entire application, the edifice of your program was built on a shaky foundation. Sometimes, the best you can do is document areas you know are subject to change or have problems. If you'll be on the same project for quite a while, you might be able to incrementally improve the design and implementation. Be careful, though — it's important not to change anything the user sees, except for errors.

This ties in with testing, especially regression testing. Right after a release is a good time to prepare proper test plans and cases. The pressure to produce only user-visible features eases for a while, and the problem areas are still fresh in your mind.

A project in trouble can also serve as a learning experience for the entire development team and management. A "lessons learned" write-up might do you and your employer some good, especially if you can present it before other developers and spark a discussion and some real changes.

Lastly, provide programmer's documentation on your projects. This is something you don't often see on small projects. Remember all the things you couldn't figure out when you first came on to this project? Try to write them up so you don't have to come back to help the next person once you finally move on.

These tips should help you survive a troubled project, or at least suggest when you should abandon a sinking ship. With increased experience, you should be able to use more of the former and less of the latter, and be able to command the consulting fees worthy of someone able to snatch victory from the jaws of defeat.

4.2.5 "Revamp Your Current Job"

by Peter Alexander

If you're not satisfied with your job description,
you can change it — without switching companies.

Your skills are in short supply. At least one in ten information technology positions in the U.S. is vacant, and most organizations predict creating more information systems jobs in the next five to ten years — a million estimated new jobs by 2005. Both the Internet and the Year 2000 problem are gobbling up human resources, which exacerbates the critical shortage. And software developer turnover is an expensive problem for employers, one that hampers their ability to innovate, compete, and grow.

In short, there's never been a better time to get more of what you want from your employer.

You may have considered switching jobs, but you should also consider reshaping your existing job to suit you better. Most jobs can be tweaked or revamped to be more satisfying, and organizations are willing to make changes to keep employees happy.

Before you barge into your boss's office, think about what would make a significant difference to your satisfaction. More money usually comes to mind first; but while you may deserve a raise and you may be able to get one, a salary boost doesn't usually affect the real drivers of job satisfaction, such as training, flexible schedules, an active role in the organization's overall effort, and a positive corporate culture.

Now is a good time to assess your values to determine what makes your work rewarding, where you want to go, and how to get there. Start by examining what may be unsatisfying about your job:

Are you off track?   When you think about your long-term goals, you may decide that your best role is technical wizard. Keeping up with new technologies, and having opportunities to use them will be a high priority. Or you may decide that you want to move up in technical management, in which case leadership training and assignments that develop leadership skills would be important. Or you may aspire to get out of the back room and into the mainstream of the organization, bringing your technical knowledge to bear on such areas as marketing, business development, and strategic planning.

No matter which future you envision for yourself, opportunities probably exist with your current employer. And your company will likely provide training and job experience to move you in the direction you want to go.

Some companies, including some conservative financial institutions, have set up technology playgrounds where software engineers can get their hands on beta software, even when it has nothing to do with their jobs. Such employers recognize that being on the cutting edge is what keeps some technical professionals from burning out (and many recognize that it's hard to predict which new technologies will become highly relevant to their business). Many companies are well aware that effective technical management is just about as rare as it is necessary, and are more than willing to train technical people who have an interest in management. And almost all organizations desperately need software experts who can effectively present ideas to upper management, serve on cross-functional teams, interact with customers, and be part of team marketing and selling efforts.

Do you wish you had a life?   Even if you like your job, you may think it makes too many demands on your personal and family time. Many organizations that give lip service to family values make it difficult for people to actually take advantage of family-friendly policies; those who leave work at 5:00, take maternity or paternity leave, or sometimes work from home fear that they'll be considered slackers or will be penalized for not being workaholics.

It's usually easy to modify a job to accommodate family needs, and a small change might make a large difference in how you feel about your job. More employers recognize that you're more than a set of technical skills, and they're flexible about when, and even where, their employees work.

Are your skills going to waste?   This is a common complaint with technical professionals. You like a challenge. You are motivated by doing difficult tasks well. Slogging along on work that doesn't stimulate your brain is demotivating and demoralizing. If you feel burned out because you're not using your highest skills, it's time to ask for a change.

It's generally not necessary to change jobs to get a sense of achievement back into your work. You may have a problem or idea that you've wanted to work on, and that your manager will let you spend part of your time tackling. Your manager may have a challenging assignment that would take you out of the monotony zone for part of each day or week. You may find that developing and using a new, nontechnical skill gives your work a new significance and challenge.

Do you feel like you're just picking up whatever they throw over the wall? It's not unusual for software engineers to feel like reactive order takers, a feeling that does not sit well with intelligent, self-motivated, and experienced people. The cure is having more frequent information about the big picture, and more interaction with clients, customers, and users. You won't feel powerless and passive when you understand your organization's overall strategic direction, the changing demands of the marketplace, and the particular pressures of the competition, and you have a say in setting the goals and making the decisions.

Some organizations pair developers up with their peers in other areas of the business, such as marketing and finance. They understand that software professionals will come up with better solutions when they know the broad context of their work and when their ideas are solicited early in the planning and implementation stages.

Do the cultural expectations of your organization leave you cold? Even if you find the work interesting and challenging, you may be uncomfortable with the culture of your department. Technical experts sometimes think they must put up with a bad fit because their value is perceived as primarily technical. You don't need to put up with an unfriendly, overly competitive, or discriminatory environment.

Customs and traditions often linger long after they serve any useful purpose and long after anyone remembers how they got started. If you are uncomfortable with the unwritten rules of behavior, chances are that others in your work group are turned off or offended, too. It's relatively easy to introduce changes that would create a better place to work — making new hires feel welcome, communicating face-to-face instead of by memo or e-mail, discouraging malicious gossip and doomsday speculation — just by doing it.

But most changes will need the consent and cooperation of your manager. If you want more responsibility, more training, more variety, more challenge, more flexibility, or a broader perspective of the value of your job, you will need to enlist your boss's support.

Waiting for your boss to recognize that you have management potential, realize that you're torn between the demands of your work and your new baby, or see that you're the obvious choice to champion the hot new project is not going to work. Complaining, hinting, and clamming up are also not going to work.

Once you have assessed what kind of change you want, make an appointment to talk with your manager. Let him or her know that you want to discuss your job, and that you would appreciate some uninterrupted private time for the discussion.

Take your needs and aspirations seriously, and expect to be given a serious hearing. Go in with a positive attitude, and be prepared to offer concrete and constructive suggestions for how to accomplish what you want. Rather than focusing on your needs, concentrate on how the manager and the organization will benefit from what you're proposing.

Ask your boss how your ideas strike him or her, and listen carefully to the answers. If the response is cursory or noncommittal, reiterate that this issue is important to you, and ask for more information. You may be surprised to find that your manager knows about opportunities you hadn't even considered, or that he or she is willing to go to bat against company-wide policies that get in the way of your job satisfaction.

Many software engineers and project leaders are unduly skeptical about having this kind of discussion with their managers. They may see their manager as the main obstacle to their job satisfaction. In fact, problems with the boss are a leading reason technical professionals leave their jobs.

Managers at any level of an organization do not necessarily see themselves as coaches, mentors, or facilitators of professional development, but they are under the gun to retain valuable players — and in some cases their compensation is tied to their rate of retention. Even if your boss is not adept at looking out for your interests, he or she is aware of the need to keep you on board.

Unless informal communication is excellent and frequent in your organization, it's best to assume that your manager does not know what is bugging you and what would make your job more rewarding. It's up to you to speak up, as well as take the initiative in making your job — and your career — what you want it to be.

4.2.6 "Painless Dismissals: Saying Goodbye"

by Jess Wells

Using these straightforward steps toward dismissing an employee will make this uncomfortable situation less awkward for everyone.

Despite all your efforts to choose just the right team member, you've found a problem employee whose work is substandard and whose bad attitude is infecting the rest of the crew. Dealing with this situation is as important as anything on the management roster. An improperly handled dismissal can destroy team morale and potentially make your company vulnerable to a retaliatory lawsuit. In the overwhelming majority of termination lawsuits, employees sued not because they thought the action was unlawful, but because they felt the methods used to discipline or discharge them were unfair.

In the U.S., an individual is employed "at will," which means the employer can fire the employee with simple notification for any reason. This is especially true when the company includes a basic statement to this effect in its hiring contracts. There is no law that protects poor performers, regardless of their race, sex, nationality, or disability.

With proper documentation and procedures, you can weed out poor performers with minimal risk of reprisal. On the other hand, no amount of gentle treatment at termination time can make up for a company culture that is rife with discrimination. The procedures for recruiting, hiring, promoting, and rewarding employees must be in step with anti-discrimination laws (obtainable through your local labor department office).

Assuming that your company policy and the enforcement of that policy is equitable and reasonable, the first step to take when firing someone is to alert the human resources department to the pending histrionics. If you don't have a human resources department, be sure to discuss your desire to fire the employee with your boss long before you actually let the ax fall. There's nothing like disciplining a troublesome employee that will start rumblings in a workgroup. Discussing your plans with your boss and with human resources will ensure the problem is identified as the employee's. Otherwise, you will look like a manager who is having trouble controlling your group. Make sure your boss and human resources both agree with your plans, and that they receive copies of your correspondence with the employee.

Document Your Displeasure

An important factor in an effective termination is documentation that shows your repeated attempts to receive reasonable performance of clearly stated tasks, and the employee's repeated failure to comply.

Employers often adopt a progressive, three-step discipline policy that includes the following:

- An oral counseling session that is also documented in writing
- A written warning
- Suspension or termination

When counseling the employee and giving a written warning, take the following steps:

- State the specific problem.
- Briefly review the background information.
- Outline actions the employee must take to correct the problem.
- Provide a deadline to correct the problem.
- Inform the employee of the consequences for failure to correct the problem.
- Provide an opportunity for the employee to comment.

You can't simply say, "I've told you about this hundreds of times." Instead, you must provide written memos outlining specific instances. Include the date the task was assigned, the date of delivery, and any evidence of poor performance. Attach copies of poorly constructed memos, improperly formulated specs, and incorrectly written code. In each instance, you must provide a measurable goal and a deadline that could have been met by a good performer. Make sure a copy of the memo goes to the employee, human resources, your boss, and your own files. Sometimes these memos can go a long way to solving your problem. Employees might not know that you are displeased with their work. They may not have understood the assignment or the standards of excellence you expect them to achieve. Evidence of shortcomings may be all they need to rise to the challenge.

In fact, performance evaluations should be an ongoing activity throughout the year, and they should involve at least two levels of management. Review by another level of management above your own is also recommended for disciplinary actions: it is important that your boss knows the challenges you face.

You must also impose these disciplinary measures consistently across the work force. If you don't treat similar cases in a like manner, employees may infer a personal discrimination.

Conduct a Security Assessment

If you don't see an immediate turnaround in the employee's performance, or if you begin to see a further deterioration in his or her attitude, conduct a security assessment to analyze your company's vulnerability. Does the employee have keys to rooms that hold delicate equipment? Is the employee a pivotal member of a product development team that is working on a tight deadline?

A disgruntled employee can do terrific damage. In some companies, developers have access to nearly every computer and can access company information anonymously. Work with human resources and your company's security team to derive ways to protect assets. It may be possible to create a new repository for the database or to quietly restrict the employee's access to certain areas. You may want to add another member to the development team who will assist the troublesome employee in completing the task on deadline.

On the other hand, it's very difficult to surreptitiously build a firewall around a problem employee. Often, your best bet is to change terminated employees' phone-in codes and passwords so they no longer have access to computers. At the same time, be discreet and appropriate in security use. Escorting an employee off the property, for example, can give the impression that he or she is guilty of a serious offense. Casting such a false light can land you in court for defamation.

Investigate the Decision

In the case of an egregious or potentially dangerous situation, immediately suspend the employee with pay, pending an investigation by human resources. Everyone wants to be treated fairly, so provide the employee with an opportunity to state his or her side of the case. Human resources may also want to gather information by interviewing other members of the team.

Evaluate Alternatives to Dismissal

You can take the following steps as an alternative to termination:

Leave of absence. This is especially effective if the employee is having personal problems. For example, California's Labor Code Section 1025 states that employers with 25 or more employees must reasonably accommodate an employee who wants to enter a drug or alcohol rehabilitation program.

Reassignment. Sometimes the classic Peter Principle gets in the way: an employee is advanced until he or she reaches a point of incompetence. Reassigning that person to a less difficult task may make all the difference you need. Sometimes reassigning an employee to another manager may provide the right chemistry for excellence. However, there is no reason to shuffle a nonperformer from workgroup to workgroup. This just has the potential to spread the headache throughout the company — so be careful.

A Guide to a Good Good-Bye

- Enforce written policies in a consistent, even-handed manner.
- Conduct reviews on a regular schedule and ensure honest, objective, and consistent appraisals.
- Adopt a two-tiered review of appraisals.
- Document disciplinary actions.
- Impose discipline in a consistent, nondiscriminatory manner.
- Permit review of personnel files by employees.
- Take prudent, respectful security precautions.
- Consider alternatives to termination.
- Gather all significant documents.
- Ensure due process.

- Review termination with several levels of management.
- Have a final paycheck prepared.
- Conduct a termination meeting.
- Explain benefits.
- Gather company property such as keys and equipment.
- Document the termination meeting.

Part-time status. This lets you continue to use the employee's skills, but removes the employee from a high-stress situation that he or she can't handle. It does not, however, free up space for you to bring in another employee.

Layoff. While poor performers should be the first to go in a layoff, be very careful about hiding the elimination of a bad apple through a layoff. The job function itself must be eliminated, putting you in a position where you cannot reasonably replace the poor performer without restructuring the job. Frequently it is just better to tell the truth about the firing.

Look on the Bright Side

Keep in mind that poor performers are glaringly obvious to everyone on the team, and there's little that's more demoralizing to hard workers than people who aren't pulling their weight. By cutting a poor performer loose, you may actually boost morale within your team — if you do it in a respectful, firm, and clear way. The message you send to your workgroup is that excellence is rewarded, slackers should look elsewhere, and you have the intestinal fortitude and sense of justice that it takes to handle the situation properly.

Remember that every problem is also an opportunity. If the troublesome employee is eliminated, what will your team look like? How will you best use their skill sets? Will this be an opportunity for an overall reshuffling of personnel or a streamlining of procedures? Rather than hiring another employee with the same skill set, does this open an opportunity to develop a team more in keeping with the company's new direction? Work with both your employees and with upper management on these ideas. It will be clear to your employees that you want to use them to their best advantage. It will be obvious to your boss that you have the overall company objectives in mind.

Retrieving Equipment

If an employee retains company equipment, write to that person and request immediate return of the materials. Don't withhold the employee's paycheck or deduct the cost of the equipment. Filing legal action against the employee for the recovery of the equipment can sometimes lead to retaliatory lawsuits.

Make It a Quick, Clean Good-Bye

The most important factor in the proper handling of a discharge is the actual meeting during which the termination takes place. Procedures that are construed to be publicly humiliating, abusive, or vague can result in additional problems.

As a manager, you may or may not want to do the firing yourself. Letting someone else do it may make it less stressful for you, but it also opens up the situation to their agenda, which may be to gather information on you as a manager from the employee. Consider whether you trust your human resources officers, or whether the employee is likely to become hostile, before making your decision to turn the dirty work over to someone else.

Even if you decide to do it yourself, make sure a member of the human resources staff is in agreement, and has provided you with the necessary paperwork. If you don't have a human resources department, find one of the books available on the marketplace that contain sample release letters and other documents. You also want to be sure that, if possible, your boss or a member of the human resources team is in the room during the termination meeting. You don't want the situation to become a my-word-against-his-or-hers battle without witnesses. Some additional points to keep in mind follow.

1. *Stay calm.* The meeting should be businesslike and brief. At the same time, its duration should reflect the employee's standing: two minutes with a 20-year employee seems terribly unfair.

2. *Have the final paycheck prepared and be sure it follows company severance policies and state law.* Be prepared to explain the contents or have the human resources representative explain it.

3. *Use a private, neutral place.* Try to use a hard-walled room and keep the door closed so other employees can't witness the conversation. It's best to choose neutral territory, since you may need to leave the room at the end of the meeting to let the employee regain his or her composure.

4. *Meet before lunch or at the end of the day so the employee can exit easily.*

5. *Be brief.* Give a reason for the termination but don't list the days and details of specific failings. These should have been discussed during disciplinary actions.

6. *Get to the point.* For example, you might say, "There's nothing more that either of us can do to make this work. I've decided to terminate your employment." (What you say will depend on the circumstances and your management style.)

7. *Don't encourage hopes that there might be a change of heart.*

8. *Don't justify or argue.* Remember that you've given up trying to remedy the situation, so lectures are not required.

9. *Don't suggest self-improvement.* What the employee does after termination is not your concern.

10. *Don't apologize.* Accept and acknowledge the employee's feelings by saying something like, "I know this is difficult for you, but my decision stands."

11. *Don't waste time talking to relieve your own anxiety.*

12. *Don't suggest that you don't agree with the decision.*

13. *Don't say anything that could be construed as hostility or discrimination.*

14. *Make arrangements for the return of company property, equipment, and keys.*

If your company has a non-compete or confidentiality agreement, show it to the employee and remind him or her of its importance. Provide information on the conversion of benefits, or mention that this information will be mailed.

There are several rules for a smooth dismissal. Be sure you have policies that are based on fairness. Make sure those policies are enforced fairly. Provide performance reviews frequently, and gather thorough documentation of poor performance. With these things in mind, dismissals can be a relatively painless part of improving your software development team.

Chapter 5

Operations and Support

5.1 Best Practices for the Operations and Support Workflow

As the name suggests, the purpose of the Operations and Support workflow is to perform the activities required to successfully operate and support your software. During the Transition phase you will continue to develop operations and support plans, documents, and training manuals, reworking them based on the results of testing. During the Production phase your operations staff will keep your software running, performing necessary backups and batch jobs as needed, and your support staff will interact with your user community whom are working with your software. Without effective operations and support processes your software will quickly become shelfware — it isn't enough to simply build software effectively, you also have to run it effectively.

5.1.1 Operations

Once your system is delivered, it goes into production and is run by your operations staff. The reality for most organizations is that they have several systems running in production, and large organizations have hundreds and sometimes thousands. This fact was a major motivator for the Operations and Support Workflow — operations is a difficult and complex endeavor, something that Scott W. Ambler points out in "The Secret Life of Software

Operations." This article begins with a description of what your operations staff typically do, including:

1. *Operate the systems within your organization.* This includes scheduling software jobs to run at various times of day and creating, testing, deploying, and scheduling scripts and programs to perform critical tasks.

2. *Real-time performance monitoring of systems.* The goal of this effort is to detect production problems before they occur.

3. *Installation of new or updated systems into production.* For more details, read Chapter 2, which describes the Deployment workflow.

4. *Technical infrastructure management.* Your operations department will by actively involved in the evaluation, acceptance, and purchase negotiation of technical infrastructure components including hardware and software. It also includes physical environment management, such as power management, network management, physical security, disaster recovery, and air conditioning are typically the purview of operations. Management of documents — including network architecture diagrams, system operations guides, and job documentation — is an also important part of these efforts.

5. *Log management.*

6. *Deployment quality gate.* Your operations staff is responsible for ensuring that your system will deploy successfully into production without adversely affecting existing systems.

5.1.2 Support

You've delivered your application to your user community and now you're finished, right? Wrong! From the point of view of your users things have just started. Now they expect that someone will support the application that you just delivered. That someone may even be you. The objective of application support is to respond to incoming requests from users, to identify a resolution for the request, and then to oversee the implementation of that resolution. Application support is critical to the success of your application — although developers put an application into production, your support engineers keep it there. In "Ignore Help Requests at Your Own Peril" Scott W. Ambler describes best practices for effective support. He describes practices for respond to the support request, determining a resolution, and resolve the issue. He also describes how to organize the support process within your organization, overviewing the two main support-flow models: the frontline/backline model and the touch-and-hold model. He also describes what to look for in support tools, and finishes with advice for effective support, such as:

- Projecting the image that every support request is critical to the requester
- Recognizing that support engineers are the sales team for your application
- Recognizing that your objective is to support your user community
- Recognizing that the support request is not resolved until the requester is satisfied

Constance Fabian-Isaacs and P.J. Raymond provide advice for developing effective help facilities in "How Helpful is Your Help?" Help information is your first line of defense, one that can dramatically reduce the need for support within your organization when developed effectively. Why is online help, or even printed help documentation, important? Good help assists your users while they learn your software, guiding them through a process, helping them to perform a task, and improving their understanding of what your system does. The reality is that no matter how intuitive an application might be, no matter how good the user interface, most users will feel insecure if there is no help. Furthermore users are quickly frustrated with systems that provide poorly written, incomplete, or badly organized help — in other words, the authors imply that you cannot do a slipshod job. The authors describe best practices for developing help facilities. First, you must recognize that people typically use help to quickly answer a specific question, often along the lines of "How can I get this to do what I need it to do — today?" They suggest that you begin with your users, understanding who is going to be using your program and what they will be doing with it. This sort of information is typically conveyed by your use case model. When designing effective help, the authors believe that nothing is more revealing than an effective usability study, and when you do one, you will often discover common complaints (that should be addressed) such as:

- Difficult navigation — users can't find what they're looking for
- Overuse of fonts, colors, paragraph styles, and pointless graphics — developers made the help facility pretty instead of useful
- Poorly written
- Poor understanding of the audience — it was either too technical or not technical enough
- Incomplete instructions — the help wasn't helpful

Another important aspect of system support efforts is having an effective help desk within your organization. A help desk is a combination of call management and problem resolution. It keeps track of who is calling, why, and, most importantly, how the calls are resolved. Jessica Keyes in "Getting Real Help from a Help Desk" describes some of the fundamentals of doing so. Although the article is somewhat old, it covers the basics. But you'll need to read between the lines a bit. First, Keyes argues that you need to gather a team to make the build-or-buy decision, typical software purchasing best practices apply regardless of the type of software you are buying. Second, she points out that even if you buy a help/support desk solution, the knowledge base will be delivered as a blank slate; there is no free ride or magic silver bullet for support. Your help desk will have the mechanism for handling knowledge, but it will be your staff's task — be they a developer or a support engineer — to load the knowledge base with the information that will ultimately solve user problems. When loading the knowledge base of a help desk, it's important to keep in mind exactly how your users interact with their software because the difference between how "typical" users operate their systems and how programmers or power users do can be surprising. In other words, you may need to invest the time to observe how your users work with your system if you want to develop effective help, something that you can do during user testing (see Chapter 3). Finally, Keyes suggests that your project team make an effort to incorporate the automated help desk into your application, making it easy for your users to access.

Jacques Surveyer takes a look at look at support from the point of view of users in "Developer Angst: Product Support." He provides an interesting take on software support because he examines it in a way that developers can readily understand: product support for software development tools. He begins with the installation process, often where you need the most support, pointing out that a bad experience will quickly change software into "underused-ware" or "dead-on-the-shelf-ware." He summarizes product support strategies taken by software vendors, strategies that you may want to emulate, including online support forums; web-based public knowledge bases; ftp sites stocked with patches, samples, and templates; and trial software that you can download. Surveyer correctly observes that a critical factor in technical support is the skill level of the technical support staff, underlining the importance of documentation as well as training and education for your support staff (a topic described in detail in Chapter 2). Surveyor believes that product support efforts should address the critical needs of users, including:

- Reducing incidents of support with more robust, reliable program releases
- Reducing need for support through better documentation and training
- Reducing problem duration with better online support
- Determining the state of the system and nature of problem quickly and efficiently
- Remotely debugging tough problems
- Including self-help through computer telephony and online support programs

5.2 The Articles

5.2.1 "The Secret Life of System Operations"

by Scott W. Ambler

It's no good putting software into production if you can't keep it there.

What happens to software once you've delivered it? It goes into production and is run by your operations staff. Most organizations have several systems running in production — in fact, large organizations often have hundreds, sometimes thousands. Managing all of these systems is a complex task, one that is the purview of the Operations and Support workflow of the Enterprise Unified Process (EUP). This month, I'll explore the role of system operations within your organization, examining what your operations professionals do, what their focus is, and how they fit into your overall software development efforts.

Figure 5.1 presents the enhanced life cycle for the EUP, first presented in *Software Development's* October 1999 issue, and explored in detail in CMP Books' *Unified Process* series edited by Larry Constantine and myself. As you can see, the major efforts for the workflow begin in the Construction phase, when you'll start working on any system documentation required for operations (see "Place Tab A in Slot B," *Thinking Objectively,* June 2001, in Chapter 2 of this book). Naturally, the majority of the Operations and Support workflow effort occurs in the Production phase, after your system has been made available to your users.

Figure 5.1   The Enhanced Life Cycle for the Enterprise Unified Process

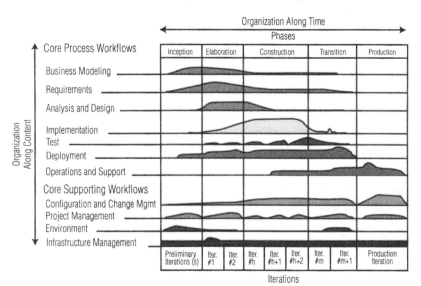

Your Operations Department

What does your operations department do? A heck of a lot of stuff, once you start looking into it; most important of which is keeping your organization's systems working, ideally 24 hours a day, seven days a week. This includes scheduling software jobs to run at various times of day, a task that has gotten much harder in the past few years as organizations become more global — you can't run a nightly batch job when there isn't any night. Operations staff will often act as developers: creating, testing, deploying and scheduling scripts and programs to perform critical tasks such as system backups.

Operations staff will also perform real-time performance monitoring of systems as they're running to try to detect glitches before they occur, including performance problems that can occur when servers or portions of your network become overloaded, or security breaches, such as attempted attacks by hackers.

Once a problem is detected, your operations staff will react accordingly. First, they must determine what the problem actually is by tracing jobs; doing dumps of memory, logs or databases; recording and analyzing actions taken by users; and analyzing communication activities. To do this, your operations staff will usually employ tools such as Computer Associates' Unicenter TNG (www.ca.com) and IBM's Tivoli (www.tivoli.com). Sometimes the operations staff can resolve the problem immediately; at other times, the problem can be traced to a specific system or department and therefore can be better addressed by another team. Occasionally, the problem must be documented and submitted to your configuration and change management process.

Installation and Deployment

The successful installation of new or updated systems into production is one of your operations department's critical responsibilities. They will often be actively involved in your project team's deployment efforts (see "Effective Software Deployment," *Thinking Objectively,* Nov. 1999, and Chapter 2 of this book), and will often be responsible for managing the deployment process. This will include the distribution and installation of hardware and software, both initial program loads (IPLs) and installation of any fixes or patches to existing software.

To successfully install new items into production, your operations department must understand the existing technical infrastructure, and deal with activities such as software, hardware and network inventory management. Your operations department will be actively involved in the evaluation, acceptance and purchase negotiation of technical infrastructure components.

Physical environment management, including but not limited to power and network issues, physical security, disaster recovery and air conditioning, is typically the purview of operations. Document management — including network architecture diagrams, system operations guides and job documentation — is an important part of these efforts. Accurate documentation and models are critical to the success of your operations efforts because they enable your staff to perform an impact analysis of proposed changes to your production environment. Without a solid understanding of what's currently in production, you can't possibly determine the potential risks of changes, nor can you address problems effectively once they occur. For discussions of effective modeling and documentation techniques, you should visit the Agile Modeling homepage (www.agilemodeling.com).

Log management is also an important part of system operations. Various types of logs — such as job logs, history/ transaction logs, database logs, problem logs, message logs and system audit logs — are produced by various aspects of your technical infrastructure. The logs are used by operations staff for problem resolution and general system monitoring, and therefore must be managed appropriately.

Smooth Operation

What's important to your operations staff? Their primary concern is to guarantee the smooth operation of your organization's technical environment within defined service levels. This includes security issues: the physical security of your organization's computing infrastructure, as well as electronic security. Operations staff must be able to recover your system from problems, as well as troubleshoot to determine the cause of errors. The configuration capabilities and deployment strategy for your system will also be of concern to operations staff, particu-. larly during your project's transition phase.

Operations Quality Gate

Most operations groups will have a set of defined criteria that your system must pass before it's deployed into production. This is often called the operations quality gate, and the effort to verify your system in this manner is referred to as operations testing. Operations testing will verify that a system will work in your production environment without adverse effects on other systems. In other words, you want to prove that your system plays well with others. From the point of view of the Unified Process, operations testing typically occurs in the Transition phase of your project, although it can also take place in the Construction and even

Elaboration phases. For example, if your organization uses new technologies, such as Web services or Enterprise JavaBeans, as part of your architectural prototyping efforts in the Elaboration phase, you may want to run your prototype through operations testing to ensure that it will work in your actual environment.

First, identify the criteria against which your software will be tested. Operations staff are critical project stakeholders in your project — people who should be involved with it from the very beginning. They should be able to define critical constraints for your system — constraints that you need to know about when you're first building your system. Furthermore, you may discover that you need to negotiate changes to your production environment, such as introducing new technologies or upgrades to existing facilities, to support your system. These alterations often need to be started sooner rather than later.

Never Underestimate Operations

System operations is a complex activity that's critical to the success of your IT organization. It's no good putting software into production if you can't keep it there, and your operations staff are the people who do just that. Little has been written about software operations, as you can see by the dearth of resources listed in the sidebar, and I think that's a shame. To deploy your system successfully and keep it running in top form, you need to look at the whole information technology picture: System operations may play a supporting role, but it's a crucial one.

Suggested Resources for Software Operations

- Information Technology Infrastructure Library, `www.itil.co.uk`
- Information Technology Service Management Forum, `www.itsmf.com`
- *The Unified Process Transition and Production Phases.* Edited by Scott W. Ambler and Larry Constantine (CMP Books, Fall 2001), `www.ambysoft.com/transition ProductionPhase.html`
- The Enterprise Unified Process, `www.ronin-intl.com/publications/ unifiedProcess.htm`
- *More Process Patterns.* Scott W. Ambler (Cambridge University Press, 1999), `www.ambysoft.com/moreProcessPatterns.html`

5.2.2 "Ignore Help Requests at Your Own Peril"

by Scott W. Ambler

After development ends, your support staff and process are key to application success.

You've delivered your application to your user community and now you're finished, right? Wrong! From your users' point of view, things have just started: Now they expect that someone will support the application you just delivered — and that someone may even be you.

The objective of application support is to respond to incoming requests from users, to identify a resolution for the request, and to oversee the implementation of that resolution.

Although developers put an application into production, support engineers keep it there, making your support staff and process key to your application's ultimate success. By helping your users solve problems, the support staff directly influences your users' productivity — and a productive user base is any organization's greatest asset.

The Support Process Pattern

The input to the support process is a support request from someone whom I call a requester. A support request may be in the form of a phone call, an e-mail message, a fax or an entry into a support request database (likely via a Web page). Furthermore, there are several types of support requests: Users may ask questions ranging from how to use your application to how to obtain training for that application; someone may submit a change request, which describes either a new application feature or a potential defect; a user may also request an environment change, such as a hardware upgrade or operating system upgrade; or the request could indicate that a software license has expired.

Support Task #1: Respond

Three main tasks comprise the support process. First, respond to the support request by communicating with the person making it. Your support engineers should immediately acknowledge each support request upon receipt, so the requester will know that the request is being looked at and by whom, and be given either a solution on the spot or an estimate of when to expect one. Never forget that your users will judge your application based on the speed and accuracy of your support personnel's responses. The best support engineers respond promptly and politely, convincing the requester that this problem is the most important issue they have to deal with.

Support Task #2: Determine a Solution

There are four primary resolution strategies: provide information, identify training for the requester, describe hardware and/or software upgrades, and create a software change request (SCR) that potentially leads to a change in your application. To select an effective combination of these four strategies, the support engineer first works with the requester to gather information and determine the request priority; then simulates the problem if necessary, and perhaps escalates or refers the problem to someone with greater authority if required.

Often overlooked when deploying an application, a problem reproduction environment (a copy of your application that simulates user problems) is an essential support tool. Support engineers will often have the requester walk them through a problem while they simulate it on their own computer. By simulating a potential problem, the support engineer gains a better understanding of what the requester is describing. In this way, the engineer can determine if there is a problem with the application or with the requester's hardware or software configuration, or if the requester needs further training to use the application effectively.

Occasionally, a support engineer will encounter support requests that he either doesn't know how to resolve or doesn't have the authority to resolve. When this occurs, the support engineer will confer with a more experienced support colleague, potentially his manager, and perhaps a few developers to determine a resolution. When a support request is escalated, the support engineer should remain involved to expand his knowledge of the application and to avoid a support request escalation when a similar issue pops up.

Support Task #3: Resolve the Problem

Your support engineers need to understand a wide range of issues pertaining to your application and your corporate environment. They must be able to assign requesters to training courses and therefore will need access to your organization's human resource systems that perform this function; they need the ability to request upgrades to the hardware and/or software configurations of requesters; and they need access to your organization's change control system to input new features or eradicate bugs.

The output of the support process is a solution provided to the requester. Furthermore, a software change request (SCR) can be created so that new requirements and bug fixes may be implemented in future versions.

Make Your Customers Happy: Distribute a Support User's Guide

And remember, he who proofs his own copy has a fool for an editor.

One way to improve your support services is to create and distribute a Support User's Guide detailing your application's support process from your users' point of view. This document will describe:

- The services provided and hours of availability
- How to obtain support
- Who is authorized to obtain support, and how often
- The turnaround time by priority
- How requests are resolved
- Tips for obtaining the best service, including basic troubleshooting steps, a list of information to have handy when you contact support, and the best times to call

Deploy your support user's guide as part of your overall application package. Many organizations choose to include this information as part of the application itself, either as an information screen built into the application or as a Web page on their internal network.

Defining Your Support Environment

How do you organize the support process within your organization? First, you need to choose a support-flow model, also known as a call-flow model. This is the process through which support engineers receive requests, find solutions and return answers to the requester. There are two basic strategies to choose from: the front-line/back-line model and the touch-and-hold model.

With the front-line/back-line model, often called the tiered model, support staff are organized into two groups: a large group of less-experienced support engineers who take incoming support requests and try to resolve them within a short period of time, and a small group of experienced support staff who handle the difficult requests fielded to them by the front-line staff. This model utilizes experienced staff efficiently, provides a handy way to train new staff, offers a career path for support engineers and supplies users with a predictable model. Its main disadvantage is that more than one person may deal with the support request, potentially decreasing the quality of the service provided to the requester.

The touch-and-hold model promotes a more individual approach — the support engineer who responds to the initial support request handles it directly, though occasionally requiring collaboration with experts for a given issue. The success of this model depends on getting the right support request to the right support engineer, perhaps through an automated phone menu. The advantages are clear: Fewer handoffs reduce the occurrence of repetitive requests; support engineers have greater opportunities to increase their skillsets; and throughput is higher due to fewer handoffs between support engineers. However, this model has several drawbacks: Support engineers must command a reasonably high level of technical expertise; your organization must have access to a large pool of good support engineers; and service can be uneven because of support personnel's varying levels of expertise.

Choosing a Support Toolset

Set up a full-featured support environment before or during the transition phase of your project.

Alone or in concert, these seven tools will make life easier:

- An automatic call-distribution system (a phone system that distributes calls to support engineers in an efficient manner by requiring requesters to work through a menu of options)
- A customer tracking system, containing basic information about the people submitting support requests, which maintains a support history for each requester
- A defect tracking system that details known trouble spots and potential workarounds, with their current status
- A fax-back system that allows requesters to call in and request information to be faxed back to them
- A knowledge-base system that lists solutions to previously resolved problems
- A support-request tracking system that records information about support requests
- A Web site to provide users with access to your knowledge base so they can attempt to resolve their own issues, as well as access to your support request tracking system so they can submit a support request electronically

---

Secrets of Support Success

If you take the following tips and techniques to heart, you'll increase your chances of success at supporting your system once it's in production:

1. *Every support request is critical to the requester.* The most successful support engineers are those who recognize that from the requester's point of view, the only thing that the support engineer should be concentrating on is resolving their problem.

2. *Support engineers are the sales team for your application.* When your support engineers project a positive image of your application — they teach users "neat tricks" to use it

more effectively and do their best to resolve requests efficiently — your users will be satisfied with your application. On the other hand, if your support engineers have a bleak attitude or bad-mouth the application, your user community will quickly become disenchanted with it and with your support staff.

3. *Your objective is to support your user community.* The main objective of every information technology department should be to support their user community. Support should be your IT department's first priority — not the last.

4. *The support request is not resolved until the requester is satisfied.* This is a basic customer service issue, based on the precept that truncated service transactions result in unnecessary grief and frustration for the requester. To close a support request, you must first ask the person who made it whether he feels that the resolution met his needs.

Not only do you need to develop and then deliver your application to your user community, you also need to keep it running once it's in production. Your organization's approach to system support is an important part of your overall production processes, one that is ignored at your own peril. Successful software developers take support issues into account when they're building systems, and ideally, they work with support staff to ensure that their needs are met. Effective support engineers enable effective users, and effective users are what defines the success of your system. I prefer to work on successful applications, don't you?

References and Recommended Reading

More Process Patterns–Delivering Large-Scale Systems Using Object Technology. Ambler, S. W. (Cambridge University Press, 1998).

Realizing the Object-Oriented Life Cycle. Baudoin, C. and Hollowell, G. (Prentice Hall PTR, 1996).

Practical Software Maintenance: Best Practices for Managing Your Software Investment. Pigoski, T. M. (John Wiley and Sons, Inc., 1997).

The Art of Software Support: Design and Operation of Support Centers and Help Desks. Tourniaire, F. and Farrell, R. (Prentice Hall PTR, 1997).

5.2.3 "How Helpful is Your Help?"

by Constance Fabian-Isaacs and P.J. Raymond

An online help system that provides clear, easy-to-find answers that users need is key to your applications' success.

Why do software developers immediately start looking for the garlic and a cross when someone mentions online help? It's probably because they hope they have created a software product so intuitive that online help isn't necessary. However, no matter how intuitive an application might be, most users will feel insecure if there is no help. In addition, they are quickly frustrated with a product that provides poorly written, incomplete, and badly organized assistance. Even products with sophisticated functionality and elevated potential have been abandoned or replaced because users simply couldn't figure them out.

Most computer users prefer the "try it for themselves" method of software training. When they can't figure something out, they turn to the online help for a quick answer to their immediate questions. If the online help answers their questions, you can be sure they'll continue to use the software and its successive upgrades. Conversely, if the help doesn't measure up, they'll think twice before they use the software again. In corporate software, user adoption of your application is the key to your success.

You're a user. You know what you like and what you don't. For one thing, you don't go to a program's online help for intellectual stimulation. Nor are you interested in solving the great mystery of online navigation. What you want is what any user wants: a quick answer to, "How can I get this to do what I need it to do — today?'

How can you be sure you've provided the best online assistance possible for your software product? There are a number of ways. First, you could hire a consultant who specializes in online documentation to evaluate your system and make recommendations. Next, you could try usability testing with a variety of users outside of your company or with peers who are not involved in the programming. Last, you could run your own evaluation of the help system following the guidelines found in this article. Sound familiar? It's when you start thinking of your online help system as an application within an application that you know you're on the right track; it requires equal attention.

Begin with Your Users

Who is going to be using your program and what will they be doing with it? Such simple questions, yet the answers can have an extreme impact on the acceptance of your software and help system. If your audience will be comprised of entry-level personnel, you wouldn't want to confuse them with volumes of technical instructions.

How do you know your audience is made up of entry-level personnel? First, do your homework. Not that you must know each of your users on a first name basis, although in a small corporation you might already, but you must take the time to identify some common elements your users share. How experienced with computers are your users? Have they used previous versions of your software? Are they experts in the process? If the program supports composition analysis of elements in a metal, and your audience is comprised of metallurgists, the tone of your help is going to be very different than if your users are receiving clerks accepting shipments of special metals.

You don't necessarily need a stalking campaign to find out about your users. Some information might have been gathered in earlier stages of development. You can write a questionnaire, observe users in their native habitat, or your online help consultant can perform a professional audience analysis. If you're going to prepare the audience analysis yourself, however, grab your garlic and cross and keep these points in mind:

- What are the personal characteristics of the users (for example: age range, gender, educational level and average work experience)?
- What function within the organization do the users perform?
- What are the goals of the users or purpose of the tasks they are performing?
- What is the computer skill level of the users?

- What is the task-related skill level?
- Are the users process experts?
- How is the software used to accomplish tasks?

This is not an exhaustive list. For more information on user analysis, check out *Designing Windows 95 Help* by Mary Deaton and Cheryl Lockett Zubak (Que Corp., 1996).

Hire a Consultant

Even if you take the easy way out by hiring an experienced consultant to do audience analysis and evaluate your help system, you must not abdicate your responsibility. Before you hire someone, be familiar with what a quality help system looks like and what it does. In other words, keep reading this article, and pay particular attention to the Who to Call for Help and Evaluation Tips sidebars on this page. Then you'll know who to call and what you're paying them to do so you can set some parameters for them.

Who to Call for Help

You've decided your application deserves a quality help system, but you don't have enough time to do it yourself. Who should you call?

There are individual writers, consultants, and companies that specialize in technical documentation, but online delivery is a specialized field within the technical writing industry. An online specialist can build an entire online help system, design and develop the paper manuals, and perform every task from user studies to final publication. How do you find these wizards of the word? The password is "online."

- The Internet is a good place to start. Many online documentation specialists have home pages. Don't rely on this completely, however, as just as many specialists do not. Do a search for WinHelp, online documentation, help, and so forth.
- Contact WinWriters, publishers of the WinHelp Journal. Many consultants advertise there.
- Help authoring software companies maintain lists of consultants and writers who are certified in the use of their products.
- The Society for Technical Communicators (STC) can make recommendations from within its membership.
- Local writer's organizations often have referral lists.

Usability Testing

Usability testing is expensive. If you've done any testing on other portions of your software, you know that already. This doesn't mean that you shouldn't do it. You should. Nothing is more revealing than an effective usability study, whether your user sampling is taken from the public at large or from individuals within your organization who have not worked on the program.

Suspend disbelief for a moment, and imagine you're developing a program for the accounting department. With a limited budget, you can do a "snapshot" study to find out what your users might need. Start by selecting one senior member and one novice from the available group. Find 30 minutes to interview each of them at the beginning of the project. You want to know who they are within the organization. What is their general education level? What tasks will they accomplish with your software? What kind of help do they think they'll need? How will your software fit into the present task structure? What help will they need to integrate the new software into that structure?

Once you've developed a working prototype, ask your subjects to test drive the new program. Your help developer can stand quietly by and watch the users struggle with the prototype. Resist the overwhelming temptation to show them how to run the program. Take lots of notes. What is in the prototype that keeps your users looking for assistance? Are there specific places where users are distracted from completing the task? Do you need to add a step-by-step procedure to talk users through a complicated action? Although it will not take the place of a detailed usability study, this less expensive snapshot study can offer valuable clues as to what direction your help should point.

Whether you do usability testing, hire a consultant, or both, you still need to know the requirements of a quality help system. You need to know what you can expect from your help system and what you cannot. When you're armed with that information, you can save your garlic to ward off the real monsters.

Evaluation Tips

Put these questions to your online help:

- *Is it easy to read?* If it takes a master's degree to understand your help, you must rewrite and simplify it. Even if your users are degreed, they prefer to get their information in a quick and easy way.
- *Is it complete?* This is a tricky question. You need to be aware of your users' abilities before you know if you've put enough in your help.
- *Make sure there are no steps missing from your procedures.* Follow each step just as it is written. If you accomplish the task without requiring further information, it's good. If not, make sure the help answers the following basic questions: What is this? What does it do? How do I do it? What do I do next?
- *Does the help file contain any useless graphics or unnecessary information?* Everything in your help file should be pertinent to the application.
- *Does it pass the three-click test?* Online navigation is a help developer's biggest challenge. The way online help is accessed can make navigation appear unimportant. However, studies have shown that users will give the help three clicks before they give up.

What Is Good Online Help?

Before you go to the project manager and suggest hiring a consultant or performing a usability test, it's important to understand the requirements for a quality help system. Good online help assists your users while they learn your software. It can guide them through a process, help them perform a task, and aid them in understanding what your program does. Online help makes it possible for them to employ your software to complete their tasks. It does all this with as little user effort as possible.

Even the best help system can't spin straw into platinum, nor can it make a poorly designed system function better. A thoroughly researched and well-planned help system works hand-in-hand with an application to produce a product that will have your marketing department — or your clients and users — dancing in the aisles. To gain an understanding of good online help, pay attention to high-quality help systems you see in other applications and development tools.

For an excellent commercial product example, take a look at Quicken, a financial software package developed by Intuit. A corporate package with an excellent help system (and a growing commercial niche in oil well treatment) is CADE Office developed by Schlumberger Dowell.

Bad Press

To date, there has been a lot of bad press in the area of online help. This is because help files that are less than helpful exist. In fact, we work with help all the time, and we have opened some online help that has been so poorly constructed that we gave up trying to use the application. Is it any wonder there are some reluctant users out there?

The advent of sophisticated authoring software made it even easier to bypass some basic planning where online help is concerned — especially the authoring products that start with a document. Trying to single-source manuals and online help is asking for trouble, as the two are written differently. Where manuals tend to be read in a linear, logical way, online help is randomly accessed. With that said, here are some of the complaints reported by users:

- Difficult navigation: they just can't find what they're looking for
- Overuse of fonts, colors, paragraph styles, and pointless graphics, like those shown in Figure 5.2
- Poorly written: so filled with jargon that a dictionary of the latest buzz words is required
- Either too technical or not technical enough
- Incomplete instructions

These are very generalized complaints of online help. To avoid many of them, talk to your users. In the writing field, it's called "know your audience." Knowing your users as readers and information assimilators is quite different from knowing them as people who work with your software. It's like knowing friends on the soccer field vs. knowing them in a classroom. The more you know about how your users process information, the better you can provide the information they need.

Discussions with the users should provide some clues about how they typically learn the software. Do they prefer tutorials or "how to" procedures? Do they want the background and theoretical basis explained in detail, or do they just want to get on with the task? If they have used other kinds of similar software, what are their complaints about the help style and tone? Be prepared for some diverse opinions within your user group.

Figure 5.2   Overuse of Fonts, Colors, Paragraph Styles, and Graphics

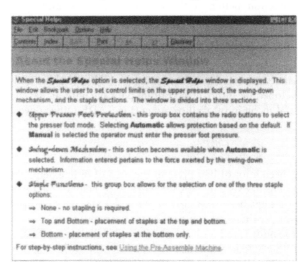

The Good, the Bad, and the Confusing

How you deliver your online information requires as much forethought as how you deliver your program. There are several elements to consider while planning your help, including design, content, navigation, and meeting user needs.

Design.   A high-quality information delivery system should start with a specification just like your application. The plan should state what the help will and will not include, how it looks, and what it should say.

Content.   First and foremost, the content of your help system depends on your use analysis. In the absence of good audience analysis, there is a tendency to include everything — in effect, burying the user under lines of unnecessary information. There is also a tendency to go down the middle of the road, in effect, missing the users on either side by only writing for the typical user. Often, information is missed that your less-experienced users need. In addition, more complex techniques, features, and procedures are not included — thereby missing your advanced users. Unfortunately, there is no best level to shoot for in providing help. The level of explanation and content complexity is determined exclusively by your user analysis. Regardless of the level of help you're providing, there are some common elements shared by every well-designed help system: the writing and the overall style.

Further Reading

Managing Your Document Projects. JoAnn T. Hackos (John Wiley and Sons Inc., 1994) ISBN 0-471-59099-1

Designing and Writing Online Documentation, Second Edition. William K. Horton (John Wiley and Sons, 1995) ISBN 0-471-11921-0

How to Communicate Technical Information: A Handbook of Software and Hardware Documentation. Jonathan Price and Henry Korman (Benjamin/Cummings, 1993) ISBN 0-8053-6829-9

Developing Online Help for Windows 95. Scott Boggan, David Farkas, and Joe Welinske (International Thomson Computer Press, 1996) ISBN 1-8503-2211-2

Designing Windows 95 Help. Mary Deaton and Cheryl Lockett Zubak (Que Corp., 1996) ISBN 0-7897-0362-9

Standards for Online Communication. JoAnn T. Hackos and Dawn M. Stevens (John Wiley and Sons, 1997) ISBN 0-471-15695-7

WinWriters. (WinHelp Journal, 3415 Soundview Dr. W., Seattle, WA 98199)

The writing must be clear and concise, and the text must be grammatically correct. Keep the tone conversational, regardless of the user's intellectual level. Again, users don't go to the online help to be intellectually challenged, they go there to solve a problem. Jargon should be avoided as if it were a poisonous snake. This might mean defining specific terms in your plan. While "data" may be a suitable term in your mind, in the minds of others it can mean the friendly android on "Star Trek: The Next Generation."

Style is as varied as the words chosen and writing techniques employed. It includes color and font selections, help window designs, the look of a bulleted list, how step-by-step procedures will read, the use of abbreviations, and other visual packaging. These decisions must be made at the start of the help project. Define project standards, add them to your help system specifications, and make sure every member of the development team is familiar with it. Beyond this, the focus of your help system should be determined by your users.

Navigation.   Navigation is the process of finding information within the help system. The information is only useful if the user can find it at a critical moment. As an industry standard, users should be able to reach an answer within three mouse clicks, as shown in . If they can't, they're likely to give up.

Consistent navigation requires planning. Again, your user profile is going to be the key in determining how your users look for help. Keep the navigation design simple. Never strand your users. Provide a link back to a familiar site, such as the contents page, thereby always leaving users in command of the situation.

Above all, be consistent throughout your product and, if possible, your entire product line. Once you get people used to finding information in a certain way, don't baffle them by changing their path. If you have multiple writers working on the help, make sure they are in sync and that they follow established guidelines.

Figure 5.3   Users Should Find Their Answers in Three Mouse Clicks

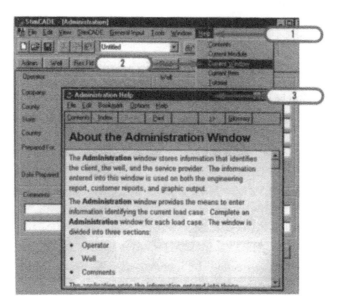

Meeting User Needs.   The application, the help system, and the paper manual's sole purpose is meeting the needs of users. In terms of providing good help, the only way to ensure you're meeting their needs is to directly expose your online help writers to your users. Without direct exposure to an audience, the comedian never knows if the joke will get a laugh or a hiss. Without direct exposure to the audience, the help writer will never be able to design a system that meets the needs of users.

Evaluation Strategy

Chances are good that you won't have the resources available to do everything you want to do with your help system in the first version. The application is usually a living entity that goes on to other versions, and so is the help system. Narrowing the scope of your help will maintain quality. Plan and budget for enhancing the help as you go so it can evolve with the application. You wouldn't put an antique motor in a race car; why would you want to create a help system and then make it obsolete by not planning for enhancements and improvements?

   To evaluate your help, ask yourself: What are the users looking for? What are they having trouble with? Has the audience profile changed? Your answers will help you plan a smooth evolution process. Developing audience profiles and determining what users need is not an all-or-nothing proposition. Again, strategy and planning are required. Review the first phase of the help system shortly after its completion. Were the basic specification objectives met? Reevaluate the help system after the application has been in use for a while. Gather user feedback. Conduct a user satisfaction survey. Review complaints or compliments received by the customer service or technical service departments. Part of your strategy and planning should allow for conducting evaluation studies.

When It's Soup

A well-developed help system will complement your application, reduce user frustration, and improve productivity. Targeting the help based on an understanding of user needs increases the chance that they'll get the correct answer the first time. You know what good help is; save the garlic for the soup pot.

5.2.4 "Getting Real Help from a Help Desk"

by Jessica Keyes

A help desk solution can be great support for your client/server application — if you understand how to develop its knowledge base.

Some people call the help desk the "killer app" of the 1990s. A Nolan Norton & Co. study, performed late in 1994, found the cost of not having a help desk is between $6,000 and $15,000, per year, per PC. This is the cost of lost productivity as users turn to each other for help, experience downtime, or incorrectly perform computer tasks. When a help desk is accurately and quickly handling all of a company's support calls, the entire work force is more productive. This boosts profitability and promotes employee satisfaction.

But what does the help desk mean for you as a developer of client/server applications? Your company's help desk solution — be it off-the-shelf or home-grown — will influence the way users learn and use your client/server application. Understanding how a help desk works, and how to integrate it with your system, is critical to your application's success.

What Is a Help Desk?

A help desk is a combination of call management and problem resolution. It keeps track of who is calling, why, and, most important, how the calls are resolved. Contact management software, no matter how sophisticated, only performs half of that job. It's the intelligent information on how to solve system problems that is the heart of the help desk. The knowledge base, rather than the help desk analyst, must act as the expert. Today's entry of a rule for that nasty driver problem the accounting department is having may just solve next week's emergency for the person from marketing. As a new help desk knowledge base is used, more and more information is stored there.

To Build or Buy

If your organization doesn't have a help desk, you can champion the idea to better support your client/server application. Since the implementation of a help desk takes a real commitment from management, the first step is to develop a strong case for its introduction. The best way to approach this is to secure one or more champion users. Next, gather a team to make the build or buy decision. Include user representatives, information technology professionals, managers, and at least one person who is savvy in artificial intelligence.

Given the proliferation of help desk software on the market — the Gartner Group forecasts that this market will grow from today's $160 million to $500 million in 1997 — it is well worth your time to weigh the pros and cons of buying an off-the-shelf solution or growing your own.

Essentially, making the build or buy decision requires consideration of the same variables in each case. If you buy the solution, you want to make sure certain features are present. If you build the solution, you want to make sure your development staff has the capability of engineering these same features.

The majority of organizations restricted by time and resources will opt to buy a help desk solution. If you decide to do this, you will be confronted with close to 100 help desk vendors, some of them mom and pop operations, all playing their competitive shell game. To be successful requires you to be smart, wary, and to have the time and resources to carefully evaluate each vendor's product.

Not all help desk software is alike. Some of the smarter vendors have infused artificial intelligence into their products, enabling support analysts to provide faster, better answers. Since anyone can hang an "artificial intelligence inside" label on the box, the evaluation team needs to delve well below the shrink-wrap to make sure the software is indeed as smart as the vendor says it is.

Most important, evaluate the software and the vendor's support of it. Vendors should answer their own phones on the first ring and solve your installation or usage problems within an hour. If this isn't the case, ask if they're using their own software to resolve customer problems. A help desk company not using its own software is suspect.

The Help Desk Expert

Even if you buy a help desk solution, the knowledge base will be delivered as a blank slate. It will have the mechanism for handling knowledge, but it will be the developer's task — an application developer, an expert systems developer, or a help desk analyst — to load the knowledge base with the nuggets of information that will ultimately solve user problems. On the other hand, if you don't know or can't control what software and hardware the users are working with, the resulting knowledge base will have superfluous information that is expensive and time-consuming to maintain — essentially a kluge.

Knowledge base development, therefore, must be as carefully planned as any of the client/ server systems you build. While some automated help desks masquerade a traditional database as a knowledge base, this is truly an insufficient solution. A database stores facts and figures, but you need a bona fide knowledge base to store intelligence.

Help desk systems are usually fitted with an artificial intelligence engine that can consist of one or several elements. Decision trees, expert systems, case-based reasoning, neural networks, and fuzzy logic are used separately or together to help the automated help desk come up with answers to any tricky questions.

Knowledge about a certain topic is stored in a series of rules and objects. The artificial intelligence engine has the ability to move backward and forward through those rules to find one or more solutions to a specific problem.

While most help desk systems provide the ability to access any and all help files from the menu bar, this information is, for the most part, unusable as input for building a knowledge base. Help file information is just plain text. Information stored in a knowledge base, on the other hand, is often in a rule-format such as this very simple example:

```
If the screen is flickering
and the VGA is on
then cf=60 driver error;
cf=30 bad circuit
```

NOTE: where `cf` means confidence factor percentage

The help desk developer has two choices when it comes to preloading the knowledge base. The first is to do nothing at all, or to manually load the knowledge base rules from textual information captured in whatever automated help desk logs are on hand. The second option, albeit more difficult, is to use artificial intelligence to convert those help files. I'm assuming here that every client/server system built in-house has help files as well. For example, some neural networks can read the text of a loan application. By reading whole batches of applications, the neural network develops rules that help it determine which applications meet the qualifying criteria and which applications do not. These rules are available for review by the audit department. More important for the help desk developer, the rules generated by the neural network can be imported into the help desk's knowledge base.

To perform this same feat in a help desk environment would require an artificial intelligence programmer to develop the neural network. It would also require some patient non-artificial intelligence programmers to separate those help files into digestible segments for input into the neural network. Given the complexity and resource requirements of these tasks, my recommendation is to start from scratch unless you can talk the help desk vendor into performing this feat for you.

Benefiting from the Help Desk

All application development teams should make a wholesale effort to incorporate the automated help desk into their client/server application. For the most part, today's help desks stand apart from the individual application. The user experiencing a problem has only his phone for solace. I recommend a more proactive approach.

That menu bar says **Help**, doesn't it? So how about providing some unique help-enabling facilities. The first I would recommend is an automatic e-mail facility that users can work with to send a question or problem directly to the help desk operations center. If you really want to be creative, enable users to "print screen" directly into the e-mail, thus showing the specific problem they're encountering.

Some of the more robust off-the-shelf help desks provide LAN access to the help desk knowledge base. There's probably no better way to solve a user's problem than to let him or her pose the problem and have the automated help desk resolve it. If you pick the right software, this is one of those rare cases where it is actually easier to do it than to say it. Given the artificial intelligence nature of the help desk, a few vendors have added the discipline of natural language into the help desk mix. Instead of typing cryptic messages or using difficult interfaces, the user can just type "my screen is flickering." This solution provides enormous productivity raising potential.

Probably the best idea to come along in a long time is the Internet. Companies realizing the potential of this new paradigm have turned it inwards to create vast intranet networks.

This provides an opportunity to deploy the help desk across the entire breadth and depth of the organization — as well as externally to outside staff and customers.

Another option is to use case-based retrieval technology, which enables users to directly access troubleshooting tips and product information via the World Wide Web — without having to wait to contact a help desk analyst.

Finally, tout the help desk as an integral component of your application. How to get help should not only be part of the online help function, but part of the manual and training, too.

With decreasing budgets and limited resources, the systems we develop today have to achieve more with less. From a software development perspective, this translates into building systems that are not only function-rich, but building systems that guide the user through these functions as well. Help desks, those built as integral components to a system and those that function with people at the other end of a telephone, are an important part of this cost vs. function equation.

How Is Your Software Being Used?

When loading the knowledge base of a help desk, it's important to keep in mind exactly how your users interact with their software. The difference between how "typical" users operate their systems and how programmers or power users do can be surprising. These statistics from a 1995 New Art Inc. survey reveal a discrepancy between computer power and productivity derived from that power. These statistics have ominous implications for the work load of the help desk staff and the productivity of the organization as a whole. More important, the statistics provide some insight into how users typically use and think about software — which is likely the way they'll use and think about your next application.

- 85% of all users are under trained in the software deployed on their computers
- Users utilize only 27.5% of the functionality of their software
- 65% of users are using an outdated version of their software
- 23% of users use their PCs for word processing only
- 85% of users indicate they spend more time than they should on formatting (using word processing, presentation graphics, desktop publishing programs)
- 90% of users indicate PC software, particularly Windows-based software, is hard to use, not intuitive, and takes too much time to perform required functionality
- 74% of users indicate PC software bugs are prevalent and affect productivity
- 68% of users indicate they continue to have problems with getting corporate data to the PC for analysis
- 90% of users admit their PC software requests for purchase are a result of advertising blitzes rather than careful consideration of actual requirements on their part.

5.2.5 "Developer Angst: Product Support"

by Jacques Surveyer

---

*Many software vendors have lost sight of critical developer
needs as their support plans proliferate.*

It's 3:00 a.m., the morning before the big milestone meeting, and your program is just not working. You are already on a workaround of a workaround. The manual says, "Do this," and the computer says most emphatically, "No way, kiddo!" Talk about developer anxiety — you need a remedy and fast. You need bug solutions pronto. Who are you going to call for help in exterminating those software blue bugs? Ghostbusters? Men In Black? The software vendor's product support? I know developers who laugh hysterically, even maniacally, at the latter notion.

"Developers' Angst and Anxiety" (*Software Development Industry Watch*, Apr. 1998) examined developer angst caused by two forces: waves of rapid change in development paradigms and technology coupled with ever-shorter development cycles. This article takes a look at the software frontlines — product support — where software vendors' promises meet developers' expectations or frustrations.

With new resources like the World Wide Web, powerful online help and support, easy-to-use interactive wizards and tutorials, and documentation crammed onto easily accessible CDs, product support should be reaching new levels of effectiveness and user satisfaction. One case in point, the Microsoft Project 98 group found that its extensive help system and tutorials reduced support calls and costs, despite a most ambitious upgrade to the program. Despite software vendors' acknowledgment of this win-win situation — lower costs to them but also happier customers — documentation quality and usability remain problematic. So my question is, how, between lip and cup, does product support get spilled?

Out of Box Experience: Installation

This is where software can quickly change into "underused-ware" or "dead-on-the-shelf-ware." There are three bugaboos. First, *n*-tier and web applications are smearing a program over several machines in a network, so software is just harder to install and implement. Second, more software depends on tie-ins to specific hardware such as computer telephony, voice recognition, fault-tolerant OLTP with clusters and RAID drives, fail-over systems, and distributed applications. Finally, software is more integrated. With Enterprise Resource Planning (ERP) systems from vendors like Baan, Peoplesoft, SAP, data warehousing, and middleware come the need to interface more different kinds of software in more different ways than ever before. Making those handshakes and interfaces work flawlessly is no small feat. So it is interesting to see how vendors support their software during installation and startup.

Table 5.1 shows a mix of service offerings, ranging from Borland's free support during installation to Oracle's and SAP's support tied to maintenance plans. This latter policy dovetails with the high-end philosophy that you are buying a solution and not a program. For example, Oracle, SAP, and Sybase see almost as much of their revenues coming from support and consulting services as they do from software licensing fees. As one support manager put it, "We are not in product support. Along with our training and consulting groups, we are in the business of development assistance." However, if that were the case, I would expect to see a more uniform provision of installation expertise among vendors.

Table 5.1 Support Policies for Developer Tools

	Platinum	Borland	IBM	Lotus	Microsoft	Oracle	SAP	Sybase
Installation (Getting started manual)								
Registration required	no	yes	no	no	yes	yes	yes	yes, online
Free installation support	yes	yes	0 to 60 days	30 to 60 days	two cases	no	no	two cases
Installation support experts	no	yes	no	yes	some	no	yes	yes
Registration Benefits (Product upgrade notice)								
Required for product support	yes	no	no	no	yes	no	yes	yes
Automatic e-mail notification of service packs and patches	no	no	pay for	pay for	yes	no	yes	yes
Automatic e-mail notification of product upgrades	no	U.S. only	no	yes	yes	no	yes	yes
Type and amount of free support	none	none	none	30 to 60 days	two cases	none	none	two cases
Registration info is private and not sold to mailing lists by default	yes	no	yes	no, shared	no, shared	yes	yes	yes
Online Support (Web site, technical faxback, FTP site)								
Access to product knowledge base	pay for	free web	free	free web	some free	free web	pay for	free web
Access to complete "bug" base	free web	no	free web	pay for	pay for	pay for	pay for	free web
Frequency of updates	daily	weekly	daily	weekly	daily	weekly	varies	daily

Table 5.1   Support Policies for Developer Tools (Continued)

	Platinum	Borland	IBM	Lotus	Microsoft	Oracle	SAP	Sybase
Paid Support (Telephone support, user groups)								
Cost per incident	N/A	$90 to $170	$180 to $270	$35 to $500	$20 to $150	N/A	N/A	$50 to $125
Cost for unlimited calls per month	N/A	$40K/yr.	no	reseller	$700	maint. fee	N/A	no
Able to download state of system	yes	some	yes	no	no	no	yes	no
Able to remotely debug system	yes	on site	yes	no	some	yes	on site	some
If case involves product bug, is it handled for free?	N/A	yes	some	yes	some	N/A	N/A	yes
Certification for technical staff	yes	some	some	yes	yes	some	yes	yes
How often are skills refreshed?	quarterly	quarterly	yearly	yearly, and with product updates	constantly	yearly, and with product updates	yearly, and with some product updates	quarterly
Other services (Conferences, training seminars, consulting services, certification)								
Books and CDs	CD	no	both	no	both	both	no	CDs
Measured mentoring	some	ad hoc	some	yes	some	some	third-party	some
Guaranteed system delivery	some	not yet	yes	some	third-party	some	third-party	contract

Startup

Getting up to speed quickly and effectively is the critical technical success factor in a lot of development work. Client/server and web application development have put a premium on not only applying old techniques but developing in new contexts. Thus, it is encouraging to see that most software vendors have expanded traditional support strategies, such as bulletin boards and online support forums, to include web-based support such as public knowledge bases; ftp sites stocked with patches, samples, and templates; plus trial software that you can download. It has never been easier to try out software: first by downloading and testing fully operable (but time-limited) software, then by carefully scanning the knowledge bases for

FAQs, bug reports, and coding tips that give the best possible insights into the software's strengths and weaknesses.

Some software vendors are helping new users get started by going beyond manuals and documentation on CDs or training seminars. They are offering measured mentoring. In this type of training, a vendor's expert joins a development team on-site for a period of time. The mentor is available to solve problems and to impart methods and tips on how to use the software most effectively. What keeps both sides focused is the measurement of the development team's skills, before and after using a mentor, with a skills survey.

Finally, as development shifts from make to buy (Gartner Group predicts a 25% increase in the use of packaged software over the next two years), vendors' support and consulting business will grow. The nature of that type of consulting and support is changing, as we see in . More vendors are offering guaranteed delivery of systems. This is an important trend because vendors like JDEdwards, who have product lines very similar to Synon or Netron, are growing at a faster rate. One of the keys to JDEdwards's success is guaranteed delivery ensured by the participation of its system engineers from the design process all the way through to system implementation. However, the development assistance available at the high end with ERP or frameworks is not necessarily matched with uniform support services for low-to-midrange tools or for individual developers.

On the Frontlines

For the individual developer or small development team, much of only suggests the labyrinth required to navigate and determine required vs. available support. First, the support plans vary quite widely in cost and structure, depending on product, operating environment, time (8 a.m. to 8 p.m. weekdays vs. 7 days x 24 hours support), accessibility and level of expertise, plus other value-added services. Even simple help is not simple. For example, Borland offers unlimited free support during installation but then charges for support thereafter. Sybase and Microsoft offer two free incidents of support and then charge for future ones. Lotus offers 30 to 60 days of free support triggered by the time of the first call. Pricing varies so much that I decided to highlight just two options.

Some vendors, like SAP, Platinum, and Oracle do not ordinarily offer support on an incident basis. Instead, their support is based on a maintenance fee (usually a percent of the software license fee); however, most vendors offer support on a defined time period. The cost per incident still varies widely among vendors, depending on the product and operating system. Developers looking to get unlimited calls during a short period of time — say the last month of a development project — find a mixed bag of services. Most software vendors' support plans are not geared to responding to these peak needs.

Of even more concern is problem duration and what methods are provided to reduce waiting-to-debug time. Several vendors, such as Borland, Microsoft, and Sybase, provide free web access to their knowledge bases where tips, bug reports, and workarounds are posted for do-it-yourself problem diagnosis. Software for providing this self-help is getting more sophisticated. Inference Corp. offers CaseSolution and CasePoint software, which not only allow natural language query of local and web-based knowledge bases, but also log all queries and escalate unresolved issues to designated technical support staff with all the details. In general, the speed and sophistication of the search engine, plus the frequency and completeness with which "bug" bases are updated, are a critical factor in these self-help solutions. Unfortunately, the provision of such services also varies widely.

If users do call product support, one of the crucial tie-ups is communicating the nature of the problem and the state of the user's system. I would like to fax or ftp my registry, config, ini, coding, and other relevant files directly to the technical support person. Better still, I would like to permit the technical support staff to remotely access my machine(s) (through the World Wide Web or PC Anywhere) and either debug directly or upload all the relevant files for problem resolution. The last thing I want is to play a game of telephone tag around "reproducing the problem." Unfortunately, as shows, the willingness or capability of software vendors to reduce problem duration is mixed to poor.

Another critical factor in technical support is the skill level of the technical support staff. To some extent, it is a case of getting what you pay for — some vendors charge extra for access to their more sophisticated support staff. However, if a vendor has its own certification program, we expect its support staff to master those skill levels and to refresh skills on a quarterly basis.

To help time-pressed developers, some vendors offer "proactive" support, which can include automatic e-mail notification of service packs or major bug fixes for registered users of their products. Some vendors, like SAP, provide web-based help agents that send registered customers relevant news that is posted to their forums or knowledge bases. In general, the World Wide Web, Java applets, and user-customized agent technology offer the promise of not only innovative, proactive support but also the ability to shorten the debug problem duration — a win-win situation for users as well as software vendors.

Mixed Support

As my review and table show, vendors' support for users is decidedly mixed. In trying to meet the varying support needs and their own cost and pricing models, vendors' support plans have proliferated in complexity. In many cases software vendors have lost sight of critical needs:

- Reduce the incidents of support with more robust, reliable program releases
- Further reduce support through better documentation and training
- Reduce problem duration with better online support
- Define quickly the state of the system and nature of problem
- Remotely debug tough problems
- Allow more smart self-help by computer telephony and smart online support programs.

True, vendor moves to proactive support and an attitude of nurturing development assistance and client problem resolution are most welcome. However, myriad support programs have resulted in very mixed levels of support. As developer time and talent become an increasingly scarce commodity, software vendors with more innovative and effective support policies are going to gain a significant competitive advantage.

Chapter 6

Infrastructure Management

6.1 Best Practices for the Infrastructure Management Workflow

A significant difference between the Enterprise Unified Process (EUP), described by this book series, and the initial lifecycle for the Unified Process is the recognition that most organizations have more than one software project that they need to manage. The reality is that software project teams are dependent on the infrastructure of your organization and on one another from a resource sharing point of view. At the same time, within their defined scope software project teams are also independent of one another and free to make decisions in an appropriate manner. In short, for a software process to be truly effective it must include activities that support the successful management of portfolios of software projects. The Infrastructure Management workflow was specifically added to EUP to focus on the management and support of cross-project issues.

The activities of infrastructure management are summarized in Table 6.1, and, as you can see, there are a wide variety of important activities that this workflow encompasses. In this chapter we will focus on architectural issues such as security, and software process management, and support, as well as strategic reuse management and support. The other activities of this workflow were covered in *The Unified Process Elaboration Phase* and *The Unified Process Construction Phase*, Volumes 2 and 3 in this book series. During the Transition phase, and at the beginning of the Production phase as well, you are likely to perform project retrospectives (see Chapter 4, Best Practices for the Project Management Workflow) in which you will discover what practices worked well and what did not work so well — learning that you should feed back into your software process improvement efforts. Although organization/enterprise-level architectural modeling and strategic reuse management and support were covered in Volume 3, we would like to take the opportunity in this volume to discuss a topic that impacts both of these efforts: effective use of open source software.

Table 6.1   The Aspects of Infrastructure Management

Activity	Definition
Strategic Reuse Management and Support	The identification, generalization and/or development of, and support of potentially reusable artifacts.
Software Process Management and Support	The identification, documentation, and support of a software process to meet your organization's unique needs. This is often the responsibility of a Software Engineering Process Group (SEPG). The software process itself may be tailored to meet the specific needs of an individual project as part of the Environment workflow.
Enterprise Modeling	The modeling of the requirements for an organization and the identification and documentation of the environment that the organization operates within. The purpose of enterprise modeling is to understand the business of the organization to direct the development of a common, reusable architecture that supports the needs of your organization and to direct your programme management efforts.
Organization/ Enterprise-Level Architectural Modeling	The development and support of both a domain architecture that supports the business of your organization and a technical/system architecture that provides the underlying technical infrastructure for your systems. These models enable your Enterprise Application Integration (EAI) efforts, providing guidance for developing new applications based on a common architecture and for integrating legacy applications into overall infrastructure.
Standards and Guidelines Management and Support	The identification, development/purchase, and support of the standards and guidelines to be followed by software professionals. These standards and guidelines may be tailored to meet the specific needs of a project team as part of the Environment workflow.
Programme Management	The management of the portfolio of software of an organization, including legacy software that exists in production, software projects currently in development, and proposed software projects awaiting development.

6.1.1 System Security

System security is a critical issue that must be addressed by every application and is in fact an issue that is typically driven at the enterprise level. Security policies are often described as part of your overall enterprise requirements model, if one exists, or as part of your common corporate development guidelines — either way security typically falls under the purview of the Infrastructure Management workflow. Mike Rothman discusses security from the point of view of developing an Internet-based application in "Who's That In My App?" Rothman points out that making applications available to people outside the enterprise — effectively what you are doing when deploying a system to the Internet — greatly increases the risk of loss, requiring new methods to protect a company's private data. A crucial aspect of application security is determining who can be trusted, and although a firewall repels attacks on a network level, it doesn't know how an application uses the network or which users need to access the application. In other words, a firewall authenticates network users, not application users. You may need to develop or purchase a Public Key Infrastructure (PKI) — the technology that issues, manages, and validates digital certificates — for use in addition to your firewall to meet your security needs. Rothman's article provides an excellent overview of the security issues that you will face as well as potential solutions for addressing those issues.

In "Intrusion Detection" Alexandra Weber-Morales presents complementary advice to Rothman's by exploring intrusion detection systems (IDS) technology. She points out that the most common methods of breaching security are social engineering (fraudulent or deceptive requests for confidential information), viruses or worms, Trojan horses, hostile web content (applets, Active X, JavaScripts), physical access to machines, and remote attacks across the Internet. IDSs are critical because they sniff out remote attacks in progress as well as the presence of Trojan horses and worms. Once a breach has been detected (depending on the product), an IDS can generate real-time alerts, dynamically reconfigure routers or firewalls, and/or display security trends as graphical reports in real time. The article lists several best practices for security design within your application:

- Least privilege
- Fail-safe defaults
- Economy of mechanism
- Complete mediation
- Open design
- Separation of principle
- Least common mechanism
- Psychological acceptability

6.1.2 Reuse Through Open Source Software (OSS)

It is very rare to find an organization that doesn't want to foster reuse in its software development projects, thereby reducing development and maintenance costs, increasing quality, and improving time to market. Unfortunately most organizations struggle to achieve this goal, even though a vast source of reuse is available only a mouse-click away in the form of open source software (OSS). These collaborative efforts in which people improve the original software by adapting it for different environments, fixing bugs, and publicly sharing their modifications are, in many ways, the epitome of code reuse on an international scale. The term OSS was popularized in 1998 to refer to some forms of free software, although not all OSS is truly considered "free," depending on its type of licensing. To be truly considered free, OSS must conform to the following four freedoms (Stallman, 2001):

- *Freedom 0*. The freedom to run the program, for any purpose.
- *Freedom 1*. The freedom to study how the program works and adapt it to your needs. Access to the source code is a precondition for this.
- *Freedom 2*. The freedom to redistribute copies, so you can help your neighbor.
- *Freedom 3*. The freedom to improve the program and release your improvements to the public, so that the whole community benefits. Access to the source code is a precondition for this.

Perhaps the most striking aspect of the free software movement is the worldwide availability of often talented software developers willing to contribute their time, energy, and creativity to free software. The vast majority of these developers hold down full-time day jobs, and some of them may even work for you. In "Reuse Through Internal Open Source" Scott W. Ambler addresses the issue of how your organization benefit from the open source movement. He first suggests that you investigate the OSS that is available, evaluate it against your needs, and reuse whatever fits best. You'll often discover that significant portions of your proposed technical infrastructure is available for free. You can also benefit from the open source movement is to start a project of your own, particularly if you need something that is common to many organizations but you do not want to develop it completely on your own. Third, you could start an internal open source project within your organization by setting up a private open source environment within your own intranet, as opposed to a public one on the Internet. Internal OSS goes beyond traditional approaches to reuse — such as project-driven reuse, repository-driven reuse or items being declared reusable — approaches that often flounder because they don't motivate developers. Many of your best developers are likely developing public OSS in their spare time that your competitors are taking advantage of, with internal OSS efforts you may be able to redirect their energies towards something you can use.

Warren Keuffel describes his views of OSS in "Arts and Crafts Software." He draws parallels between the rise of the Arts and Crafts movement and the ascendancy of OSS. He believes that the OSS movement is fueled, in large part, by programmer dissatisfaction with the industrial-software world, as exemplified by Microsoft. Keuffel describes how Richard Stallman, founder of the Free Software Foundation (FSF), embraces a view of how society is bettered by recognizing the efforts of the craftspeople who come together — often in their own self-interest, it is true — to create or improve a program. With OSS the construction and design of the program is equally as visible to anyone who cares to inspect it and even use it. You know exactly what you are getting and can improve upon anything that doesn't meet your exact needs.

In "The Ethics of Free Software" Bertrand Meyer examines the negative side of the OSS movement. He believes that free software advocates often condemn commercial software vendors (meaning most of the industry) on the basis of moral absolutes, presenting themselves as generous benefactors of humanity. They reduce all software-related moral issues to one aspect, a special notion of "freedom," as though nothing else mattered. Meyer points out that some, although not all, "free" software is taxpayer-funded, coming from developers who have the comfort of a salary from an institution that can not legally go bankrupt, such as a state university. It is easy to be morally superior from a well-protected ivory tower. He brings up a very serious ethical issue that arises in the design of free software that are "copycat" versions of commercial software. Meyer states that it is legal, and perhaps ethical, to start from someone else's design and reimplement it. However, it is profoundly unethical not to acknowledge this origin.

Regardless of the ethical issues surrounding OSS, one fact remains: OSS is here to stay and can often prove to be a significant source of reuse on software projects. For example, in *The Unified Process Construction Phase* (Volume 3), we published a collection of articles written by Scott Ambler on the topic of persistence frameworks. At `http://www.ambysoft.com/per-sistenceLayer.html` Ambler provides links to several OSS products that are based on his design, as well as commercially available software products. Persistence is a significant aspect of any technical infrastructure — do you want to build it yourself, download it for free in the form of OSS, or pay for it?

6.1.3 Software Process Improvement (SPI)

An important part of the Infrastructure Management workflow is software process improvement (SPI), something that is typically a cross-project task (unlike process tailoring, covered in Volume 1, *The Unified Process Inception Phase*, which focuses on adapting your software process to reflect the exact needs of your project). In "Software Process Improvement: 10 Traps to Avoid" Karl Wiegers describes 10 common traps that can undermine your SPI program. These traps are:

- *Trap #1:* Lack of Management Commitment
- *Trap #2:* Unrealistic Expectations
- *Trap #3:* Time-Stingy Leaders
- *Trap #4:* Inadequate Time and Resources Devoted to Training
- *Trap #5:* Achieving a CMM Level Becomes the Primary Goal
- *Trap #6:* Failing to Scale Formal Processes to Project Size
- *Trap #7:* Excluding Project Team Members from Assessments
- *Trap #8:* Stalling on Action Plan Implementation
- *Trap #9:* Process Improvement Becomes a Game
- *Trap #10:* Expecting Defined Procedures to Make People Interchangeable

Once you've avoided the common SPI traps you still need to get on with the actual work of improving your software process. Wiegers describes best practices for doing so in "Process Improvement That Works." Wiegers believes that at its core, SPI is simple: you need to consistently apply the practices that give you good results and change the practices that cause problems. This requires honest introspection, something that you can do by performing a retrospective (see Chapter 4) and careful analysis to identify the reasons behind your previous projects' successes and shortcomings. He advises that you should define your desired business objectives, assess your current processes, your problems, and your project outcomes. Armed with assessment insights and a knowledge of software industry best practices, such as those presented in this book series, you can then set realistic improvement goals. To succeed at SPI Wiegers suggests that you begin by focusing on the pain because pain is the best motivation for changing the way people work. Effective communication should permeate your process improvement activities — you must articulate the price being paid for your current process shortcomings. This might include blown schedules, missing functionality, massive overtime, high product support costs, unhappy customers, or low morale. Successful SPI efforts get practitioners involved in developing realistic new procedures and are treated like a project, giving it the structure, resources, and respect that any development project needs. Finally, you should focus on improving your business results by selectively and creatively applying the guidance from existing frameworks such as the Capability Maturity Model (CMM), the Unified Process, and agile software processes (Chapter 7) such as Extreme Programming (XP) (Beck, 2000) and Agile Modeling (AM) (Ambler, 2002).

An interesting question to ask is whether your goal should be to optimize your software development efforts as the CMM suggests or whether it should be something else. In "Beyond Optimizing" Jim Highsmith does exactly this. Structure or subversion? Control or creativity? Engineering or art? Software developers, consultants, and managers have been arguing the sundry sides of this apparent dichotomy for decades. To many, the rigid progression of successive levels of maturity so lauded today represents the ultimate surrender of creative programming to procedural bean-counting. Jim Highsmith posits that the model of organic adaptation best yields that elusive balance at the boundary between order and chaos where you can find both manageability and flexibility in the same place. Highsmith argues that repeatable, standardized processes reflect the attitude of software development traditionalists who believe in optimizing management practices characterized by rigorous rules and tight control. Optimization solved yesterday's software delivery problems; however, today software project managers must deliver concrete results in shorter time frames while being constantly bombarded with myriad changes and risk-laden decisions. Highsmith contends that for complex, e-business-like projects — those defined by high speed and uncertainty — that while some optimizing practices are necessary, they are also insufficient. It is adaptation practices that are essential to your success. To succeed in the transition from an optimizing to an adaptive perspective, you need to define an organic organizational model to replace your mechanistic one (as typified by the Unified Process). Second, you should adopt a new adaptive management style, one he has labeled leadership-collaboration to replace the command-and-control style that permeates optimizing organizations. Highsmith believes that what we need is a new framework — patterns and connectivity — and a new philosophy — organic and adaptive — to succeed. This article is important because it provides a different look at both SPI and the motivations behind it, as well as sets the initial groundwork for looking beyond the Unified Process to agile methodologies, the topic of the next chapter.

Do adaptive software processes work? Are adaptive software principles something you should consider adopting as part of your SPI efforts? Nike certainly believes so, as Warren Keuffel describes in "Just Doing It." Nike's management realized a flexible and always-current enterprise data model for product information would provide a firm foundation on which to build the information technology infrastructure it needed to maintain a competitive position. But previous efforts to build such a model had failed. Nike brought in consultant Jim Highsmith as project manager because of his work in adaptive software development (ASD) processes (Highsmith, 2000). The key concept behind ASD is that the traditional, deterministic plan-build-revise cycle must be replaced with an adaptive model that focuses on an iterative speculate-collaborate-learn model. To bring ASD into Nike, Highsmith created a feeling of chaos by making the team establish its own strategies and objectives during the first cycle. The teams were deliberately encouraged to accept that details in the early stages would be fuzzy and were told they were expected to make lots of mistakes but that they should make them and correct them early. The purpose of this cycle was to force closure on issues and learn from mistakes. In later cycles the level of anxiety and discomfort diminished as the participants became more comfortable with their responsibilities. However, 80% of the work was accomplished in the first two cycles, which created what Highsmith calls the "groan factor." The heavy load, uncertainty, and chaotic atmosphere results in participants making greater contributions, both creatively and productively, than would occur in more traditional environments. It worked for Nike; perhaps it will work for you.

Larry Constantine finishes this chapter with his article "Unified Hegemony," in which he describes his experiences at a five-day international conference on the convergence between usage-centered design and UML/UP. The article should motivate your SPI efforts because it takes a very realistic look at both of these techniques and finds them wanting. Constantine reports that in the eyes of many, one of the great strengths of UML is that it is comprehensive, although the reality is that, despite its size and complexity, much is left out of UML. The UML is weak in its support of use cases and lacking in support for user interface design and in practice proves to be a particularly poor match for usage-centered and task-driven design approaches. He also reports that although the arguments for a common notation are straightforward — who really wants to argue about the shape of bubbles and lines? — the case for a uniform process seems harder to make. Notation and modeling are far more rigorous and better understood, but when it comes to software process, every development group has its own distinct story. The Unified Process was intended as a template which could be cut down, edited and tailored to suit varying projects, constraints, and cultures. Unfortunately, to do this you have to read the books and understand pretty much the whole of the Rational Unified Process (RUP) product (Rational Corporation, 2001) before you can tailor it down. He points out that as one might expect of anything pretending to unify complex development processes, the UP, like UML, borrows freely from almost anywhere and everywhere, often without credit. For example, so-called logical prototypes are easily recognized as interface content models in disguise, on which they were based, though scarcely an acknowledgement is in sight. Even worse, general consensus at the conference was that the claim to be using the Unified Process translates, on careful listening, into not much more than owning the CD-ROM and using the vocabulary in casual conversation. In practice, then, the good intentions and worthy goals of unification have to be weighed against the failures of UML and the UP to offer well-developed models or methods for task-driven user interface design and efficient and in-depth support for the full range of modern development processes and practices. Constantine suggests that at some point customization within the framework of UML and the UP becomes a procrustean process and that taking a different approach may be a better option for you. In other words, you may want to look beyond the Unified Process.

6.2 The Articles

6.2.1 "Who's That In My App?"

by Mike Rothman

---

*Conducting secure business-to-business transactions
takes more than a firewall.*

Enterprises everywhere have automated processes for e-business. Companies have long used enterprise resource planning applications such as SAP R/3 or PeopleSoft, along with collaboration applications like Lotus Notes, to move paper-pushing procedures online. The next step is to integrate suppliers and customers across corporate boundaries by using the Internet.

When only internal users accessed these applications, security threats were contained and risk was manageable. Opening applications to new constituencies outside the enterprise greatly increases the risk of loss, requiring new methods to protect a company's private data.

What Is Trust?

One crucial aspect of application security is determining who can be trusted. This is different from determining a user's identity, commonly called authentication. Either before or after a user is authenticated, you must decide if the identity presented is trustworthy. More importantly, you must also ascertain whether that identity belongs to a trusted group who can access a particular application or perform a specific function. This is commonly called authorization.

A trust policy is much more powerful than the traditional notion of user names and passwords. A trust policy not only verifies that a user is on a list, it provides a framework for determining what sources of user data can be trusted and which entities can issue user credentials that allow application access. It enforces policies that determine credential eligibility, and it can deny access by invalidating the credentials of an entire group or a single user if those policies are violated. In the business-to-business (B2B) world, where there are many users from many sources (both internal and external to the organization), there is no longer one list of user accounts.

Most trust policies are implemented at the network or server level. Yet applications contain the code that accesses and processes all sensitive data such as purchase orders, prices, revenues, customers, employees, salaries and so on. Therefore, the trust policy must be managed and enforced at the application level. Unfortunately, defining and enforcing a trust policy is easier said than done, as each application presents unique challenges.

Application data often passes from the user through several tiers of application architecture, especially with Web-based applications. Every application has its own list of user accounts (separate from network accounts), which must be managed by a system administrator.

User authorization and credential mapping are key to maintaining data security and the ensuing transactions. For example, consider the case of Alpha Manufacturing, which buys parts from Beta Supply. Alpha also uses Gamma Processing to handle its payroll, benefits and hiring. Alpha would like to give SAP R/3 access to Beta Manufacturing, so that Beta Manufacturing can view its inventory and weekly build plans over the Internet to implement a "just in time" zero inventory process with Beta Supply. Alpha also wants to give Gamma Processing direct access to its PeopleSoft data to handle day-to-day benefit change requests.

In this case, Alpha's trust policy can allow R/3 system access to a certain subset of Beta's users without having to manage them directly. Beta can manage the credentials, and Alpha can trust them. Alpha's trust policy can dictate similar rules for PeopleSoft access; in this case, for only Gamma's users.

Doesn't My Firewall Do That?

A firewall repels attacks on a network level — it doesn't know how an application uses the network or which users need to access the application. The firewall authenticates network users, not application users. Most internal company users are authenticated by a firewall or VPN and access various resources from there. The enterprise may also control which machine traffic can pass from the corporate network user on the outside, as well as encryption, which scrambles data as it passes through the Internet to the firewall.

In contrast, most outside B2B users are given access to a specific application or set of applications. Applications, which typically have carte blanche to pass traffic through a firewall as needed, are expected to check these users against their own access control list, since the users wouldn't have a corporate network account. Traffic for these applications is often passed in the clear with viewable text on the internal-side network (after the firewall gateway has decrypted the data stream).

An application-level trust policy allows security administrators to designate a specific set of outside user certificates that can access an application. The trust policy, managed by the administrator, also determines where and how to establish user certificate validity. This is part of an essential strategy to address security beyond the network level, in the application itself. Without application-level security, hackers can pass through a secured network to the application database, with their connection securely encrypted by the VPN to give them privacy as they compromise data.

For example, the VPN might allow secure connections between Gamma and Alpha's servers to implement secure human resources management. Without strong security at the application level, a compromise at Gamma's site endangers Alpha's application data. With application security and a trust policy in place, only the holders of trusted credentials can access the application and its data regardless of who has access to the VPN. These trusted credentials are called digital certificates.

What About PKI?

Public Key Infrastructure (PKI) forms the technology that issues, manages and validates digital certificates. A digital certificate issued by a certificate authority (CA) binds a public key to a specific user and details the operations it can be used for, as well as its validity duration. It also identifies the CA that issued it with the issuer's signature. This public key can be used in concert with its associated private key to authenticate the user and perform cryptographic operations. A certificate authority as implemented at a single company is itself the issuer of certificates, and everyone in the company will often trust that issuer because it is internal.

However, as PKI use grows and complicated structures of CAs need to interoperate, the situation gets much trickier. The complexity increases as B2B applications require dealing with the CAs of outside parties, which may be implemented with the technology of a different PKI vendor. Since a PKI is concerned only with the issuance and management of certificates, it has little notion of their use: It can't understand the business implications of employing that certificate to validate a transaction representing real economic value.

A PKI implements a trust policy by simply trusting another CA. This is a process called cross-certification, in which each PKI is modified to trust another CA, creating a link between them. As many of these trust links are created between many companies, a complex "web of trust" forms. All certificates in this web are trusted for those purposes the certificate allows. While this process meets the needs of PKIs, it doesn't meet the needs of business process embodied in applications.

A Bad Example

Alpha Manufacturing has determined that it should apply strong security when its sensitive data needs to be seen by a third party, especially across public networks. However, Alpha doesn't want to manage Beta's and Gamma's user population in addition to its own. Beta's and Gamma's digital certificate users should be granted access to only those applications they need to use.

If Alpha Manufacturing employed the typical PKI process of cross-certifying with Beta and Gamma in a web of trust, all certificates from both companies would be trusted for all purposes. Even worse, Beta and Gamma could end up trusting each other's certificates without even knowing it. They would have gone through an overly complex cross-certification and still not have the answer to their simple problem.

A trust policy allows you, on a per-application basis, to simply add a CA to a list of trusted issuers by including its root or sub-tree certificate, which identifies a CA for the purpose of checking the validity of a user certificate; no cross-certification is required. This list can be on a global or a per-application basis. Allowing a sub-tree certificate means that only a portion of a CA's certificates can be trusted, so that a set of certificates can be designated and agreed upon between two companies for specific inter-enterprise requirements. Beta and Gamma would allow a certain percentage of this group to have access to Alpha's applications, and Alpha would automatically allow only those users access to the appropriate applications without having to know all their names and account information in advance. And, as business relationships are formed and terminated, root keys can be added and removed from the lists simply and easily. Cross-certification is more difficult to modify. With a trust policy, business policy, rather than PKI technology, dictates who is trusted.

Today's critical applications must undergo a transformation to allow access to external and internal parties. This creates unprecedented risk to system integrity — and offers unprecedented opportunity to streamline the value chain. If you don't provide a means for strong trust, private and sensitive data will certainly be exposed.

6.2.2 "Intrusion Detection: Focus on E-Development & Security"

by Alexandra Weber Morales

The latest salvo in a decades-old battle for secure systems.

The assessment is harsh but familiar: "There is little question that contemporary, commercially available systems do not provide an adequate defense against malicious threat. Most of these systems are known to have serious design and implementation flaws that can be exploited by individuals with programming access to the system."

Though the words from this computer security study commissioned by the U.S. Air Force could have been written in 2000, a subsequent sentence puts them in historical context: "While there are growing requirements for interconnecting computer systems into networks, the dimensions of the security problem are unknown." Indeed, in 1972, when James P. Anderson wrote the report — and even a decade later — the military's security specialists could not have predicted the degree to which heterogeneous networks would ramble across the globe.

"I don't believe that anyone in defense circles, which are at the root of a lot of what we know about security, could ever have foreseen the impact that the World Wide Web has had. And some folks in defense were blindsided by the whole notion of distributed systems," says Rebecca Bace, a security consultant and researcher in Scotts Valley, California. Bace has been in the field since 1989, when she was tapped to lead the National Security Agency's Computer Misuse and Anomaly Detection research program.

Today, numbers describing the expanding dimensions and costs of the computer security problem are readily available. According to the Computer Security Institute, in its annual report with the FBI on what might aptly be termed "e-crime," rates of attack have risen steadily for the past three years. Of the 521 security practitioners surveyed in 1999, 30 percent reported intrusions by outsiders and 55 percent reported unauthorized access from insiders. Faced with such statistics, security professionals are looking past firewalls and virus protection to the latest well-hyped offering: intrusion detection systems.

Playing in Traffic

The most common methods of breaching security are social engineering (fraudulent or deceptive requests for confidential information), viruses or worms, Trojan horses, hostile web content (applets, Active X, JavaScripts), physical access to machines and remote attacks across the Internet. Intrusion detection systems (IDS) sniff out remote attacks in progress as well as the presence of Trojan horses and worms. Once a breach has been detected (depending on the product), an IDS can generate real-time alerts, reconfigure routers or firewalls on the fly and convert log entries into reports displaying security trends graphically. In addition to host- and network-based IDS, vulnerability and file integrity assessment are two other key approaches.

A host-based IDS processes audit data derived from user, application and system activity (with electronic commerce over the World Wide Web, the interaction between users and applications requires increased monitoring). A network-based IDS, on the other hand, not only watches signs such as device state transitions tracked in network management logs, but it also employs sniffers to read source and destination information contained in packet headers, scanning the data for attack signatures.

These signatures are unique sequences of system commands, such as a move, then a rename, followed by an invocation of the file. Or, at a more complex level, a pattern of bytes on a certain port number can indicate that a Trojan horse such as Back Orifice, a malicious program released in 1998 that allows remote control of a PC running Windows, is functioning. The fidelity of matching attack signatures depends, however, on how comprehensive the database is. Indeed, the prospect of constant updates makes this method of intrusion detection attractive to vendors who watched the growth of the antivirus market.

"Eight years ago, antivirus software was all shareware. Intrusion detection is still in its infancy, but in the next few years we expect it to become as ubiquitous as virus protection is now," says Rob Graham, chief technical officer for Network ICE Inc., a San Mateo, California-based company targeting not only the corporate borderless network market but also, with its $39.95 combination IDS and personal firewall offering, the end-user cable modem and digital subscription line market.

Questions on when, where and how to use IDS abound: Should the IDS sit in front of or behind the firewall? Will a suite of network- and host-based products perform better than an assemblage of best-of-breeds? What is an acceptable incidence of false positives? Will there be a noticeable drain on performance? What is the product's scalability? How often should the attack signature database be updated? Is it ethical — or efficient — for vendors to use hackers to try to crack their IDS?

"This is where a lot of IDS vendors are right now," laughs Bace. "If your value-add is that you keep track of all of the hacker threat out there, in that case, yeah, you can afford to hire them. These are folks who are totally enchanted with the notion of finding new trouble. Internet Security Systems and Axent and Network Associates have parlayed that into a wonderful business case — and I'm not slamming that; it's just that it isn't sufficient. Hackers aren't going to enable the consistency of process that's key to hardening the trustworthiness of your software."

Matters of State

In addition to signature databases, some IDSs come with scripting languages that allow users to define additional events to track. Many also store state information for a given connection, which lets them trigger on conversations as well as single packets. But statefulness isn't everything.

"Some folks believe intrusion detection is simply a linear pattern-match exercise — and it isn't," says Bace. "When you start dealing with heavily distributed systems, you have Poisson effects associated with the arrival time of messages. Poisson is a traffic analysis concept that says that when events need to be consolidated at a particular point in space, you'll have some randomization of the arrival times of those messages."

Atomic signatures are simple enough to deal with, but when multiple indicators from even a single stream must be analyzed, the detection process becomes much more complicated. The difference between trouble and benign activity often comes down to the ordering of the event stream. In race conditions, for example, a check and an access take place in sequence, with a write in the intervening slice rather than after the access, where it should normally occur.

According to Prof. Eugene Spafford, director of Purdue University's Center for Education and Research in Information Assurance and Security (CERIAS), analyzing event-stream ordering requires recording not only when things start but when they end.

"When opening a file on some Unix systems, we need to record not only when the call to open it was made, but also when the file was actually opened and whether the name was mapped to the underlying system — because the two change in some attacks," Spafford says. "Ordering requires a finer-grained time stamp than what's used. Currently, the system clock doesn't have the right resolution. It's a very minor change to add a sequence field; for every system audit event you just add one to it. That's not done, but it can make a huge difference."

In the end, without measures preventing the surveillance of sensitive settings in the first place, says Bace, a stateful IDS may not make much difference. And cache space and performance limitations place an additional burden on issues of state.

"Some of the early failures that we saw were in statistics rather than attack signatures. You'd have these immense matrices characterizing activity not only for every user on the system but also for every file object, every process. These would grow incredibly quickly until you'd run out of memory," explains Bace.

Unforgiving Hosts

Even today, Spafford dismisses the feasibility of logging all packets, a feature that NetworkICE's Rob Graham boasts allows his product to prevent intruders from avoiding detection by using long, slow scanning.

"It's not viable," Spafford says. "If you've got a network of 15,000 machines (which is not a lot for some organizations), and you're doing e-commerce and office applications, what kind of disk farms do you need to have to save every packet over any length of time? It may work for a very narrow environment, but not in general."

"Many systems really miss the boat," continues Spafford, whose CERIAS ranks as the nation's preeminent security think tank. "They don't catch insider misuse, they don't work on ATM networks, they don't work on hubs that don't broadcast, they don't work with virtual private networks, encrypted traffic or enterprises where you have more than one route into the network for load sharing or fault tolerance. Those kinds of systems have a limited lifetime with the continuing evolution of networks."

For these reasons, many experts prefer focusing on host- and application-level security rather than debating whether network sniffers offer sufficient statefulness.

"You can do a lot of cool things in host-based intrusion detection that you can't do from the network side," Bace says. "When I'm inside the host watching an operating system audit trail, I can tell when people transition identities and see how much resource they've consumed. From a network point of view, you can't determine what the ultimate state is on the endpoint. You can see a hack go across, but you can't lay your hands on evidence of whether it worked or not, and exactly what the reach was. It could easily be blocked at the host level, and you'd never know."

Fail-Safe Basics

The experts agree that IDS is still immature — and it's detecting the failure of software engineers to learn robust programming lessons first taught in the 1970s.

That's why Matt Bishop, associate professor at the University of California, Davis department of computer science, is assembling a compendium of seminal papers in computer security (on CD-ROM and at http://seclab.cs.ucdavis.edu/projects/history/seminal.html). According to Bishop, developers too often overlook the early work and waste time rediscovering problems and solutions.

"Vulnerabilities have been around since the first software. There were two seminal studies in the 1970s about this. One was done by Bob Abbott and a group of people at Livermore Laboratories. They surveyed about 10 systems and built a classification scheme for the vulnerabilities they found. The Information Sciences Institute project, under Richard Busbee, published a similar study two years later. Their goal was to automate the detection of vulnerabilities. They didn't succeed, but they developed a very interesting classification of security flaws."

But that work lay dormant in the 1980s, according to Bishop — abandoned in favor of the belief that the technology at the time allowed the construction of secure systems without any vulnerabilities. It soon became evident that this was not true.

"You can't build systems without vulnerabilities," says Bishop, "and even if you could, you'd have problems with the operators and misconfigurations and such. In 1991, the folks at Purdue came out with a taxonomy of security flaws. I wrote one at the same time. Carl Landware, in the late 80s, had come out with one as well. They all boil down to this: Essentially, nothing's changed. The flaws described in the taxonomies were quite different, but you could basically map them on to one another. I'm coming up with a new one now, and again, I'm not seeing any development in the field. Techniques for writing good code and testing for vulnerabilities are not being used. Intrusion detection will help us spot things, but it's too late. We've got to build better code."

Many security professionals, though, are tired of hearing the same harangue about quality code at every conference keynote address. Bishop does acknowledge that "we're beginning to get a handle on how to scan programs for potential race conditions; once we've got a list of potential ones, we can go in and eliminate them." But, he notes, a classic attack from the late 1970s — buffer overflow — is still successfully penetrating systems today.

"As an adversary, I have a much easier task than you have as a security developer," Bace explains. "I only have to find one hole; you have to make sure there are none. A wonderful hacker is not someone who understands how to protect the system. The hacker might be able to engineer workarounds for those areas he knows how to attack, but there's no guarantee that what he's seen represents the entire universe of problems."

In her book *Intrusion Detection* (Macmillan Technical Publishing, 1999), Bace urges developers to reacquaint themselves with a 25-year-old paper by Jerome H. Saltzer and Michael D. Schroeder ("The Protection of Information in Computer Systems," *Proceedings of the IEEE*, Vol. 63, No. 9, Sept. 1975), in which the authors enumerate eight fail-safe security design principles. They are:

1. *Least privilege.* Relinquish access when it's not required.

2. *Fail-safe defaults.* When the power goes off, the lock should be closed.

3. *Economy of mechanism.* Keep things as small and simple as possible.

4. *Complete mediation.* Check every access to every object.

5. *Open design.* Don't attempt "security by obscurity," as Bace puts it; assume the adversary can find your hiding places.

6. *Separation of principle.* Don't make privilege decisions based only on a single criterion; use the onion-skin model.
7. *Least common mechanism.* Minimize shared channels.
8. *Psychological acceptability.* Make security painless, transparent and ubiquitous.

Both Bishop and Spafford concur with Bace that following these principles would go a long way toward eliminating the "penetrate-and-patch" mentality that prevails among software vendors today.

The current approach — trying to keep pace with all the attacks as the number of weaknesses multiplies — is fundamentally backward, Spafford laments: "The next generation of Windows has 60 million lines of code. How can it possibly be designed to be secure?"

Resources

The COAST (now CERIAS) Intrusion Detection Hotlist online at `http://www.cs.purdue.edu/coast/ids/` is probably the most comprehensive listing of intrusion detection and other computer security resources on the World Wide Web, compiled by professor Eugene Spafford and his faculty and staff at Purdue University in West Lafayette, Ind.

The seminal work by Jerome H. Saltzer and Michael D. Schroeder naming eight security principles that are still relevant today ("The Protection of Information in Computer Systems," *Proceedings of the IEEE,* Vol. 63, No. 9, September 1975) is reprinted online at `http://www.mediacity.com/~norm/CapTheory/ProtInf/index.html`.

Though it's a bit out-of-date, the Computer Security Institute's Intrusion Detection System Resource page at `http://www.gocsi.com/intrusion.htm` contains a hard-hitting interview with five IDS vendors, a roundtable discussion and a list of tough questions to ask IDS vendors.

The University of California, Davis Computer Security Laboratory (web page at `http://seclab.cs.ucdavis.edu`) has been designated a Center of Academic Excellence in Information Assurance Education by the National Security Association.

The site contains a wealth of current and past projects, as well as a collection of seminal papers in computer security.

Future Fears

Increasingly complex, monolithic operating systems are not, however, the biggest risk on the horizon. While Internet security has been reinvented by the Java virtual machine, which already emulates IDS in its method of code verification by stack inspection, problems with mobile code only look to get worse. With embedded systems attached to heterogeneous networks, intruders no longer stand to simply gain access to information or financial transactions — now they could conceivably control real-time systems or safety-critical devices. In addition, even the rigidly bureaucratic, stiffly secure Department of Defense has found itself in potentially compromising positions with commercial off-the-shelf components that have been built quickly under market pressures and don't comply with its iron-clad requirements.

"There's a huge demand for security software in general, but there hasn't been enough real research done," says Spafford. "The result is products that aim to meet a market demand. Customers want more features rather than strong security, so vendors introduce more complexity, which leads to a greater likelihood of failure. We've seen this in firewalls, and we're going to start to see it in intrusion detection."

6.2.3 "Reuse Through Internal Open Source"

by Scott W. Ambler

A properly run, "ownerless" collaboration lowers development and maintenance costs while protecting your unique software from the prying eyes of the outside world.

I haven't found an organization yet that doesn't want to foster reuse in its software development projects, thereby reducing development and maintenance costs, increasing quality and improving time to market. Unfortunately, most struggle to achieve this goal, even though a vast source of reuse is available only a mouse click away in the form of open source projects. These collaborative, public efforts, in which people improve the original software, adapt it for different environments, fix bugs and share their modifications with the rest of the world are, in many ways, the epitome of code reuse on an international scale.

A great place to learn about open source is OpenSource.org (www.opensource.org), a non-profit organization dedicated to supporting and evolving the open source movement. Collab-Net (www.collab.net) also provides tools and services based on open source tools and principles, and SourceForge (sourceforge.net) is a free open source hosting service. A quick search on the Web will find other organizations that offer a wealth of information, tools and services. The book *Open Sources: Voices from the Open Source Revolution*, edited by Chris DiBona, Sam Ockman and Mark Stone (O'Reilly Publishing, 1999), is worth reading; in the spirit of the open source community, it is also published online in its entirety at www.oreilly.com/catalog/opensources/book/toc.html.

An interesting example of an open source project is Osage: Persistence Plus XML (osage.sourceforge.net). Osage is a persistence layer written in Java, supporting JDBC-based object-relational mapping to enable experienced Java developers to quickly implement database access in their applications. It generates SQL for basic CRUD (create, retrieve, update and delete) operations, maps Java objects into a relational database, maps object relationships (associations) and generates persistent object identifiers (keys). The design of Osage, in part, is based on my articles about persistence layers, many of which have appeared in *Software Development* over the years and have now been reprinted in *The Unified Process Construction Phase* (CMP Books, 2000), a book edited by Larry Constantine and myself. I have had little input into Osage other than that due to lack of time on my part, but I've been very impressed with the project to date.

Joining the Effort

So how can your organization benefit from the open source movement? First, investigate the software that is available, evaluate it against your needs, and reuse whatever fits best. Infrastructure software, such as Osage, is often immediately usable by a wide range of companies because it addresses a common technical need, in this case, the persistence of Java objects into a relational database. However, do exercise care with open source software. As Bertrand Meyer reveals in "The Ethics of Free Software" (*Software Development,* March 2000, and on page 191), you could be burned waiting for fixes or changes that don't materialize in a timely manner. Organizations that do decide to reuse existing open source software should be prepared to share any changes that they make by submitting them back to the project — open source is a give-and-take proposition.

The second way you can benefit from the open source movement is to start a project of your own. Perhaps your organization requires software that you believe could fill a popular need, and after looking into both commercially and freely available software, you discover that you're the first to have thought of it. You start building the software and quickly realize that, while you can develop basic functionality quickly, some of the more complex functionality will incur a significant investment to both develop and maintain. You may decide to place your existing work in the public domain as an open source project, perhaps hosted by a company such as SourceForge, in the hope that others with similar needs will get involved and extend your work.

Third, you could start an internal open source project within your organization by setting up a private open source environment within your own intranet, as opposed to a public one on the Internet. You would make your work available to others within your organization, allowing them to evolve it and then share their changes as they see fit. This is true, honest teamwork between developers — other project teams become involved if it is to their advantage, not because they are forced to by senior management. Your work must have an intrinsic value to the developers, however, by solving a problem that others are struggling with and doing so with sufficient quality. A properly run internal open source project allows you to achieve reuse within your organization, reducing your development and maintenance costs, while protecting your unique software from the prying eyes of the outside world, thereby safeguarding your intellectual property.

Indeed, internal open source, when implemented properly, reflects many common reuse practices (as I described in *Thinking Objectively,* "Reuse Patterns and Antipatterns," The *Unified Process Elaboration Phase,* Chapter 3). To throw some pattern and antipattern names around, internal open source results in the development of robust artifacts through self-motivated generalization while supporting and enhancing a reuse-friendly culture. It goes beyond traditional approaches to reuse — such as project-driven reuse, repository-driven reuse or items being declared reusable — approaches that often flounder because they don't motivate developers. Why do I believe that internal open source is attractive to developers? Most existing open source projects are efforts that developers work on in their spare time — if developers are willing to invest their own time working on open source software (OSS) then it isn't much of stretch to think that they would be willing to invest company time on an internal project.

Managing Internal Open Source

How do you run an internal open source project? Start by identifying a vision and general architecture for your efforts and then build an initial version of the software following your typical development process. This initial version need not be complete, but it should provide some initial value to the people who download it, while reflecting the overall vision so as to provide guidance to developers who choose to evolve it. A project page, or set of pages for large efforts, that links to your project's artifacts (for example, the project overview, the source code, frequently asked questions and licensing definitions) for the software, should be set up on your intranet. Ideally, the definition of usage should be fairly straightforward because your software should only be used within your organization, although issues such as chargebacks (and politics in general) can get in the way. And if you're bogged down defining your own internal usage license, your organization's culture likely won't allow you to successfully develop internal open source software — or any other software.

Identify a project or team leader who will be responsible for shepherding the effort as well as accepting submitted changes. Shepherding often simply entails staying actively involved with the project's newsgroup, discussing suggested solutions and their potential impacts, communicating the vision, and trying to put people together who are working on similar issues. Changes need to be reviewed for applicability as they are submitted and then should be made available to the overall project. Larger projects will have hierarchies of people involved: Some will be allowed to directly submit their changes, whereas others, often people new to the effort, will first submit their changes through some sort of quality gate.

Contrary to popular belief and to their commonly chaotic appearance, open source projects are often well organized. Although not directed at nonproprietary projects, I recommend *Adaptive Software Development: A Collaborative Approach to Managing Complex Systems* by James A. Highsmith III (Dorset House, 1999) for a fresh perspective on how to be successful at developing software.

What tools do you need to make an internal open source project successful? Luckily, not many. You'll need a code repository, typically a version-control tool such as CVS (which is itself OSS) or Microsoft's SourceSafe, from which people may check out and submit code and other project artifacts. To facilitate communication between developers, you will need a newsgroup and/or a mailing list. Defect-tracking software enables developers to post identified problems and their solutions. Your organization likely has all of this software in place already; however, any of it can easily be obtained at no cost over the Web (once again, as OSS) if needed.

Making It Work

To ensure success, first inform developers that the software is available for their use either through an internal marketing campaign or by word of mouth. Second, apply internal open source not only to code but also to documentation templates, internal standards and guidelines, and common software models. Third, focus on quality and not quantity — two or three reusable programs employed by several projects offer more value than 20 or 30 projects gathering electronic dust. Fourth, overcome cultural and political obstacles. Forget cost chargeback schemes, forget complex management processes, forget endless meetings and instead focus on developing software in a collaborative manner. Fifth, be prepared to keep an eye on individual developers: Programmers should be plugging away at internal open source because it makes sense to do so for their current, primary project, not simply because they want to ignore their assigned work.

6.2.4 "Arts and Crafts Software"

by Warren Keuffel

Is Richard Stallman the reincarnation of William Morris?

By the time you read this, the house I've been building for the last six months should be finished. It's a small bungalow, heavily influenced by my interest in the Arts and Crafts movement of the nineteenth century. Architecture inspired by the Arts and Crafts movement flourished between 1910 and 1930. Also known as Craftsman-style, Arts and Crafts arose partly as a rebellion against the ornate architectural excesses of the Victorian era but also as a way of celebrating the contributions of skilled craftsmen to the construction of homes — which was in itself a reaction against the industrialization of society. Building in the Arts and Crafts tradition, then, frequently means exposing and focusing attention on craft elements such as fine joinery, for example.

What relevance, you may be asking yourself, does an obscure architectural movement have for Software Development readers? A fair question, and the answer is this: Frequently, we can find clues to guide us through the present to the future if we look at the past objectively. During the design and construction of this home, I have frequently been struck by the parallels between the rise of the Arts and Crafts movement and the ascendancy of open-source software (OSS). For example, consider the time when England was at the peak of her world power as a center of industry and commerce during Queen Victoria's reign, and compare today's software world, where, until recently, Microsoft occupied the same center-of-the-universe role.

Other parallels abound. The industrial revolution made reasonably-priced, mass-produced household goods available to the average person, just as the personal computer revolution in general, and Microsoft in particular, made computers accessible to the average person. The cities of industrial England were filled with overworked and underpaid immigrants, a situation that mirrors the high-tech industry's continuing efforts to avoid retraining American engineers in favor of buying votes in Congress to open the gates for increasing numbers of green-carded foreign engineers. And in response to the social ills of industrial England, the Arts and Crafts movement arose, seeking to make people aware that many long-standing craft traditions were in danger of being swept away by industrialization.

Squalid Tenements vs. Splendid Homes

The open-source software movement is fueled, in large part, by programmer dissatisfaction with the industrial-software world, as exemplified by Microsoft. But how can one compare the squalid tenements of the English midlands to the splendid homes occupied by legions of Microsoft stock-option millionaires? It's easy to forget that for every Microsoftie on easy street, there are dozens of Microserfs — often temporary workers — that make the Microsoft money machine the success that it is. My intent here is not to bash Microsoft's success but rather to illuminate what the past can tell us about what the future may hold. One of the best ways to accomplish that is to focus on the individuals who exerted significant influence over their respective movements. In Arts and Crafts, that honor would undoubtedly be awarded to William Morris, and in open software, the accolades — with equal justification — would accrue to Richard Stallman.

Renaissance Men

William Morris, it is said, possessed the enthusiasm and energy of 10 of his contemporaries. He was a poet, designer, typographer, manufacturer — and in later life, a socialist. Morris is often incorrectly linked to Victorian design ideals, but in reality he was a staunch opponent of all that the industrial, Victorian era of England represented. He placed a high value on art and on the value of craftsmanlike endeavor. He felt strongly that the artifice and shoddy workmanship inherent in manufacturing for profit served to corrupt manufacturing, and that the solution was to focus on the honesty of craftsmanship. Although Morris celebrated medieval values, his work as a wallpaper and textile designer and manufacturer reflected a commitment to a holistic philosophy in which the health of artistic endeavors served as a litmus test for the health of society. Morris was no Luddite, because he valued and used machinery throughout his career — such as for textile production — but he fought industrialization which resulted in dehumanizing the worker, making him or her nothing more than a cog in a vast industrial machine. For example, Morris rejected workmanship in which beauty only existed as a superficial attribute designed to sell goods; thus he eschewed ornate decoration and surface veneers that served only to camouflage the true nature of the item. Instead, he argued that superficially attractive goods created by an industrial machine — and society — which later discarded not only the shoddy goods but the workers that made them, degraded both the worker and society. These thoughts, not surprisingly, later led him to embrace socialism.

Stallman, founder of the Free Software Foundation, embraces a similar view of how society is bettered by recognizing the efforts of the craftspeople who come together — often in their own self-interest, it is true — to create or improve a program. Stallman is chiefly responsible for the Emacs editor, but he has contributed to several other projects within the Free Software Foundation.

Uncanny Resemblance

Within the software world, Stallman is no less recognized than Morris was in the art world. He received the Grace Hopper Award from the Association for Computing Machinery in 1991 for his development of the first Emacs editor in the 1970s. He was awarded a MacArthur Foundation fellowship in 1990 and received an honorary doctorate from the Royal Institute of Technology in Sweden in 1996. In 1998, he received the Electronic Frontier Foundation's Pioneer award along with Linus Torvalds. And in 1999, he received the Yuri Rubinski Award.

There's even an uncanny physical resemblance between the two men, which you can see for yourself at these Web sites:

- www.ccny.cuny.edu/wmorris/morris.html
- www.lib.utexas.edu/hrc/morris.jpg
- www.gnu.org/people/rms.jpg
- www.gnu.org/people/saintignucius.jpg

The Free Software Foundation's ideals, as developed by Stallman, are what, more than anything, bring to mind the battles that Morris fought in the nineteenth century. Stallman's battles against commercial software can be summed up in his famous dictum, "free speech, not free beer." That is, the issue is liberty, not price — an effort that parallels Morris' efforts to free art from industrialization — and suggests a similar socialist orientation. Free software, and access to the source code, Stallman says, includes four freedoms:

- *Freedom 0.* The freedom to run the program, for any purpose.
- *Freedom 1.* The freedom to study how the program works and adapt it to your needs. Access to the source code is a precondition for this.
- *Freedom 2.* The freedom to redistribute copies, so you can help your neighbor.
- *Freedom 3.* The freedom to improve the program and release your improvements to the public, so that the whole community benefits. Access to the source code is a precondition for this.

Stallman's philosophy indirectly provides the same freedom to the programmers as Morris sought for craftspeople, to let the honesty of craftsmanship — whether in art or code — shine through to the user. With a Morris-designed chair, the construction and design are fully revealed to anyone who cares to inspect it.

Likewise, with open-source software, the construction and design of the program are equally as visible to anyone who cares to inspect it. It's the emphasis on this visibility, as well as the cooperative ethic that underlies OSS projects, that encourages comparisons of Stallman as a latter-day reincarnation of William Morris. And that is why, when I consider the construction of my Arts and Crafts home, my thoughts frequently turn to open-source software as well.

6.2.5 "The Ethics of Free Software"

by Bertrand Meyer

In an excerpt from a longer opinion piece, Bertrand Meyer challenges some open source assumptions.

One of the most exciting aspects of today's software scene is the availability of a large body of free software, from operating systems (Linux, FreeBSD) to text processing tools (LATEX, Ghostscript), graphics (GIMP), compilers (GCC), web servers (Apache) and many others. The publicity around Linux has brought into the limelight such leaders of the free and open source movement as Richard Stallman, Eric Raymond and Linus Torvalds — not just in the computer press, but also in Time, Newsweek and on prime time TV.

This could be the end of the story: free software, like commercial software, has had amazing successes, and has already established its indelible mark on the computer industry. The pioneers of free software could bask in their justly acquired glory and recognize the contributions of the other folks too. After all, the public and private can coexist peacefully in other areas; the provost of UC Berkeley doesn't spend his days denouncing Stanford's chancellor as the evil incarnate of crass commercialism.

But this isn't the end of the story. One of the characteristics of some of the most vocal free software and open source advocates is that they are not content with success; they also claim the high moral ground, decrying in strong ethical terms (examples follow, with more in the full version of this article at `www.sdmagazine.com`) the developers of commercial software. Because they have chosen to state the issue in ethical terms, it is important to follow that path and examine the ethical issues at stake.

Free, Open...

Terms such as Free and Open Source software are a source of controversy. The GNU project (at `www.gnu.org/philosophy/free-software-for-freedom.html`) chides Eric Raymond's Open Source initiatives for attempting to trademark the term "open source." It criticizes providers of free software — Apple (`apsl.html`, same directory), Berkeley Unix (`bsd.html`) and Netscape (`netscape.html`) — for not observing the exact GNU definition of "free." Here we will call software "free" if it:

- Is available from at least one source without payment
- May be used for commercial as well as not-for-profit development, even by people who have not paid for it
- Can be obtained in source code form

This is not the definition promoted by GNU, which uses "free" in a much stronger sense. My intent is not to fight over terminology, but simply to make do with the limited number of terms in English and acknowledge the many "free" software products that do not fall within the exact limits of the GNU definition.

Perhaps the most striking aspect of the free software movement is the world-wide availability of often talented software developers willing to contribute their time, energy and creativity to free software. It is this pool of enthusiastic contributors, willing to work without immediate monetary reward, that has led in part to the general feeling of goodwill surrounding the free software community.

It should be pointed out that the existence of a community of dedicated, well-intentioned and sincere defenders of a cause doesn't by itself establish the ethical value of that cause. We've had enough examples this past century of murderous movements supported by hordes of idealists to remind us that no idea can be justified by the merits of its supporters. (Conversely, a corrupt politician may sincerely support principles of democracy and freedom.)

Voices from the Revolution

Many of the contributions of the free software community are admirable. Highly disturbing, however, is its widespread slander and hatred of the commercial software world. The best known figure of free software, Richard Stallman from GNU and the Free Software Foundation (FSF), professes an absolute refusal of any notion of commercial software. Software should be free, period. A few samples from the GNU and FSF web pages include:

- "Signing a typical software license agreement means betraying your neighbor: I promise to deprive my neighbor of this program so that I can have a copy for myself." (`www.gnu.org/philosophy/shouldbefree.html`)
- "When a program has an owner, the users lose freedom to control part of their own lives." (`www.gnu.org/philosophy/why-free.html`)
- "The system of copyright gives software programs 'owners,' most of whom aim to withhold software's potential benefit from the rest of the public. They would like to be the only ones who can copy and modify the software that we use." (`www.gnu.org/philosophy/why-free.html`)
- "I think that to try to own knowledge, to try to control whether people are allowed to use it or to try to stop other people from sharing it, is sabotage. It is an activity that benefits the person that does it at the cost of impoverishing all of society. One person gains one

dollar by destroying two dollars' worth of wealth. I think a person with a conscience wouldn't do that sort of thing except perhaps if he would otherwise die." (www.gnu.org/gnu/byteinterview.html)

And so on. These are extremely strong moral indictments ("...he would otherwise die"). However, nowhere in the pages of GNU and FSF literature is there any serious explanation of why it is legitimate, for example, to make a living selling cauliflowers, or lectures (as a professor does) or videotapes of your lectures, but criminal to peddle software that you have produced by working long hours, thinking brilliantly and risking the livelihood of your family.

A Skewed Moral Perspective

Free software advocates condemn commercial software vendors (meaning most of the industry) on the basis of moral absolutes. As later citations will show, they present themselves as generous benefactors of humanity. What is striking is the reduction of all software-related moral issues to one aspect, a special notion of "freedom," as if nothing else mattered. This leads to pronouncements that would be funny if they weren't also scary. Dr. Stallman writes at www.april.org/actions/rms/10111998/texte.html that: "scientists sometimes used to be able to cooperate even when their countries were at war. I read that once American soldiers, who landed on an island of the Pacific Ocean during World War II, found a building with a note saying: 'To American soldiers. This building is a marine biology laboratory. We put all our samples and reports in order so that U.S. scientists can go on with our work.' Because, for them, they were working only for humanity. Not only for Japan. They wanted their work to be useful for humanity, regardless of the outcome of the war. But today we live in a state of civil war between small groups, in every country. In which every group acts to stop the others, hinder the others, hamper the others. It's sad."

Appalling. To cite as an ideal one alleged act of scientific chivalry from a country whose World War II atrocities are known to everyone — and to present in contrast, as a paragon of monstrosity, some corporate policies with which you disagree in today's peaceful U.S. society — shows a noxious contempt for the hierarchy of ethical values. The phrase "civil war" is particular ill-chosen. What is more scandalous: the Rape of Nanking or restrictive software licenses? Who would you rather be: a POW in a Japanese camp in 1944 or a developer unable to get hold of the source of Lotus Notes in 2000?

This is the danger of single-issue proponents: they lose all sense of perspective and start thinking that their perceived "moral" problem is the only one that counts.

In one person's case, this loss of perspective leads to extreme stances. Eric Raymond, another leader of the movement (who prefers the term "open source"), uses his web page to proselytize for gun rights. One quote will suffice, although readers interested in this propaganda can find heaps of it at www.netaxs.com/~esr/guns/gun-ethics.html and neighboring pages. In "Ethics from the Barrel of a Gun: What Bearing Weapons Teaches About the Good Life" (note the reference to ethics), Raymond writes: "There is nothing like having your finger on the trigger of a gun to reveal who you really are. Life or death in one twitch — ultimate decision, with the ultimate price for carelessness or bad choices. It is a kind of acid test, an initiation, to know that there is lethal force in your hand and all the complexities and ambiguities of moral choice have fined down to a single action: fire or not?"

Such balderdash would be easy to dismiss if it were not highly visible from the author's Open Source pages (I came across it while looking for Mr. Raymond's often-quoted essay "The Cathedral and the Bazaar") and didn't have any ethical implications.

This text will be hard to understand for people who don't live in the U.S. Perhaps the greatest U.S. tragedy today is that a minority of gun nuts (a term that Mr. Raymond applies to himself with apparent pride), supported by the powerful National Rifle Association, has managed to terrorize Congress into maintaining loose gun laws that have no equivalent in the rest of the civilized world. The official pretext — the Constitution's Second Amendment, devised in the late eighteenth century to establish a Swiss-style popular militia against the return of oppressive power — is absurd: There is no Swiss-style militia in the U.S. (guns are used for pleasure and, of course, for killing ordinary people); the U.S. political system has a remarkable combination of checks and balances making the imposition of a dictatorship rather unlikely (the historical exceptions to this observation — such as McCarthyism and institutionalized racial discrimination — were not, if memory serves us well, met by armed resistance from an outraged citizenry); and an aspiring dictator would have means of oppression, such as missiles, tanks and perhaps nuclear weapons, against which even the sophisticated guns about which Mr. Raymond raves ecstatically on his web pages would be rather powerless. But the actual results on the biggest ethical issue of all, human life, are easy for everyone to see in the headlines (in what other industrialized country do they regularly report 12-year-olds have gone on shooting rampages with rifles taken from the family home?) and, more significantly, in the statistics.

Is it right, one might ask, to make a connection between Mr. Raymond, who is entitled to his opinions, and the rest of the free software community? The answer is yes, for at least three reasons:

- His propaganda is prominent on his web pages, one of the most frequently accessed sources of information about the free software movement, to which the media's references draw countless unsuspecting visitors.
- Eric Raymond has been one of the most visible proponents of the Open Source movement, widely interviewed and cited. He is a public person; his views, unless disavowed strongly and publicly, inevitably taint the rest of the movement.
- His views have not, as far as I know, been strongly and publicly disavowed by the rest of the movement. Richard Stallman, whose differences and competition with Eric Raymond are widely known, has not — again, to my knowledge — disassociated himself from the gun propaganda.

It is high time for Richard Stallman and Linus Torvalds to state publicly that they do not endorse the views of the gun lunatics, and that their cherished notion of freedom has nothing to do with the freedom to kill children and other innocents.

Just Like the Rest of Us

The free software literature is not hampered by self-doubt. Richard Stallman announced at the start of the GNU project that: "I'm looking for people for whom knowing they are helping humanity is as important as money." (www.gnu.org/gnu/initial-announcement.html) More recently at Linux World 1999, Stallman announced that: "Although we do business to make a living and live, there are things that are above and beyond that. Such as making the world a better place." Wow! Stallman describes GNU's goals as "pragmatic idealism:" "My work on free software is motivated by an idealistic goal: spreading freedom and cooperation." (www.gnu.org/philosophy/pragmatic.html)

Call me a cynic, or blame it on my having had to read Molière's *Tartuffe* at too early an age, but when I start hearing this kind of self-eulogy I become suspicious. Although my conjectures about sainthood are based on neither personal experience nor personal encounters, I have a feeling that real saints wouldn't go around advertising their sainthood that way. What I do know is that the line is sometimes fine between self-proclaimed virtue and the desire to burn at the stake all those who dare to differ. Here indeed is GNU's view of commercial developers: "The economic argument [for charging for software] goes like this: 'I want to get rich' (usually described inaccurately as 'making a living')."(www.gnu.org/philosophy/shouldbefree.html)

So all of you reading this who develop software for a living are liars. Note that some (although clearly not all) "free" software is taxpayer-funded, coming from developers who have the comfort of a salary from an institution that can not legally go bankrupt, such as a state university. This provides a convenient vantage point for bashing commercial developers, who have often put everything at risk to pursue their ideal. Many fail miserably, gaining only ruin and divorce; some manage to "make a living;" and a few become rich, as they are indeed entitled to if their talent, effort, business sense and luck get them there. Who can deny their right to "make a living" from honest work?

Besides money, a common motivating force for software entrepreneurs is their rejection by traditional institutions, including those who support free software. Many successful industry figures have told how they went to management with a great idea, only to be rebuked. Outraged by the reaction, they left, implemented the idea as a software package and proved the idiots wrong. The motives of such people deserve respect, not abuse.

We should also respect the motives of free-software developers. Many indeed find a great reward out of working for the common good. Why deny, however, that there may be many other legitimate motives? They may include: the realization that there is no money to be made with a certain kind of software; an attempt to correct limitations of existing tools; a strategy for enlisting the help of others and foster collaboration; a desire to learn; or an attempt to increase one's marketability.

Another is the desire to make money. As Eric Raymond puts it: "I expect to be quite wealthy once the dust from the Linux IPOs has settled" (www.netaxs.com/~esr/travelrules.htm). That some companies have got rich on free software is testimony to the business acumen of their founders; it is not an indictment of those who have a different vision. A business model is not a moral imperative.

Yet another legitimate motive is the search for fame and recognition. It was amusing to hear from the publishers of Linux Journal about the letter Dr. Stallman wrote asking that the operating system and the journal be renamed "Lignux" to acknowledge Linus Torvalds' debt to GNU. Who would cast the first stone? We are all human. Just cease slandering people who have chosen other solutions.

And What About Quality?

Another issue that has obvious ethical resonances is the quality of the software that a programmer produces. Isn't it relevant, for an ethics-preoccupied software engineer, to worry about this aspect? Is it more or less important than software ownership?

GNU and other free-software products are often good or very good. Not surprisingly, some products are also so-so. (We have recently had to cancel two projects at ISE, after many months of delay, because fixes promised repeatedly over many months by the developers of two GNU products never materialized.)

The licenses that accompany these products are revealing through the warranties (or absence thereof) they offer to the user. It is indeed amusing to note where the inflammatory proclamations about freedom suddenly stop in the GNU public license, and the tone changes completely. That's where the discourse switches to the topic of software "warranties:"

"EXCEPT WHEN OTHERWISE STATED IN WRITING THE COPYRIGHT HOLDERS ... PROVIDE THE PROGRAM 'AS IS' WITHOUT WARRANTY OF ANY KIND..." (www.gnu.org/copyleft/gpl.html).

Where have we seen this before? Oh yes — in the hated "proprietary" licenses, those that "take away your freedom and mine:" no warranty of any kind; AS IS; caveat emptor.

The GNU license is neither better nor worse here. Few software providers are able to warrant their offerings the way producers of non-software artifacts do. We cannot be too harsh on GNU and consorts in this respect. But given the violence of their attacks on the software industry, and their self-positioning as freedom-defending angels, it is fair to ask of them: do you have your priorities right?

A hypothetical question. Assume two products have a similar goal, but *F* is free software. It comes with the standard no-warranty warranty. *P* is proprietary software. It costs $50 for the binary-only version, and uses the most advanced techniques of software engineering. It never crashes or departs in any way from its (mathematically expressed) specification. The seller promises you money back, plus damages, if you find any error. According to the comments cited, *F*, being the only product that preserves users' "freedom," is the ethical one. The seller of *P* is a repugnant profiteer.

Which of these solutions do you consider the more ethical? Does your answer change if the price of the product becomes $5,000? $500,000?

Auxiliary question for special credit: you think the revolutionary software development technique you have just invented can produce provably bug-free products. You need $20 million to productize it. Your university will be glad to pay for a postdoc for six months if you teach an extra course. The funding agencies tell you to get lost, but a group of investors values your idea. They expect to make a windfall, so they'll laugh if you suggest free software. Should you go with them, or is it more ethical to turn them down and devote the next five years of your life to a completely free LATEX extension for Babylonian cuneiform?

The Great Satan

One reason for writing free software deserves some consideration: hatred of the "evil empire" — Microsoft. It is not hard to understand some of the reasons for the resentment of Microsoft. The company grew unbelievably quick, and software engineers have a nagging feeling that it was partly a result of sheer luck: When IBM obtained DOS from Microsoft and hence created the modern Personal Computer industry, it didn't demand exclusivity, enabling Microsoft to sell the same solution to every IBM competitor. (It is interesting to see that IBM's mistake was based on a reasoning — we don't make money out of software products, we make money from selling "iron," that is computers — is not unlike the GNU/FSF argument that one should not sell software, but it's OK to sell computers and services.) The reputation of Microsoft among developers is not helped by the unconfirmed, but widely circulating, rumor that Bill Gates — although hailed by the popular press as the genius software engineer of all times — was, in fact, rather lousy at programming. The reputed arrogance of Microsoft in dealing with partners, competitors, computer vendors and customers does not help.

Anti-Microsoft feeling is also reinforced by the nature of the Microsoft tools; designed for the mass market, they sometimes give computer-savvy users the impression of forcing them into an intellectual stranglehold. Instead of having the Unix programmer's freedom to drive the interaction with versatile commands and scripts, you have to follow the exact scheme that the Redmond folks have devised for you.

For all that, it is easy to miss the incredible contributions of Microsoft — and its de facto partner, Intel — to the just as incredible progress of the computer industry. By establishing a mass market that enabled staggering price reductions, the so-called "Wintel" alliance has made the computer revolution possible. Fanatical advocates of Linux do not seem to realize that without Microsoft, Intel and the resulting 200 million compatible PCs, without the $500 400-MHz systems with a complete operating system, there would be no Linux. The entire computer world, including Microsoft groupies and Microsoft haters, is riding on the coattails of Microsoft. It is easy enough to lambaste Bill Gates. It is less self-flattering for the anti-Microsoft community to understand why Microsoft has reached its unique status. There was the initial stroke of luck, of course. But there was also an in-depth understanding of the market. There was a relentless effort at integration: you write a Microsoft Project plan; integrate a Microsoft Excel spreadsheet and a Microsoft Word document into it at the click of a mouse; post it on your intranet with Microsoft Front Page for your colleagues to access with Microsoft Internet Explorer; have it automatically generate an e-mail with Microsoft Outlook whenever a deadline slips; and so on. The underlying engineering effort supporting this pervasive integration is gigantic, and does more to explain Microsoft's continued success than any conspiracy theory.

In achieving this result, Microsoft, however unpopular some of its tactics may be, relied for the most part on its business acumen and its technical dedication. The losers have no one to blame but the skills of their competitor and their own myopia. Unix, in particular, had its window of opportunity circa 1989, when Windows was little more than a promise; however, Unix vendors scorned the mass market for what must at the time have looked like excellent business reasons. When they woke up a few years later, the mass market opportunity was gone.

Microsoft envy is very palpable in the current excitement around Linux. On the floor of a conference such as Linux World one can hear the constant Microsoft bashing. The jokes can be funny up to a point, but soon one starts to realize that the problem most people have is not Microsoft. It's that they are not Microsoft.

The Ethics of Acknowledgement

A point of ethics that arises in the design of free software has not yet been raised in this discussion (or in any other text that I have read): Many free-software products are "copycat" versions of commercial software. The GNU project indeed made its mark by providing quality replacements for dozen of Unix utilities, from `awk` and `yacc` to `troff` and `cc`.

In software, much of the hard work and creativity goes into specifying a system. By seeing your specification, and having access to your system, a good developer can often reimplement it with reasonable effort. Doing something that has already been done by someone else is an order of magnitude easier if only because there is an existence proof: the reimplementer knows it can be done.

It is both a boon and a bane that the interface of a product to the rest of the world, often the most difficult part of the work, is also the hardest to protect (since you cannot let customers use the product without telling them how to use it!). It's a boon for users, competitors and free-software advocates; it's a bane if you work hard only to see a more powerful competitor prosper on the strength of your ideas. (The first spreadsheet program, VisiCalc, was an immediate hit, leading to great commercial success not for its inventor but for the next implementers.)

It is legal, and it may be ethical, to start from someone else's design and reimplement it. It is profoundly unethical not to acknowledge it, whether the originator dealt in free or in commercial software.

This is not just a matter of being fair and courteous to the people who made possible your own job and hence your own little claims to fame and a great career. It is also a matter of acknowledging the tremendous contributions of commercial software. Commercial products not only save lives; more prosaically, they established the historical basis without which there wouldn't have been any free software. GNU, as we have seen, was unable by itself to build an operating system; the paragon of evil, Microsoft, provided the economic basis that made Linux possible. There would also not have been a GNU (and a GCC, a Linux, a Bison, and so on) if there hadn't been a Unix in the first place, arising from the genius of two AT&T Bell laboratories researchers — Ken Thompson and Dennis Ritchie — working in a proprietary context.

Thompson and Ritchie, by the way, derived many of their ideas from Multics, a sixties' research project from MIT. The cycle is complete: Commercial software builds on public software, and free software builds on commercial software. Sometimes you want one kind, sometimes the other. Both can be bad; both can be admirable. Both result from the hard work of skilled, thorough, dedicated and often idealistic software enthusiasts. It's the same people on both sides of the fence: the passionate "hackers" who think software, dream algorithms, eat data structures, drink objects and discuss, long through the night, the pros and cons of generating code for a machine with a clever instruction prefetch scheme.

Mongering hatred of the members of one of these two complementary communities is unproductive and unethical.

A Course of Action

What should be done? Everyone should:

1. Recognize the major contributions of the free software community.
2. Accept that both commercial and free software have a role to play, and that neither will ever go away.
3. Be respectful of the authors of good free software.
4. Try to convince them to apply the reciprocal goodwill.
5. Refuse and refute the moral defamation of commercial software developers. If you are a software developer, be proud of your profession.
6. Call the extremists' bluff by questioning their moral premises. Re-establish ethical priorities.

7. Refuse the distortion of moral values and the use of free software as a pulpit from which to spread ideologies of violence.

8. Demand (in the spirit of faithful advertising) that the economic origin of "free" software be clearly stated.

9. For Microsoft, whose unique position in the community creates unique responsibilities: promote a more open attitude towards the rest of the world. Open up; you can afford to.

10. For everyone: focus on quality. Work with every competent person — free or commercial software developers — to address the increasingly critical, and increasingly ethical, issue of software quality.

11. Strive to combine the best of what the two communities have to offer.

6.2.6 "Software Process Improvement: 10 Traps to Avoid"
by Karl Wiegers

Surviving in the increasingly competitive software business requires more than hiring smart, knowledgeable engineers and buying the latest development tools. You also need to use effective software development processes, so those smart engineers can systematically use the best technical and managerial practices to successfully complete their projects. More organizations are looking at software process improvement as a way to improve the quality, productivity, and predictability of their software development, acquisition, and maintenance efforts. However, software process improvement efforts can be derailed in many ways, leaving the members of the organization jaded, frustrated, and more committed than ever to the ways of the past.

Here are 10 common traps that can undermine a software process improvement program. Learning about these process improvement killers — and their symptoms and solutions — will stop them from bringing your initiative to its knees.

Trap #1: Lack of Management Commitment

Symptoms: While individual groups can improve the way they do their work through grass roots efforts, sustainable changes across an organization require management commitment at all levels. Senior managers may claim to support process improvements (how can they say otherwise?), but they may not really be willing to make short-term sacrifices to free up the resources required for the long-term investment. Larger organizations must establish alignment between senior management and one or more layers of middle managers.

If you're leading the software process improvement effort, you might obtain senior management commitment, but get resistance from middle managers. In this case you'll be forced to spend time and energy debating the importance of software process improvement with people who should only have to be educated, not sold.

Such mixed signals from management make it hard for team leaders and software developers to take the effort seriously. Watch out for lip service and buzzwords masquerading as commitments. Lower-level managers who assign their least capable people (or none at all) to the program are sending a clear sign that the lack of management commitment is about to foil your effort.

Solutions: Managers at all levels need to send consistent signals about software process improvement to their constituencies. Executives must be educated about its costs, benefits, and risks so they will have a common vision and understanding of this complex area of software development. Commitments need to be aligned along the organizational hierarchy, so that managers are not working at cross purposes, and a reluctant manager cannot sabotage the effort through inaction. Make sure that commitments from management translate into resources devoted to software process improvement, realistically defined expectations of the process group and the engineering staff, and accountability for the results.

Management commitment to software process improvement also affects the morale and dedication of people who are working to advance the cause of better processes in the organization. When management objectives change with the wind and the staff devoted to facilitating process improvement is downsized, those affected may be embittered at having months or years of their technical careers sidetracked for nothing. Once burned in such a fashion, they may be reluctant to step forward the next time the organization is looking for people to enable change.

Trap #2: Unrealistic Expectations

Symptoms: Excessive enthusiasm by ambitious managers can also pose risks to the improvement program. If the goals, target dates, and results expected by managers are not realistic, the software process improvement effort is ultimately set up for failure. Managers, particularly those with little software experience, may not appreciate the effort and time involved in a large-scale software process improvement effort such as one based on the Software Engineering Institute's five-level Capability Maturity Model (CMM). These managers may be confused about how process improvement frameworks like the CMM relate to other software engineering approaches, such as a specific object-oriented methodology. They may focus on issues of pressing importance to them that are not realistic outcomes of the process improvement effort. For example, a manager may hope to solve current staff shortages by driving the organization to reach CMM Level 2, which typically leads to higher software productivity and quality. However, since it can take two years or more to reach Level 2, this is not an effective solution to near-term staffing problems.

Management needs to understand that the behavioral changes and organizational infrastructure that are parts of a successful software process improvement program cannot be mandated or purchased. Catchy slogans like "Level 5 by '95" or "Six Sigma by '96" are not constructive. In an unhealthy competitive environment, process improvement can become a contest: Department A sets an objective of achieving CMM Level 3 by the end of 1997, so the head of Department B says that they can do it by the middle of 1997. With rare exceptions, such behavior is neither inspiring nor motivating.

Solutions: Educate your managers to help them understand the realities of what a serious process improvement initiative will cost and what benefits they might expect. Collect data from the software literature on results that have been achieved by other companies with effective improvement programs and the investments those companies made over a specified time period. Every organization is different, so it's risky to promise an eight-fold return from each dollar invested just because you read that another company actually achieved that level of success. Use data available from the software literature or from other areas of your own company to help your managers develop realistic expectations and set reasonable, even ambitious, goals. Software process improvement is no more of a magic silver bullet than any other single software tool or technology.

Trap #3: Time-Stingy Leaders

Symptoms: When a senior manager states that he or she is committed to improving the software processes used in the organization, most project leaders will say that they are too — whether they mean it or not. However, successful software process improvement initiatives require project leaders to adjust their schedules to permit team members to devote some time to improvement activities. A project leader who claims to believe in software process improvement but who treats it as a burden added on top of other project activities is sending conflicting signals.

Even if team members are permitted to work on improvement tasks, these tasks often get low priority, and "real work" can easily squeeze process improvement activities out of a busy engineer's schedule. Project leaders may respond to the pressure of delivering the current product by curtailing the effort that should go into upgrading the organization's process capability.

Solutions: You need to have consistent, active commitment at all stages of management; a bottleneck anywhere in the organizational hierarchy can bring the software process program to a screeching halt. One way to achieve consistency is through an interlocking management commitment process as a corporate or organizational policy. Top managers publicly state their goals and priorities (including software process improvement), and people at the lower management levels write their goals and priorities to support those of their superiors.

Senior management must make it clear that project leaders will be evaluated on the effectiveness of their process improvement activities, as well as on the success of the software projects themselves. Software project planning needs to account for the staff resources that are being devoted to design and implement the new software processes. In small organizations with shallow management hierarchies, the first-level manager is the most critical factor in the success of any process improvement effort. If this person doesn't make software process improvement a visible priority, it just isn't going to happen.

One way to keep a program viable is to treat all software process improvement activities as mini projects, to give them the visibility and legitimacy they need for success. Write an action plan for each mini project. This plan identifies resources, states timelines, itemizes deliverables, clarifies accountability, and defines techniques to assess the effectiveness of new processes implemented as a result of each mini project.

The need to treat improvement activities with the respect afforded to technical projects does not require extensive documentation; most action plans can be written in just one or two pages. Don't try to solve every process problem in your group at once. Instead, concentrate on the two or three top priority items, as determined through some process assessment mechanism, then tackle the next three, and so on down the line.

Project leaders can't just assign their least effective people to the software process improvement efforts, either. We all want to keep our best people working on technical projects. However, if good people and respected leaders are not active contributors, the process improvement outputs generated will have less credibility with the rest of the organization.

Trap #4: Inadequate Time and Resources Devoted to Training

Symptoms: A process improvement initiative is at risk if the developers, managers, and process leaders do not have adequate skills and training. Each person involved must understand the general principles of process improvement, the CMM and other pertinent software process improvement methodologies, change leadership, software measurement, and related areas.

Inadequate knowledge can lead to false starts, well-intentioned but misdirected efforts, and a lack of apparent progress. This can undermine the improvement effort. Without training, the organization's members will not have a common vocabulary and understanding of how to assess the need for change or how to interpret specialized concepts of the improvement model being followed, such as the CMM or ISO 9001. For example, "software quality assurance" means different things to different people; training is needed to achieve a common understanding of such terms among all participants.

Solutions: Training to support established process improvement frameworks can be obtained from various commercial sources (such as consultants or training vendors), or you can develop training yourself. Different participants in the software process improvement activities will need different kinds of training. If you are using a CMM-based approach, the process improvement group members should receive two to three days of training on the CMM. However, four hours of training about software process improvement using the CMM will be enough for most participants.

If you become serious about software process improvement, consider acquiring training in other key software improvement domains: setting up a software engineering process group, establishing a metrics program, assessing the process capability of a project team, and action planning. Use commercial sources of training wherever possible. This way you avoid having to create all of your own training materials. Table 6.2 identifies several companies that specialize in process improvement training and consulting.

Table 6.2   Process Improvement Consulting Firms

The Process Group
P.O. Box 870012
Dallas, Tex. 75287
Tel: (214) 418-9541

Process Enhancement Partners Inc.
711 Nob Hill Trail
Franktown, Colo. 80116-8717
Tel: (303) 660-9400

Process Inc. US
P.O. Box 1988
Annapolis, Md. 21401
Tel: (301) 261-9921

TeraQuest Metrics Inc.
12885 Research Blvd., Suite 207
Austin, Tex. 78750
Tel: (512) 219-0478

Ronin International
www.ronin-intl.com
Tel: (303) 883-6624

Trap #5: Achieving a CMM Level Becomes the Primary Goal

Symptoms: Organizations that adopt the CMM framework for process improvement risk viewing the attainment of a specific CMM maturity level as the goal of the process improvement, rather than as one mechanism to help achieve the organization's real business goals. Software process improvement energy may be focused on a race to the level *N* rating, when some energy should perhaps be devoted to other problem areas that can contribute quickly to the quality, productivity, people, and management issues facing the organization.

Sometimes, a company is in such a rush to reach the next maturity level that the recently implemented process improvements have not yet become well established and habitual. In such cases, the organization might actually regress back to the previous maturity level, rather than continue to climb the maturity ladder as it is attempting to do. Such regression is a sure-fire way to demoralize practitioners who are eager to move steadily toward a superior software engineering culture.

Solutions: In addition to aiming at the next CMM level, make sure your software process improvement effort is aligned with corporate business and technical objectives. Mesh the process improvement activities with any other improvement initiatives that are underway, such as ISO 9001 registration, or with an established software development framework already in use. Recognize that advancing to the next CMM maturity level can take one to three years. It is not feasible to leap from an initial ad hoc development process to a supersophisticated engineering environment in one fell swoop. Your goal is not to be able to chant, "We're Level 5! We're Level 5!" Your goal is to acquire improved software processes and more capable development engineers so that your company can prosper by offering higher quality products to your customers more efficiently than before.

Use a combination of measurements to track progress toward the business goals as well as measure the progress of the software process improvement program. Goals can include reducing project cycle times and product defect levels. One way to track software process improvement progress is to perform low-cost interim assessments to check the status of your project teams in various CMM key process areas (such as requirements management, project planning, and software configuration management). Over time, you should observe steady progress toward satisfying both CMM key process area goals and your company's software success factors. This is the outcome of a well-planned and well-executed program.

Trap #6: Failing to Scale Formal Processes to Project Size

Symptoms: A small organization can lose the spirit of the CMM (or any other process model) while attempting to apply the model to the letter, introducing excessive documentation and formality that can actually impede project work. This undermines the credibility of software process improvement, as team members look for ways to bypass the official procedures in an attempt to get their work done efficiently. People are reluctant to perform tasks they think add little value to their project.

Solutions: To reach a specific CMM maturity level, you must demonstrate that your organization is satisfying all the goals of each key process area defined at that maturity level. The process definitions your group develops should be no more complicated or elaborate than they need to be to satisfy these goals. Nothing in the CMM says that each procedure must be lengthy or documented in excessive detail. Strive for a practical balance between documenting procedures with enough formality to enable repeatable project successes, and having the flexibility to get project work done with the minimum amount of low-value overhead effort.

This non-dogmatic view doesn't mean that smaller organizations and projects cannot benefit from the discipline provided by the CMM. It simply means that the practices recommended by the CMM should be scaled rationally to the size of the project. A 20-hour project should not demand eight hours of project planning just to conform to a CMM-compliant "documented procedure." Your process improvement action teams should provide a set of scalable processes that can be applied to the various sizes and types of projects your group undertakes.

Trap #7: Excluding Project Team Members from Assessments

Symptoms: If process capability assessments (often led by the software engineering process group) are conducted without adequate participation by the software development staff, they turn into audits. This can lead to a lack of commitment, buy-in, and ownership of the assessment findings by the project team. Assessment methods that depend solely on the responses to a CMM-based questionnaire can overlook important problem areas that should be addressed. Outside "experts" who purport to identify your group's process weaknesses based on insufficient practitioner input will have little credibility with your technical staff.

Solutions: Process change is a cultural change, and the ease of this cultural change depends on the extent of the team's involvement with the process assessment and action planning activities. Include a free-form discussion with a representative group of project team members as part of the assessment process whenever time permits. This discussion can identify problem areas that might relate to CMM practices that were not covered by an assessment questionnaire, but which can still be profitably addressed. For example, software testing is not addressed by Level 2 of the CMM, but if poor testing practices are hurting a project in a Level 1 organization, you should do something about that soon. Similarly, topics may come up in a project team discussion that are not part of the CMM at all, including management or organizational issues, lack of resources for acquiring tools, and so forth.

Use your software engineering process group to actively facilitate the change efforts of your project teams, not just to audit their current process status and report a long, depressing list of findings. Identify process liaisons or champions in the project teams to augment the assessment activities of the process group. Those process liaisons can also help drive effective changes into the project team's behaviors and technical practices. The project team must understand that the software engineering process group is doing process improvement with the members of the project team, not for them or to them.

Trap #8: Stalling on Action Plan Implementation

Symptoms: Action plans might be written after a process assessment, but little progress is made on them because management does not make them a clear priority, assign individuals to work on them, or otherwise take them seriously. Managers may never mention the action plans after they are written, so team members get the message that achieving improved processes by implementing the action plans is really not important. The lack of progress on improvement plans is frustrating to those who actually want to see progress made, and it devalues the investment of time and money made in the process assessment itself.

Solutions: As with Trap #3, a good way to turn plans into actions is to treat improvement activities as miniprojects. Concentrating on just two or three improvement areas at a time avoids overwhelming the project team. You need to measure progress against the plans, and to measure the impact of each action plan on the business results achieved. For example, a plan to improve the effectiveness of unit testing performed by the programmers might include an interim goal to acquire test automation tools and train developers in their use. These interim goals can be tracked easily. The desired business outcome of such an action plan should be a specific quantitative reduction, over some period of time, in the number of defects that slip through the unit testing quality filter.

If your project leaders never seem to make much progress against their action plans, you may need to implement a management oversight function to encourage them to take software process improvement more seriously. For example, in a particular organization I know of, all project leaders must report the status of their software process improvement action plans, every three months, to a multilevel management steering committee. When this occurs, no one wants to be embarrassed by reporting little or no progress on his or her plans. From one perspective, such periodic reporting reflects appropriate management accountability for the commitments that others have made to improve their software processes. From another, this approach represents a "big stick" strategy for enforcing software process improvement, which is best avoided unless action plans simply are not being implemented. Your culture will determine the most effective techniques for driving action plans to completion. The management oversight approach did achieve the desired results in the aforementioned organization.

Trap #9: Process Improvement Becomes a Game

Symptoms: Yet another way that software process improvement can falter is when the participants pay only lip service to the real objective of improving their processes. It creates the illusion of change while actually sticking with business as usual for the most part. The focus is on making sure a process audit is passed, rather than on really changing the organization's culture for the better. Software process improvement looks like the current flavor of the month, so group members just wait for this latest fad to pass so they can get back to working in their old familiar ways. Sometimes, the quest for ever-higher process maturity levels becomes a race. Project teams go through the appropriate motions in an attempt to satisfy some aspect of the CMM, but time is not provided for the group to really internalize the corresponding behaviors before management sets its sights on the next CMM maturity level.

Solutions: To succeed with software process improvement, focus on meeting organizational and company objectives with the help of improved software processes. Do not simply try to conform to the expectations of an established framework like the CMM, ISO 9001, or the Malcolm Baldrige quality award. It is not enough to simply create documented procedures to satisfy the letter of some improvement framework; you must also satisfy the spirit of the framework by actually following those procedures in your daily project work.

The CMM talks about institutionalizing process improvements, making new practices routine across the organization. Organization members must also internalize improved procedures, becoming committed enough to the new processes that they would not consider going back to their old ways of building software. As a process change leader, identify the behaviors you would expect to see throughout the organization in each improvement area if superior processes are successfully internalized and institutionalized. As a manager, your group members need to understand that you are serious about continually striving to improve the way they build software; the old methods are gone for good. Continuous improvement means just that, not a one-shot game we play so that someone's checklist can be filled in properly.

Trap #10: Expecting Defined Procedures to Make People Interchangeable

Symptoms: Managers who have an incomplete understanding of the CMM may expect that having repeatable processes available (CMM Level 2) means that every project can expect to achieve the same results with any set of randomly assembled team members. They may think that the existence of a defined process in the organization makes all software engineers equally effective. They might even believe that working on software process improvement means that they can neglect technical training to enhance the skills of their individual software engineers.

Solutions: Individual programmers have been shown to have a 10-to-1, 20-to-1, or even higher range of performance (quality and productivity) on software projects. Process improvements alone can never equalize such a large range of individual capability. You can close the gap quite a bit by expecting people to follow effective defined processes, rather than using whatever methods they are used to. This will enable people at the lower end of the capability scale to achieve consistently better results than they might get other wise. However, never underestimate the importance of attracting, nurturing, and rewarding the best software engineers and managers you can find. Aim for software success by creating an environment in which all team members share a commitment to quality and are enabled — through superior processes, appropriate tools, and effective team interactions — to reach their peak performance.

As you chart a course to improve your software process capability, be aware of the many minefields lurking below your organization's surface. Your chances of success increase dramatically if you watch for the symptoms that identify these traps as a threat to your process improvement program and make plans to deal with them right away. Process improvement is succeeding at many companies. Make yours one of them by controlling these risks — and others — as well as you can.

6.2.7 "Process Improvement That Works"

by Karl Wiegers

Software process improvement is simple: consistently apply the practices that give you good results, and change the practices that cause problems. So why do so many development organizations fail to keep up with their SPI efforts?

Many development organizations are climbing onto the software process improvement (SPI) bandwagon, but too many of them are falling back off again. To get a zero return on your SPI investment, follow this simple procedure:

- Spend money and time on process assessments, consulting services, and training seminars.
- Create a big honkin' binder of procedures and tell all team members they must follow all of the procedures starting immediately.

- Hear senior management decree, "Make it so!"
- Watch the binders gather dust as team members never really change the way they work.

Here are some lessons from the process improvement trenches that can help you avoid this exercise in futility. I'll share practical tips for how to approach SPI, along with descriptions of the basic process improvement steps.

What Is Process Improvement?

At its core, process improvement is simple: consistently apply the practices that give you good results, and change the practices that cause problems. This requires honest introspection and careful analysis to identify the reasons behind your previous projects' successes and shortcomings. Your primary motivation should be to achieve specific business results through better software development and management approaches. You can use established process improvement frameworks like the Software Engineering Institute's Capability Maturity Model for Software (CMM) to guide your efforts. Remember, though, your objective is not simply to satisfy the model's expectations.

The Process Improvement Cycle

Figure 6.1 illustrates an overall SPI cycle. After defining your desired business objectives, assess your current processes, problems, and project outcomes. Armed with assessment insights and a knowledge of software industry best practices, you can then set realistic improvement goals. Select a small set of appropriate practices that will address your current process shortcomings and move you toward your goals. Identify a project or two on which to pilot new processes and make adjustments before officially rolling them out.

Figure 6.1   The Software Process Improvement Life Cycle

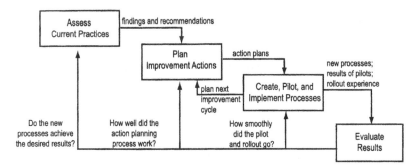

Planning how you will implement new ways of working greatly increases your chance of success. The hardest part is actually implementing an action plan; if you don't, nothing will really change. Give the new processes some time, then see whether they're easing the problems those improvement actions targeted. Hard data about process benefits is more convincing than subjective perceptions. Then continue the improvement cycle with the next most pressing need. Process improvement is a journey, not a destination.

Focus on the Pain

Pain is the best motivation for changing the way people work. I don't mean external or artificially induced pain, but rather the very real pain we sometimes experience from our current methods. One way to encourage people to change is to persuade them that the grass will be greener in the intended future state. A more compelling motivation is to point out that the grass behind them is already on fire.

The assessment helps reveal the points of pain and major risks facing your projects. An assessment can be a simple brainstorming session in which your team members identify barriers to improving their productivity and quality. Alternatively, you can invest in a semiformal evaluation by an external consultant or in a rigorous formal process appraisal conducted according to an established process model such as the CMM. Such formal appraisals are expensive and time-consuming, but they thoroughly evaluate your current practices against some process standard.

In my experience, a process assessment doesn't usually reveal major surprises. Most groups are already aware of their problem issues and behaviors. Having an external party conduct the assessment legitimizes it, because the external party is free of the development organization's politics, historical tensions, and personalities. The assessment lets you confront the uncomfortable problem situations directly. An assessment should never be a forum for finding fault or blaming individuals for past problems.

Performing an assessment can also demonstrate management's commitment to process improvement. Be sure to follow through on the assessment's findings and recommendations. If you don't, you'll lose the money and time you've spent on the assessment, as well as credibility with team members.

An assessment usually identifies more improvement opportunities than you can tackle at once. "Focus" is a key word in process improvement. It takes longer than you probably think to devise better processes and make them part of the way your group routinely operates. I once saw a highly motivated, 20-person project team undertake seven improvement areas concurrently. Resources were spread thin, priorities were unclear, and the team accomplished little, despite the members' enthusiasm.

State your process improvement objectives in terms of the desired business results. For example, a goal could be to eliminate incorrect builds being handed off from development to system testing, not merely to write a build-and-promote procedure. The SPI activities are a means to an end, not an end in themselves. Your managers should be able to articulate how they expect the group's behaviors and results to be different if the SPI program succeeds.

Based on your top priority goals, pick two or three improvements to address initially. If you complete them quickly, great; go back to the assessment report and select the next area to work on. Don't try to do too much right out of the gate. Large organizations can undertake several change initiatives concurrently across multiple projects, but each project team should focus on just a few areas at a time.

Communicate, Communicate, Communicate

People naturally resist changing the way they work, because they have a comfort level with familiar (if not always effective) practices and a fear of the unknown. Concern about burdensome process overhead that stifles creativity and delays delivery is also common, but the fear normally exceeds the reality. Your team members might also experience a sense of failure because the assessment identified process shortcomings, even though they've been working as hard as they can. Customers and other external groups might view the SPI program as raising barriers that will make it harder for them to get what they want from developers.

To address these issues, communication should permeate your process improvement activities. Articulate the price being paid for your current process shortcomings. This price might include blown schedules, missing functionality, massive overtime, high product-support costs, unhappy customers, or low morale. Explain to skeptics what benefits the improvement activities will provide to individuals, the project team, the company, and customers. Allay the fear of overwhelming change by stressing that new processes will be selected thoughtfully, created by the team members themselves, and rolled out gradually. Look for "allies" who are willing to try new procedures and document templates, provide feedback, and help lay the groundwork for successful change.

Trumpet your achievements to the team members and other stakeholders. Publicly recognizing the individuals who contributed to each successful change demonstrates that constructive participation in the SPI program is desired. Analyze unsuccessful change attempts to understand why they struggled and adjust your approaches accordingly.

A key SPI operating principle is "Gentle pressure, relentlessly applied." Keep your improvement goals and status visible to the team. Stress how the SPI goals align with your organization's business goals. Set aside time during team meetings to review the process improvement progress. Periodically report successes to management to bolster their support for the effort.

A kiss of death is to launch an improvement program with great fanfare at the beginning of the year, then never mention it again until you see whether or not you reached your goals at year's end. You won't. Working on project activities will always be more important to most team members than contributing to process improvement. Managers must frequently remind the team that SPI work is important and valued.

Organize for Process Improvement

Organizations that are serious about SPI often set up a three-level organizational infrastructure to make it succeed (as shown in Figure 6.2), but you should adapt these ideas to your organization. This structure shouldn't be any more complicated than necessary to ensure that sensible improvement actions are identified, initiated, and implemented effectively. The management steering committee (MSC) commits resources and sets direction and priorities. It might also identify a "process owner" for each improvement area, a manager who is responsible for achieving improvements and provides continuity as individual working groups come and go.

Typical MSC members include the organization's senior manager, the manager who is responsible for the SPI program, the individual leading the SPI effort, and selected project or department managers. Getting several management levels to participate actively in the MSC indicates that the organization is taking process improvement seriously. The MSC's responsibilities include:

- Setting improvement area priorities
- Chartering working groups to address specific improvement areas
- Monitoring activities and status
- Assessing the impact of the improvement actions completed to date
- Managing process improvement risks and breaking down barriers

Figure 6.2 A Typical Process Improvement Organizational Structure

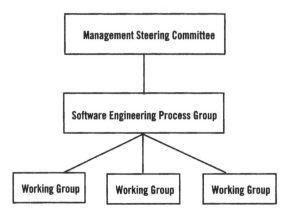

The software engineering process group (SEPG) coordinates the various process improvement actions. The SEPG acts as management's agents to implement the process improvement program. A large organization's SEPG should have a full-time manager, some full-time software process specialists, and a rotating cast of practitioners who participate on a part-time basis for a year or so.

Process specialists often come out of the testing and quality assurance ranks, but several SEPG members should have substantial development experience. Project management experience is a needed perspective, also. These qualifications will give the SEPG more credibility with developers and managers than if it is viewed as a bunch of theoreticians who don't know how real software development gets done.

Process Improvement Resources

Books:

- Perhaps the best known SPI resource is *The Capability Maturity Model: Guidelines for Improving the Software Process* by Mark C. Paulk, Charles V. Weber, Bill Curtis, and Mary Beth Chrissis (Addison-Wesley, 1995). Even if you don't want to formally apply the CMM, it contains useful guidelines for process improvements.

- *CMM Implementation Guide: Choreographing Software Process Improvement* by Kim Caputo (Addison-Wesley, 1998) provides many recommendations for putting the CMM into practice and includes a CD with useful process-related artifacts.

- My book, *Creating a Software Engineering Culture* (Dorset House, 1996), takes a less formal approach, describing case studies of many improvements that small software groups made.

- Steve McConnell's *Rapid Development: Taming Wild Software Schedules* (Microsoft Press, 1996) describes dozens of best practices to consider incorporating into your software process.

Web Sites:

- The Software Engineering Institute's web site (www.sei.cmu.edu) has many useful technical reports you can download on a wide variety of software engineering and process improvement topics.
- Brad Appleton has a rich set of process improvement links available at www.enteract.com/~bradapp/links/sw-proc-links.html.
- My web site, www.processimpact.com, has templates for the strategic and tactical action plans described in this article. It also lists many magazine article references and links to software process and quality improvement resources.

—*Karl Wiegers*

SEPG members learn a lot about assessments, process improvement frameworks, writing good processes and procedures, and influencing change. The human and organizational issues of change management are at least as important as the technical aspects of process improvement. Effective SEPG members are good communicators who can adapt their approaches to individual situations. They are also well-organized, patient, and flexible. They are skilled facilitators who lead fruitful discussions on sensitive topics with diverse participants, some of whom probably don't believe in SPI and would rather not participate.

The SEPG serves as a resource to all those involved in the process improvement program. The group's expertise, resources, and outside connections accelerate the change initiative because practitioners involved in the effort have a place to go for help. SEPG members typically perform the following functions:

- Develop strategic and tactical improvement action plans.
- Lead or participate in process assessments.
- Coordinate and facilitate process improvement working groups.
- Collect and disseminate literature and information on industry best practices.
- Accumulate process assets, such as procedures, templates, checklists, and work product examples, and share them across the organization (see my article, "Improve Your Process with Online 'Good Practices,'" *The Unified Process Inception Phase,* Chapter 6).
- Review new processes, procedures, and templates that working groups create.
- Lead improvement activities that span the entire organization, such as metrics and training programs.

It's not a good idea to have the SEPG write all the new procedures and inflict them on the project teams. This classic "throw it over the wall to land on the victims' heads" approach almost always fails. Instead, get practitioners involved in developing realistic new procedures through their participation in process improvement working groups, also called process action or process improvement teams. A working group is an ad hoc group of about three to six project representatives who address a specific improvement area. Their deliverables typically include a description of the processes currently being used in that area, as well as new processes and process assets. A working group's efforts might lead to new processes for just one project, or they could develop processes for an entire organization.

Scope each working group's objectives such that it can complete its tasks within about three months. If the working group goes on for too long, the members may lose their enthusiasm and turnover is likely. You can always re-charter it or convene a new group for the next round of improvement actions. Try to get all practitioners and project leaders involved in a working group at some point (although not all at once). This will help give all team members a sense of ownership toward the new processes. A member of the SEPG can launch each group and facilitate its initial meetings. However, it's important for the development organization to adopt ownership of its improvement program and sustain its own working group efforts after the SEPG removes the training wheels.

Plan Your Actions

Treat your SPI program like a project, giving it the structure, resources, and respect that any development project needs. Two useful planning components are an overall strategic software process improvement plan and a tactical action plan for each working group. Some people balk at writing plans, viewing them as wasteful process bureaucracy and overhead. However, writing the plan isn't the hard part. The hard part is thinking, asking, listening, understanding, negotiating, and thinking some more. Actually, writing the plan is mostly transcription at that point. I've found that plans help keep even simple projects on course and provide something against which I can track my progress.

Table 6.3 suggests a template for a strategic SPI plan, which guides the organization's long-term improvement activities. The organization's process improvement leader typically is the prime author of this plan, although members of the SEPG and key managers should review and approve it. Adapt this template to serve your own SPI planning needs.

Each working group should write an action plan, using a standard template, that describes what the group intends to accomplish and how. The action plan should identify:

- Business or technical goals to be accomplished, which should trace back to the overall goals expressed in the strategic SPI plan
- Measures to tell if the process changes have had the desired effects
- Organizational scope of these process changes
- Participants, their roles, and their time commitments
- How often and to whom the group will report status, results, and issues
- Any external dependencies or risks
- The target completion date for all activities
- A list of action items, identifying for each the individual owner, date due, purpose, activities, deliverables, and resources needed

Limit the number of action items in each plan to 9 or 10 specific, small actions. This will help you scope the working group's efforts to just a few months.

Steer to Success

Process improvement leadership is a steering function, guiding the organization first to accept that better practices are needed and then to successfully implement them. This steering requires stable goals and constancy of purpose. Ever-changing improvement objectives confuse and frustrate practitioners, who might throw up their hands and say, "Tell me when you figure out what you really want." Avoid being distracted by a quest for higher CMM levels; focus instead on improving your business results by selectively and creatively applying the guidance from existing frameworks such as the CMM.

Table 6.3   Template for a Strategic Software Process Improvement Plan

Purpose
> Acronyms
> Reference Documents

Overview

Executive Summary

Business Case for SPI Initiative
> Business Rationale
> Guiding Principles

Process Improvement Goals
> Short-Term Goals
> Guiding Principles

Assumptions, Risks, and Barriers

Organization for Process Improvement
> Organizational Scope
> Management Steering Committee
> Software Process Improvement Leader
> Software Engineering Process Group
> Working Groups
> Process Owners
> SPI Consultant

Criteria for Success

Improvement Agenda
> Selection of SPI Activities
> Current SPI Activities
> Process Improvement Roadmap

Decide how serious you are about SPI and allocate resources accordingly. Organizations that spend less than 3% or 4% of their budget on process improvement (including training, assessments, consultants, SEPG staffing, and working groups) are dabbling. Organizations that invest 7% or 8% are pretty serious, and spending more than 10% of your budget indicates a major commitment. Track the time actually spent on SPI activities to see if the planned work is really getting done and whether your current resource level is consistent with your objectives.

Recognize the reality of the learning curve — the short-term performance drop that results as you learn new work methods and incorporate them into everyone's personal processes. It will take time for individuals to internalize new and better ways of working, and for the organization as a whole to institutionalize new methods as routine practice. The time and money you spend on SPI is a strategic investment in the long-term success of your organization, and those resources aren't available for immediate project use. Take satisfaction in small victories and celebrate your successes. Keep trying to do your project work better tomorrow than you did it yesterday, and you'll come out ahead. That's all process improvement is really about.

6.2.8 "Beyond Optimizing"

by James A. Highsmith III
Edited by Larry Constantine

In an adaptive organization, the role of rigor is to provide just enough structure to prevent chaos but not enough to dampen the creativity of your collaborative networks.

According to the Software Engineering Institute, the optimizing organization is the epitome of software development practices. Today it seems every development group wants to earn that coveted accolade of SEI Level 5. "Successful companies," states Bill Roetzheim in "Customized Process Improvement" (*Focus on Project Management,* Mar. 1999), "standardize every business process to the point where an average employee can be successful simply by following the outlined process." Yuck. Will all you average employees out there who want to spend your careers following regulated, simplistic rules please raise your hands?

Repeatable, standardized processes reflect the attitude of software development traditionalists who believe in optimizing management practices characterized by rigorous rules and tight control. Optimization solved yesterday's software delivery problems. However, today software project managers must deliver concrete results in shorter time frames while being constantly bombarded with myriad changes and risk-laden decisions. On complex, e-business-like projects — those defined by high speed and uncertainty — I contend that while some optimizing practices are necessary, they are also insufficient. It is adaptation practices that are essential. This issue of adaptation vs. optimization changes the perspective of project managers from a mechanical view that lets you predict the future, follow a plan with minimal deviation, and drive out ugly process variations to an organic view in which the determinants of success are creativity, innovation, fast learning, skilled problem-solving, and effective decision-making.

The transition from an optimizing to an adaptive perspective involves defining an organic organizational model to replace our mechanistic one; describing a new adaptive management style, one I've labeled leadership-collaboration, to replace the command-and-control style that permeates optimizing organizations; and finally, examining the role of rigor in adaptive organizations.

The Biology of Organizations

Biological metaphors are hot, mechanical metaphors are not — at least in recent management literature. Kevin Kelly characterizes newer organizational systems as having lack of central control, autonomous subunits, high connectivity, and nonlinear causality in *Out of Control: The New Biology of Machines, Social Systems and the Economic World* (Perseus Press, 1995). These systems are more adaptable, evolvable, and resilient says Kelly. Arie De Geus in *The Living Company: Habits for Survival in a Turbulent Business Environment* (Harvard Business School Press, 1997) writes that the machine metaphor has long shaped management thinking, our notions of control, and our approach to people. De Geus describes how viewing companies as a collection of living beings shapes management thinking in distinctly different ways.

Mechanical thinking results in process thinking. Organic thinking results in pattern thinking. The difference between processes and patterns is key to understanding the organic nature of organizations. Visualize the traditional input-process-output diagram with a feedback loop that includes a control block. This picture has dominated our view of mechanical and electronic control systems, and unfortunately, our view of organizational systems. The process is known — step, step, step. The control block is likened to a thermostat in a heating system, adjusting temperature based on measurements and a plan (the set temperature) — all mechanical, rule-based, predictable, and controllable.

The Software Engineering Institute's (SEI) Capability Maturity Model (CMM) is the pinnacle of the optimizing viewpoint. The CMM and its highly structured, process-centric managerial cousins (like business process reengineering) attempt to counteract uncertainty by admonishing people to be more certain. It is about as effective as telling a raging Mt. Everest storm to desist.

If the SEI were a business with five products — from the basic Level 1 model to the luxury Level 5 model — why has selling fewer than 10 luxury models in 15 years been considered successful? The software development community is characterized by the SEI and strict process adherents as being undisciplined and remaining in a state of immaturity. But maybe, just maybe, we aren't undisciplined or immature after all. Another explanation for the handful of Level 5 organizations is that there are only a half-dozen environments in the world that are stable and predictable enough for the "optimizing" approach to work.

In reality, solutions to complex problems are highly dependent on initial conditions and variable inputs, and the rules are either heuristic or nonexistent. Complex systems give rise to perpetual novelty that, in turn, resists canned solutions. For example, great chess players don't follow rules; they understand "patterns" of past play that indicate what future moves may be beneficial. Following the 14 recommended steps in a requirements definition process does not guarantee success — it is not a process in the sense of an algorithm. The 14 steps define a pattern that increases the odds of a favorable outcome, but are in no way a guarantee. Requirements definition is not a repeatable process that you can measure and refine to the point of statistical control. It is a pattern that you must continuously adapt as you learn from your environment.

Processes are limited to a discrete set of acceptable inputs; patterns can deal with variety and ambiguity. Processes imply you don't have to think; patterns challenge your creativity and problem-solving abilities. Processes are measured; patterns are assessed. Processes are controlled; patterns are learned from, adapted, and influenced. Processes are mechanical; patterns are organic.

The Leadership-Collaboration Management Model

Saying, "We are an adaptable organization" doesn't make it so — even if you're Star Trek's commander Jean-Luc Picard. Adaptability involves profound cultural changes. Dee Hock coined the word "chaordic" to describe adaptable organizations, those balanced on the edge between order and chaos. Hock, the former CEO of Visa International, who presided over Visa's growth to $7.2 billion transactions and $650 billion annually, said simply and effectively, "Simple, clear purpose and principles give rise to complex, intelligent behavior.

Complex rules and regulations give rise to simple, stupid behavior." ("Institutions in the Age of Mindcrafting," 1994 Bionomics Annual Conference in San Francisco, Calif.).

The leadership-collaboration model embraces Hock's chaordic idea. In this model, leadership replaces command and collaboration replaces control. Managers who embrace the leadership-collaboration model understand their primary role is to set direction, to provide guidance, to facilitate the decision-making process, and to expedite connecting people and teams.

Adaptive organizations are messy, anxiety-ridden, exciting, exuberant, bubbling, and redundant — they are just this side of chaotic, but not quite there. Adaptive organizations listen to the world around them — their customers, suppliers, employees, competitors — and respond to what they learn, not to what some process rule told them. Control-oriented managers revel in structure; collaborative managers revel in connectivity and real-world ambiguity.

Leadership-collaboration style managers believe in people and passion. Ardent "structure" proponents confuse structure and skill — they deem unstructured to be unskilled. In "The Commando Returns" (*Software Development Management Forum*, Mar. 1999), Dave Thielen falls into this trap when he argues that "average" programmers need more structure than "above-average" ones. First, I abhor the concept of an "average" person. If you create the right environment and align capabilities and roles, everyone can be the best they can be, to paraphrase the Army slogan. Second, while structure can support and leverage skill, I don't think increasing structure makes up for skill deficiency. For example, if I have trouble articulating good questions, no amount of "structure" will turn me into a good systems analyst; it will merely leave me a poor — and grouchy — systems analyst. There is a place for structure, but substituting it for skill isn't that place.

Another underappreciated aspect of skill arises from knowledge management — the concepts of tacit and explicit knowledge. At a simple level, explicit knowledge is codified, or documented, and tacit knowledge is that still in your head. Best practices may be written down, but it takes tacit knowledge (from experience, know-how, thought, judgment, and more) to bring them to fruition. Explicit knowledge provides you with the rules, tacit knowledge provides you with the deeper understanding that tells you when to break or bend the rules. You can no more become a good programmer from reading a C++ book than become a golfer by reading a treatise by Tiger Woods.

Proponents of process and structure assume that knowledge can be written down, encapsulated in little "knowledge" objects (called best practices), and plunked into peoples' brains just as reusable code is plunked into the next application. But whether you are a professional golfer or a professional software developer, the essence of your skill is tacit — it can't be written down and plunked into the next recruit. The essence of skill isn't what we record on paper; it's defined by proficiency, mastery, virtuosity, savvy, and artistry. Tacit knowledge-transfer takes time, energy, and face-to-face apprenticeship. Structure is not a substitute for skill.

Rigor in an Adaptive Organization

In the twenty-first century, we will need to move beyond arguments about unstructured vs. disciplined approaches to software development. We need a new framework. The science of complex adaptive systems (whether the components are neural networks in the brain or team members in a project) provide a clue to the role of rigor in an adaptive organization. Complex adaptive systems generate emergent (creative and innovative) results while teetering at the edge of chaos. This phenomenon, this tiny edge hovering between the twin abysses of stability and chaos, is driven from connectivity and information flow, not isolation and rules. "When systems of any kind (for example, beehives, businesses, economies) are poised on the edge of chaos between too much structure and too little structure, they 'self-organize' to produce complex adaptive behavior," writes Shona Brown and Kathleen Eisenhardt in *Competing on the Edge* (Harvard Business School Press, 1998). Too much structure reduces problem solving and innovation; too little creates chaos and ineffectiveness.

In an optimizing organization, the role of rigor is to control, raising predictability to a statistical plateau. In an adaptive organization, the role of rigor is to provide just enough structure to prevent chaos but not enough to dampen the creativity of our collaborative networks. "A little bit less than just enough" is my guideline for implementing rigor. If people and their passion are the true core of any development effort, then rigor must be wielded with a deft touch, not brute force.

Surviving in an E-Business World

In our world brimming with both remarkable opportunity and frightening uncertainty, we need an adaptive model of both project and organizational management. We need a model that views rigor as a balancing mechanism rather than a goal. We need a model that draws creativity and innovation out of people's passion, because when structure drives out passion we have failed as leaders. Individual practices of the CMM (for example, requirements management and configuration control) aren't obsolete, it's the framework (maturity levels) and philosophy (predictability and control) that are outdated. What we need is a new framework — patterns and connectivity — and a new philosophy — organic and adaptive — that sustain developers in our quest to tilt at the windmills of complexity.

6.2.9 "Just Doing It"

by Warren Keuffel

How Nike uses its "Just Do It" corporate message to create an effective software development process.

Few advertising campaigns proclaim a company's culture to the world as much as Nike's "Just Do It." Nike makes certain that as many people in as many cultures as possible hear and see professional athletes deliver the company's message. When a company's culture is advertised so pervasively and proudly, a peek behind the scenes at its software development processes can prove interesting.

Like many fast-growing companies, Nike found its ability to deliver manufacturing and financial information lagged behind the delivery of its latest products. And it wasn't just shoes; even though the footwear business dominates the company's image and manufacturing activities, Nike also has significant lines of business in athletic equipment and sports apparel. Nike's management realized a flexible and always-current enterprise data model for product information would provide a firm foundation on which to build the information technology infrastructure it needed to maintain a competitive position. But previous efforts to build such a model had failed. The reasons will be familiar to some of you: development was done by a part-time, techie-only team; the team attempted to provide a static snapshot of a company's dynamic activities; and a central group dictated requirements for a distributed company.

Rather than repeat past mistakes, Nike embarked on an effort to build a global product model. This model would incorporate the core data that would underlay any local implementation of that data. Funded and driven by the footwear division, Nike's vice president of finance, Bob Harold, sponsored an effort that would prove to be radically different from any other development initiative at Nike. The chief architect of the global product model, Jerry Gordon, knew the conservative culture of Nike's information technology organization would require a radical change in process if the project was to succeed.

Adaptive Software Development

To sparkplug that culture change, Gordon brought in consultant Jim Highsmith as project manager. Highsmith's work with adaptive software development (ASD) processes had caught Gordon's attention during earlier consulting engagements. (I have written previously about ASD [see "Adapting Personal Processes," *Tools of the Trade*, July 1997]; if you're interested in learning more, you can check out www.ksinc.com.) One of the first tasks facing Highsmith was how to bring Nike's major divisions — footwear, apparel, equipment, logistics, finance, and retail — together for a coordinated effort. Each division has its own information technology organization. While conservative, these organizations had performed well for Nike using the traditional "plan, analyze, define, build, test and install" life cycle approaches. In recent years, they've experimented with JAD and RAD with good success in client/server projects.

The key concept behind ASD is that the traditional, deterministic plan-build-revise cycle must be replaced with an adaptive model that focuses on an iterative speculate-collaborate-learn model. Speculation acknowledges that the probability of making mistakes with traditional planning is high, so it's best to postulate a general idea of where the project is going. The collaboration phase stresses ASD's emphasis on realizing that you can't tightly control software development projects and expect great software to emerge. ASD advocates a management style that recognizes emergent software development exists on the edge of chaos. In the learning phase, value is attached to the products of the two prior phases, and the activities in the speculation phase adapt to the information gathered in the prior phases and cycles.

Chaos is encouraged in ASD. It's seen as a necessary step on the path — particularly through early iterations of the speculate-collaborate-learn cycle. But chaos is uncomfortable for many people. For conservative information technology folks, it's especially difficult. However, those in the Nike business units, where the cutting-edge culture reigns supreme (they do take "Just Do It" to heart), found the chaos exhilarating.

Nike's Global Product Model

For the global product model project, Gordon assembled a team charged with development a core data model that would embody the data attributes common to all implementations of a given entity. For example, the team defined the product entity as containing attributes for ID (key); color specification; and codes for dimensions, status in the development process, design location, development location, and so on. But attributes for business-specific data such as whether a shoe had an air sole would be left for the individual lines of business to add — on top of the corporate core data model.

The team that developed this core data model was drawn from organizations that would ultimately be using the core data as the basis for their lines of business or function-specific tasks. Thus, the project team had to represent all cells of a matrix that included the footwear, equipment, and apparel lines of business in one dimension; and the functions of finance, sales and marketing, management, and customers in the other. The team was charged with providing a common face to the data for each cell.

In addition, the team needed to create a data model that would provide a seamless flow of product information. A reengineering effort within the footwear division provided the initial impetus for the global product model, as footwear was losing the ability to track its products. Problems stemmed from product conception, to design and manufacturing, to distribution. Nike later extended the footwear reengineering effort to meet the needs of the other lines of business.

Thus, the core data model received support from several quarters. This satisfied the requirement of achieving management support, most notably from the CIO and senior managers in finance. With this high-level support, the team was created. It consisted of six full-time and six half-time employees from both technical and business backgrounds. In addition, another eight to ten quarter-time employees were assigned to the project. These individuals, most of whom were managers or leads with extensive experience in their lines of business, were organized into subteams.

From September 1996 through January 1997, the team developed a global product model. It devoted one week to the model, then it broke up into subteams that met once or twice weekly. In addition, the whole team would gather for a group meeting every Thursday. Highsmith established three iterative cycles; each with clearly defined objectives.

In the first cycle, Highsmith created a feeling of chaos by making the team establish its own strategies and objectives — in essence, by giving each team a blank sheet of paper. Because most people flounder when placed in situations without clear directions, they felt very uncomfortable when charged with establishing the direction of their teams. As a result, the teams were deliberately encouraged to accept that details in the early stages would be fuzzy. The teams were told they were expected to make lots of mistakes, but that they should make them and correct them early. The purpose of this cycle was to force closure on issues and learn from mistakes.

In the subsequent cycles, the level of anxiety and discomfort diminished as the participants became more comfortable with their responsibilities. However, 80% of the work was accomplished in the first two cycles, which created what Highsmith calls the "groan factor." The heavy load, uncertainty, and chaotic atmosphere results in participants making greater contributions, both creatively and productively, than would occur in more traditional environments. The objective, Highsmith says, is to load as much anxiety as possible onto the front end of the project, when people are at their most energetic. In traditional projects, most anxiety occurs as the final deadline nears.

Positive Results

The results of each iteration were presented twice: once to the technical staff and once to the business staff. Because (or perhaps in spite of) the "Just Do It" culture at Nike, the many, inevitable mistakes found during the presentation following the first cycle were not used to bludgeon the project. Instead, a positive attitude prevailed. Everyone understood that it was necessary to make mistakes to get a good product, but it was better to make them early in the process.

Gordon says, in his opinion, Nike was happy with the results of the global product model effort. He wonders, however, whether ASD would fare as well in an organization that didn't have the same culture. He recommends that other, non-technical areas of business could benefit from the ASD principles. However, Highsmith suggests there are scalability issues that must also be addressed.

Any process that makes people uncomfortable carries with it many risks. Some participants may go back to their groups with negative reports of team direction. Some may attempt to play politics with upper management and sabotage the project. Without good facilitation, some participants may flounder and get nowhere. But for organizations with an energetic culture, such as what Nike is famous for, chaotic development may bring greater regards than tradition team management methods provide. Try the ASD principles in your next project, and see if you can "just do it."

6.2.10 "Unified Hegemony"

by Larry Constantine

No one wants to be the grinch who stole unification, but a truly rational perspective demands airing of the problems of a universal process.

It is virtually impossible to be an informed manager of software development today without being aware of the "U" word. It's on the covers of books, in articles in our trade magazines and prominently featured in the titles of conferences and conference presentations. Where once the marketplace of ideas was enamored with objects, now it seems ready to devour anything claiming to be unified. The acronymic derivatives of the "U" word do a dizzying dance before our eyes — UML, UP, RUP, EUP, USDP — and we wonder whether we should celebrate our emancipation, bemoan our homogenization or snicker cynically at the exaggeration.

Perhaps this trend is merely the technological echo of the zeitgeist abroad in the larger world. A divided Germany has reunified. The Europeans have their Union. Even in the often divisive world of competitive sports, "A World in Union," the inspirational theme song debuted at the World Cup in South Africa in 1996, now opens Rugby Union matches around the globe. And today, theoretical physicists stand poised (as they have for decades) on the threshold of a grand unification, the theory of everything that eluded even Einstein.

In the smaller universe of software development (there are only about 6 million of us developers worldwide), the leading theme songs are UML (Unified Modeling Language) and the UP (Unified Process). These purport to give developers and their managers a common notation for representing their ideas and a universal process for translating ideas into software. A few stalwarts notwithstanding, hardly a skeptical voice is raised and scarcely a dissonant note is heard amidst the unison chorus heralding the arrival of this new age of software development unity. No one wants to be the grinch who stole unification, but a truly rational management perspective demands consideration of some of the problems as well as the benefits of unified this or unified that.

The issues in unification are fresh in my mind because my company recently sponsored an international conference on the convergence between usage-centered design and UML/UP. Experts from three continents converged on tiny Rowley, Massachusetts and spent five days wrestling with the problems and solutions and providing the inspiration for this column.

Advocating Consistency

The fact is that UML and the tools that support it have much to offer software development managers. A single common notation means that results from diverse development teams and projects are more readily shared and compared. Skills also become more portable and transferable when new hires do not have to learn a proprietary scheme of representation.

The need for a common means of modeling software has been recognized by many, and I have long been an outspoken advocate for uniform conventions and consistency, particularly in the matter of notation. Electronics engineers around the world can read each other's diagrams, but the programming priesthood long shunned uniformity, with each sect portraying its problems and picturing its solutions in its own hieroglyphics.

Well before unification was a cloud in Grady Booch's eye, methodologists Meilir Page-Jones, Steven Weiss and I teamed up to tackle the problem of creating a common notation for modeling object-oriented systems, one that combined (unified) notation for object-oriented and procedural programs. Far less ambitious than UML, our notation also bore a more modest moniker (see "Modeling Object-Oriented Systems: A Uniform Object Notation," *Computer Language*, Oct. 1990). Though now little more than a historic curiosity, the Uniform Object Notation (UON), along with other pioneering notations, contributed to the dialogue and left an enduring legacy that can be seen today in UML.

Sour Notes

In the eyes of many, one of the great strengths of UML is that it is comprehensive, which, alas, it is not. Despite its size and complexity, much is left out of UML. Not surprising, considering its origins among the gurus of the object-oriented paradigm, UML provides little or no support for describing software that is not built solely from objects. Ironically, although use cases are at the very heart of modern software development practice and figured prominently in the evolution of UML, the current version provides no explicit and dedicated scheme for structuring the narratives that define use cases. Its most glaring fault, however, is that it completely omits any vocabulary for discussing and designing the very *raison d'être* of modern software: the user interface. When it comes to designing this critical aspect of software-based systems, no specific notation or diagrams are provided: not interface content models, not context navigation maps and not abstract prototypes.

Weak in its support of use cases and lacking in support for user interface design, UML is proving in practice to be a particularly poor match for usage-centered and task-driven design approaches that employ more sophisticated notions of use cases and tie them directly to the design of user interfaces. Although many groups have attempted usage-centered design with UML and its supporting development tools, most have either given up on the notation and tools or devised admittedly awkward workarounds and substitutions.

Despite its numerous omissions or oversights, UML is still complicated. One of the most popular books on the subject is, not surprisingly, Martin Fowler's slim primer, *UML Distilled* (Addison-Wesley, 1997), a kind of *Readers' Digest* introduction to the language. UML has been roundly criticized by Brian Henderson-Sellers and others of the OPEN movement for notation that is often arbitrary and far from intuitive (see Henderson-Sellers and Unhelkar, *OPEN Modeling with UML*, Addison-Wesley, 2000).

In the near term, the shortcomings can be overcome through various workarounds as long as efficiency and ease of use are not paramount. Not being evangelical adherents or doctrinal purists, many developers blithely mix tools and notations in practice. Document templates can be created for structuring use cases, which are then attached as notes to UML diagrams. Generic database systems and drawing tools can be cobbled together with scripts into ad hoc tool suites.

In the long run, of course, change will occur, but the message to the UML people and the vendors of UML-oriented tools must be clear: Support real-world practice in usage-centered and task-driven design or lose business. Managers should not have to choose between best practices in design and development on the one hand and a standardized notation supported by tools on the other.

Methodical Process

The Unified Process started life as a method but was renamed midstream, perhaps because its corporate mentors recognized that putting Rational in front of Unified Method would have yielded an amusing but commercially unwise acronym, or perhaps because methods and methodologies of the past have left a bad taste in the mouths of many managers, who are the real customers for the process.

Although the arguments for a common notation are straightforward, the case for a uniform process seems harder to make. Notation and modeling are far more rigorous and better understood than process. When it comes to process, every development group is its own distinct story. A five-person Web shop and a 300-programmer tool vendor are likely to differ in far more than just size. A four-month, time-boxed project producing a new release of a mature payroll application has little in common with a multiyear effort producing a novel programming system for automation tools. The cultural dynamics in a department full of engineers all writing embedded C++ code are poles apart from those in a mixed team of graphic artists, content creators, information architects, database analysts, HTML coders and Java wonks.

In short, it seems almost axiomatic that no single model for the software development process can work across the board. The brilliance of ISO 9001 is that it does not specify any particular process but only requires a process that is documented and practiced as documented. In all fairness, the Unified Process was intended as a template, a comprehensive guidebook that could be cut down, edited and tailored to suit varying projects, constraints and cultures. Nevertheless, to prepare a digest for your readers, you have to read the book; to tailor a slimmed down subset of the Unified Process, you have to understand pretty much the whole darned thing. The growing interest in "lightweight" methods, such as Extreme Programming (XP), reflects widespread frustrations with the heavyweights of the industry. The bureaucratic thoroughness that might be appropriate for a multiyear project by a defense contractor is probably nuclear overkill for a nimble dot-com startup.

If these are the problems, why, then, should anyone try to unify processes, and why would anyone be interested in the result? Comfort. A standard and widely recognized process — or the claim to have one — puts both managers and customers at ease. Whatever concerns your customers have, the reassuring answer becomes just "Oh, we use the Unified Process." After all, it covers everything. For managers, great comfort and confidence comes with an approach that is not only supported by software and courseware but tells everyone on a project just what they should be doing and when and to whom they hand off what. Whether the process is right, appropriate or efficient is secondary to its ritualized reassurance and formulaic nature. A plug-and-play process that comes on a CD-ROM is almost irresistible. Just buy the CD-ROM, send your people to some courses, and you, too, can join the UPpies!

Whether the process is truly unified or not, the storyline is most definitely not. The exact content and scope of the Unified Process remains a somewhat elusive matter. There is Philippe Krutchen's book (*The Rational Unified Process*, Addison-Wesley, 2000) and there is Ivar Jacobson's book (*The Unified Software Development Process*, Addison-Wesley, 2000), and most readers find little in common between them. Then, too, there is the official Rational Unified Process, which is a commercial product residing on a CD-ROM and in training courses and in the minds of marketers. Like all commercial products, its content is whatever those good folks want it to be.

Indeed, Rational has achieved such a commanding lead in both the tools and process areas that the RUP has become almost synonymous with the UP. One-stop shopping for tools, training, consulting and performance support has strong management appeal. End-to-end integration of tools and performance-support infrastructure, to the extent that it works as advertised, offers powerful advantages to developers and their managers. Rational has, in a sense, become the Microsoft of process unification: a force to be reckoned with irrespective of the merits and opinions. For decision makers, going with the clear market leader is often the safest and simplest route. If things go well, obviously you had the wisdom to choose the best. If things go badly, you escape blame because you went with the winner.

The management decisions may seem straightforward, but adding to the UP learning curve for developers — and to the need for training — is a maddening insistence on inventing new names for old ideas and redefining established terms that already have widely accepted meanings. As one might expect of anything pretending to unify complex development processes, the UP, like UML, borrows freely from almost anywhere and everywhere, often without credit. So-called logical prototypes, for instance, are easily recognized as interface content models in disguise, on which they were based, though scarcely an acknowledgement is in sight. You may think you understand what a storyboard or a scenario is, but such terms get usurped for idiosyncratic usage in the UP.

Modern Language

One manifestation of the hubris of contemporary methodologists is their insistence on referring to their congeries as languages. Today's developers are offered not a unified modeling notation but a Unified Modeling Language; not a pattern collection but a pattern language.

Natural and unnatural languages might, indeed, have some lessons to teach us in our search for unification. In a twist of multilingual irony, English, not French, has become the lingua franca of commerce and travel. As *L'Académie Française* fights a rear guard action to keep the mongrel hordes of foreign words at bay, English has no academy, no border patrol, and happily embraces all comers, giving it the richest vocabulary of any natural language.

Only the French would claim French to be a logical language, but logical languages have been devised. Esperanto, perhaps the best known of the many artificial and rational languages, has been around since 1887, but Zamenhof's dream of a world united by a common language seems more distant than ever, and only a tiny minority (less than two million worldwide) are fluent speakers of Esperanto.

UML is no Esperanto. It is best described as a collection of disparate models and the notations for their expression supporting object-oriented analysis and design. If it is a language, it is hardly a universal one, because it has no vocabulary for user interface design and is limited to object-speak.

Reality Check

So, is the revolution over? Has a new and united world order in notation and method arrived? Should working managers "UP-grade" their processes and teach their developers to mumble UML? Perhaps. The CD-ROMs and courses are surely selling well, but, as Germans quickly learned after reunification, the reality of the doing is somewhat different from the selling.

Being a columnist, consultant and conference presenter affords me abundant opportunities to get the inside stories of companies that have bought the big "U." If my sources are at all typical, scant little has changed since the era of early CASE tools. Many companies seem to be using UML tools not to design but to document. Often the claim to be using the Unified Process translates, on careful listening, into not much more than owning the CD-ROM and using the vocabulary in casual conversation. Even among the serious and dedicated users, an increasing number express frustration with the overhead involved in using the tools and the methods and the difficulty within both when trying to follow best practices for product usability. In practice, then, the good intentions and worthy goals of unification have to be weighed against the failures of UML and the UP to offer well-developed models or methods for task-driven user interface design and efficient and in-depth support for the full range of modern development processes and practices.

The salvation of the unified agenda is that UML has a built-in mechanism for introducing variations on its uniform themes. For many but not all problems, the solution may be to define new elements and concepts as so-called stereotypes or extensions of existing notions and notations within UML. The UP, to its credit, invites customization within certain limits. At some point, however, customization within the framework of UML and the UP becomes a procrustean process. Buying a different frame or getting a more comfortable mattress may sometimes be a better option.

Chapter 7

Beyond the Unified Process — Agile Software Processes

Introduction

This book series is based on several premises. First and foremost is the premise that the Unified Process isn't complete, a concept that we've addressed in detail. Not only is the Unified Process missing a phase, Production, and two workflows, the Operations and Support workflow and the Infrastructure Management workflow, it is also missing a wide range of activities in its existing workflows. This book series has presented myriad articles to address these shortcomings. The second premise, not addressed sufficiently until now, is that the Unified Process may not be right for you. No single software process will meet the needs of every single project team, no matter how many best practices it encompasses. What are your other options? What do you do when you find that you've tried the Unified Process, you're at the end of a project and have discovered that the Unified Process isn't a good fit for your organization? Where do you go next? Currently your most viable alternatives to the Unified Process fall are the various agile software processes.

7.1 Towards Agility

Larry Constantine defines the setting for this chapter in "Methodological Agility" by stating that managers need to understand not only the league leaders like the Unified Process but also its agile competitors. These competitors include processes such as Extreme Programming (XP) (Beck, 2000), Adaptive Software Development (ASD) (Highsmith, 2000), Dynamic System Development Methodology (DSDM) (Stapleton, 1997), and Agile Modeling (Ambler, 2002). Instead of the prescriptive approach favored by the Unified Process, he notes that philosophy is also a critical component of nearly all the agile methods. The general rules of the agile game are relatively simple:

- Work in short release cycles.
- Do only what is needed, without embellishment.
- Don't waste time.
- Describe the problem simply in terms of small, distinct pieces, then implement these pieces in successive iterations.
- Develop a reliable system by building and testing with immediate feedback.
- Start with something small and simple that works, then elaborate on successive iterations.
- Maintain tight communication with clients and among programmers.
- Test every piece in itself and regression-test continuously.

Constantine believes that these rules are easier to learn and master than the Unified Process. He also explores the potential benefits of agile software processes, such as early results, reduced overhead, and more reliable code. He points out that tales of success far outnumber sob stories, of course, at least for well-trained teams working on appropriately focused projects. To be successful at agile software processes Constantine believes that not only do you need skilled and speedy developers, but you need ones of exceptional discipline, willing to work hard with someone sitting beside them watching every move. He believes that the agile processes do not readily scale up beyond a certain point. Like the Unified Process, the agile software processes aren't perfect, but they are applicable in many situations and are something you should consider adopting in whole or in part.

Jim Highsmith and Martin Fowler describe the philosophies underlying agile software processes in "Agile Manifesto," an article that summarizes material presented in Fowler's online article "The New Methodology" http://www.martinfowler.com/articles/new-Methodology.html. The Agile Manifesto (Agile Alliance, 2001a) is the result of a gathering on February 11–13, 2001, at The Lodge at Snowbird ski resort in the Wasatch mountains of Utah where 17 methodologists met to talk, ski, relax, and try to find common ground. One thing this group wanted to accomplish was to restore a balance in software processes — they embrace modeling, but not merely to file away some diagram in a dusty corporate repository. They embrace documentation, but not to waste reams of paper in never-maintained and rarely used tomes. They embrace planning, but recognize the limits of planning in a turbulent environment. The Agile Manifesto is defined by four simple value statements — the important thing to understand is that while you should value the concepts on the right hand side you should value the things on the left hand side (presented in italics) even more. A good way to think about the manifesto is that it defines preferences, not alternatives. The Agile Alliance values:

- *Individuals and interactions* over processes and tools
- *Working software* over comprehensive documentation
- *Customer collaboration* over contract negotiation
- *Responding to change* over following a plan

These values in turn lead to a collection of twelve principles, principles that define what it is for a software process to be considered agile. These principles (Agile Alliance, 2001b) are:

- Our highest priority is to satisfy the customer through early and continuous delivery of valuable software.
- Welcome changing requirements, even late in development. Agile processes harness change for the customer's competitive advantage.
- Deliver working software frequently, from a couple of weeks to a couple of months, with a preference to the shorter time scale.
- Business people and developers must work together daily throughout the project.
- Build projects around motivated individuals. Give them the environment and support they need, and trust them to get the job done.
- The most efficient and effective method of conveying information to and within a development team is face-to-face conversation.
- Working software is the primary measure of progress.
- Agile processes promote sustainable development. The sponsors, developers, and users should be able to maintain a constant pace indefinitely.
- Continuous attention to technical excellence and good design enhances agility.
- Simplicity — the art of maximizing the amount of work not done — is essential.
- The best architectures, requirements, and designs emerge from self-organizing teams.
- At regular intervals, the team reflects on how to become more effective, then tunes and adjusts its behavior accordingly.

Martin Fowler argues for light-weight, or more agile, software processes in "Put Your Process on a Diet." This article is interesting because it explores in detail many of the philosophies of agile development. Many of the detractors of agile software development point focus on the reduced amount of documentation produced during development. Fowler believes that reduced documentation isn't the real issue, that it is merely a symptom of two much deeper differences. First, agile methods are adaptive rather than predictive. Heavy/prescriptive methods tend to try to plan out a large part of the software process in great detail for a long span of time, which works well until things change. Heavy methods therefore resist change whereas agile methods welcome change. Second, agile methods are people-oriented rather than process-oriented, explicitly working with peoples' nature rather than against it. So if planning isn't effective, how you control projects in an unpredictable world? Fowler believes that you need an honest feedback mechanism that can accurately tell you what the situation is at frequent intervals, and that the key to this feedback is iterative development. Why are agile methods better than prescriptive methods? Fowler reiterates the beliefs of Alistair Cockburn (2001) when he makes the point that predictable processes require components that behave in a predictable way, but unfortunately people are not predictable components and furthermore

Cockburn's studies of software projects have led him to conclude that people are the most important factor in software development. Fowler argues that agile/adaptive approaches are good when your requirements are uncertain or volatile because if you don't have stable requirements you aren't a the position to have a stable design and follow a planned process. Agile processes rely on you having confidence in your developers. If you consider them to be of low quality and motivation Fowler suggests that you choose a heavy/prescriptive approach.

In a follow-up article Martin Fowler looks at the role of modeling in "Is Design Dead?," a summary of a larger article by the same name posted at `http://www.martinfowler.com/articles/designDead.html`. In this article, Fowler discusses two approaches to design, evolutionary and planned. With evolutionary design your system's design grows as it is implemented. Design is part of the programming process, and as the program evolves, the design changes. Planned design, on the other hand, is counter to this. Following this approach designers think through big issues in advance, an approach often referred to as big design up front (BDUF). Designers don't need to write code because they aren't building the software, they're designing it. Fowler discusses two of the common slogans within XP community: "Do the simplest thing that could possibly work" and "You aren't going to need it" (YAGNI), manifestations of the XP practice of simple design. He discusses Kent Beck's (2000) four criteria, in order of importance, for a simple design:

- It runs all the tests.
- It reveals all the intention.
- There is no duplication.
- It uses the fewest number of classes or methods.

Fowler continues with a discussion of refactoring (Fowler, 1999), arguing that it is needed to keep the design as simple as you can, so you should refactor whenever you realize you can make things simpler. He also argues that you should ease into patterns, a concept adopted by Agile Modeling (AM)'s practice Apply Patterns Gently (Ambler, 2002), concentrating on when to apply them (not too early), implementing the pattern in its simplest form first and then adding complexity later, and not being afraid to remove a pattern that isn't pulling its weight. He also points out that changing the design doesn't necessarily mean changing the diagrams, providing the following advice for ongoing documentation:

- Only use diagrams you can keep up to date without noticeable pain.
- Put the diagrams where everyone can easily see them, such as on a wall. Encourage people to edit the wall copy with a pen for simple changes.
- Pay attention to whether or not people are using them. If not, throw them away.

Agile software processes seem too good to be true, and, as we all know things, that seem too good to be true often are. Scott W. Ambler in "Extreme Lessons Learned" reports on the experiences of a very agile project (albeit a small one). At Software Development East 2000, a conference sponsored by CMP Media, the publisher of *Software Development* magazine and this book series, the organizers decided to have its speakers and attendees develop a system for a nonprofit organization, in this case the redeployment of the Hydrocephalus Association's Web site (`www.hydroassoc.org`). With an undefined and constantly changing team, many of whom did not have experience in the technologies being applied and none of whom had worked together previously, a fairly sophisticated web site was developed over a very short period of time. The lessons learned, many of which are clearly best practices that you can apply on your projects, included:

1. Initial preparation pays off.
2. Kickoff meetings help the team to gel.
3. Too many people on a project is just as bad as too few: Staff your project with the right people at the right time.
4. The first step in obtaining reusable artifacts is to look for them.
5. Don't commit to a schedule until you know you have a chance of meeting it.
6. Lying to senior management isn't ideal, but sometimes it's your best option.
7. Define a "good things to know" list for developers new to the project.
8. Consider maintenance issues while you are developing your system.
9. Set development standards and guidelines early in the project.
10. Your artifacts may be meaningless to others.
11. Simple models are often the best models.
12. Develop a minimal set of artifacts.
13. Prove your approach by developing an end-to-end prototype.
14. Set user interface conventions early in the project.
15. Identify common aspects of your system, and develop them early, so they may be reused.
16. Be prepared to bring new people into the project part way through it.
17. Be prepared to lose people during your project.
18. Co-locate your team in a shared working space.
19. Users can and should play active roles on your development teams.
20. Bring in an expert for a short time to get you through a difficult situation.
21. One bad decision can kill a software project.
22. Backup your work on a regular basis.
23. Decision makers must be close to the situation to be effective.
24. Users, not developers, should drive the prioritization of new system features.

7.2 Agile Software Processes

The Agile Manifesto (Agile Alliance, 2001a) merely describes the philosophies behind agile software development, it doesn't define the software process itself. The most famous, or infamous, depending on your point of view, agile software process is Kent Beck's (2000) Extreme Programming (XP) methodology, a process described by Warren Keuffel in his article aptly titled "Extreme Programming." XP encourages programmers to select the most important features and developing them to completion within a short time frame. A team begins by putting together a collection of desirable features, as defined by the customer, each of which consists of a user story described on one index card. User stories are not detailed documentation, rather they are merely a reminder to have a conversation with your users to obtain detailed requirements. An XP team proceeds to iterate through an analysis-design-implementation-test cycle for each story, frequently producing a new release — perhaps daily, perhaps monthly. XP requires intensive customer involvement; ideally, a customer is assigned to full-time participation with the team. Testing is a core activity in XP, not an afterthought, and test cases are actually developed before any "real coding" begins (an approach often called test-first design). XP also requires that developers work in pairs, addressing the common inability of programmers to write their own tests and dramatically improving productivity along the way (two heads working together are better than two heads working separately). XP advocates multiple builds per day, each of which is followed by automatically running all of the accumulated test cases to verify that nobody has broken the system. The end result of XP is that you have working software very early in your project lifecycle, often on the first week, and it continues to work as it evolves because you're not allowed to break it.

In a two-part series, Mary Poppendieck describes the lean programming process in "Lean Programming Part 1" and "Lean Programming Part 2." Based on the concepts promoted by Lean Production (see *The Machine That Changed the World: The Story of Lean Production*, by James P. Womack, Daniel T. Jones and Daniel Roos, New York: Rawson and Associates, 1990) Lean Programming promotes software development based on the following ten principles:

1. Eliminate waste.
2. Minimize inventory.
3. Maximize flow.
4. Pull from demand.
5. Meet customer requirements.
6. Do it right the first time.
7. Empower workers.
8. Ban local optimization.
9. Partner with suppliers.
10. Create a culture of continuous improvement.

Poppendieck argues that these rules, adapted to logistics, customer service, healthcare, finance and even construction over the last two decades, have proven their worth. More recently, they have found their way into software project management. Her articles are "must reads" for anyone serious about increasing the agility of their software development efforts.

In two articles entitled "Extreme Modeling" and "A Closer Look at Extreme Modeling," Scott W. Ambler lays the foundation for what would later become Agile Modeling (Ambler, 2002). The first article asks the question "What types of models would you need to create a business application?" and, like Larry Constantine in "Unified Hegemony" (Chapter 6), comes to the conclusion that the Unified Modeling Language (UML) is lacking. In the second article Ambler delves deeper into the modeling process itself, exploring principles and practices for being more effective. He believes that models don't kill projects, people kill projects. He points out that regardless of what the name may imply, modeling is a fundamental part of the Extreme Programming (XP) software process but that many developers are unsure how they can include modeling while remaining sufficiently "extreme." The answer lies in the fundamental principles of what was then called the Extreme Modeling (XM) methodology, now called Agile Modeling (AM). These principles (http://www.agilemodeling.com/principles.html) are summarized in Table 7.1. The principles of AM form a basis from which effective modeling practices (http://www.agilemodeling.com/practices.htm) are derived, summarized in Table 7.2. It is important to understand that with the exception of a catchy name nothing about Agile Modeling is truly new, instead it is a repackaging of concepts that many software professionals have been following for years. Both articles provide an interesting look at an agile approach to modeling, and provide a perfect example for how something can evolve very quickly and effectively — the development of AM is clearly following what Martin Fowler calls an evolutionary design process over a planned design process, providing an example of how agile principles actually work in practice.

Table 7.1   The Principles of Agile Modeling

Core Principles	Supplementary Principles
Assume Simplicity	Content Is More Important Than Representation
Embrace Change	Everyone Can Learn From Everyone Else
Enabling the Next Effort is Your Secondary Goal	Know Your Models
Incremental Change	Know Your Tools
Maximize Stakeholder Investment	Local Adaptation
Model With a Purpose	Open and Honest Communication
Multiple Models	Work With People's Instincts
Quality Work	
Rapid Feedback	
Software is Your Primary Goal	
Travel Light	

Table 7.2   Agile Modeling Practices

Core Practices	Supplementary Practices
Active Stakeholder Participation	Apply Modeling Standards
Apply The Right Artifact(s)	Apply Patterns Gently
Collective Ownership	Discard Temporary Models
Consider Testability	Formalize Contract Models
Create Several Models in Parallel	Model to Communicate
Create Simple Content	Model to Understand
Depict Models Simply	Reuse Existing Resources
Display Models Publicly	Update Only When It Hurts
Iterate To Another Artifact	
Model in Small Increments	
Model With Others	
Prove it With Code	
Use the Simplest Tools	

There is a wide variety of agile software processes for you to consider. The ones mentioned in this chapter — Adaptive Software Development (ASD), Agile Modeling (AM), Dynamic System Development Methodology (DSDM), and Extreme Programming (XP) — are merely the tip of the iceberg. Other agile methods include Scrum (http://www.controlchaos.com/), Crystal Clear (http://crystalmethodologies.org/), and Agile Testing (http://www.testing.com/agile/). The point to be made is that you have options. You can chose to abandon the Unified Process in favor of a more agile approach or use agile techniques to improve the Unified Process.[1] It's your choice — choose to succeed.

7.3 The Articles

7.3.1 "Methodological Agility"

by Larry Constantine

Managers who want to play today's game need to understand not only the league leaders, but also the nimble competitors.

Software development today can seem like a strange game. At one end of the field, in scruffy jerseys of assorted color and stripe, lurk the unruly rabble representing the methodless chaos that all too often passes for programming in many organizations; at the other end, we see the advancing phalanx of the heavyweight team, a bright letter U emblazoned on the chest of each hulking Goliath. These true heavyweights of modern software development — the Unified Process and its supporting player, the Unified Modeling Language — were subject to critical scrutiny recently in Management Forum ("Unified Hegemony," Chapter 6).

Between the contrasting extremes of libertarian license and methodological muddling, the center of the process playing field is currently dominated by the real crowd-pleasers of modern software development: a small group of relatively young, fast-moving players — the so-called lightweight processes, with names like XP, Crystal, Scrum, and FDD. To be both correct and *au courant*, however, we should follow the lead of a group of the foremost coaches and promoters of these processes who met in February at Snowbird, Utah, to discuss their current interests and future prospects. Wishing to shed the negative connotations of the

---

1. How to apply Agile Modeling (AM) practices on a Unified Process project are described at http://www.agilemodeling.com/essays/agileModelingRUP.htm.

term lightweight, they agreed to hereafter refer to their sundry methods as "agile" processes. Agile it is, then. After all, who would want to risk being considered the 98-pound weaklings of software development?

Agile Players

Managers who want to play today's game need to understand not only the league leaders like RUP, the Rational Unified Process, but also the agile competitors. A complete comparison of all the agile processes is beyond the scope of Management Forum; there are just too many, and they differ in too many details. In any case, Martin Fowler has already provided a concise overview in this magazine ("Put Your Process on a Diet," in this chapter), and more detail can be found along with useful links in an expanded version available on the Web (www.martinfowler.com/articles/newMethodology.html). In this column, I'll stick to a management perspective and focus on some of the common pluses and minuses of the agile processes.

The archetype of these agile athletes of software development is XP, short for Extreme Programming (see Kent Beck's *Extreme Programming Explained,* Addison-Wesley, 2000). Undoubtedly the best known of the agile processes, in many respects it typifies this diverse bunch. Like nearly every other methodology — light, heavy or middleweight — XP and its agile teammates are really mishmashes of tricks and techniques, plus methods, models and management formulas, along with tools, practices and even a bit of philosophy. Some advocates argue that, because the pieces were all concocted to complement each other, you have to buy the whole assorted package of any given method, but many practitioners simply pick and choose the parts that work for them and toss the bits they don't like.

The hallmarks of XP, as with most of the agile processes, are that it's more people oriented than process oriented, and that it emphasizes flexible adaptation rather than full description. Along with the need for agility, the stress on effective teamwork puts a premium on good management and leadership skills. Success with most of the agile approaches requires particularly close, hands-on management aimed at smoothing the process and removing impediments.

Oddly enough, one of the more controversial aspects of XP teamwork is also one of its best-established best practices: pair programming. Also known as the dynamic duo model, pair programming puts two developers in front of a single screen. By providing instantaneous inspection of each line of code, the technique radically reduces bugs and cuts the overall cost of programming. Pioneered by C/C++ guru P. J. Plauger and popularized by yours truly ("The Benefits of Visibility," *Computer Language,* Sept. 1992; reprinted in *The Peopleware Papers,* Prentice Hall, 2001), pair programming is a useful technique with a solid track record.

Philosophy is also a critical component of nearly all the agile methods. XP itself is built around a set of core values: simplicity, communication, testing and fearlessness. (Yes, fearlessness.) Jim Highsmith's Adaptive Software Development, which has also been classified with the lightweight processes, is more framework and philosophy than prescribed practices, especially compared to such precisely delineated approaches as XP or Peter Coad's Feature-Driven Development (FDD).

The rules of the game are relatively simple: Work in short release cycles. Do only what is needed, without embellishment. Don't waste time in analysis or design; just start coding. Describe the problem simply in terms of small, distinct pieces, then implement these pieces in successive iterations. Develop a reliable system by building and testing with immediate feedback. Start with something small and simple that works, then elaborate on successive iterations. Maintain tight communication with clients and among programmers. Test every piece in itself and regression-test continuously.

Although some programmers and their managers may think of agile methods as a license to hack, it should be clear that following the philosophy and practices takes genuine discipline. I have heard some managers refer to XP as structured hacking, and that may not be far from the truth.

The Pros

Perhaps the biggest selling point of the agile processes is their weight. With far less heft than the leading heavyweights, they're easier to learn and master. That doesn't mean that agile processes are easy, any more than it suggests that they can substitute for programming skills and developmental discipline — but it does mean that there is less to explain about the processes themselves.

Reduced overhead is another strong point. Unlike the more heavy-duty processes that emphasize diverse deliverables and numerous process artifacts, the agile processes concentrate on code. Design is on-the-fly and as needed. Index cards and whiteboard sketches take the place of a slew of design documents, and brief, stand-up confabs replace protracted meetings.

Early results are yet another benefit of agile processes. With short release cycles that produce a fully functional system on every iteration, clients can begin using a simplified, working core with limited but useful capability early in a project.

For clients, managers and developers alike, agile methods can offer a major potential payoff in minimal defect injection and leakage rates: the number of bugs created in the first place and the number that sneak past successive phases of development. More reliable code means more up-time and cheaper development, requiring less support and maintenance.

The simple philosophies of the agile processes appear to translate fairly well into practice. Despite — or because of — their streamlined structure, agile processes have worked well in a variety of real-world projects. Tales of success far outnumber sob stories (but, of course!), at least for well-trained teams working on appropriately focused projects.

What Goes Around

What are the risks and shortcomings of the agile methods? Readers who have been around long enough or have a sufficient grounding in the history of programming may be experiencing a strong sense of deja vu. Some 30 years ago, IBM touted so-called chief programmer teams [see F. T. Baker's "Chief Programmer Team Management of Production Programming," *IBM Systems Journal*, 11 (1), 1972]: small, agile groups headed by a strong technical leader who could hold the implicit architecture in mind without resorting to much explicit design. Applications were constructed with thorough inspection and testing through successive refinements. The objective: To have working code at all times, gradually growing it through successive enhancements into a full-scale working system.

Like XP and its agile teammates, chief programmer teams also enjoyed early victories for awhile, but the model ultimately foundered on the shoals, caught between the Charybdis and Scylla of charisma and scale. Led by gifted technical managers and applied to problems of modest size, the approach worked, but there are only so many Terry Bakers in the world, and not every problem can be sliced and diced into the right pieces for speedy incremental refinement.

The same issues challenge today's agile methods. There are only so many Kent Becks in the world to lead the team. All of the agile methods put a premium on having premium people and work best with first-rate, versatile, disciplined developers who are highly skilled and highly motivated. Not only do you need skilled and speedy developers, but you need ones of exceptional discipline, willing to work hell-bent-for-leather with someone sitting beside them watching every move.

Scale is another problem. When I surveyed colleagues who are leaders in the light methods world, they agreed that the agile processes do not readily scale up beyond a certain point. A few brave XP efforts with teams of 30 developers have been launched, but the results are not yet in. Alistair Cockburn claims that his family of methods, known as Crystal, has been used for larger projects, but the general consensus is that 12–15 developers is the workable upper limit for most agile processes. The tightly coordinated teamwork needed for these methods to succeed becomes increasingly difficult beyond 15 or 20 developers.

All the agile methods are based on incremental refinement or iterative development in one form or another. The basic premise is that it's easier to add capability to a compact base of well-written existing code than to build a complete application in one fell swoop. Within the prescribed short-release iterations of agile processes, a small team can do only so much. Systems that total some 250,000 lines of code may be achievable over many such iterations, but a million lines is probably out of reach. Moreover, some projects and applications cannot, for all practical purposes, be broken into nice and neat 30-, 60- or 90-day increments.

What's the Use?

My informants in the agile process community also confirmed what numerous colleagues and clients have been suggesting all along. XP and the other light methods are light on the user side of software. They seem to be at their best in applications that aren't GUI-intensive. As methodologist Alistair Cockburn told me, this "is not a weak point — it is an absence." User-interface design and usability are largely overlooked by the agile processes — a failing shared with the bulk of their big-brother behemoths in the heavyweight arena.

Some, like XP, do explicitly provide for user or client participation in pinning down initial requirements through jointly developed scenarios, known as user stories. However, in keeping with an emphasis on minimalist design and repeated refinement, when it comes to user interface design, the agile processes favor somewhat simplistic forms of iterative paper prototyping rather than model-driven design or thorough forethought. Especially with XP, which relies so heavily on testing, GUI-intensive projects pose particular problems. Testing of user interfaces is labor-intensive and time-consuming; automated user-interface testing is difficult, if not impossible, except at the most elementary level. True usability testing requires repeated testing with numbers of users under controlled settings. User or client reactions to paper prototypes are no substitute and can even be completely misleading — what people will say they like or claim is feasible when they see a paper sketch will often prove unworkable in practice.

Iterative prototyping is an acceptable substitute for real user-interface design only when the problems aren't too complicated, there aren't too many screens with too many subtleties, and a rather pedestrian and uninspired solution will suffice. Software with intricate user-interface problems or for which usability will be a major factor demands a more sophisticated, model-driven approach. This is where usage-centered design enters the picture (see Constantine and Lockwood's *Software for Use*, Addison-Wesley, 1999).

When Lucy Lockwood and I began developing usage-centered design (U-CD) in the early 1990s, we didn't set out to create a lightweight process. Our philosophy has always been simply to use whatever tools and techniques helped us design more usable systems in less time. We aren't surprised, then, that U-CD is increasingly mentioned in company with the agile processes.

Where usage-centered design parts company from some of the agile processes is in its emphasis on modeling and on driving the user interface design and development by the models. First, we build profiles of the roles users play in relation to the system; these directly inform the task model, which captures the nature of the tasks to be supported by the system. The task model — collections of interrelated use cases in simplified, abstract form — directly drives how information and capability are collected and arrayed on the user interface.

In its most agile incarnation, usage-centered design works some of the same card magic that powers XP (see Ron Jeffries' "Card Magic for Managers," *Management Forum*, Dec. 2000). We model task cases on index cards, thus keeping them short and sweet to facilitate easy collection and distribution. We shuffle the cards to prioritize them by business and end-user importance. We sort them into related groups that help us construct complete usage scenarios and that guide the collection of user interface components into screens, pages or dialog boxes. The same task cases that steer the user interface design are grist for the programming mill that grinds out the objects and methods that power the software. As always, we focus on user intentions and system responsibilities to help distinguish real user needs from mere wants and wishes. In short, usage-centered design probably qualifies as an agile process, even if it wasn't conceived with that in mind. Moreover, it supplies a critical piece missing from other methods — an effective and efficient scheme for designing highly usable user interfaces.

I'll leave you with some simple advice. If you're ready to leave behind both ochlocracy and bureaucracy, then it's best to join the agile few and heed the words of the venerable William of Occam: "It is vain to do with more what can be done with less."

7.3.2 "The Agile Manifesto"

by Martin Fowler and Jim Highsmith

Facilitating change is more effective than attempting to prevent it.
Learn to trust in your ability to respond to unpredictable events; it's
more important than trusting in your ability to plan for disaster.

Formation of the Agile Alliance

On February 11–13, 2001, at The Lodge at Snowbird ski resort in the Wasatch mountains of Utah, 17 people met to talk, ski, relax and try to find common ground. What emerged was the Agile Software Development Alliance.

A bigger gathering of organizational anarchists would be hard to find, so what emerged from this meeting was symbolic — a Manifesto for Agile Software Development — signed by all participants. Although the Manifesto provides some specifics, a deeper theme drives many

Alliance members. At the close of the two-day meeting, Extreme Programming mentor Bob Martin joked that he was about to make a "mushy" statement. Though tinged with humor, Bob's sentiments were shared by the group — we all enjoyed working with people who shared compatible goals and values based on mutual trust and respect, promoting collaborative, people-focused organizational models, and building the types of professional communities in which we would want to work.

The agile methodology movement is not anti-methodology; in fact, many of us want to restore credibility to the word. We also want to restore a balance: We embrace modeling, but not merely to file some diagram in a dusty corporate repository. We embrace documentation, but not to waste reams of paper in never-maintained and rarely used tomes. We plan, but recognize the limits of planning in a turbulent environment. Those who brand proponents of XP, Scrum or any of the other agile methodologies as "hackers" are ignorant of both the methodologies and the original definition of the term (a hacker was first defined as a programmer who enjoys solving complex programming problems, rather than someone who practices ad hoc development or destruction).

Early on, Alistair Cockburn identified the general disgruntlement with the word light: "I don't mind the methodology being called light in weight, but I'm not sure I want to be referred to as a 'lightweight' attending a 'lightweight methodologists' meeting. It sounds like a bunch of skinny, feebleminded people trying to remember what day it is." So our first task was to come up with a new adjective that we could live with. Now our processes are "agile," even if some of us are a bit creaky.

The result of this meeting (and the ensuing frenzied online interaction) was the Agile Manifesto (see sidebar). While the purpose and principles of the Manifesto were developed by the entire group, we (Jim and Martin, both authors of the Manifesto) have added, for this article, our own interpretations and explanations.

The Manifesto for Agile Software Development

Seventeen anarchists agree:

We are uncovering better ways of developing software by doing it and helping others do it. Through this work we have come to value:

- Individuals and interactions over processes and tools.
- Working software over comprehensive documentation.
- Customer collaboration over contract negotiation.
- Responding to change over following a plan.

That is, while we value the items on the right, we value the items on the left more.

- We follow the following principles:
- Our highest priority is to satisfy the customer through early and continuous delivery of valuable software.
- Welcome changing requirements, even late in development. Agile processes harness change for the customer's competitive advantage.
- Deliver working software frequently, from a couple of weeks to a couple of months, with a preference to the shorter timescale.

- Business people and developers work together daily throughout the project.
- Build projects around motivated individuals. Give them the environment and support they need, and trust them to get the job done.
- The most efficient and effective method of conveying information to and within a development team is face-to-face conversation.
- Working software is the primary measure of progress.
- Agile processes promote sustainable development. The sponsors, developers and users should be able to maintain a constant pace indefinitely.
- Continuous attention to technical excellence and good design enhances agility.
- Simplicity — the art of maximizing the amount of work not done — is essential.
- The best architectures, requirements and designs emerge from self-organizing teams.
- At regular intervals, the team reflects on how to become more effective, then tunes and adjusts its behavior accordingly.

Kent Beck, Mike Beedle, Arie van Bennekum, Alistair Cockburn, Ward Cunningham, Martin Fowler, James Grenning, Jim Highsmith, Andrew Hunt, Ron Jeffries, Jon Kern, Brian Marick, Robert C. Martin, Steve Mellor, Ken Schwaber, Jeff Sutherland, Dave Thomas

www.agileAlliance.org

The Agile Manifesto: Purpose

We are uncovering better ways of developing software by doing it and helping others do it. We value:

- *Individuals and interactions* over processes and tools
- *Working software* over comprehensive documentation
- *Customer collaboration* over contract negotiation
- *Responding to change* over following a plan

This statement has a number of fascinating aspects, not the least of which was getting 17 people to agree to it. First, the word *uncovering*. While this was a group of experienced and recognized software development "gurus," the word *uncovering* was selected to assure (or frighten) the audience that the Alliance members don't have all the answers and don't subscribe to the silver-bullet theory.

Second, the phrase "by doing it" indicates that the members actually practice these methods in their own work. Ken Schwaber (a proponent of Scrum) told of his days of selling tools to automate comprehensive, "heavy" methodologies. Impressed by the responsiveness of Ken's company, Jeff Sutherland (Scrum) asked him which of these heavy methodologies he used internally for development. "I still remember the look on Jeff's face," Ken remarked, "when I told him, 'None — if we used any of them, we'd be out of business!'"

Third, this group is about helping, not telling. The Alliance members want to help others with agile methods, and to further our own knowledge by learning from those we try to help.

The value statements have a form: In each bullet point, the first segment indicates a preference, while the latter segment describes an item that, though important, is of lesser priority. This distinction lies at the heart of agility, but simply asking people to list what's valuable doesn't flesh out essential differences. Roy Singham, Martin's boss at ThoughtWorks, put it well when he said that it's the edge cases, the hard choices, that interest him. "Yes, we value planning, comprehensive documentation, processes and tools. That's easy to say. The hard thing is to ask, "What do you value more?"

The Alliance recognizes the importance of process and tools, with the additional recognition that the interaction of skilled individuals is of even greater importance. Similarly, comprehensive documentation is not necessarily bad, but the primary focus must remain on the final product — delivering working software. Therefore, every project team needs to determine for itself what documentation is absolutely essential.

Contract negotiation, whether through an internal project charter or external legal contract, isn't a bad practice, just an insufficient one. Contracts and project charters may provide some boundary conditions within which the parties can work, but only through ongoing collaboration can a development team hope to understand and deliver what the client wants.

No one can argue that following a plan is a good idea — right? Well, yes and no. In the turbulent world of business and technology, scrupulously following a plan can have dire consequences, even if it's executed faithfully. However carefully a plan is crafted, it becomes dangerous if it blinds you to change. We've examined plenty of successful projects and few, if any, delivered what was planned in the beginning, yet they succeeded because the development team was agile enough to respond again and again to external changes.

The Agile Manifesto: Principles

Our highest priority is to satisfy the customer through early and continuous delivery of valuable software. In a recent workshop, a software development manager questioned the feature or story approach to iterative cycle planning. "But aren't requirements specifications and architecture documents important?" he asked. "Yes," Jim replied, "They are important, but we need to understand that customers don't care about documents, UML diagrams or legacy integration. Customers care about whether or not you're delivering working software to them every development cycle — some piece of business functionality that proves to them that the evolving software application serves their business needs."

Implementing a "customer value" principle is one of those "easier said than done" activities. Traditional project management practices assume that achieving a plan equals project success equals demonstrated customer value. The volatility associated with today's projects demands that customer value be reevaluated frequently, and meeting original project plans may not have much bearing on a project's ultimate success.

Welcome changing requirements, even late in development. Agile processes harness change for the customer's competitive advantage. The growing unpredictability of the future is one of the most challenging aspects of the new economy. Turbulence — in both business and technology — causes change, which can be viewed either as a threat to be guarded against or as an opportunity to be embraced.

Rather than resist change, the agile approach strives to accommodate it as easily and efficiently as possible, while maintaining an awareness of its consequences. Although most people agree that feedback is important, they often ignore the fact that the result of accepted feedback is change. Agile methodologies harness this result, because their proponents understand that facilitating change is more effective than attempting to prevent it.

Deliver working software frequently, from a couple of weeks to a couple of months, with a preference for the shorter timescale. For many years, process gurus have been telling everyone to use an incremental or iterative style of software development, with multiple deliveries of ever-growing functionality. While the practice has grown in use, it's still not predominant; however, it's essential for agile projects. Furthermore, we push hard to reduce delivery cycle time.

However, remember that deliver is not the same as release. The business people may have valid reasons for not putting code into production every couple of weeks. We've seen projects that haven't achieved releasable functionality for a year or more. But that doesn't exempt them from the rapid cycle of internal deliveries that allows everyone to evaluate and learn from the growing product.

Business people and developers work together daily throughout the project. Many folks want to buy software the way they buy a car. They have a list of features in mind, they negotiate a price, and they pay for what they asked for. This simple buying model is appealing, but for most software projects, it doesn't work. So agile developers respond with a radical change in our concept of the requirements process.

For a start, we don't expect a detailed set of requirements to be signed off at the beginning of the project; rather, we see a high-level view of requirements that is subject to frequent change. Clearly, this is not enough to design and code, so the gap is closed with frequent interaction between the business people and the developers. The frequency of this contact often surprises people. We put "daily" in the principle to emphasize the software customer's continuing commitment to actively take part in, and indeed take joint responsibility for, the software project.

Build projects around motivated individuals, give them the environment and support they need and trust them to get the job done. Deploy all the tools, technologies and processes you like, even our agile processes, but in the end, it's people who make the difference between success and failure. We realize that however hard we work in coming up with process ideas, the best we can hope for is a second-order effect on a project. So it's important to maximize that first-order people factor.

For many people, trust is the hardest thing to give. Decisions must be made by the people who know the most about the situation. This means that managers must trust their staff to make the decisions about the things they're paid to know about.

The most efficient and effective method of conveying information with and within a development team is face-to-face conversation. Inevitably, when discussing agile methodologies, the topic of documentation arises. Our opponents appear apoplectic at times, deriding our "lack" of documentation. It's enough to make us scream, "the issue is not documentation — the issue is understanding!" Yes, physical documentation has heft and substance, but the real measure of success is abstract: Will the people involved gain the understanding they need? Many of us are writers, but despite our awards and book sales, we know that writing is a difficult and inefficient communication medium. We use it because we have to, but most project teams can and should use more direct communication techniques.

"Tacit knowledge cannot be transferred by getting it out of people's heads and onto paper," writes Nancy Dixon in *Common Knowledge* (Harvard Business School Press, 2000). "Tacit knowledge can be transferred by moving the people who have the knowledge around. The reason is that tacit knowledge is not only the facts but the relationships among the facts

— that is, how people might combine certain facts to deal with a specific situation." So the distinction between agile and document-centric methodologies is not one of extensive documentation versus no documentation; rather a differing concept of the blend of documentation and conversation required to elicit understanding.

Working software is the primary measure of progress. Too often, we've seen project teams who don't realize they're in trouble until a short time before delivery. They did the requirements on time, the design on time, maybe even the code on time, but testing and integration took much longer than they thought. We favor iterative development primarily because it provides milestones that can't be fudged, which imparts an accurate measure of the progress and a deeper understanding of the risks involved in any given project. As Chet Hendrickson, coauthor of *Extreme Programming Installed* (Addison-Wesley, 2000), remarks, "If a project is going to fail, I'd rather know that after one month than after 15."

"Working software is the measure of progress because there's no other way of capturing the subtleties of the requirements: Documents and diagrams are too abstract to let the user 'kick the tires,'" says Dave Thomas, coauthor of *The Pragmatic Programmer* (Addison-Wesley, 1999).

Agile processes promote sustainable development. The sponsors, developers and users should be able to maintain a constant pace indefinitely. Our industry is characterized by long nights and weekends, during which people try to undo the errors of unresponsive planning. Ironically, these long hours don't actually lead to greater productivity. Martin and Kent Beck have often recalled working at companies where they spent all day removing errors made late the previous night.

Agility relies upon people who are alert and creative, and can maintain that alertness and creativity for the full length of a software development project. Sustainable development means finding a working pace (40 or so hours a week) that the team can sustain over time and remain healthy.

Continuous attention to technical excellence and good design enhances agility.
When many people look at agile development, they see reminders of the "quick and dirty" RAD (Rapid Application Development) efforts of the last decade. But, while agile development is similar to RAD in terms of speed and flexibility, there's a big difference when it comes to technical cleanliness. Agile approaches emphasize quality of design, because design quality is essential to maintaining agility.

One of the tricky aspects, however, is the fact that agile processes assume and encourage the alteration of requirements while the code is being written. As such, design cannot be a purely up-front activity to be completed before construction. Instead, design is a continuous activity that's performed throughout the project. Each and every iteration will have design work.

The different agile processes emphasize different design styles. FDD has an explicit step at the beginning of each iteration in which design is executed, usually graphically with the UML. XP places great emphasis on refactoring to allow the design to evolve as development proceeds. But all of these processes borrow from each other: FDD uses refactoring as developers revisit earlier design decisions, and XP encourages short design sessions before coding tasks. In all cases, the project's design is enhanced continually throughout the project.

Simplicity — the art of maximizing the amount of work not done — is essential. Any software development task can be approached with a host of methods. In an agile project, it's particularly important to use simple approaches, because they're easier to change. It's easier to add something to a process that's too simple than it is to take something away from a process that's too complicated. Hence, there's a strong taste of minimalism in all the agile methods. Include only what everybody needs rather than what anybody needs, to make it easier for teams to add something that addresses their own particular needs.

"Simple, clear purpose and principles give rise to complex, intelligent behavior," says Dee Hock, former CEO of Visa International. "Complex rules and regulations give rise to simple, stupid behavior." No methodology can ever address all the complexity of a modern software project. Giving people a simple set of rules and encouraging their creativity will produce far better outcomes than imposing complex, rigid regulations.

The best architectures, requirements and designs emerge from self-organizing teams. Contrary to what you've heard, form doesn't follow function: Form follows failure. "The form of made things is always subject to change in response to their real or perceived shortcomings, their failures to function properly," writes Henry Petroski, civil engineering professor and author of *The Evolution of Useful Things* (Vintage Books, 1994). Stuart Brand writes that the "form follows function" idea has misled architects into believing that they could predict how buildings would actually be used.

Petroski's views are similar to one of the two key points of this principle — that the best designs (architectures, requirements) emerge from iterative development and use rather than from early plans. The second point of the principle is that emergent properties (emergence, a key property of complex systems, roughly translates to innovation and creativity in human organizations) are best generated from self-organizing teams in which the interactions are high and the process rules are few.

At regular intervals, the team reflects on how to become more effective, then tunes and adjusts its behavior accordingly. Agile methods are not something you pick and follow slavishly. You may start with one of these processes, but we all recognize that we can't come up with the right process for every situation. So any agile team must refine and reflect as it goes along, constantly improving its practices in its local circumstances.

Jim has been working with a consulting company to develop an Adaptive Software Development–Extreme Programming combination methodology. The first team to use it modified it immediately. Martin has worked with a number of teams at ThoughtWorks to tailor Extreme Programming practices to various project situations. Trust in people, believing that individual capability and group interaction are key to success extends to trusting teams to monitor and improve their own development processes.

Toward an Agile Future

Early response to the Agile Manifesto has been gratifying. Several e-mails expressed sentiments such as, "My product manager has already posted the Manifesto on her wall." Many of Martin's colleagues at ThoughtWorks have popped in to say how much they shared the values.

One question that arose immediately was whether or not the Alliance was a precursor to what one conference attendee tagged a Unified Lightweight Methodology. Absolutely not! While the group believes that a set of common purposes and principles will benefit the users of agile methodologies, we are equally adamant that variety and diversity of practices are necessary. When it comes to methodologies, each project is different and each project team is different — there's no one-size-fits-all solution.

What of the future? We can confidently say that we don't know. Agility is all about trusting in one's ability to respond to unpredictable events more than trusting in one's ability to plan ahead for them. We also know that the personal relationships formed by our collaboration matter far more than the document that we've produced. One thing is clear: we've only just started.

7.3.3 "Put Your Process on a Diet"

by Martin Fowler

As a reaction to cumbersome approaches to development, new methodologies have appeared. These methods attempt a compromise between no process and too much process, providing just enough to gain a reasonable payoff.

NOTE: This is an abridged version of a longer paper posted at `www.martinfowler.com/articles/newMethodology.html`.

Most software development is a chaotic activity characterized by the phrase "code and fix." The software is written without much of an underlying plan, and the design of the system is cobbled together from many short-term decisions. This actually works pretty well while the system is small, but as it grows, it becomes increasingly difficult to add new features. Furthermore, bugs begin to mushroom in number and difficulty. A typical sign of such a system is a long test phase after the system is "feature complete." This plays havoc with schedules.

We've lived with this style of development for a long time, but we've also had an alternative for a long time: methodology. Methodology imposes disciplined, detailed process — with a strong emphasis on planning, inspired by other engineering endeavors — upon software development to make it more predictable and efficient.

Methodologies have been around for a long time, but they haven't been noted for being terribly successful. They are even less noted for being popular. The most frequent criticism is that they are bureaucratic; there is so much that needs to be done to follow the methodology that the whole pace of development slows down. Hence they are often referred to as heavy methodologies, or, to use consultant Jim Highsmith's term, "monumental" methodologies.

As a reaction to cumbersome approaches to development, a new generation of methodologies has appeared in the last few years. Although they have no official name, they are often referred to as light methodologies, signaling a clear alternative to the heavyweight methodologies. For many, the appeal of these lightweight methodologies is based on their reaction to the bureaucracy of the heavy methodologies. These new methods attempt a useful compromise between no and too much process, providing just enough to gain a reasonable payoff.

The most obvious difference with lightweight methodologies is that they are less document-oriented, emphasizing less extraneous paperwork for a given task, and more code-oriented, proclaiming that the key part of documentation is source code.

I don't think, however, that this is the key point about lightweight methods. Lack of documentation is a symptom of two much deeper differences:

- *Light methods are adaptive rather than predictive.* Heavy methods tend to try to plan out a large part of the software process in great detail for a long span of time, which works well until things change. Their nature, therefore, is to resist change. The light methods, however, welcome change. They try to adapt and thrive on change, even to the point of changing themselves.

- *Light methods are people-oriented rather than process-oriented.* They explicitly work with peoples' nature rather than against them and emphasize that software development should be an enjoyable activity.

I'll explore these differences in more detail so that you can understand what an adaptive and people-centered process is like, learn its benefits and drawbacks, and decide whether it's something you should use as a software developer or customer.

Predictive vs. Adaptive

The usual inspiration for software development methodology is some form of engineering, say civil or mechanical. Such disciplines, sensibly, put a lot of emphasis on planning before building. A series of drawings precisely indicates what needs to be constructed and how it should be put together. Many design decisions, such as how to deal with the load on a bridge, are made as the drawings are produced. The drawings are then handed over to a different group to be built. It's assumed that the construction process will follow the drawings. In practice, the constructors will encounter problems, but these are usually small.

Since the drawings specify the pieces and how they are put together, they act as the foundation for a detailed construction plan. Such a plan can outline the tasks to be done and the dependencies that exist between them, making a reasonably predictable schedule and budget possible. It also explains in detail how the construction should be done, allowing the builders to focus on the physical implementation.

So we have two fundamentally different activities: design, which is difficult to predict and requires expensive and creative people, and construction, which is easier to predict. Once we have the design, we can plan the construction. Once we have the plan for the construction, we can then deal with construction more predictably. In civil engineering, construction is much bigger in both cost and time than design and planning.

The approach for many software methodologies is this: We want a predictable schedule that can use people with lower skills, so we must separate design from construction. Therefore, we must figure out how to design software so that the construction can be straightforward once the planning is done.

What form does this plan take? For many, this is the role of design notations such as the Unified Modeling Language. If we can make all the significant decisions using UML, we can build a construction plan and then hand these designs off to coders as a construction activity.

But herein lie two crucial issues: Can you get a design that is capable of turning the coding into a construction activity? And if so, is construction sufficiently larger in cost and time to make this approach worthwhile?

All of this brings a few questions to mind. First, how difficult is it to get a UML-like design into a state that can be handed over to programmers? A UML-like design can look very good on paper, yet be seriously flawed when you actually program the thing. The models that civil engineers use are based on years of practice that have been enshrined in engineering codes. Furthermore, the key issues, such as the way forces play in the design, are amenable to mathematical analysis. The only checking we can do of UML-like diagrams is peer review. While this is helpful, it leads to errors in the design that are often only uncovered during coding and testing. Even skilled designers, as I consider myself to be, are often surprised when we turn such a design into software.

The second issue is that of comparative cost. When you build a bridge, the cost of the design effort is about 10% of the job, with the rest being construction. In software, the amount of time spent in coding is much, much less. Steve McConnell, author of *Code Complete* (Microsoft Press, 1993) and chief software engineer at Construx Software, suggests that, for a large project, only 15% of the project is code and unit test, an almost perfect reversal of the bridge-building ratios. Even if you lump in all testing as part of construction, then design is still 50% of the work. This raises important questions about the nature of design in software compared to its role in other branches of engineering.

Resources to Slim Down Your Software Process

From chaos theory to freeware, approaches to systematic yet unbureaucratic development abound.

The method that has gotten the most attention in recent years is Extreme Programming (XP), popularized by Kent Beck. The roots of XP lie in the Smalltalk community; in particular, in the close collaboration of Beck and Ward Cunningham in the late 1980s.

XP begins with four value — communication, feedback, simplicity and courage — and then builds to a dozen practices (such as iterative planning, pair programming, simple design and unit testing), which XP projects should follow. Many of these practices are tried and tested, yet are often forgotten by many, including most planned processes. XP not only resurrects these techniques, but weaves them into a synergistic whole where each one is reinforced by the others. While Kent Beck's *Extreme Programming: Embrace Change* (Addison-Wesley, 1999) is the key manifesto of XP, there are other resources:

- Ron Jeffries, Ann Anderson and Chet Hendrickson's *Extreme Programming Installed* (Addison-Wesley, 2001).
- Kent Beck and Martin Fowler's *Planning Extreme Programming* (Addison-Wesley, 2001).
- www.xprogramming.com
- www.extremeprogramming.org
- www.egroups.com/group/extremeprogramming

The Crystal Family

Author Alistair Cockburn believes that different kinds of projects require different kinds of methodologies; therefore, Crystal is not a single methodology, but a "family" of approaches. The Crystals share XP's human orientation, but are people-centered in a different way. According to Cockburn, many people find disciplined processes hard to follow. Instead of emulating XP's high level of discipline, Cockburn seeks the least disciplined methodology that can still succeed, consciously trading off productivity for ease of execution. Although Crystal is less productive than XP, Cockburn believes more people will be able to follow it.

End of iteration reviews are crucial in Crystal, making the process self-improving. Iterative development also helps find problems early, enabling speedy corrections. Crystal emphasizes people monitoring and tuning the process as they develop. For more information, go to members.aol.com/acockburn.

Open Source

Open source is a style of software, not a process; however, there is a definite way of doing things in the open source community, and many of these approaches are as applicable to closed source projects as they are to open source. In particular, the open source process is geared toward physically distributed teams, which is important because most adaptive processes stress co-located teams. Most open source projects have one or more individuals who maintain the project, while the debugging is highly parallel, with many people sending patches to the maintainer when they find a bug. The process for open source hasn't yet been extensively examined, but there are a few references:

- Eric Raymond's evolving book, *The Cathedral and the Bazaar*, found at www.tuxedo.org/~esr/writings/cathedral-bazaar.
- Karl Franz Fogel's *Open Source Development with CVS* (Coriolis Open Press, 1999).

Adaptive Software Development

Jim Highsmith, in his book *Adaptive Software Development* (Dorset House, 1999), applies ideas that originate in the world of complex adaptive systems — commonly referred to as chaos theory — to software development. Adaptive Software Development doesn't provide the kind of detailed practices that XP does, but it does provide the fundamental groundwork for why adaptive development is important, while revealing the consequences of such an approach at the deeper organizational and management levels.

Scrum

Scrum aims to stabilize requirements during iterations by dividing a project into 30-day "sprints." Before beginning each sprint, you define the functionality required for that 30-day period and then leave the team to deliver it. Scrum literature primarily focuses on the iterative planning and tracking process. It's very similar to the other lightweights in many respects and should work well with the XP's coding practices. See the following Web sites for more information: www.controlchaos.com and jeffsutherland.com/scrum/index.html.

Feature Driven Development

Feature Driven Development (FDD) was developed by the long time OO guru Peter Coad. Like the other adaptive methodologies, it focuses on short iterations that deliver tangible functionality. In FDD's case, iterations are two weeks long. FDD has five processes: three of them (develop an overall model, build a features list and plan by feature) are done at the beginning of the project. The last two (design by feature and build by feature) are completed within each iteration. See Coad's *Java Modeling in Color with UML* (Prentice Hall, 1999) for more information.

Other Approaches

There are a number of other papers and discussions about light methods. While these may not be full methodologies, they do offer insights into this growing field. For more information, check out www.bell-labs.com/cgi-user/OrgPatterns/OrgPatterns and www.computer.org/software/so2000/s4toc.htm.

These kinds of questions led Jack Reeves ("What is Software Design," C++ *Users Journal,* Feb. 1992) to suggest that, in fact, the source code is a design document and that the construction phase is actually the use of the compiler and linker. Indeed, anything that you can treat as construction can and should be automated.

This thinking leads to some important conclusions:

- In software, construction is so cheap that it can be considered free.
- In software, all the effort is in design, thus development requires creative and talented people.
- Creative processes are not easily planned, so predictability may well be an impossible target.
- We should be wary of applying the traditional engineering metaphor to building software. It's a different kind of activity and requires a different process.

Morphing Requirements

There is a refrain I've heard on every problem project I've run into. The developers come to me and say "the problem with this project is that the requirements are always changing." I find it surprising that anyone is surprised by this. In building business software, requirements changes are the norm. The issue is what we do about it.

One route is to treat changing requirements as the result of poor requirements engineering. The idea behind requirements engineering is to fully understand the requirements before you begin building the software, get a customer sign-off to these requirements, and then set up procedures that limit requirements changes after the sign-off.

But just trying to understand the options for requirements can be tough. It's even tougher when the development organization doesn't provide cost information on the requirements. It's analogous to asking for a sun roof on your car only to discover that the salesman can't tell you if it will add $10 or $10,000 to the cost. Without any idea of the cost, how can you figure out whether you want to pay for that sun roof?

Estimation is hard for many reasons. Part of it is that software development is a design activity, and thus it's hard to plan and determine cost. Another reason is that the basic materials keep changing rapidly. And, finally, so much depends on who is involved; individuals are hard to predict and quantify.

Software's intangible nature also cuts in. It's very difficult to see what value a software feature has until you use it. Only when you use an early version of some software do you really begin to understand which features are valuable and which are not.

This leads to the ironic point that people expect that requirements should be changeable. After all, software is supposed to be soft. Requirements aren't just malleable, they ought to be so. It takes a lot of energy to get customers of software to fix requirements. It's even worse if they've ever dabbled in software development themselves, because then they "know" that software is easy to change.

But even if you could settle all that and really get an accurate, stable set of requirements, you're probably still doomed. In today's economy, the fundamental business forces are changing the value of software features too rapidly. What might be a good set of requirements now will not be a good set in six months. Even if the customers can fix their requirements, the business world isn't going to stop for them. And many changes in the business world are completely unpredictable. Everything else in software development depends on the requirements. If you can't get stable requirements, you can't get a predictable plan.

There are some software development projects where predictability is possible. Organizations such as NASA's space shuttle software group are a prime example of where software development can be predictable. It requires a lot of ceremony, plenty of time, a large team and stable requirements. There are projects out there that are space shuttles; I don't think much business software fits into that category, however. For most business software, you need a different kind of process.

One of the big dangers is to pretend that you can follow a predictable process when you can't. People who work on methodology aren't very good at identifying boundary conditions: the places where the methodology passes from appropriate to inappropriate. Most methodologists want their methodologies to be usable by everyone, so they don't understand nor publicize their boundary conditions. This leads to people using a methodology in the wrong circumstances.

Organic Process

How do we control ourselves in an unpredictable world? We need an honest feedback mechanism that can accurately tell us what the situation is at frequent intervals. The key to this feedback is iterative development. This is not a new idea. Iterative development has been around for a while under many names: incremental, evolutionary, staged, spiral and so on. The key to iterative development is to frequently produce working versions of the final system that have a subset of the required features. These working systems are short on functionality, but should otherwise be faithful to the demands of the final system. They should be fully integrated and as carefully tested as a final delivery.

There is nothing like a tested, integrated system for bringing a forceful dose of reality into any project. Documents can hide all sorts of flaws. Untested code can hide plenty of flaws. But when people actually sit in front of a system and work with it, then flaws become truly apparent, both in terms of bugs and in terms of misunderstood requirements.

Iterative development makes sense in predictable processes as well, but it is essential in adaptive processes because they must be able to deal with changes in required features. This leads to a style of planning where long-term plans are very fluid, and the only stable plans are those made for the short-term: a single iteration. Iterative development gives you a firm foundation in each iteration that you can base your later plans on.

Putting People First

One of the aims of traditional methodologies is to develop a process where the people involved are replaceable parts. With such a process you can treat people as resources who are available in various types. You have an analyst, some coders, some testers, a manager. The individuals aren't as important as the roles. That way, if you plan a project it doesn't matter which analyst and which testers you get, as long as you know how many you have and how the number of resources affects your plan.

But are the people involved in software development replaceable parts? One of the key features of lightweight methods is that they reject this assumption.

Perhaps the most explicit rejection of people as resources comes from object technology specialist Alistair Cockburn. He makes the point that predictable processes require components that behave in a predictable way. People are not predictable components. Furthermore, his studies of software projects have led him to conclude that people are the most important factor in software development.

Although Cockburn is the most explicit in his people-centric view of software development; the notion of people first is a common theme with many thinkers in software. The problem, too often, is that methodology has been opposed to the notion of people as the first-order factor in project success.

This creates a strong positive feedback effect. If you expect all your developers to be plug-compatible programming units, you won't try to treat them as individuals. This lowers morale (and productivity). The good people look for a better place to be, and you end up with what you desire — plug-compatible programming units.

The Self-Adaptive Process

I've discussed how a project's developers adapt the software frequently to meet the changing requirements of its customers. There is another angle to adaptiveness — that of the process changing over time. A project that begins using an adaptive process won't have the same process a year later. Over time, the team members will find what works for them and alter the process to fit.

A consequence of this is that you should never expect to find a single corporate methodology. Instead, each team should not just choose their own process, but should also actively tune their process as they proceed with the project. While both published processes and the experience of other projects can act as an inspiration and a baseline, the developers' professional responsibility is to adapt the process to the task at hand.

Should You Go Light?

Using a light method isn't for everyone. There are a number of things to bear in mind if you decide to follow this path. However, these new methodologies are widely applicable and should be used by more people than those that currently consider them.

In today's environment, the most common methodology is code-and-fix. Applying more discipline than chaos will almost certainly help, and the lightweight approach has the advantage that it is much less of a step than using a heavyweight method. Simpler processes are more likely to be followed when you are used to no process at all.

One of the biggest limitations to these new methodologies is how they handle larger teams. Cockburn's Crystal methodology has been used by teams of up to 50 people, but there is little evidence as to how you can use an adaptive approach, or even if such approaches work at all, beyond that size.

I hope I've made it clear that adaptive approaches are good when your requirements are uncertain or volatile. If you don't have stable requirements, then you aren't in the position to have a stable design and follow a planned process. In these situations, an adaptive process may be less comfortable but more effective. The biggest barrier is often the customer. Help the customer understand that following a predictive process when requirements change is as risky to them as it is to development.

If you have more than 50 people, you should use a traditional predictive process, and if you have changing requirements, you should use an adaptive process, right? What if you have both a large project and changing requirements? I don't have a good answer to this, so I'd suggest you seek a second opinion. I can tell you that things will be very difficult, but I suspect you already know that.

If you are going to take the adaptive route, trust your developers and involve them in the decision. Adaptive processes rely on you having confidence in your developers. If you consider them to be of low quality and motivation, on the other hand, choose a predictive approach.

7.3.4 "Is Design Dead?"

by Martin Fowler

Extreme programming (XP) strives for simple code — but simplicity is still a complicated thing to find.

NOTE: This is an abridged version of the article posted at `www.martinfowler.com/articles/designDead.html`

Extreme programming (XP) challenges many common assumptions about software development. One of the most controversial is its rejection of significant effort in up-front design, in favor of a more evolutionary approach. To its detractors, this is a return to "code and fix" development — usually derided as hacking. To its fans, it's often seen as a rejection of design techniques, principles and patterns. Don't worry about design. If you listen to your code, good design will appear.

I'm at the center of this argument. Much of my career has involved graphical design languages — like UML and its forerunners — and patterns. I've even written books on both UML and patterns. Does my embrace of XP mean I recant what I've written, cleansing my mind of all such counter-revolutionary notions?

I don't expect I can leave you dangling on the hook of dramatic tension. The short answer is no. The long answer is the rest of this article.

Planned and Evolutionary Design

In this article, I'm going to describe two styles of design used in software development: evolutionary and planned design. Perhaps the most common is evolutionary design. Essentially, it means a system's design grows as the system is implemented. Design is part of the programming process, and as the program evolves, the design changes.

In its common usage, evolutionary design is a disaster. The design ends up being the aggregation of ad hoc tactical decisions, each of which makes the code harder to alter. In many ways, you might argue this is no design — certainly, it usually leads to poor design. Not only does this make the software harder to change, it also makes bugs both easier to breed and harder to find and safely kill. This is the "code and fix" nightmare, where the bugs become exponentially more expensive to fix as the project goes on.

Planned design is counter to this. Designers think through big issues in advance. They don't need to write code because they aren't building the software, they're designing it. So they can use a design technique like UML that gets away from programming details and lets them work at a more abstract level. Once the design is done, they can hand it off to someone else to build.

The planned design approach has been around since the 70s, and lots of people have used it. It's better in many ways than code-and-fix evolutionary design, but it has some faults. The first is that it's impossible to think through all the issues you need to deal with when you're programming. So when the programmers find things that question the design, they start coding around it — and entropy sets in. And even if the designer hasn't moved on to another project, it takes time to sort out the design problems and alter the code accordingly.

The second fault, and the biggest cause of headaches on software projects, is changing requirements. One way to deal with it is to build flexibility into the design. However, this requires insight into what kind of changes you expect. A design can be planned to deal with areas of volatility, but that won't help (and can hurt) any unforeseen changes. So you have to understand the requirements well enough to separate the volatile areas, and my observation is that this is very hard. Many unforeseen requirements changes occur due to changes in the business. Those can't be prevented, no matter how careful you are.

The Enabling Practices of XP

XP is controversial for many reasons. One of the key red flags is that it advocates evolutionary rather than planned design. At the core of understanding this argument is the software change curve, which says that as the project runs, it becomes exponentially more expensive to make changes.

The change curve is usually expressed in terms of phases: "A change made in analysis for $1 would cost thousands to fix in production." The exponential change curve means evolutionary design can't work. It also conveys why planned design must be done carefully, because any mistakes there would face the same exponentiation.

The fundamental assumption underlying XP is that it's possible to flatten the change curve enough to make evolutionary design work. This flattening is both enabled and exploited by XP. Specifically, you can't use XP to exploit the flattened curve without using it to enable the flattening. This is a common source of the controversy over XP. Many people criticize the exploitation without understanding the enabling. Often, the criticisms stem from experience, where the critics didn't do the enabling practices that allow the exploiting practices to work. As a result, they were burned. Now, when they see XP, they remember the fire.

There are many parts to the enabling practices. At the core are the practices of testing and continuous integration. Without the safety provided by testing, the rest of XP would be impossible. Continuous integration is necessary to keep the team synchronized, so you can make a change without worrying about integrating it with other people. Together, these practices can have a big effect on the change curve.

Refactoring has a similar effect. People who refactor their code in the disciplined manner suggested by XP find a significant difference in their effectiveness, compared to doing looser, more ad hoc restructuring.

Jim Highsmith uses the analogy of a set of scales in his summary of XP in the February 2000 issue of the Cutter Consortium's *E-business Application Delivery* newsletter (www.cutter.com/ead/ead0002.html). On one tray is planned design, and refactoring is on the other. In more traditional approaches, planned design dominates because the assumption is you can't change your mind. But as the cost of change lowers, you can do more of your design later as refactoring. Planned design doesn't go away completely, but there is a balance of the two design approaches.

These enabling practices of continuous integration, testing and refactoring provide a new environment that makes evolutionary design plausible. However, we haven't yet figured out where the balance point is. I'm sure that, despite the outside impression, XP isn't just test, code and refactor. There is room for designing before coding. Some of this is before there is any coding, but most occurs in the iterations before coding for a particular task. Still there is a new balance between up-front design and refactoring.

The Value of Simplicity

Two of the greatest rallying cries in XP are the slogans "Do the simplest thing that could possibly work" and "You aren't going to need it" (known as YAGNI). Both are manifestations of the XP practice of simple design.

YAGNI is usually described by saying that you shouldn't add any code today that will only be used by a feature that is needed tomorrow. On the surface, this sounds simple. The issue comes with such things as frameworks, reusable components and flexible design. Such things are complicated to build, and you pay an extra up-front cost to build them, in the expectation you'll gain it back later. This idea of building flexibility up-front is seen as key to effective software design.

However, XP's advice is not to build flexible components and frameworks, but to let them grow as needed. For example, if I want a money class today that handles addition but not multiplication, then I build only addition into the money class. Even if I'm sure I'll need multiplication in the next iteration, and understand how to do it easily, I'll still leave it until the next iteration.

One reason for this is economic. If I have to do any work that is only used for a feature that is needed tomorrow, I'll lose time for features that need to be done today. The release plan says what needs to be worked on now. Working on other things is contrary to the developers' agreement with the customer. It's up to the customer to decide what extra work should be done — and that still might not involve multiplication.

This economic disincentive is compounded by the chance of getting it wrong. However certain I may be about how this function works, I can still get it wrong — especially without detailed requirements. Working on the wrong solution early is even more wasteful than working on the right solution early.

The second reason to use a simple design is that it is easier to understand than a complex design. Any system modification is made harder by added complexity. This adds a cost during the period between when the more complicated design was added and when it was needed.

Now this advice strikes many people as nonsense, and they're right to think that. Right providing they imagine the usual development world, where the enabling practices of XP aren't in place. However, when the balance between planned and evolutionary design alters, then YAGNI becomes good practice (and only then).

So, to summarize, you don't want to spend effort adding new capability that won't be needed until a future iteration. And even if the cost is zero, you still don't want to add it because it increases the cost of modification. However, you can only sensibly behave this way when you're using XP or a similar technique that lowers the cost of change.

What on Earth is Simplicity?

So we want our code to be as simple as possible. That doesn't sound like a difficult argument. After all, who wants to be complicated? But of course this begs the question, "What is simple?"

In *Extreme Programming Explained* (Addison-Wesley, 1999), Kent Beck gives four criteria for a simple system. Here they are in order (most important first):

- It runs all the tests.
- It reveals all the intention.
- There is no duplication.
- It uses the fewest number of classes or methods.

Running all the tests is a pretty simple criterion. No duplication is also straightforward. The tricky one has to do with revealing the intention. What exactly does that mean? It comes down to the clarity of code. XP places a high value on code that is easily read; "clever code" is a term of abuse. But one person's easily read code is often considered clever by another.

In his "Patterns and XP" paper presented at XP 2000 in Sardinia, Italy, Josh Kerievsky points out a good example of this. He looks at possibly the most public XP code of all — JUnit. JUnit uses decorator patterns to add optional functionality, such as concurrency synchronization and batch setup code, to test cases. By separating this code into decorators, the general code becomes more clear than it otherwise would be.

But you have to ask yourself if the resulting code is really simple. For me it is, but I'm familiar with the Decorator pattern. But for many who aren't, it's quite complicated. Similarly, JUnit uses pluggable methods that most people initially find anything but clear. So might we conclude that JUnit's design is simpler for experienced designers, but more complicated for less experienced people?

I think the focus on eliminating duplication — both with XP's mantra of "Once and Only Once" and the *Pragmatic Programmer's* (Andrew Hunt and David Thomas, Addison-Wesley, 1999) recommendation "Don't Repeat Yourself" (DRY) — is one of those obvious and powerful pieces of good advice. Just following that alone can take you a long way. But it isn't everything, and simplicity is still a complicated thing to find.

The best take I heard on all this came from Robert Martin. His advice was not to get too hung up about what the simplest design is. After all, you can, should and will refactor it later. In the end, the willingness to refactor is much more important than knowing what the simplest thing is right away.

Does Refactoring Violate YAGNI?

This question starts with the point that refactoring takes time but doesn't add functionality. Since the point of YAGNI is that you're supposed to design for the present, not the future, is refactoring a violation? The answer is no.

YAGNI simply ensures that you don't add complexity that isn't immediately needed. This is part of the practice of simple design. Refactoring is needed to keep the design as simple as you can, so you should refactor whenever you realize you can make things simpler.

Simple design exploits XP practices and is also an enabling practice. Only if you have testing, continuous integration and refactoring can you practice simple design effectively. At the same time, keeping the design simple is essential to keeping the change curve flat. Any unneeded complexity makes a system harder to change in almost all directions. People aren't good at anticipating, however, so it's best to strive for simplicity. But people won't get the simplest thing the first time, so you need to refactor to get closer to the goal.

Patterns and XP

The JUnit example leads me inevitably to patterns. The relationship between patterns and XP is interesting, and it's a common question. Kerievsky argues that patterns are underemphasized in XP, but it's worth mentioning that for many people, patterns seem to conflict with XP.

XP may be a process for development, but patterns are a backbone of design knowledge, knowledge that is valuable whatever your process may be. Different processes may use patterns in different ways. XP emphasizes both not using a pattern until it's needed and evolving your way into a pattern through simple implementation. But patterns are still a key piece of knowledge.

My advice to XP developers (XPers) using patterns would be to learn about patterns, concentrate on when to apply them (not too early), concentrate on how to implement the pattern in its simplest form first, then add complexity later, and don't be afraid to remove a pattern that isn't pulling its weight.

UML and XP

Of all the questions I get about my involvement with XP, one of the biggest revolves around my association with the UML. Aren't the two incompatible?

In many ways, yes. Certainly, XP de-emphasizes diagrams to a great extent. Although the official position is along the lines of "use them if they're useful," there is a strong subtext of "real XPers don't do diagrams."

I think the issue comes from two separate causes. One is that some people find software diagrams helpful, and some don't. The danger is that both sides think the other is incorrect. Instead, we should just accept that some people will use diagrams, and some won't.

The other issue is that software diagrams tend to get associated with heavyweight processes. Such processes require you to spend a lot of time drawing diagrams that don't help and can actually cause harm. Thus, people should be advised how to use diagrams well.

First, know why you're drawing the diagrams. The primary value is communication. Effective communication means selecting important things and neglecting the less important. This selectivity is the key to using the UML well. Don't draw every class, only the important ones. For each class, don't show every attribute and operation, only the important ones.

Don't draw sequence diagrams for all use cases and scenarios, only the important ones. You get the picture.

A common problem with using diagrams is that people try to make them comprehensive. The code is the best source of comprehensive information, as it's the easiest thing to keep in sync. For diagrams, comprehensiveness is the enemy of comprehensibility.

A common use of diagrams is to explore a design before you start coding it. Often, you get the impression that such activity is "illegal" in XP, but that is not true. Many people say that when you have a sticky task, it's worth getting together to have a quick design session first. However, when you do such sessions, keep them short, don't try to address all the details, and treat the resulting design as a sketch, not as final. [See Ron Jeffries, Ann Anderson and Chet Hendrickson's *Extreme Programming Installed* (Addison-Wesley 2000) for more information about the quick design session.]

The last point is worth expanding. When you do some up-front design, you'll inevitably find that some of its aspects are wrong — and you only discover this when coding. That isn't a problem if you change the design at that point. The trouble comes when people think the design is done, and then don't take the knowledge they gained through the coding and run it back into the design.

Changing the design doesn't necessarily mean changing the diagrams. It's perfectly reasonable to draw diagrams that help you understand the design and then throw the diagrams away. Drawing them helped, and that is enough to make them worthwhile. They don't have to become permanent artifacts. In fact, the best UML diagrams are not artifacts.

A lot of XPers use CRC cards. That doesn't conflict with UML. I use a mix of CRC and UML all the time, using whichever technique is most useful for the job at hand. Another use of UML diagrams is ongoing documentation. In its usual form, this is a model residing on a CASE tool. The idea is that keeping this documentation helps people work on the system. In practice, it often doesn't help at all. Instead, it takes too long to keep the diagrams up to date, so they fall out of sync with the code. And they're often hidden in a CASE tool or a thick binder, so nobody looks at them. So my advice for ongoing documentation is this:

- Only use diagrams you can keep up to date without noticeable pain.
- Put the diagrams where everyone can easily see them, such as on a wall. Encourage people to edit the wall copy with a pen for simple changes.
- Pay attention to whether or not people are using them. If not, throw them away.

The last aspect of using UML is for documentation in a situation where one group hands over a project to another. Here the XP point is that producing documentation is a story like any other, and thus its business value is determined by the customer. Again, the UML is useful here, providing the diagrams are selective to help communication. Remember that the code is the repository of detailed information, and the diagrams act to summarize and highlight important issues.

So, Is Design Dead?

Not by any means, but its nature has changed. XP design looks for the following:

- A constant desire to keep code as clear and simple as possible.
- Refactoring skills so you can confidently make improvements as needed.

- A good knowledge of patterns — not just the solutions, but also appreciating when to use them and how to evolve into them.

- Knowing how to communicate the design to the people who need to understand it, using code, diagrams, and above all, conversation.

That is a fearsome selection of skills. But then being a good designer has always been tough. XP doesn't really make it any easier, at least not for me. But I think it does give us a new way to think about effective design, because it's made evolutionary design a plausible strategy again. And I'm a big fan of evolution — otherwise who knows what I might be?

7.3.5 "Extreme Lessons Learned"

by Scott W. Ambler

How total strangers built a working system in just three days.

Think you've got it tough on your current project? What if you were assigned to deliver a system with roughly 25 HTML pages, many of them interactive, with a team of developers who had never worked together before, most of whom had no experience in the selected technology, were not familiar with the problem domain, were not available full time, had no clear reporting structure, and were working for free? Did I mention that we only had three days in which to deliver a working system that was to be presented to our users in front of thousands of our peers on the fourth day? Is that "eXtreme" enough for you? Welcome to the first SD Project, developed at the Software Development East 2000 (www.sdexpo.com) conference, held the last week of October 2000 in Washington D.C.

This year the conference decided to have its speakers and attendees develop a system for a nonprofit organization — in this case, the redeployment of the Hydrocephalus Association's Web site (www.hydroassoc.org). The effort was led by Ken Pugh, of Pugh-Killeen Associates (www.pughkilleen.com), one of the speakers at the conference, and organized by Shabnam Malek, Conference Manager for the Software Development Media Group. I'm proud to say that the effort was successful, although not without a few hiccups. By the end, we all (re)learned several interesting lessons about software development.

The Initiation Phase

The project began several weeks prior to the conference; Shabnam lined up VA Linux (www.valinux.com) to provide equipment and development tools for the team. Ken developed an initial technical specification — in coordination with Jim Kranz, a board member of the Hydrocephalus Association — and then formulated a list of development tasks and the skills required to complete those tasks. Shabnam also asked the conference speakers, via e-mail, to volunteer. Ken distributed his documents to the volunteers, so we could familiarize ourselves with the effort before arriving at the conference. This initial preparation by a few people enabled the rest of the team to hit the ground running.

The core of the development team got together on Sunday evening to discuss the project, to understand the scope, and simply to meet everyone else. This was effectively a project kick-off meeting held over dinner. At dinner, we quickly realized that the composition of the team wasn't ideal; there were no Perl programmers among us, and few of us had Linux experience. In short, we were top heavy with managers and analysts, and desperately short of programmers. This situation is typical of many projects: Senior management had effectively made a technical decision to use Linux and Perl without first consulting the development team. Luckily, we actually required Perl as it was the only CGI scripting language supported by all the potential host systems, and Linux is a great operating system. Also, we likely had several people more than we needed at the beginning of the project; we had front-loaded the project with staff, but in the end, we were glad to have everyone on board.

Luck was on our side when Lorah McArdle, copy editor at *Software Development* magazine, hunted down some code for us and sent Ken the URLs for some sites with Perl code on them. Ken then downloaded an appropriate example after selecting it based on its description. With a little bit of investigation, you can often find reusable artifacts appropriate for your project team.

On Monday morning, we began by defining the initial scope and planning the project, and it quickly became obvious that we had more to do than we could handle — we were working on an unrealistic schedule. Typical software project. We had suspected this the night before, but it wasn't confirmed until we actually started planning. It was about this time that Shabnam, effectively senior management for the project, popped in to see how things were going. She was eager to know if we would have the system running in time for the presentation she had scheduled on Thursday. Wanting to soothe her fears, I told her that everything was on track and there was nothing to worry about: I lied and she went away happy. I usually want to be honest with everyone involved in a project, but by this time, the important factors (schedule, team, environment) were carved in stone. Worrying Shabnam would only slow us down.

Monday was a tutorial day, so the core team focused on building the foundation upon which the other volunteers would operate. We developed a list of good things to know about the project (a project overview, our goals, the site URL and our working directories) and posted it on the walls. This would help us to integrate new people into the project easily, an important goal considering people would join the project for only a few hours at a time. We also defined naming standards for the HTML fields, and we adopted some Perl coding conventions we found online because we felt that consistency was important as someone other than us would have to maintain the system over time.

We then developed a user interface flow model, also called a navigation map, which showed the HTML pages and how to traverse between them. We posted it on the wall, so everyone could see it and change it as the project progressed. The model was a collection of sheets of paper connected by masking tape, which indicated the pages that you could navigate to. Each piece of paper revealed the purpose of the HTML page, its name (for example, `dona-tions.html`), whether it was an input form or static text, and its current development status. This model was simple; we clearly didn't use a CASE tool, yet it was vital to our project's success because it was user interface intensive (it's a Web site). User interface flow diagrams are not yet part of the Unified Modeling Language (UML), but you can read more about them and their use in my book, *The Object Primer, Second Edition* (Cambridge University Press, 2001), and in *Software For Use* (Larry L. Constantine and Lucy Lockwood, ACM Press, 1999).

We tried a similar approach with the initial project plan but had much less success. We taped some flip chart paper to the wall and put sticky notes on the paper, one note for each task that we needed to accomplish. Although this effort allowed us to get a better handle on what needed to be done, it was abandoned on Tuesday once we lost the person leading the planning effort. The project plan was kept as simple as possible, but the reality was that the developers were focused on writing software, not updating a management document. They quickly migrated to an even simpler task list that they maintained throughout the effort. In short, the important artifacts of one set of team members were meaningless to others and therefore not kept current; you need to focus on developing and maintaining only a minimal set of artifacts.

The Lessons We Learned

1. Initial preparation pays off.
2. Kickoff meetings help the team to gel.
3. Too many people on a project is just as bad as too few: Staff your project with the right people at the right time.
4. The first step in obtaining reusable artifacts is to look for them.
5. Don't commit to a schedule until you know you have a chance of meeting it.
6. Lying to senior management isn't ideal, but sometimes it's your best option.
7. Define a "good things to know" list for developers new to the project.
8. Consider maintenance issues while you are developing your system.
9. Set development standards and guidelines early in the project.
10. Your artifacts may be meaningless to others.
11. Simple models are often the best models.
12. Develop a minimal set of artifacts.
13. Prove your approach by developing an end-to-end prototype.
14. Set user interface conventions early in the project.
15. Identify common aspects of your system, and develop them early, so they may be reused.
16. Be prepared to bring new people into the project part way through it.
17. Be prepared to lose people during your project.
18. Co-locate your team in a shared working space.
19. Users can and should play active roles on your development teams.
20. Bring in an expert for a short time to get you through a difficult situation.
21. One bad decision can kill a software project.
22. Backup your work on a regular basis.
23. Decision makers must be close to the situation to be effective.
24. Users, not developers, should drive the prioritization of new system features.

The Elaboration Phase

On Monday, we set the architecture for the system and proved that it worked by developing an end-to-end prototype (a data input form). This was important for several reasons: It familiarized the team with the technology they were using, it provided working examples that people could copy and modify, and it assured both project and senior management that the project was realistic.

In parallel, we developed sample HTML forms to work from. One form set the general layout and color scheme for each page, something that was copied extensively once we finalized the Web site's look and feel later in the project (in the middle of the construction phase). Another form provided examples of input fields for common information, such as a person's name and address, which was needed on several pages. This helped set the look and feel of the input form pages, enforced the naming conventions that had been set previously, and provided a reusable asset that could be applied throughout the project. Our construction efforts benefited dramatically by our decision to identify and develop common reusable assets early in the project.

The Construction Phase

With the basic architecture, guidelines and code examples in place, we were able to start the Construction phase on Tuesday morning. We luckily had our own workroom that contained all the development workstations and provided enough wall space to post our models and plans. Had the team been separated from one another, a typical situation that most developers face with cubicles, we would not have been able to produce as much software that quickly. We also had the benefit of our user, Jim Kranz, being actively involved with the project. He edited some of the HTML pages, particularly the ones that were static text, and reviewed the effort as it progressed. He also helped improve and then finalize the site's look and feel, enabling the team to apply that style to all the HTML pages. He naturally assisted in explaining the goals of the system and provided insight into the requirements. It was easy for our user to become an active and productive member of the team, once we found a productive role for him.

On Wednesday, a Perl expert became involved with the project for a short time — until that point, the team had been learning as they went and were struggling. The expert reviewed some of the source code and provided critical insights that got the programmers going in the right direction. With a small investment of time, the team was able to effectively leverage the knowledge of this expert tenfold.

That evening, disaster was narrowly averted. Due to miscommunication, a manager at VA Linux sent someone to pick up our equipment on Wednesday evening. They thought that we only needed the equipment until Thursday morning, which was true because the presentation was early Thursday afternoon; however, someone had translated that to mean they could pick everything up Wednesday night. Fortunately, some of the team were still there (we were just about to leave for dinner), and we were able to set everything straight.

The near disaster only proved one of my core beliefs: Our industry has such a dismal success rate, in part, because it's so easy to kill a project with one bad decision. In this case, the decision maker was far away from the situation, and the team he had sent didn't have sufficient knowledge to make the right call, forcing people near the situation (the project team) to override the original decision. Had we not been able to prevent VA Linux from taking the equipment, we very likely would not have been able to deliver in time for the presentation on Thursday (I doubt everything was fully backed up).

The Transition Phase

The presentation occurred on Thursday as originally planned, even though the system had not yet been deployed. The users had not yet identified an ISP to host the new version of the site, and, therefore, we couldn't deploy and test the site until we knew the exact operational environment. Although Perl is a cross-platform language, we still needed to validate that our system would work on the chosen platform.

The Production Phase

At Software Development West 2001 (www.sdexpo.com), to be held the second week of April in San Jose, California, a group of volunteers will develop an updated version of the site. By that time, the system will have operated for several months and our users will have identified and prioritized new requirements. Time will tell. I look forward to sharing a new set of lessons learned with you after SD West.

Special Thanks to the Team

We'd like to thank the following people (my apologies if I missed anyone) who worked on the project:

- Ken Pugh, Brad Niemann, Timothy Wright, Ravi Muttineni, Lou Russell, Larry Meinstein, Robert Hall, Brahma Sen, Ahura Hazan-Fuchs and Rod Spradlin.
- Special thanks go out to Fremont, California-based VA Linux (www.valinux.com), who supplied the equipment and software that we used to develop the system. This project would not have been possible without their generous support.
- Also, thanks to Ken Pugh who took the time to provide me with feedback to help improve the accuracy of this column.

7.3.6 "Extreme Programming"

by Warren Keuffel

Like those who snowboard, skydive and skateboard, people who develop software in "Internet time" often find themselves in a do-or-die mode of operation.

Extreme sports, in which competitors vie with each other in dreaming up even more outrageous exploits, have captured the public's eye. Parachutists jump off bridges, tall buildings and cliffs. Skydivers strap snowboards to their feet and surf the sky. Water-skiers take off their skis and go over jumps with bare feet. The list goes on, limited only by how daring — or stupid — people can be.

The software development analogue to extreme sports is sometimes found in the shops of those who develop software in "Internet time." Some efforts succeed with spectacular results. Others crash and burn with equally spectacular pyrotechnics. For those of us interested in learning from these pioneers, successful, thoughtful, repeatable models for doing so have been slow in arriving. As with most cutting-edge practices, the understanding — and the discipline — have lagged behind. Microsoft's "eat your own dog food" model has been widely emulated, often without an understanding of how and why it works — and does not work — other than because someone decides that "if it's good enough for Microsoft, it'll be good enough for us."

Microsoft's development model revolves around market-driven and dynamic requirements, use of daily builds and heavy reliance on peer pressure among the members of the development team. It's an expensive way to go, though, because assigning a "testing buddy" to each developer forms a core concept in how Microsoft implements its method. In Microsoft's culture, these practices have worked in the past, enabling the company to get software that is "good enough" to market soon enough to grab crucial early market share — even if consumers have learned that the first two releases of a product are usually still beta quality.

I've written in the past about Jim Highsmith's Adaptive Software Development (ASD) models that emphasize a chaotic atmosphere to encourage creativity and productivity in an environment where requirements are constantly changing. To briefly recapitulate, the key concept behind ASD is that the traditional, deterministic plan-build-revise cycle must be replaced with an adaptive speculate-collaborate-learn model. Speculation, in ASD, acknowledges that the probability of making mistakes with traditional planning is high, so it's best to postulate a general idea of where the project is going. The collaboration phase realizes that you can't tightly control software development projects and expect great software to emerge. Instead, ASD advocates a management style that recognizes that successful software development exists on the edge of chaos. Finally, in the learning phase, value is attached to the products of the two prior phases; activities in the next speculation phase adapt to the information gathered in prior cycles.

Chaos is encouraged in ASD, and is seen as a necessary step on the path — particularly through the early iterations of the speculate-collaborate-learn cycle. But chaos is, by its nature, uncomfortable, and for conservative IT folks, it does not come easily. However, those who have taken the plunge have found the chaotic environment exhilarating and reinforcing.

Consultant Kent Beck describes another rapid development model in *Extreme Programming Explained: Embrace Change* (Addison-Wesley, 2000). Beck, who hails from Smalltalk-land and who is heavily pattern-focused, targets Extreme Programming (XP) at the needs of small teams confronted with vague and changing requirements.

Beck maintains that it is possible to develop software using techniques that minimize the cost of making changes late in the development life cycle. Instead of planning, analyzing and designing for the future, Beck encourages programmers to adopt a method which emphasizes selecting the most important features and developing them to completion within a short time frame. Here's Beck's prescription for making this possible.

Story Time

A team begins by putting together a collection of desirable features, as defined by the customer, each of which consists of a use case (or portion thereof) that can comfortably be described on one index card. Beck calls these feature fragments "stories." The customer then decides which features, or stories, are desired in the first iteration, a decision based not only on the stories themselves but also on the length of time it will take to implement each story. Thus, each release incorporates only that functionality requested by the customer. Beck calls a collection of stories a metaphor, which becomes a shared vision for developers and customers alike.

The team proceeds to iterate through an analysis-design-implementation-test cycle for each story, frequently producing a new release — perhaps daily, perhaps monthly. A unique concept advanced by Beck for XP is that all code for each story is developed by a team of two programmers working on one machine. This two-person team first develops a test case for the story, taking into account the functional tests, which are provided by the customer. An important characteristic of XP teams is that there is no division of labor among analysis, development and testing. All members of the team perform all of these duties at appropriate times in the development of individual stories.

As with other similar intensive programming methods, XP requires equally intensive customer involvement; ideally, a customer is assigned to full-time participation with the team. Customers help develop the list of stories, using their knowledge of the functional requirements for the project. Each story must have an accompanying functional test, which the customer must supply. But if customers can't or won't cooperate, XP teams should realize that perhaps the project is not a high priority with the customer and move on to other tasks.

Testing is a core activity in XP, not an afterthought. Test cases are developed before any coding is begun, and XP addresses the common inability of programmers to write their own tests by specifying that each story be developed by a two-person team. This helps ensure that more than one perspective goes into both the testing and implementation of each story.

Constant Building

XP shares with Microsoft the "daily build" philosophy, but goes one step further and advocates multiple builds per day, each of which is followed by automatically running all of the accumulated test cases. As the growing system repeatedly passes the also-growing repertoire of tests, the team, including the customer, gains more and more confidence in the integrity of the system. If a change breaks the test suite, the system reverts to the previous build until the new changes complete the test suite satisfactorily. In addition, the modularity of the system — and how it is implemented — helps ensure that if requirements change, new stories will be written to meet those new requirements.

If you're interested in learning more about XP, Beck describes it in detail in the October 1999 issue of *IEEE Computer* ("Embracing Change with Extreme Programming," *IEEE Computer*, Vol. 32, No. 10). Despite several successful case studies described in the article, Beck is quick to point out that XP is still very much a work in progress. He suggests that it's applicable initially to small or medium systems where requirements are vague and volatile. He expects that as XP matures it will find its way into larger projects.

Since development at Internet speed doesn't appear to be going away anytime soon, I find it gratifying that people are paying attention to repeatable, measurable methods that can absorb the volatility that characterizes much of today's software development environment.

7.3.7 "Lean Programming; Part 1"

by Mary Poppendieck

Assembly-line production techniques apply to software, too.

About the time of the 1980 NBC documentary "If Japan Can, Why Can't We?," I was the system manager of a videocassette manufacturing plant, and our Japanese competition was selling superior products at much lower prices. We knew we needed to make dramatic changes or close up shop, but we didn't know what to change.

As far as we could tell, we were doing everything right. Optimized forecasting methods determined economic lot sizes, and the latest manufacturing requirement, planning software, launched the plant's daily schedules. A sophisticated computer system analyzed our quality control results and process parameters to pinpoint the causes of defects.

We did have some quality problems, and it took a month to fill most orders. Special orders were another matter, however: The division vice president would often call to expedite them for important customers.

We moved in-process videocassettes from one workstation to another on carts, and we used a lot of carts. There was never enough room to store them all at the next workstation, so carts full of inventory would get misplaced. Videocassettes piled up in front of testing stations. Whenever a process drifted out of control, it took a while to discover that we were producing a marginal product. We had plenty of rework stations.

All in all, we had about a month's worth of work-in-process inventory. At the time, we blamed our inability to rapidly fill orders on bad forecasts from marketing. Later, we were surprised to learn that the real culprit was our in-process inventory. Today, it's a truism that the average supply-chain shipping time is about the same as the average level of inventory in the chain.

Lean Production

In 1935, Kiichiro Toyoda, the son of brilliant inventor Sakichi Toyoda, founder of the Toyoda Spinning and Weaving Company Ltd., dreamed of providing vehicles to the general public. After a hiatus imposed by World War II, he chartered Taiichi Ohno to design an efficient production system for high-quality automobiles. Over the next 30 years, Ohno developed the Toyota Production System (the *d* morphed into a *t* when the company reached the import stage), now known worldwide as Lean Production (see *The Machine That Changed the World: The Story of Lean Production*, by James P. Womack, Daniel T. Jones and Daniel Roos, New York: Rawson and Associates, 1990). The foundation of Ohno's system is the absolute elimination of waste in both product and process.

Although Ohno learned from Henry Ford's pioneer work in assembly-line flow, he didn't have the customer base to imitate the U.S. practice of manufacturing in so-called "economic," or large lot sizes. Ohno was captivated by U.S. supermarkets, however, where a small quantity of every product was placed on shelves that were rapidly replenished. He decided to place inventory "supermarkets" throughout his plant, thus dramatically lowering the "waste" of in-process inventory. He named these inventory supermarkets *kanban*.

Chronological Bibliography

All you ever wanted to know (and more) about Lean Production: from pioneer tomes to expanded concepts of "lean thinking."

Quality Control Handbook by Joseph M. Juran. New York, NY: McGraw Hill Book Company, 1951 (now in its fourth edition).
This handbook is considered the standard reference in the field of quality. Like Deming, Juran consulted mainly in Japan during the 1950s and 60s.

Managerial Breakthrough by Joseph M. Juran. New York, NY: McGraw-Hill Book Company, 1964.
Widely ignored when it was first published, this book is now considered a landmark treatise on continuous improvement.

Quality Is Free by Philip Crosby. New York, NY: McGraw-Hill Book Company, 1979.
We used this book to launch our plant's TQM program. Deming never liked the zero-defects approach advocated in this book, and it contains little about statistical quality control. However, many corporate executives got the quality message from Phil Crosby.

Toyota Production System, Practical Approach to Production Management by Yasuhiro Monden. Norcross, Georgia: Industrial Engineering and Management Press, 1983.
This is the classic book on Lean Production.

Zero Inventories by Robert W. Hall. Homewood, IL: Dow Jones-Irwin, 1983.
Robert Hall, a professor at Indiana University, understood the just-in-time concept earlier than most academics. This book is still considered the definitive work on JIT.

Out of the Crisis by W. Edwards Deming. Cambridge, MA: MIT Press Center for Advanced Engineering Study, 1986.
This is the classic in which Deming outlined his famous 14 points.

The Deming Management Method by Mary Walton and W. Edwards Deming. New York, NY: Perigee Books, 1986.
Probably the most comprehensive book on Deming and his management approach.

Toyota Production System — Beyond Large Scale Production by Taiichi Ohno. Cambridge, MA: Productivity Inc. Published in Japanese in 1978; in English in 1988.
This is an explanation of JIT by its inventor. The English version arrived after JIT had become widespread in the U.S.

The Machine That Changed the World: The Story of Lean Production by James P. Womack, Daniel T. Jones and Daniel Roos. New York, NY: Rawson and Associates, 1990.
This landmark book about the Toyota Production System was the first to associate the term "lean" with manufacturing.

Lean Thinking by James P. Womack and Daniel T. Jones. New York, NY: Simon & Schuster Inc., 1996.
A follow-up on the story of lean production, this book extends the lean concept

throughout an enterprise, revealing how the "lean principles" of value (as defined by the customer), value stream, flow, pull and perfection can be applied. Software development is implicitly included.

Because Ohno's automobile manufacturing plant evolved from the highly successful Toyoda spinning and weaving company, he already knew how to avoid making a bad product. Sakichi Toyoda had invented an automatic shut-off mechanism that stopped a weaving machine the minute it detected a flaw (such as a broken thread). Ohno expanded this concept into car manufacturing, insisting that each automobile part be examined as soon as it was processed, stopping the line immediately when a defect was found.

To maximize product flow, workers who knew the process — not desk-bound engineers — created standard work sheets, which included cycle times, *kanban* shelf space for each item and multilevel workflow. Production workers operated like a relay team, handing the baton to the next person in line. This "just-in-time" system required close teamwork and exquisite choreography: When the process stalled, teammates were expected to help each other reset a machine or recover from a malfunction.

Ohno's aggressive elimination of waste led him to the twin values of rapid product flow and built-in quality. Over time, he discovered that these two values led to the production of the highest quality, lowest cost, shortest lead-time products available.

Total Quality Management

At about the same time Ohno was revolutionizing auto production, American management guru W. Edwards Deming was teaching quality management in Japan. In fact, the Total Quality Management (TQM) movement that Deming spawned can't be separated from Ohno's Lean Production. Deming's photo hangs in the lobby of Toyota's headquarters — in a larger image than that of founder Sakichi Toyoda. Deming's "profound knowledge," Ohno's "lean production" and "flexible manufacturing," and Toyoda's spirit of creativity and invention have inspired a powerful management movement that revitalizes the business model for optimal efficiency.

Deming maintained that poor quality was engendered by systems that thwarted the workers' desire to do good work. He taught the Japanese managers how to empower production workers to investigate problems and systematically improve business processes, stressing teamwork and long-term, trust-based connections with suppliers. Deming's vision emphasized a culture of continuous improvement of both process and product.

Paradigm Shift

When we first heard about Lean Production at the videocassette manufacturing plant, we thought it was a hoax. Get rid of safety stock, don't run machines at full capacity and have suppliers deliver small lots on a daily basis? Though it went against the wisdom of the day, we were desperate enough to give Lean Production a try. In the end, it saved our business.

The critical step was a carefully planned changeover from push scheduling to pull scheduling. We decided that we couldn't do it partway — we had to switch cold turkey, over a weekend. The entire plant held its collective breath as the pull system went into effect, but the workers knew what to do — they had developed the methods themselves. The first week packout accuracy was 92%, and it improved from then on. We were able to fill special orders in two weeks, so the vice president could stop expediting them. We had lots of extra space, and quality had never been better.

Simple Rules

In a January 2001 *Harvard Business Review* article titled "Strategy as Simple Rules," Kathleen Eisenhardt describes how smart companies thrive in a complex business environment: by establishing a set of rules that define — not confine — direction. She suggests that instead of complex processes, simple communication strategies can best enable people to seize fleeting opportunities in rapidly changing markets.

The basic practices of Lean Production and TQM might be summed up in these 10 points:

1. Eliminate waste.
2. Minimize inventory.
3. Maximize flow.
4. Pull from demand.
5. Meet customer requirements.
6. Do it right the first time.
7. Empower workers.
8. Ban local optimization.
9. Partner with suppliers.
10. Create a culture of continuous improvement.

These rules, adapted to logistics, customer service, healthcare, finance and even construction over the last two decades, have proven their worth. More recently, they have found their way into software project management.

Lean Programming

Lightweight methodologies, adaptive software development and Kent Beck's Extreme Programming techniques have, in effect, applied the simple rules of Lean Production to software development. The results, which I call Lean Programming, can be as dramatic as the improvements in manufacturing engendered by the Ohno- and Deming-based efficiency movements of the 1980s. The Chrysler C3 project, which used Extreme Programming, with its characteristic focus on teamwork, customer feedback and continual reintegration, is a prime example of this new methodology.

Lean Rule #1: Eliminate Waste

The first rule of Lean Programming is to eliminate waste. A value stream analysis identifies all activities in the process and delineates the specific value they add to the final product. The value analysis then attempts to find a different, more efficient way to produce the same value.

The documents, diagrams and models produced as part of a software development project are often consumables — aids used to produce a system, but not necessarily a part of the final product. Once a working system is delivered, the user may care little about the intermediate consumables. Lean principles suggest that every consumable is a candidate for scrutiny. The burden is on the artifact to prove not only that it adds value to the final product, but also that it is the most efficient way of achieving that value.

Lean Rule #2: Minimize Inventory

Contrary to popular belief, inventory is wasteful: It consumes resources, slows response time, hides quality problems, gets lost, degrades and becomes obsolete. The inventory of software development is documentation that isn't a part of the final program. Take requirements and design documents, for example. How important are they to the final product? If you compare them to in-process inventory, it's striking to note that the hours expended to create these documents form a major component of the product's cycle time. Just as inventory must be diminished to maximize manufacturing flow, so, too, must requirements and design documents be reduced to maximize development flow.

There are many wastes associated with excess documentation: the squandering of time spent creating and reviewing reports, and the unnecessary work involved in change requests and associated evaluations, priority setting and system changes. But the biggest waste of all is that of building the wrong system if the documentation doesn't correctly and completely capture the user's requirements.

We know that users are relatively inefficient at envisioning the details of a system from most documents, and are even less likely to correctly perceive how a system will work in their environment until they actually use it. Even if users could predict exactly how the system should operate, it's unlikely that the way the system is supposed to work months before it's delivered will be exactly the way users need it to work throughout its life span. All of these factors must be considered when we evaluate the value of documentation.

Lean Rule #3: Maximize Flow (Reduce System Response Time)

In the 1980s, TQM principles taught us how to make products in hours instead of days or weeks. Indeed, rapid product flow shortened cycle times by several orders of magnitude. During the 1990s, e-commerce projects were often able to accomplish in weeks what used to take months or years in the traditional software development world. Yes, in some sense they cheated, exploiting the absence of an established customer base, which allowed unchecked expansion built upon sometimes shoddy components. And many paid the price for this gold rush: A number of the early e-commerce firms, funded largely by speculation, died natural deaths brought on by poor management, code that was anything but robust and lack of discipline. Nevertheless, in the last five years, an abundance of useful software with extremely short cycle times has been deployed.

In his article, "Reducing Cycle Time" (*Management Forum*, Aug. 2000), Dennis Frailey proposes trimming software development cycle time using the same techniques employed to reduce manufacturing cycle time. He suggests looking for and reducing accumulations of work in process, or WIP. Just as in manufacturing, if you reduce WIP, you trim the cycle time. To do this, Frailey recommends using the familiar Lean Production "small batch" and "smooth flow" principles.

Iterative development is basically the application of these principles to programming. In this method, small but complete portions of a system are designed and delivered throughout the development cycle, with each iteration taking on an additional set of features. From start to finish, cycle time of any iteration varies from a few weeks to a few months, and each iteration engages the entire development process, from gathering requirements to acceptance testing.

Lean Rule #4: Pull From Demand (Make Decisions as Late as Possible)

In our videocassette manufacturing plant, we used to think that it would be ideal if our marketing department could forecast exact market requirements. A lot of work went into sophisticated techniques to more accurately predict the future. Then one day we realized that we were doing the wrong thing: It would not be ideal if we had a perfect forecast. Instead, we should relinquish our dependence on forecasts by reducing system response time so dramatically that the system could adequately respond to change, obviating the need for prediction.

In a market in which volatile technology requires constant product upgrades, Dell Computer has a huge advantage over its keenest competitors because it doesn't forecast demand; rather, it responds to it by making-to-order in an average of 10 days. While Dell holds only days' worth of inventory, its competitors maintain weeks' worth. Dell's ability to make decisions as late as possible gives the company a significant competitive edge in a fast-moving market.

Software development practices that keep requirements flexible as close to system delivery as possible provide a competitive advantage. In a volatile business environment, users can't accurately forecast their future needs. Freezing the design early in a development project is just as speculative as forecasting. Software systems should be designed to respond to change, not predict it.

Lean Rule #5: Meet Customer Requirements (Now and in the Future)

In his 1979 book, *Quality Is Free,* Philip Crosby defines quality as "conformance to requirements." The 1994 Standish Group study "Charting the Seas of Information Technology — Chaos" notes that the most common cause of failed projects is missing, incomplete or incorrect requirements. The software development world has responded to this risk by amplifying the practice of gathering detailed user requirements and getting user sign-off prior to proceeding with system design. However, this approach to defining user requirements is deeply flawed.

I worked on one project in which the customer wanted a complex system delivered in 10 months. Time was of the essence — 10 months or bust. Yet, because the project emanated from a government agency, the contract required sign-off on an external design document before internal design and coding could begin. Several users were involved, and they dragged their feet on signing the documents, concerned that they might endorse something that would later prove to be a mistake. Since there was no easy way to change things after the design documents were signed, they took two months to approve the design. And who can blame them? Their jobs depended on getting it right. So, halfway into a very tight schedule, over two months of time and a lot of paper were wasted in obtaining user sign-off on design documents.

Instead of encouraging user involvement, user sign-off tends to create an adversarial relationship between developers and users. Users are required to make decisions early in the development process and are not allowed to change their minds, even when they do not have a clear concept of how the system will work or how their business situation may develop in the future. Understandably reluctant to make these commitments, users will instinctively delay decisions to as late in the process as possible. Note that this instinct is in line with Lean Rule #4: Make decisions as late as possible.

The most effective way to accurately capture user requirements is through iterative system development. Developing core features early and obtaining customer feedback in usability demonstrations of each iteration results in a far more correct definition of customer requirements. If we realize that requirements will necessarily change over time, systems must be designed to evolve as necessary.

Coming Soon

Next month, I'll explain Lean Rules #6 through 10. These points are: do it right the first time by providing for change, empower workers and drive out fear, declare measurements the enemy by banning local optimization, partner with suppliers and, finally, create a culture of continuous improvement.

7.3.8 "Lean Programming; Part 2"

by Mary Poppendieck

W. Edwards Deming's Total Quality Management still rings true for software

---

Last month I described the origins of Lean Production and Total Quality Management, the paradigm shift that revolutionized business in the 1980s, and discussed its application to software development, which I call "Lean Programming. Lean Production, which evolved from Taiichi Ohno's efficient system for creating high-quality automobiles (the Toyota Production System), is based on the absolute elimination of waste, in both product and process. However, Ohno's revolutionary contributions can't be separated from W. Edwards Deming's teachings on quality management. While Ohno sought to eliminate waste and improve production in the years following World War II, Deming taught Japanese managers how to empower workers to investigate problems and systematically improve business processes. The movement, Total Quality Management (TQM), emphasizes a culture of continuous improvement of both process and product.

The basic practices of Deming's TQM movement and Ohno's Lean Production can be summed up in these 10 points:

1. Eliminate waste.
2. Minimize inventory.
3. Maximize flow.
4. Pull from demand.
5. Meet customer requirements.
6. Do it right the first time.
7. Empower workers.
8. Ban local optimization.
9. Partner with suppliers.
10. Create a culture of continuous improvement.

In part one, I discussed points one through five. The final five rules of TQM and Lean Production follow.

Lean Rule #6: Do It Right the First Time (Incorporate Feedback)

Before Lean Production arrived at our videocassette manufacturing plant in the early 1980s, we occasionally had output of marginal quality. To identify and correct this, we tested to find good products and reworked bad products. After implementing the Do It Right the First Time rule, we closed down rework stations and stopped trying to test quality into the product after the fact. Instead, we made sure that each component was good at every handoff by employing tests and controls throughout the manufacturing process. In this way, we could detect when a product was drifting away from the specifications and stop production before any bad products were made.

"Do It Right the First Time" does not mean "Freeze the Spec." On the contrary, product (and software project) specifications change constantly. Lean discipline demands instantaneous adaptation to changing market conditions, which is best effected with a flexible product architecture that readily accommodates manufacturing change, techniques for monitoring that detect errors before they occur and tests that are designed before manufacturing begins.

In his "Industrial Software Metrics Top 10 List" published in the September 1987 issue of *IEEE Software*, Barry Boehm notes that it costs 100 times more to find and fix a problem after software delivery than in the early stages of design. This observation and the "Do It Right the First Time" rule have been widely used to justify the decision to develop a detailed system design before code is written.

The problem with this approach lies in the assumption that customer requirements are static and can be defined by a predetermined system. Because requirements do change — and frequently — throughout the life of most systems, they cannot be adequately fulfilled by a rigid design. "Do It Right" has also been misinterpreted as "don't allow changes." In fact, once we acknowledge that change is a fundamental customer requirement, it becomes clear that "Doing It Right" requires that we provide for change at all stages of a project's life cycle.

If we acknowledge that customers may not know what they want at the beginning of development and that their needs might change midstream, we must incorporate a method of obtaining customer feedback during development. Instead, most software development practices include a complex "change control process" that discourages developers from responding to user feedback. Far from ensuring a quality result, these change-resistant processes actually get in the way of "Doing It Right."

Lean Programming employs two key techniques that make change easy. Just as Lean Production builds tests into the manufacturing process to detect when the process is broken, Lean Programming builds tests into the beginning of the development process. As programming proceeds and changes are made, the unit and regression tests are run. If the tests don't pass, programming is stopped until the problem is found and corrected. A comprehensive testing capability is the best way to accommodate change throughout the development process.

The second technique that facilitates change is refactoring, or improving the design of existing software in a controlled and rapid manner. With refactoring, initial designs can focus on the basic issue at hand rather than speculate about other features that may be needed in the future. Later in the process, refactoring techniques can incorporate these additional features as they are required, making it easy to accommodate the future if and when it becomes the present.

Lean Rule #7: Empower Workers

A basic principle of Lean Production is to drive decisions down to the lowest possible level, delegating decision-making tools and authority to the people "on the floor." As Paul Adler noted in his article, "Time-and-Motion Regained" (*Harvard Business Review*, Jan.–Feb. 1993), when Toyota took over GM's manufacturing plant in Fremont, California, in 1983, it inherited workers with the worst productivity and absenteeism record in the industry. Within two years, those same workers, organized into teams trained in work measurement and improvement techniques, had doubled their quality and productivity scores.

Often when software development environments underperform, the instinctive reaction is to impose more rigid processes, specifying in greater detail how people should do their jobs. Lean Production principles suggest exactly the opposite approach. When there are problems in manufacturing, a team of outside experts is not sent in to document in more detail how the process should be run. Instead, people on the manufacturing floor are given tools to evaluate and improve their own areas. They work in collaborative teams with the charter to improve their own processes and the links to nearby processes for which they are suppliers or customers. Their supervisors are trained in methods of forming and encouraging work teams to solve their own problems.

Lean Programming similarly prizes people and collaborating teams over paperwork and processes. It focuses on methods of forming and encouraging teams to address and resolve their own problems, recognizing that the details must be determined by the people doing the work.

Software development involves the handoff of information at least once (from user to programmer) and often more than once (from user to designer to programmer). One school of thought holds that it's best to transfer all such information in writing, but in fact, a great amount of tacit knowledge is lost by handing off information on paper. It's far more effective to have small collaborating teams work across the boundaries of an information handoff, minimizing paperwork and maximizing communication.

Lean Rule #8: Ban Local Optimization

In the 1980s, the worst enemy of Lean Production was often the accounting department. We had big, expensive machines in our plant, and the idea that they should not be run at full capacity was radical, to put it mildly. The accountants didn't want to abandon our daily work-in-process (WIP) inventory reports just because there was virtually no WIP to report.

A generation of accountants had to retire before it became acceptable to run machines below full capacity, and designing machines for rapid changeover rather than highest throughput remains a tough sell even today. After 20 years, Lean Production is still counterintuitive to those who lack a broad business view.

In this context, let's examine the role of managing scope in a software development project. Project managers have been trained to focus on managing scope, just as we in manufacturing concentrated on maximizing machine productivity. However, Lean Programming is fundamentally driven by time and feedback. In the same way that localized productivity optimization weakens the overall manufacturing process, so focus on managing scope impairs project development.

Think about it — holding the scope to exactly what was envisioned at the beginning of a project offers little value to the user whose world is changing. In fact, it imparts anxiety and paralyzes decision-making, ensuring only that the final system will be outdated by the time it's delivered. Managing to a scope that's no longer valid wastes time and space, necessitating inefficient issue lists, extensive trade-off negotiations and multiple system fixes. However, as long as limiting a project to its original scope is a key project management goal, local optimization will flourish — at the expense of the project's overall quality.

Lean thinking dictates that scope will take care of itself if the domain is well understood and there is a well-crafted, high-level agreement on the system's function in the domain. Scope will take care of itself if the project is driven in time buckets that aren't allowed to slip. Scope will take care of itself if both parties focus on rapid development and problem-solving, and adopt waste-free methods of achieving these goals.

Lean Rule #9: Use Evolutionary Procurement (Partner with Suppliers)

Lean Production didn't remain within the confines of the manufacturing plant. Once the idea of partnering with suppliers was combined with an understanding of the value of rapid product flow, Supply Chain Management was born. People began to realize that it took tons of paper to move material between companies. Moreover, the paperwork was more expensive than one might expect, as was the ensuing delay in product flow. Today, by cutting the cost of business-to-business transactions, Web portals have generated billions of dollars in savings.

Supply Chain Management made companies take a close look at their business-to-business contracts. All too often, they focused on keeping the companies from cheating each other. In addition, it was common to pit one vendor against another to ensure supply and to obtain the lowest cost. Again, Lean Production changed this paradigm. Deming taught that trust-based relationships with single suppliers create an environment that best benefits both companies.

Throughout the 1980s, companies revitalized their supply chains by reducing the number of suppliers they used and working as partners with those who remained. The high quality and creativity of these supply chain partnerships far outweighed the putative benefits of competitive bidding and rapid supplier turnover. Partner companies helped each other improve product designs and product flows, linking systems to allow just-in-time movement of goods across several suppliers with little or no paperwork. The advantages of this collaborative supply-chain relationship are lasting and well documented.

Wise organizations realize that traditional software development contract practices generate hidden wastes. As the manufacturing world revealed in the 1980s, trusted relationships with a limited set of suppliers can yield dramatic advantages. Freed from the adversarial relationship created by a concentration on controlling scope and cost, software development vendors can focus on providing the best possible software for their customers, stabilizing requirements as late as possible in the development process to provide the greatest value for the available funds.

Lean Rule #10: Create a Culture of Continuous Improvement

When software development seems to be out of control, organizations often hasten to increase their level of "software maturity" with awards and certifications. This might seem to be in line with good manufacturing practice, in which ISO 9000 certification and Malcolm

Baldridge awards are sometimes equated with excellence. However, these process-documentation programs indicate excellence only when the documented process excels in the context of its use.

In many software development projects today, excellence means the ability to adapt to fast-moving, rapidly changing environments. Process-intensive approaches such as the higher levels of Software Engineering Institute's (SEI) Capability Maturity Model (CMM) may lack the flexibility to respond rapidly to change. In a recent e-mail advisory (*E-Projects in India,* Cutter Consortium's e-Project Management Advisory Service, March 1, 2001), Jim Highsmith highlights the tension between such heavyweight methodologies and the lightweight development models inspired by Lean Production.

One suspects that process-documentation certification programs may stifle, rather than foster, a culture of continuous improvement. Deming would probably turn over in his grave at the tomes of written processes substituting for his simple Plan-Do-Check-Act approach:

- *Plan:* Choose a problem. Analyze it to find a probable cause.
- *Do:* Run an experiment to investigate the probable cause.
- *Check:* Analyze the data from the experiment to validate the cause.
- *Act:* Refine and standardize based on the results.

Iterative development can effectively employ the Plan-Do-Check-Act method. During the first iteration, the handoff from design to programming or programming to testing may be a bit rough. It's OK if the first iteration provides a learning experience for the project team, because the subsequent iterations will allow the team to improve its process. In a sense, an iterative project environment becomes an operational environment, because processes are repeated and Deming's techniques of process improvement can be applied from one iteration to the next.

Product improvement is also enhanced in the iterative process, particularly if refactoring is used. In fact, refactoring provides a tremendous vehicle to apply the principle of continuous improvement to software development.

However, we need an improvement model that can span more than a single project. We must improve future project performance by learning from existing ones. Here again, Lean Production can point the way. During the 1980s, the set of practices summarized in the 10 rules of Lean Production were adopted widely across most manufacturing plants in the U.S. and Europe. These practices then spread to service organizations, logistics organizations, supply chains and beyond. In these multiple domains, application of Lean Production principles has engendered remarkable and continuing success.

The simple tenets of Lean Production have effected dramatic improvements in a myriad of industries. Applied to software project management as Lean Programming, these practices will lead to the highest quality, lowest cost, shortest lead-time software development possible.

7.3.9 "Extreme Modeling"

by Scott W. Ambler

Design is fundamental to the XP process, regardless of what the name may imply.

Did you decide to read this column simply because the headline included the word "Extreme?" If so, then you have likely fallen victim to the Extreme Hype (EH) surrounding eXtreme Programming (XP)—an important and growing movement within the software engineering community, despite the hoopla. For many software development teams, XP makes eXtreme Sense (XS) because it encompasses a collection of proven principles and practices of software engineering that few projects can do without. However, when taken at eXtreme Face Value (XFV), XP appears to be little more than a thin veneer atop hacking. Nothing could be further from the truth. Over the past year, I have noticed an eXtreme misUnderstanding (XU) in the software development community: Many believe that XP practitioners do little or no modeling. My experience has shown that this is simply not the case. Instead, XP practitioners take an adaptive approach to all aspects of development, including modeling. This month I examine XP, instead of taking it at XFV, to resolve any XUs regarding modeling by discussing an extreme modeling process that makes XS. Also, I'll cut out the eXtreme Abbreviations (XA) because I hope I've made my eXtreme pOint (XO) about the EH surrounding XP.

XP is simply a collection of interrelated principles and practices, some of which focus on basic activities such as configuration management, but many of which focus on the communication and cultural aspects between team members and between the team and the organization in which it operates. XP's pair programming, collective ownership and position on coaching help to promote teamwork and communication between team members, and its focus on understanding the requirements and inclusion of a user representative as an active member of the team promotes communication with other parts of the organization.

Not Just a Hack

Working closely with users as equals? Working as a team, not as a lone genius? XP sounds like it's more than hacking to me. Instead, XP is a well-thought-out software process worthy of consideration.

Now let's look at XP's approach to modeling. To quote Kent Beck from *Extreme Programming Explained* (Addison-Wesley, 2000): "We will continually refine the design of a system, starting from a very simple beginning. We will remove any flexibility that doesn't prove useful." Contrary to the claims of some of XP's detractors, you do in fact invest time modeling when taking an XP approach. XP recognizes that it is significantly more productive for a developer to draw some bubbles and lines to think through an idea, or to compare several different approaches to solving a problem, than it is to simply start hacking out code. Where XP differs from many software processes, or at least how many software processes such as the Rational Unified Process (RUP), the OPEN Process and my own Object-Oriented Software Process (OOSP) are typically implemented, is that it doesn't require the development and maintenance of a monolithic model of what you are building. Instead, XP's philosophy is to invest just enough effort into understanding what it is you intend to build and then to build it to see whether your design is right. In short, XP suggests that you take an iterative approach — as does RUP, OPEN and OOSP — it's just that XP is a little more blatant about it. XP practitioners believe that you shouldn't invest time generalizing your design because it isn't clear yet whether the extra code that you will need to write and test will actually be necessary. Instead, you should develop for today's problem and trust that you can solve tomorrow's problem tomorrow by refactoring your code as needed. However, XP practitioners aren't stupid: If the impact of a change is likely to be severe, they will invest the resources to reflect a likely change in their design from the beginning — an excellent compromise.

XP and Business Models

What types of models would you need to create a business application? I have been trying to answer this question for years, at least from the point of object-oriented software, and my answer, presented in Figure 7.1, depicts the latest incarnation of the solution to the detailed modeling process pattern. Adapted from my latest book, *The Object Primer*, Second Edition (Cambridge University Press, 2001), Figure 7.1 illustrates what I consider to be the primary artifacts that software developers may create while building object-oriented business software. (For simplicity's sake, I have left out project management artifacts such as estimates and testing artifacts such as test cases.) The boxes in the diagram represent potential development artifacts such as essential use case models and activity diagrams. The lines depict the major relationships between artifacts; for example, information in your analysis class model drives the development of information in your design class model. These relationships are important because they reveal how you are likely to iterate between development of the artifacts. For instance, you may be working on your use case model and find that it makes sense to develop a sequence diagram, which in turn leads you to change your class model. The highlighted boxes indicate artifacts that are described by the industry-standard Unified Modeling Language (UML), developed and maintained by the Object Management Group (www.omg.org).

Figure 7.1   Detailed Object Modeling (2000).
The primary artifacts software developers need to create while building object-oriented business software.

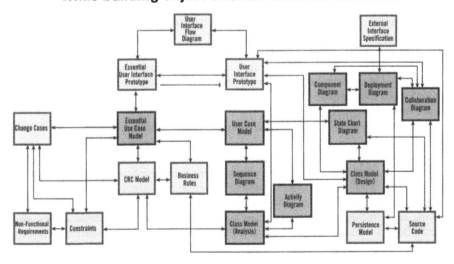

The adaptation in Figure 7.1 is the addition of the "External Interface Specification," which encompasses the design of how to integrate your system with another one, perhaps through an application programming interface (API), a data file or simply a shared database. Although I believed I had a fairly comprehensive answer, I quickly discovered on a recent project that I was missing this artifact and that it was critical to the project's success. The lesson to be learned, one taken from James Highsmith's latest book *Adaptive Software Development* (Dorset House, 1999), is that, although you can begin a project with a reasonably good approach, you need to be prepared to adapt to the situation at hand.

XP in Practice

So how can you use the information contained in Figure 7.1 on an XP project? First, understand that although there are many modeling artifacts available, you probably won't need to create them all. Just like you wouldn't order every item on the menu when you eat at a restaurant, you don't need to gorge yourself on every model available. Instead, you should apply only the modeling techniques that enable you to better understand the software that you are building. For example, essential user interface prototypes enable you to better understand the requirements for a user interface; however, if your user interface needs are well understood, then this technique likely offers little value for your team, and you shouldn't apply it. Similarly, activity diagrams are useful for discerning the flow of complex business logic, but they aren't very valuable if the workflow is straightforward.

Second, just because you need an artifact, doesn't mean that you have to create a formal version of it. I often draw an activity model or a sequence diagram on a white board as part of understanding whatever it is that I'm modeling, but I won't formalize it using a CASE tool. Instead, if I want permanent copies for later reference, I may take a snapshot of these diagrams with a digital camera or simply create a hand drawing. Don't get me wrong, I'll use CASE tools when they add value to my development efforts. For example, TogetherSoft's Together/J (www.togethersoft.com) can be valuable on Enterprise JavaBean (EJB) projects because of its round-trip integration with Java and I-Logix's Rhapsody (www.ilogix.com) for development of embedded software due to its focus on real-time modeling. In short, sometimes a whiteboard or a paper napkin is a sufficient modeling environment, whereas only a complex CASE tool addresses the needs of a project team other times.

Third, having a variety of artifacts at my disposal actually makes modeling easier. The greater the selection of models available, the greater the chance that you will find one that meets your specific needs. If you need to cut a piece of wood in half and your toolkit only contains a hammer and screwdriver, you'll have a significantly harder time than if your toolkit also included saws, wrenches and pliers. I only need a saw for that specific job, but it doesn't hurt to have a wide range of tools at my disposal. Granted, you need to be skilled at using these tools to be effective: If you try to cut the wood using a wrench, then having a saw in your toolkit wasn't useful. When I develop business software I often need to model the user interface, which is why Figure 7.1 includes several artifacts that focus on this issue. I often need to work with some sort of data storage mechanism, such as a relational database (RDB) or objectbase, to persist my objects, which is why I included a persistence model. I am far more effective as a developer when I have these artifacts available to me because I can use the right tool for the job. Your project team needs people who are trained and experienced at applying these techniques; not everyone needs to be expert at everything, but you should strive to have a team with a wide range of skills. In fact, if you are unable to put together a team with the requisite skills to complete the job, or at least a team that has the ability to learn any missing skills as work progresses, then you shouldn't attempt the project at all.

Suggested Resources

Books and URLs to pump up your design and process skills

Extreme Programming (XP)

The XP Web site, www.extremeprogramming.org, is a good place to learn about XP, but the best source of information is Kent Beck's book, *Extreme Programming Explained: Embrace Change* (Addison-Wesley, 1999), a 1999 Software Development Productivity award winner.

Essential Modeling

The book *Software For Use: A Practical Guide to the Models and Methods of Usage-Centered Design* (ACM Press, 1999), 1999 Jolt winner, written by Larry Constantine and Lucy Lockwood, is the best source of detailed information on this topic. My own book, *The Object Primer, 2nd Edition: The Application Developer's Guide To Object Orientation* (Cambridge University Press, 2000) also presents a good overview of essential modeling techniques and object modeling techniques in general.

Refactoring

Martin Fowler's *Refactoring: Improving the Design of Existing Code* (Addison-Wesley, 1999) presents a large collection of strategies for refactoring object-oriented source code.

The Unified Modeling Language (UML)

The Unified Modeling Language Reference Manual (Addison-Wesley, 1998), written by the Three Amigos (James Rumbaugh, Grady Booch and Ivar Jacobson), is an excellent resource for any serious developer because it explains the various parts of UML in great detail. However, to learn how to apply the techniques of UML, I suggest my book, *The Object Primer, 2nd Edition, UML Distilled: Applying the Standard Object Modeling Language* (Addison-Wesley 1997) by Martin Fowler and *Fundamentals of Object-Oriented Design in UML* (Dorset House, 2000) by Meilir Page-Jones.

Software Process

Begin with James Highsmith's *Adaptive Software Development: A Collaborative Approach to Managing Complex Systems* (Dorset House, 2000), which presents an interesting and new look at how to be successful at software development. Highsmith examines the cultural aspects of software development and suggests practices and principles that reflect the realities of the complex and changing environment in which modern software development exists. Small teams should stick with *Extreme Programming Explained*, whereas larger teams likely need something along the lines of Philippe

Krutchen's *The Rational Unified Process: An Introduction,* Second Edition (Addison-Wesley, 2000). However, to extend the Rational Unified Process (RUP) for large-scale, real-world development, I would then follow up with CMP Books' *Unified Process Series* — *The Unified Process Inception Phase, The Unified Process Elaboration Phase* and *The Unified Process Construction Phase* — all published in 2000 and coedited by myself and Larry Constantine. You will also find *The Process Patterns Resource Page,* `www.ambysoft.com/processPatternsPage.html`, and the OPEN Consortium's Web site, www.open.org.au, valuable.

Real-World Implications

What are some of the other interesting implications of Figure 7.1? The fact that not all of the boxes are highlighted implies that UML is not sufficient for the real-world needs of application developers, something that the OMG should attempt to address as they evolve UML. The figure also indicates that software development is both serial and iterative. It's serial because as you traverse the diagram from left to right, the focus of the artifacts starts at requirements, shifts to analysis, then design and then finally to implementation. (I have always argued that source code is an incredibly detailed model of your software.) Development is also iterative because you can quickly move back and forth between artifacts. I am often in a situation where a user describes a requirement to me, and I internally analyze what they are telling me, formulate a design that fulfills the requirement and even begin thinking about how I will code it — all within a matter of seconds. That's about as iterative as you are going to get. My belief is that although the concepts of requirements, analysis and design are all important, what you are really doing is modeling and constantly changing your focus as you do so. At times, it's important to identify what the users want or need (requirements), identify what you can deliver (analysis) and describe how you intend to build the software (design). The reality is that these concepts are intertwined. Modeling is serial in the large and iterative in the small. Finally, it's clear that software development is hard. You need software professionals that recognize this fact — ideally, professionals who are skilled at working with several of the artifacts indicated in the diagram.

Modeling is an important part of software development, one that is a fundamental part of XP, regardless of what the name may imply. Models don't kill projects, people kill projects. The best software professionals have a wide range of techniques in their development toolkit, and they know when and how to apply them effectively.

NOTE: Extreme Modeling (XM) is now known as Agile Modeling (AM) — visit `www.agilemodeling.com` for details.

7.3.10 "A Closer Look at Extreme Modeling"

by Scott W. Ambler

A lightweight methodology adapted from heavyweight processes.

Models don't kill projects, people kill projects. Regardless of what the name may imply, modeling is a fundamental part of the extreme programming (XP) software process. However, many developers are unsure how they can include modeling while remaining sufficiently "extreme." The answer lies in the fundamental principles of the extreme modeling (XM) methodology ("Extreme Modeling," this chapter) now called Agile Modeling (AM) (www.agilemodeling.com).

XM is a lightweight methodology built on existing and proven modeling approaches that are adapted from common heavyweight software processes. The secret to XM isn't the modeling techniques themselves, but how they're applied on a software project. And to understand XM, you must first understand its values, principles and practices.

XM Values

The values of XM are the values of XP: communication, simplicity, feedback and courage. Models promote communication between project stakeholders (for example, developers, users, project managers, senior management and so on). It's important that developers understand that models are critical for simplifying both software and the software process — it's much easier to explore an idea, and improve upon it as your understanding increases, by drawing a diagram or two instead of writing tens or even hundreds of lines of code. With respect to feedback, Kent Beck says it best in *Extreme Programming Explained* (Addison Wesley Longman, 2000): "Optimism is an occupational hazard of programming, feedback is the treatment." By communicating your ideas through diagrams, you quickly gain feedback, enabling you to act on that advice. Finally, courage is important because you need to make important decisions and be able to change direction by either discarding or refactoring your work when some of your decisions prove inadequate.

XM Principles

Where XP includes principles such as incremental change, assuming simplicity, open and honest communication, local adaptation, and traveling light, XM extends them with several modeling-specific principles. If a picture is worth a thousand words, then a model is worth 1024 lines of code, a term I picked up from Karl Wieger's *Software Requirements* (Microsoft Press, 1999). You can explore design alternatives more effectively by drawing a couple diagrams on a whiteboard with your peers than you can by sitting down and developing code samples. Using multiple models to develop software is another XM principle that you need to apply, because each model describes a single aspect of your software. You should also apply the right model; for example, a UML activity diagram is useful for describing a business process, whereas the static structure of your database is better represented by a physical data or persistence model. And to be successful at applying multiple models, you must both know your models and know your tools, the tools in this case being the various models that you have at your disposal, as well as any diagramming or CASE tools.

It's important to model first, that is, think through a problem before you begin to code the solution; 10 minutes of modeling can often save you several hours of coding. Software professionals also reuse existing artifacts: Perhaps you can take advantage of an existing enterprise requirements model, business process models, physical data models or even models of how systems are currently deployed within your user community. It's true that these models either don't exist or are out of date in many organizations, although you're often likely to uncover reasonably accurate models with a bit of research.

A crucial principle of XM is that you should have a limited number of contract models. Contract models are often required when an external group controls an information resource that your system requires, such as a database, legacy application or information service. A contract model is something that both parties should mutually agree to and mutually change over time if required. Examples of contract models include the detailed documentation of an application programming interface (API), a file layout description, an XML DTD or a physical data model describing a shared database. As with a legal contract, a contract model often requires a significant investment of resources to develop and maintain; you must ensure that it's accurate and sufficiently detailed. Your goal is to minimize the number of contract models for your system to conform to the principle of traveling light.

XM Practices

The practices of XM are also a superset of those of XP. XP's small releases, metaphor, simple design, refactoring and other practices are all applicable to modeling. Very likely XM's most important practice is simple tools: The vast majority of models can be drawn on a whiteboard, on paper or even the back of a napkin. Whenever I want to save one of these diagrams (because I want to explain my design approach for a component to others or I need to erase the whiteboard so I can work on something else), I take a picture of it with a digital camera. I've also worked on several projects where we posted our drawings on an internal Web page, improving communication within the team without introducing the burden of redrawing the diagrams using a drawing package or CASE tool. In my experience, most diagrams are throwaways; their value comes from drawing them to think through an issue, and once the issue is resolved the diagram doesn't offer much value.

Most of the time, a whiteboard and markers are my best modeling tool alternative. I'll use a drawing tool such as Visio if I need to create "pretty" diagrams to present to important project stakeholders. And occasionally, I'll use a CASE tool such as TogetherSoft's Together/J (www.togethersoft.com) or Rational Rose (www.rational.com) — if and only if they provide value to my programming efforts. Both of these tools generate scaffolding code — to manage associations between objects, for example — a tedious task that I prefer to have automated. If you find that you primarily use your CASE tool to document your system then you probably aren't getting much benefit from it. You're not following the XP and XM principle of traveling light, either. Your goal is to develop software, not documentation; therefore, simple tools such as a whiteboard and digital camera are often a better choice than a complex CASE tool. Another downside of CASE tools are the licensing costs and the cost of training and education to learn how to use them appropriately. If a tool doesn't provide positive value then it doesn't make sense to use it

XP's simple models practice is related to XP's simple tools practice. When you consider the diagrams of the Unified Modeling Language (UML), or traditional diagrams such as Entity-Relationship Diagrams (ERDs) or structure charts, you quickly realize that most of the time you only require a subset of the diagramming notation available to you. You could choose to create complex diagrams using any of these techniques, but if a simple diagram that uses a subset of the notation, or even a modification of it, suffices then apply the simple approach. Simplicity is a fundamental value of XM.

A critical question is why do you model? The most important application of modeling is to explore the problem space, to identify and analyze the requirements for the system, or to compare potential design alternatives to identify the potentially most simple solution that meets the requirements. In other words, you model to understand. Following this practice you often develop small, simple diagrams that focus on one aspect of your software, such as the life cycle of a class or the flow between screens. This practice is supported by the XM principles of knowing your models, understanding the multiple models at your disposal, and then applying the right model for the specific issue you are trying to understand.

The secondary reasons to model are related to the XM practice of modeling for others: You model to communicate with people external to your team or to create a contract model. Because the customers for some models are outside your team, you may need to invest the time to make your model(s) look "pretty" by using such electronic tools as word processors, drawing packages or even sophisticated CASE tools. For example, your project team may need to go to senior management to obtain the necessary resources to continue a project, which might require you to present models that your manager can understand. In this case, your hand drawings are likely not sufficient, requiring you to transcribe critical diagrams into a product such as Visio or PowerPoint. Having said that, I've found that better managers often appreciate rough drawings because they realize that you didn't waste several hours or even days on cosmetic issues. However, you will almost always use an electronic tool to develop a contract model because the model must be maintained over time.

These two XM practices, model to understand and model for others, go to the heart of how much permanent documentation you should develop while modeling. I use the term "permanent documentation" to represent models that you keep for posterity's sake, either because they are contract models or because your organization's software process insists that you develop specific models. A model should be permanent if someone will need it in the future. Whenever I'm asked to develop a permanent model, I first ask who will use it and what they intend to use it for, and then I work with them to determine what critical information needs to be contained in the model. This approach helps me to keep things simple and travel light: Modeling doesn't have to imply the creation of excessive documentation. Furthermore, whenever I run across an existing permanent model, I question whether I still need it. If not, I retire it as quickly as I can to lighten my load. Your goal is to have just enough documentation and no more.

XM also includes the practice of collective modeling in which your development team works together to develop models. Most of the time you model to understand, and the best way to do this is to talk the issue through with one or more people. Often you and your modeling partner(s) will first develop throwaway diagrams to think through your design before you code. To develop the metaphor or architecture for your system, you will often need to model with a group of people to develop a solution everyone agrees on as well as one that is as simple as possible.

The final two XM practices are called modeling wall and apply patterns. A modeling wall is where you post your models for everyone to see; it should be accessible to both your development team and other project stakeholders. Your modeling wall may be physical, perhaps a designated whiteboard for your architecture diagram(s) or a place where you tape a printout of your physical data model. However, modeling walls are often virtual — for example, an internal Web page that is updated with scanned images. The apply patterns practice is exactly what it sounds like: You should learn and then appropriately apply common architectural, design and analysis patterns in your models. The application of patterns allows you to reuse the thinking processes of other developers (*Thinking Objectively*, Feb. 2000), providing significant benefit to most projects.

Extreme Modeling in Practice

So, how does XM fit into your overall development picture? If you're practicing extreme programming (XP) then it fits in quite well. If you're following a less adaptive software process, such as the Unified Process ("Effective Software Deployment," Chapter 2) then you may decide to adopt the XM principles and practices that fit in best with your organization's culture. To learn more about XM, check out www.agilemodeling.com, where I'll continue developing the concepts I've described here.

8

Parting Words

We originally undertook this book series to provide an alternative voice within the IT industry regarding the Unified Process (UP). This series has clearly succeeded at that goal, describing a new vision for real-world instantiation of the UP called the Enterprise Unified Process (EUP). Since Scott Ambler first presented the enhanced lifecycle for the Unified Process in the pages of *Software Development* in November 1999, the article that motivated this book series, we've seen the Unified Process become the de facto standard for heavy-weight prescriptive processes. In parallel we've seen the popularization of agile methodologies, such as Extreme Programming (XP), and the introduction of new methods such as Agile Modeling (AM). It's an exciting time in the software process field, and this book series has led the way for extending the UP to meet the real-world needs of modern organizations. The many articles presented in this book series represent the ideas and ideals of the leading minds in the IT industry. If you have adopted the UP willingly, or if it has been forced on you by management or your clients, one fact remains — you have alternatives available to you when applying the UP, alternatives described within the pages of *Software Development* magazine over the years (www.sdmagazine.com).

8.1 Scott's Really Bad Zen Poetry

A tradition of this book series is to inflict a really bad zen poem on you at the very end of the book, potentially making you regret having purchased the book in the first place. Does this make any sense?[1] Likely not, but we're doing it anyway. Furthermore, because we've covered two phases in this book we're punishing you with two really bad Zen poems — your suspicions are correct: software methodologists really are evil.

The Zen of Transition

Project stakeholders eagerly await their new system,
    developers, near to exhaustion, strive to get through.
Will the system meet our needs or disappoint yet again?
The setting sun rises again in the morning.

The Zen of Production

The system provides many surprises,
    disappointing to some and exhilarating to others.
Will our change requests ever be implemented?
In karate there is no first strike.

Sorry, folks. I can't help myself! ;-)

— Scott

---

1. Actually, now Scott can claim to be a published poet, giving him an incredibly good pick-up line whenever he is in a bar — there is a methodology to his madness.

Appendix A

Bibliography

Adolf, S. 2000. Lost in Chaos: Chronology of a Failure. *Software Development*, January.

Alexander, P. 1999. Revamp Your Current Job. *Software Development*, July.

Ambler, S.W. 1999. UML Deployment and Beyond. *Software Development*, April.

Ambler, S.W. 1999. Effective Software Deployment. *Software Development*, November.

Ambler, S.W. 2000. Extreme Modeling. *Software Development*, November.

Ambler, S.W. 2001. Extreme Lessons Learned. *Software Development*, February.

Ambler, S.W. 2001. A Closer Look at Extreme Moeling. *Software Development*, April.

Ambler, S.W. 2001. A J2EE Testing Primer. *Software Development*, May.

Ambler, S.W. 2001. Place Tab A in Slot B. *Software Development*, June.

Ambler, S.W. 2001. Planning for Deployment. *Software Development*, July.

Ambler, S.W. 2001. Ignore Help Requests at Your Own Peril. *Software Development*, September.

Ambler, S.W. 2001. The Secret Life of Software Operations. *Software Development*, October.

Ambler, S.W. 2000. Reuse Through Internal Open Source. *Software Development*, December.

Bach, J. 1996. Training Testers. *Software Development*, September.

Barnhart, A. 1997. Creating Good Installations. *Software Development*, September.

Black, B. 1997. Manageable Migrations. *Software Development*, July.

Boddie, J. 1999. Waste Management. *Software Development*, July.

Constantine, L. 2000. Unified Hegemony. *Software Development*, November.

Constantine, L. 2001. Methodical Agility. *Software Development*, June.

DiMaggio, L. 2000. Running a Stellar Testing Team. *Software Development*, 2000.

Fabian-Isaacs C., Raymond P. J. 1997. How Helpful is Your Help?. *Software Development*, November.

Fowler, M., Highsmith J. 2000. Agile Manifesto. *Software Development*, December.

Fowler, M. 2001. Is Design Dead?. *Software Development*, April.

Fowler, M. 2000. Put Your Process on a Diet. *Software Development*, December.

Furlong, S. 1997. Saving a Project in Trouble. *Software Development*, October.

Highsmith, J. 1999. Beyond Optimizing. *Software Development*, September.

Kaner, C. 2000. Recruiting Software Testers. *Software Development*, January.

Kerth, N. 1998. Making Lemonade from Lemons. *Software Development*, July.

Keuffel, W. 2000. eXtreme Programming. *Software Development*, February.

Keuffel, W. 2000. Arts and Crafts Software. *Software Development*, June.

Keuffel, W. 1997. Just Doing It. *Software Development*, November.

Keyes, J. 1996. Getting Real Help from a Help Desk. *Software Development*, June.

Major, M., McGregor J. D. 2000. Selecting Test Cases Based on User Priorities. March.

Margulies B. 2000. Surviving Performance Fire Drills. *Software Development*, August.

Meyer B. 2000. The Ethics of Free Software. *Software Development*, March.

Poppendieck, M. 2001. Lean Programming Part 1. *Software Development*, May.

Poppendieck, M. 2001. Lean Programming Part 1. *Software Development*, June.

Rothman, J., Wiegers, K. 2001. Looing Back, Looking Ahead. *Software Development*, February.

Rothman, M. 2001. Who's That in My App?. *Software Development*, May.

Seevers, T., Sparks R. 1998. Real-World Acceptance Testing. *Software Development*, March.

Shimeall, S., Shimeall T. 1997. Don't Waste Your Bugs. *Software Development*, March.

Surveyer, J. 1998. Developer Angst: Product Support. *Software Development*, June.

Weber-Morales, A. 2000. Intrusion Detection. *Software Development*, July.

Wells, J. 1997. Painless Dismissals: Saying Good-Bye. *Software Development*, May.

Weinberg, J. 1996. Planning the Right Rollout. *Software Development*, June.

Wiegers, K. 1999. Process Improvement that Works. *Software Development*, October.

Wiegers, K. 1996. Software Process Improvement: 10 Traps to Avoid. *Software Development*, May.

Appendix B

Contributing Authors

Adolph, Stephen Steve Adolph is a principal object technology consultant with WSA Consulting Inc. in Furry Creek, British Columbia. Since receiving his master's in computing science from the University of San Francisco in 1987, Steve has accrued development experience in call-processing software for cellular telephone systems, mobile dispatching, railway signaling and direct-to-plate systems for the printing industry, among other projects. Steve can be reached at steve@wsaconsulting.com.

Alexander, Peter Peter Alexander is a senior consultant with Blessing/White, a Princeton, New Jersey-based training firm.

Ambler, Scott W. Scott W. Ambler is the President of Ronin International (www.ronin-intl.com) a firm specializing in software process mentoring and software architecture consulting. He is a senior contributing editor with *Software Development* and author of the books *The Object Primer 2nd* (Cambridge University Press, 2001) and *Agile Modeling* (John Wiley & Sons, 2002) and coauthor of *The Elements of Java Style* (Cambridge University Press, 2000) and *Mastering Enterprise JavaBeans 2nd* (John Wiley & Sons, 2002).

Bach, James James Bach is chief engineer at Software Testing Laboratories, an independent testing facility in Seattle, Washington.

Barnhart, Andy Andy Barnhart is a consultant who specializes in Windows development. He works for Cii in Raleigh, North Carolina.

Black, Brian Brian Black is vice president of strategic services at Emergent Corp., a consulting company that focuses on highly scalable OLTP, World Wide Web, and data warehousing applications.

Boddie, John John Boddie is a senior contributor for DMR/Amdahl. He coauthored the third edition of *Managing a Programming Project* (Prentice Hall, 1997).

Constantine, Larry Larry Constantine is the director of research and development at Constantine and Lockwood Ltd. His latest book is *Beyond Chaos: The Expert Edge in Managing Software Development* (Addison-Wesley, 2001) He can be contacted on the Web at www.foruse.com.

DiMaggio, Len Len DiMaggio (ldimaggi@genuity.com) manages the software test and quality assurance department for Genuity in Burlington, Massachusetts, (formerly GTE Internetworking and BBN) and is writing a book on the implications of the Internet and World Wide Web on software testing and quality assurance.

Fabian-Isaacs, Constance Constance Fabian-Isaacs in the quality systems document specialist for Willbros USA Inc. She has more than 15 years technical writing experience and four years online documentation experience.

Fowler, Martin Martin Fowler is Chief Scientist at ThoughtWorks (www.thoughtworks.com). He is the coauthor of *UML Distilled* (Addison-Wesley, 1997), and author of *Analysis Patterns* (Addison Wesley Longman, 1997) and *Refactoring* (Addison Wesley Longman 1999).

Furlong, Steve Steve Furlong has seven years of consulting experience. One of his specialties is picking up troubled projects after everyone with any sense has bailed out. He can be reached at furlos@rpi.edu.

Highsmith III, James A. James (Jim) Highsmith is director of the Cutter Consortium's e-Project Management Practice, and author of *Adaptive Software Development: A Collaborative Approach to Managing Complex Systems* (Dorset House, 2000), which recently won Software Development's Jolt Award for Product Excellence. His book on *Agile Methodologies* will be published by Addison-Wesley in 2002. Highsmith has more than 20 years experience in consulting, software development, managing and writing.

Kaner, Cem Cem Kaner is the senior author of *Testing Computer Software* and *Bad Software: What To Do When Software Fails* (John Wiley & Sons, 1998). He consults to software publishers and practices law with an emphasis on the law of software quality. He can be reached at kaner@kaner.com.

Kerth, Norm Norman Kerth is a software engineering consultant well known for his object-oriented and distributed Internet systems. He has special interests in recovering failed projects and leading postmorta, and is author of the book *Project Retrospectives*. He can be reached at nkerth@acm.org.

Keuffel, Warren Warren Keuffel is a software engineer and writer based in Salt Lake City, Utah. He is senior contributing editor for *Software Development*.

Keyes, Jessica Jessica Keyes is president of New Art Inc., a New York City-based consultant company specializing in high technology. Keyes, the author of seven books, authored *The McGraw-Hill Multimedia Handbook*, which has been translated into Japanese and Chinese.

Major, Melissa. Melissa Major is a consultant and site manager for Software Architects. She has created testing processes for Lucent Technologies, among other companies, and has taught computer science courses for Clemson University and Limestone College in Gaffney, South Carolina.

Margulies, Benson I. Benson I. Margulies is vice president and chief technology officer for Basis Technology Corp., an internationalization services firm in Cambridge, Massachusetts. His experience ranges from secure operating systems to object-oriented databases to cable TV set-top box applications. He can be reached at benson@basistech.com.

McGregor, John D. John D. McGregor is an associate professor of computer science at Clemson University in Clemson, South Carolina and a senior partner at Software Architects, a software design consulting firm based in Collegedale, Tennessee, specializing in object-oriented techniques. He is coauthor of *Object-Oriented Software Development: Engineering Software for Reuse* (Van Nostrand Reinhold, 1992).

Meyer, Bertrand Bertrand Mayer is the Santa Barbara, California-based author of *Object-Oriented Software Construction*, second edition (1997 Jolt Award). His website is http://eiffel.com.

Poppendieck, Mary Mary Poppendieck, president of Poppendieck LLC, a consulting firm based in the Eden Prairie, Minnesota, has more than 25 years of experience as an engineer, IT manager and project manager. A pioneer in implementing just-in-time systems, Poppendieck has been a popular speaker at both local and national PMI Symposia, at Project World and at Software Development.

Raymond, P.J. P.J. Raymond is an online documentation specialist and writer with the Writers Resource Group in Tulsa, Oklahoma. She has more than 15 years technical writing experience and several years of online documentation experience.

Rothman, Johanna Johanna Rothman is the President of Rothman Consulting Group, Inc. She observes and consults on managing high technology product development. She can be reached at www.jrothman.com.

Rothman, Mike Mike Rothman is executive vice president of SHYM Technology Inc., assuming responsibility for marketing and corporate strategy. Prior to cofounding SHYM, Mr. Rothman was vice president of Global Networking Strategies at META Group, and also held positions at Ernst and Young, American Management Systems and Mobil Oil.

Seevers, Timothy Tim Seevers is an advisory programmer and team lead in software quality assurance at Lexmark International.

Shimeall, Stephen Stephen Shimeall is a senior software test engineer with Applied Microsystems Corp. in Redmond, Washington. He has been involved in the development and testing of software for more than 25 years.

Shimeall, Timothy Timothy Shimeall is an associate professor at the Naval Postgraduate School in Monterrey, California. He has also been a member of the IEEE Computer and Reliability Societies.

Sparks, Randy Randy Sparks is the software quality assurance manager at Lexmark International.

Surveyer, Jacques Jacques (Jack) Surveyer is a freelance writer and software consultant. He can be reached at http://home.inforamp.net/~jbsurv/.

Weber Morales, Alexandra Alexandra Weber Morales is Editor in Chief of *Software Development* magazine. After attending Bryn Mawr College in Pennsylvania, she spent several years as a freelance writer, primarily covering health care. She joined Miller Freeman Inc. (now CMP Media LLC) in January 1996 and spent three years traveling Latin America as chief editor of a Spanish- and Portuguese-language medical imaging technology magazine. She speaks fluent Spanish, French, and Portuguese in addition to her native English. Her interests once included mid-century internal combustion engines (she rebuilt several Volkswagens and one 1964 Chevrolet P-10) but now tend toward graphic design, music, and public transportation.

Weinberg, Jeff Jeffrey Weinberg is an eBusiness veteran with over 15 years of extensive technology consulting experience. Jeff works with startup and Fortune 1000 companies to identify communication and operational strategies that help these companies grow and meet changing needs. Jeff holds a BS in Computer Science from the University of Illinois at Chicago and an MBA from DePaul University.

Wells, Jess Jess Wells is a marketing consultant, journalist, and author based in the San Francisco Bay Area. She is the author of *Avoiding Wrongful Discharge: A Step by Step Guide* (Council on Education in Management, 1995).

Wiegers, Karl Karl Wiegers is the principal consultant at Process Impact, the author of the Jolt Productivity Award-winning *Creating a Software Engineering Culture* (Dorset House, 1996) and *Software Requirements* (Microsoft Press, 1999). Wiegers is also a contributing editor of *Software Development* magazine. He can be reached at www.processimpact.com.

Appendix C

References & Recommended Reading

Printed Resources

Agile Alliance 2001a. *Manifesto for Agile Software Development.* www.agilealliance.org

Agile Alliance 2001b. *Principles: The Agile Alliance.* www.agilealliance.org/ principles.html

Ambler, S.W. 1998a. *Building Object Applications That Work: Your Step-By-Step Handbook for Developing Robust Systems with Object Technology.* New York, NY: SIGS Books/Cambridge University Press.

Ambler, S. W. 1998b. *Process Patterns – Building Large-Scale Systems Using Object Technology.* New York, NY: SIGS Books/Cambridge University Press.

Ambler, S. W. 1999. *More Process Patterns – Delivering Large-Scale Systems Using Object Technology.* New York, NY: SIGS Books/Cambridge University Press.

Ambler, S.W. 2001. *The Object Primer: The Application Developer's Guide To Object Orientation,* 2nd Edition. New York, NY: SIGS Books/Cambridge University Press.

Ambler, S.W. 2002. *Agile Modeling*. New York, NY: John Wiley & Sons.

Ambler, S.W. & Constantine L.L. 2000a. *The Unified Process Inception Phase*. Gilroy, CA: CMP Books.

Ambler, S.W. & Constantine L.L. 2000b. *The Unified Process Elaboration Phase*. Gilroy, CA: CMP Books.

Ambler, S.W. & Constantine L.L. 2001. *The Unified Process Construction Phase*. Gilroy, CA: CMP Books.

Bassett, P. G. 1997. *Framing Software Reuse: Lessons From the Real World*. Upper Saddle River, NJ: Prentice-Hall, Inc.

Baudoin, C., and Hollowell, G. 1996. *Realizing the Object-Oriented Life Cycle*. Upper Saddle River, NJ: Prentice-Hall, Inc.

Beck, K. (2000). *Extreme Programming Explained – Embrace Change*. Reading, MA: Addison Wesley Longman, Inc.

Beck, K. & Fowler, M. 2001. *Planning Extreme Programming*. Boston, MA: Addison-Wesley Publishing Company, Inc.

Bennett, D. 1997. *Designing Hard Software: The Essential Tasks*. Greenwich, CT: Manning Publications Co.

Binder, R. 1999. *Testing Object-Oriented Systems: Models, Patterns, and Tools*. Reading, MA: Addison Wesley Longman, Inc.

Booch, G. 1996. *Object Solutions – Managing the Object-Oriented Project*. Menlo Park, CA: Addison-Wesley Publishing Company, Inc.

Booch, G., Rumbaugh, J., & Jacobson, I. 1999. *The Unified Modeling Language User Guide*. Reading, MA: Addison Wesley Longman, Inc.

Brooks, F.P. 1995. *The Mythical Man Month*. Reading, MA: Addison Wesley Longman, Inc.

Brown, W.J., McCormick, H.W. III, & Thomas, S.W. 2000. *AntiPatterns in Project Management*. New York, NY: John Wiley & Sons Ltd.

Buschmann, F., Meunier, R., Rohnert, H., Sommerlad, P., & Stal, M. 1996. *A Systems of Patterns: Pattern-Oriented Software Architecture*. New York, NY: John Wiley & Sons Ltd.

Champy, J. 1995. *Reengineering Management: The Mandate for New Leadership*. New York, NY: HarperCollins Publishers Inc.

Chidamber S.R. & Kemerer C.F. 1991. *Towards a Suite of Metrics for Object-Oriented Design*. OOPSLA'91 *Conference Proceedings*, Reading MA: Addison-Wesley Publishing Company, pp. 197–211.

Coad, P. and Mayfield, M. 1997. *Java Design: Building Better Apps and Applets*. Englewood Cliff, NJ: Prentice Hall.

Cockburn, A. (2001). *Crystal Clear: A Human-Powered Software Development Methodology for Small Teams*. http://members.aol.com/humansandt/crystal/clear/

Compton, S.B. & Conner, G.R. 1994. *Configuration Management for Software*. New York, NY: Van Nostrand Reinhold.

Constantine, L. L. 1995. *Constantine on Peopleware*. Englewood Cliffs, NJ: Yourdon Press.

Constantine, L.L. & Lockwood, L.A.D. 1999. *Software For Use: A Practical Guide to the Models and Methods of Usage-Centered Design*. New York, NY: ACM Press.

Constantine, L. L. 2000a. *The Peopleware Papers*. Englewood Cliffs, NJ: Yourdon Press.

Constantine, L. L. 2000b. *Managing Chaos: The Expert Edge in Software Development*. Reading, MA: Addison Wesley Longman, Inc.

Coplien, J.O. 1995. "A Generative Development-Process Pattern Language." *Pattern Languages of Program Design*. Reading, MA: Addison Wesley Longman, Inc., pp. 183–237.

DeLano, D.E. & Rising, L. 1998. "Patterns for System Testing." *Pattern Languages of Program Design 3*, eds. Martin, R.C., Riehle, D., and Buschmann, F., Addison Wesley Longman, Inc., pp. 503–525.

DeMarco, T. 1997. *The Deadline: A Novel About Project Management*. New York, NY: Dorset House Publishing.

Douglass, B.P. 1999. *Doing Hard Time: Developing Real-Time Systems With UML, Objects, Frameworks, and Patterns*. Reading, MA: Addison Wesley Longman, Inc.

Emam, K. E.; Drouin J.; and Melo, W. 1998. *SPICE: The Theory and Practice of Software Process Improvement and Capability Determination*. Los Alamitos, CA: IEEE Computer Society Press.

Eriksson, H-K and Penker, M. 2000. *Business Modeling with UML: Business Patterns at Work*. New York, NY: John Wiley & Sons Ltd.

Fowler, M. 1997. *Analysis Patterns: Reusable Object Models*. Menlo Park, CA: Addison Wesley Longman, Inc.

Fowler, M. 1999. *Refactoring: Improving the Design of Existing Code.* Menlo Park, CA: Addison Wesley Longman, Inc.

Fowler, M. and Scott, K. 1997. *UML Distilled: Applying the Standard Object Modeling Language.* Reading, MA: Addison Wesley Longman, Inc.

Gamma, E.; Helm, R.; Johnson, R.; and Vlissides, J. 1995. *Design Patterns: Elements of Reusable Object-Oriented Software.* Reading, MA: Addison-Wesley Publishing Company.

Gilb, T. & Graham, D. 1993. *Software Inspection.* Reading, MA: Addison Wesley Longman.

Goldberg, A. & Rubin, K.S. 1995. *Succeeding With Objects: Decision Frameworks for Project Management.* Reading, MA: Addison-Wesley Publishing Company Inc.

Grady, R.B. 1992. *Practical Software Metrics For Project Management and Process Improvement.* Englewood Cliffs, NJ: Prentice-Hall, Inc.

Graham, I.; Henderson-Sellers, B.; and Younessi, H. 1997. *The OPEN Process Specification.* New York, NY: ACM Press Books.

Graham, I.; Henderson-Sellers, B.; Simons, A., and Younessi, H. 1997. *The OPEN Toolbox of Techniques.* New York, NY: ACM Press Books.

Hammer, M. & Champy, J. 1993. *Reengineering the Corporation: A Manifesto for Business Revolution.* New York, NY: HarperCollins Publishers Inc.

Highsmith, J.A. III 2000. *Adaptive Software Development: A Collaborative Approach to Managing Complex Systems.* New York, NY: Dorset House Publishing.

Hohmann, L. 1996. *Journey of the Software Professional: The Sociology of Computer Programming.* Upper Saddle River, NJ: Prentice Hall PTR.

Humphrey, W.S. 1997. *Managing Technical People: Innovation, Teamwork, And The Software Process.* Reading, MA: Addison-Wesley Longman, Inc.

Jacobson, I., Booch, G., & Rumbaugh, J., 1999. *The Unified Software Development Process.* Reading, MA: Addison Wesley Longman, Inc.

Jacobson, I., Christerson, M., Jonsson, P., Overgaard, G. 1992. *Object-Oriented Software Engineering – A Use Case Driven Approach.* ACM Press.

Jacobson, I., Griss, M., Jonsson, P. 1997. *Software Reuse: Architecture, Process, and Organization for Business Success.* New York, NY: ACM Press.

Jones, C. 1996. *Patterns of Software Systems Failure and Success.* Boston, MA: International Thomson Computer Press.

Karolak, D.W. 1996. *Software Engineering Risk Management*. Los Alimitos, CA: IEEE Computer Society Press.

Kerth, N. 2001. *Project Retrospectives: A Handbook for Team Reviews*. New York, NY: Dorset House Publishing.

Krutchen, P. 2000. *The Rational Unified Process: An Introduction 2nd Edition*. Reading, MA: Addison Wesley Longman, Inc.

Larman, C. 1998. *Applying UML and Patterns: An Introduction to Object-Oriented Analysis and Design*. Upper Saddle River, NJ: Prentice Hall PTR.

Lorenz, M. & Kidd, J. 1994. *Object-Oriented Software Metrics*. Englewood Cliffs, NJ: Prentice-Hall.

Maguire, S. 1994. *Debugging the Development Process*. Redmond, WA: Microsoft Press.

Marick, B. 1995. *The Craft of Software Testing: Subsystem Testing Including Object-Based and Object-Oriented Testing*. Englewood Cliff, NJ: Prentice Hall.

Mayhew, D.J. 1992. *Principles and Guidelines in Software User Interface Design*. Englewood Cliffs NJ: Prentice Hall.

McClure, C. 1997. *Software Reuse Techniques: Adding Reuse to the Systems Development Process*. Upper Saddle River, NJ: Prentice-Hall, Inc.

McConnell, S. 1996. *Rapid Development: Taming Wild Software Schedules*. Redmond, WA: Microsoft Press.

Meyer, B. 1995. *Object Success: A Manager's Guide to Object Orientation, Its Impact on the Corporation and Its Use for Engineering the Software Process*. Englewood Cliffs, NJ: Prentice Hall, Inc.

Meyer, B. 1997. *Object-Oriented Software Construction, 2nd Edition*. Upper Saddle River, NJ: Prentice-Hall PTR.

Mowbray, T. 1997. *Architectures: The Seven Deadly Sins of OO Architecture*. New York, NY: SIGS Publishing, *Object* Magazine, April, 1997, 7(1), pp. 22–24.

Page-Jones, M. 1995. *What Every Programmer Should Know About Object-Oriented Design*. New York, NY: Dorset-House Publishing.

Page-Jones, M. 2000. *Fundamentals of Object-Oriented Design in UML*. New York, NY: Dorset-House Publishing.

Rational Corporation 2001. *The Rational Unified Process.* http://www.rational.com/products/rup/index.jsp

Reifer, D. J. 1997. *Practical Software Reuse: Strategies for Introducing Reuse Concepts in Your Organization.* New York, NY: John Wiley and Sons, Inc.

Rogers, G. 1997. *Framework-Based Software Development in C++.* Englewood Cliffs, NJ: Prentice Hall.

Roman, E., Ambler, S.W., Jewell, T., & Marinescu, F. 2002. *Mastering Enterprise Java Beans, 2nd edition.* New York, NY: John Wiley & Sons.

Royce, W. 1998. *Software Project Management: A Unified Framework.* Reading, MA: Addison Wesley Longman, Inc.

Rumbaugh, J., Jacobson, I. & Booch, G., 1999. *The Unified Modeling Language Reference Manual.* Reading, MA: Addison Wesley Longman, Inc.

Siegel, S. 1996. *Object Oriented Software Testing: A Hierarchical Approach.* New York, NY: Wiley and Sons, Inc.

Software Engineering Institute. 1995. *The Capability Maturity Model: Guidelines for Improving the Software Process.* Reading MA: Addison-Wesley Publishing Company, Inc.

Stallman, R. 2001. *The Free Software Definition.* www.gnu.org/philosophy/free-software-for-freedom.html

Stapleton, J. 1997. *DSDM: Dynamic Systems Development Method.* Harlow, England: Addison-Wesley Publishing Company, Inc.

Szyperski C. 1998. *Component Software: Beyond Object-Oriented Programming.* New York, NY: ACM Press.

Taylor, D. A. 1995. *Business Engineering With Object Technology.* New York, NY: John Wiley & Sons, Inc.

Vermeulen, A., Ambler, S. W., Bumgardner, G., Metz, E., Misfeldt, T., Shur, J., and Thompson, P. 2000. *The Elements of Java Style.* New York, NY: Cambridge University Press.

Warner, J. & Kleppe, A. 1999. *The Object Constraint Language: Precise Modeling With UML.* Reading, MA: Addison Wesley Longman, Inc.

Webster, B.F. 1995. *Pitfalls of Object-Oriented Development.* New York, NY: M&T Books.

Whitaker, K. 1994. *Managing Software Maniacs: Finding, Managing, and Rewarding a Winning Development Team.* New York, NY: John Wiley and Sons, Inc.

Whitmire, S. A. 1997. *Object-Oriented Design Measurement*. New York, NY: John Wiley & Sons, Inc.

Whitten, N. 1995. *Managing Software Development Projects: Formula for Success, 2nd Edition*. New York, NY: John Wiley & Sons, Inc.

Wiegers, K. 1996. *Creating a Software Engineering Culture*. New York, NY: Dorset House Publishing.

Wiegers, K. 1999. *Software Requirements*. Redmond, WA: Microsoft Press.

Wilkinson, N.M. 1995. *Using CRC Cards: An Informal Approach to Object-Oriented Development*. New York, NY: SIGS Books.

Wirfs-Brock, R., Wilkerson, B., & Wiener, L. 1990. *Designing Object-Oriented Software*. NJ: Prentice Hall, Inc.

Yourdon, E. 1997. *Death March: The Complete Software Developer's Guide to Surviving "Mission Impossible" Projects*. Upper Saddle River, NJ: Prentice-Hall, Inc.

Web-Based Resources

Agile Modeling Site. http://www.agilemodeling.com

CETUS Links. http://www.cetus-links.org

The OPEN Website. http://www.open.org.au

The Process Patterns Resource Page. http://www.ambysoft.com/processPatternsPage.html

Rational Unified Process. http://www.rational.com/products/rup

Software Engineering Institute Home Page. http://www.sei.cmu.edu

Index

Create the Software of the Future!

Learn How at the Software Development Conference

The Software Development Conference offers six full days of in-depth, unbiased, real-world training. Over 200 classes cover the spectrum of cutting-edge development, from the latest in Java technology to the team strategies you'll use to implement them. Come to one of our future Software Development events and plan the week that will change the way you work forever.

Tutorials

Start the week with your choice of our intense 1/2-day through 3 day tutorials on the languages and skills most essential to your job, such as:
- Java
- Design Patterns
- UML
- COM Design

Software Development Conference

Get hard-core instruction that will have an immediate impact on your productivity, taught by the top minds in the field. Paths include:
- C++ Programming
- E-Commerce Architecture
- Java Programming
- Open Source
- Windows DNA
- XML Development

21 Technical Paths ● 100 Exhibitors ● 200 Classes
● Expert Speakers ● Power Panels ● Roundtables ● Technical Sessions
● Career Development ● Peer Networking ● Parties

To learn more about our
future events contact us at:
800.441.8826 / 415.905.2702 / www.sdexpo.com

2001

The Unified Process Elaboration Phase

Scott W. Ambler & Larry L. Constantine, Compiling Editors

The Elaboration Phase focuses on defining, validating, and establishing the baseline architecture for a system. Subjects include developing frameworks, component architectures, designing with interfaces, using the UML effectively, working with legacy systems, modeling business rules, selecting tools, user interface prototyping, testing requirements, and managing metrics. 277pp, ISBN 1-929629-05-2

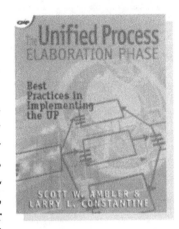

RD3564   **$34.95**

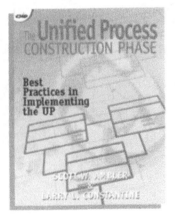

RD3565   **$34.95**

The Unified Process Construction Phase

Scott W. Ambler & Larry L. Constantine, Compiling Editors

Fill the gap between theory and practice! Implement a software process that goes beyond the UP with details of development and production. You learn best practices in implementing the UP as recommended by Software Development magazine. In the Construction Phase, you learn about the design and implementation of new systems in an iterative and incremental manner. 295pp, ISBN 1-929629-01-X

Get Connected.
Stay Informed.

e-development and security

product reviews

design center

www.sdmagazine.com
The online resource for corporate software developers.

project and process management

64-bit development zone

career and training

SOFTWARE
Development
**The People, Products and Practices
of Corporate Development**

Printed and bound by CPI Group (UK) Ltd, Croydon, CR0 4YY

22/10/2024

01777636-0002